A
TAGORE
READER

A
TAGORE
READER

Edited by

Amiya Chakravarty

BEACON PRESS : BOSTON

First published as a Beacon Paperback in 1966
by arrangement with The Macmillan Company

Beacon Press books are published under the auspices
of the Unitarian Universalist Association

Printed in the United States of America

International Standard Book Number: 0–8070–5971–4

9

UNESCO COLLECTION OF REPRESENTATIVE WORKS—
INDIAN SERIES

This book has been accepted in the Indian Translation Series of the UNESCO Collection of Representative Works, jointly sponsored by the United Nations Educational, Scientific and Cultural Organization (UNESCO), and the Government of India.

CONTENTS

INTRODUCTION

The Centennial of Tagore's birthday (1861–1961) spans an epic of great change, of new developments in the relationships between different civilizations and cultures. In spite of two major wars and many grievous disturbances, it bears witness to an increasing understanding and growth in the broad field of human ideas. Tagore's own writings as a poet, traveler, diarist, short story writer, novelist, and a commentator on international affairs came out of the ferment of the modern age while they helped to shape the course of literature in Asia and the West and deepened its resources.

Tagore's creative power, and the impact of his spiritual personality, however, had been dimly assessed outside Bengal and India. Primarily this is owing to the linguistic barrier, but one of the major reasons is that his writings, even in Bengali, and especially in English translations, were not brought into focus by any clear arrangement of materials or by the careful editing needed for an expression of his many-sided genius in a single frame of reference.

This anthology is intended to offer a fairly comprehensive view of Tagore's contribution to our times—actually it transcends any temporal standards—even though the scientific writings, intricate discussions on language and poetics, and other aspects of his thought intimately associated with local lore and color could not be represented. We remember also that no literary compilation can deal with him as a composer who blended classical Indian melodies with original modes, or as a painter whose lines and colors defy the craftsmanship of words. His great center of education and culture, Visva-

Bharati, has to be visited in order that its unique offerings to an international world can be appraised. And yet the editor has attempted, through his knowledge of Tagore, stretching over several decades, to provide glimpses of these and other essential features of his creative expression in Tagore's own words. Having traveled with him in many parts of the world, and thus had the opportunity to study the richness of his mind, the editor has a special responsibility which this edition of Tagore's writings seeks in some measure to fulfill. This volume is not a collection of Tagore's writings, nor does it attempt to be a bibliography; rather it is a selection, and the process followed in culling from the abundance of Tagore's genius a manageable amount of significant material has simply been a careful weighing on the tenuous scales of rich quality and available space.

Where Tagore made his own translations into English the material has sometimes been cut and selected, but otherwise left inviolate; where others' translations have been included, certain changes have been made for reasons of orthography, meaning, and accuracy. Some of the colloquial phrases and epigrams or puns which are not translatable have been omitted. Fidelity to the accuracy and strength of the original text has been the guiding principle.

Except for a few cases where topical considerations were more important, the material in each section has been arranged chronologically. Special procedures peculiar to an individual section have been noted in the introduction to it. American spelling has been maintained throughout, and authorial spelling of place names has been retained.

The individual introductions include relevant information concerning the context in which the original material was written, brief discussions of the contents of the section, and facts concerning translations and publication. Further clarification of names and events and emendations of the texts are provided in the notes at the back of the book. Bengali words whose meanings are not self-evident in the text of the material have been defined in the glossary.

This book is made possible by the cooperative efforts of the Sahitya Akademi, the Asia Society, UNESCO, and the Hazen Foundation, whose support provided for editorial work including a visit to India to collect materials in consultation with Rabindra-Sadan in Santiniketan. The curator of Rabindra-Sadan, Kshitis Roy, gave careful and essential help in comparing Tagore's original manuscripts and supplied information which has been used in some of the notes and the glossary. I am indebted to Krishna Kripalani, Secretary of Sahitya Akademi, New Delhi, for insights obtained from him during several discussions in India and in this country. His articles on Tagore, his notes and comments, and his general advice, and also some interpretive notes by Somnath Maitra have greatly helped in the presentation of text and comments.

The editor wishes to express thanks to Boston University, particularly the School of Theology, for many facilities granted to him during the preparation of the book; to The Macmillan Company, Allen & Unwin, Ltd., and Visva-Bharati for permission to quote extensively from their published works; to Rathindranath Tagore, the poet's son, who helped the literary enterprise with his authorization. Special acknowledgment is due to Helen Phillips Whipple, whose skill and perseverance in typing the manuscript helped immeasurably, and to Donald Junkins, who advised in all critical matters in the adaptation of translations and in the collation and preparation of the final copy of the manuscript. The book could not have been concluded without the help of friends in India and this country who prefer to remain unnamed; they guided this literary effort and identified themselves with the spirit of East-West understanding which Tagore's own writings seek to implement in a revelation of man's universal humanity.

Where the mind is without fear
and the head is held high,
Where knowledge is free;
Where the world has not been broken
up into fragments by narrow domestic
walls;
Where words come out from the
depth of truth;
Where tireless striving
stretches its arms towards
perfection;
Where the clear stream of reason
has not lost its way into the
dreary desert sand of dead habit;
Where the mind is led forward
by thee into ever-widening
thought and action —
into that heaven of freedom,
my Father,
let my country awake.

Rabindranath Tagore

Santiniketan

TRAVEL

Tagore toured the world many times during his lifetime, recording his experiences and ideas in letters, diaries, journals, and articles. The excerpts printed here are, strictly speaking, letters, but because of their pictorial quality and their reflective flavor, they have been incorporated into a separate travel chapter. In contrast to the travel literature of the last decade of Tagore's life, which contains more speculative thought and commentary on situations, these selections from the early tours contain specific references to places and people, and throw more light on the culture and history of the people he visited.

On May 3, 1916, Tagore, accompanied by C. F. Andrews and W. W. Pearson, sailed from Calcutta on a Japanese boat, S. S. *Tosha Maru*, bound for Japan, the first stop on a journey to the United States where he was to undertake an extended lecture tour. They stayed in Japan four months. *On the Way to Japan* and *In Japan* were sent to Pramatha Chaudhuri, editor of *Sabuj Patra*, who published them serially. In 1919 they were collected in a book, *Japanyatri* (A Sojourner in Japan). Much of this was translated by Pramatha Chaudhuri's wife, Indira Devi, and published in Volume III of the *Visva-Bharati Quarterly*.

Tagore sailed from Madras on July 14, 1927, for a tour of Southeast Asia, accompanied by Suniti Kumar Chatterji and Surendranath Kar. By the end of October, when the trip was completed, they had visited, in addition to other places, Java, Bali, Siam, Singapore, Penang, Malacca, and Kuala Lumpur. *Letters from Java* was serialized in *Vichitra* during 1927–1928, and issued as a book, *Jatri*, a year later. Indira Devi translated and published it in the *Visva-Bharati Quarterly*.

During Tagore's historic visit to England in 1912, Yeats read the *Gitanjali* poems (see letter of May 6, 1913, to Indira Devi) at a specially arranged reading in the Hampstead Heath home of William Rothenstein (see Note 3, page 377), and Tagore then retired to the Butterton countryside in Staffordshire where he spent some part of the summer at the home of one of Andrews' clergyman friends. The letter describing this visit was first published in the December issue of the *Tattvabodhini Patrika*, was later (1939) incorporated in the book, *Pather Sanchay (Gleanings of the Road)*, and was translated by this editor for the Summer issue, 1940, of the *Visva-Bharati Quarterly*.

In April, 1932, at the invitation of His Majesty, Riza Shah Pahlavi, Tagore journeyed by airplane to Iran, accompanied by his daughter-in-law (Pratima Devi), Kedarnath Chatterji, and this editor. The tour lasted about two months, and although Tagore was constantly traveling, he regularly sent letters to India. They were serially published in the Bengali monthlies, *Prabasi* and *Vichitra*, and were collected in 1936. They were translated into English by Surendranath Tagore, and published in Volumes II and III of the *Visva-Bharati Quarterly*.

FROM *On the Way to Japan*

A TEMPLE IN BURMA

From the glare of the outside world we entered into the ripened gloom of olden times. A broad flight of steps rose in tiers before us, covered with a canopy. On either side they were selling fruit, flowers, candles, and other sundry offerings of worship—the sellers mostly Burmese women. The colors of the flowers mingling with the colors of their silk clothes made the shades of the temple as variegated as the sky at sunset. Buying and selling are not prohibited, and Mohammedan shop-keepers are displaying their miscellaneous foreign wares. Meat and fish are not excluded either, and domestic concerns, including eating, are being carried on all around. There is no line drawn between the world and the temple; they mingle freely, but the commotion that prevails in the market is absent. Here there is no solitude, but there is privacy; no silence, but peace. There was a Burmese barrister in our party, who, when asked why fish and flesh were allowed to be bought and sold and eaten on the temple steps, replied, "Buddha has preached to us, he has told us which way lies man's salvation, and which way lies his bondage; but he never wanted to make anything good by force; no good can be done by pressure from the outside; salvation lies in one's own free will; therefore, there is no ritualistic tyranny in our temple or our society."

HONGKONG   MAY 21, 1916

The sky is overcast with clouds; the hills in the harbor of Hongkong can be seen with waterfalls coursing down their sides. It seems as if a party of giants, after putting their heads into the sea, have just raised them above the water which is trickling down their tangled hair and beards. Charlie [1] says that the scenery is like that of a Scottish lake surrounded by hills—the same green dumpy hills, the same clouds like wet blankets, the same land and seascape partially blurred by mist.

Our ship will stop here for about two days. The idea of going down to the city and staying in a hotel for the two days did not appeal to me. For a man of my lazy disposition, rest is better than comfort; happiness has its drawbacks, but peace is without sin. I remained on board, even at the risk of enduring the disturbances of loading and unloading. And I was not without my reward.

First of all, I notice the work of the Chinese laborers on the quay. They wore only blue pajamas, the rest of their bodies bare. Spare and perfectly moulded, there was not the slightest superfluity anywhere—their muscles kept rippling the beat of their work. There was no necessity of prodding them from outside, and work seemed to vibrate from their bodies like music from lutes. I never imagined that I could possibly extract so much enjoyment from the loading and unloading of cargo on a ship's pier. The work of perfect strength is very beautiful; at each stroke it beautifies the body, and that body, too, beautifies the work. The poetry of toil and the rhythm of man's body appeared before me. I can say with emphasis that no woman's figure could be more beautiful than these men's figures, because such perfect balance between strength and grace is rarely found in women. In another steamer just opposite ours, all the Chinese sailors, after their work was over, were bathing in the afternoon with their clothes off, and it was a joy to watch them.

JAPAN

One thing strikes the eye. There are crowds of people in the streets, but no confusion whatsoever. It is as if these people do not know how to shout; they even say the children of Japan do not cry. On going through the street in a car, when one is sometimes held up by rickshaws, the chauffeur waits quietly, never shouting or abusing anybody. Suddenly in the middle of the road a bicycle nearly collided with our car, under which circumstances an Indian chauffeur could not have refrained from abusing the cyclist to his heart's content, but our man took not the slightest notice. I am told by the Bengalis here, that even when there is an injury caused by a collision between two vehicles in the streets, both parties, instead of shouting and abusing each other, brush the dust off and walk away.

It seems to me that this is the main source of Japan's strength. The Japanese do not waste their energy in useless screaming and quarreling, and because there is no waste of energy it is not found wanting when required. This calmness and fortitude of body and mind is part of their national self-realization. They know how to control themselves in sorrow and tribulation, in excitement and pain; they do not allow themselves to melt and drip through every hole and opening. That is why foreigners say the Japanese are inscrutable; they are too reserved.

FROM *In Japan*

TOKYO

Immediately on arriving, I was caught in the midst of a cyclone of greetings and kind hospitality, together with which the newspapermen created a furor around me. I had almost given up hope of seeing anything of Japan through the loopholes in this wall. They crowd around you on board ship, they follow you in the streets, they crash into your room.

Pushing our way through this inquisitive crowd, at last we arrived in Tokyo town. Here we found asylum in the home of our artist friend Yokoyama Taikan.[2] Now we began to become acquainted with the heart of Japan. First of all, we had to take off our shoes at the door. We were given to understand that shoes are for the street, and only the feet for the house. We also found that dust did not belong to their houses but to the world outside. All the rooms and corridors were covered with mats under which were mattresses of hard straw, so that as no dust enters their rooms, so also no footfalls are heard. The doors are sliding doors, so there is no chance of their rattling in the wind.

Another thing is, their houses are not very large. There are as few walls and beams and windows and doors as possible. That is to say, the house does not exceed the householder, but is completely within his grasp, and easily amenable to washing and scrubbing, cleaning and polishing. . . .

When I took my seat at early dawn on a mat by the window, I realized that not only are the Japanese master-painters but they have reduced the whole of man's life to an art. They know this much, that a thing which is valuable, which has worth, must be allowed a sufficient amount of space around it. Emptiness of space is most necessary for fullness of perception. A crowd of material is most inimical to the unfolding of life. In the whole of this house there is not a single corner which is uncared for, which is superfluous. The eye is not offended by any unnecessary object; the ear is not annoyed

5

by any unwanted sound. The mind of man can spread itself out as much as it likes, and does not have to trip over things at every step.

A JAPANESE GARDEN

After going a long way from Kobe by car, we first of all entered a garden deeply filled with shade and peace and beauty. These people know what a garden means. That gardening does not mean working geometrical problems on the earth by laying down some gravel and planting trees, is realized as soon as one enters a Japanese garden. The eyes and hands of the Japanese have achieved the freshness of beauty directly from Nature; they know equally well how to see and how to make.

At the end of the shady avenue, there was some clear water in a hollowed-out stone under a tree in which each of us washed our face and hands. They then took us into a small room and placed small round straw mats on a bench where we sat down. It is customary to sit in silence for some time; you do not meet the master of the house as soon as you arrive. In order to calm and tranquillize the mind, you are invited to advance gradually, after resting by degrees in two or three rooms, to the real meeting ground. All the rooms are silent as if wrapped in the shades of eternal evening; nobody says a word. The charm of this shadowy quiet silence gradually works upon the mind. . . .

There was practically no furniture in the rooms, yet one felt as if they were full of something, and resonant. There is perhaps a single picture or a single vessel somewhere in the room. The guests examine it carefully and satisfy themselves in silence. A real thing of beauty requires a large open space; to keep beautiful things crowded together is to insult them. . . .

The host appeared and told us that for special reasons he had assigned to his own daughter the duty of serving the tea. After bowing to us, she proceeded. From her entrance to every stage of tea-making, everything seemed to be performed in rhythm: washing, drying, lighting the fire, opening the lid of the tea-pot, taking down the vessel of hot water, pouring out the tea into cups, placing them before the guests. Every act was performed with such poise and grace that it must be seen to be believed. Every utensil belonging to this tea-ceremony is rare and beautiful. It is the duty of the guests to turn these vessels around and around and observe them carefully; each possesses a special name or history. The amount of care lavished on these deserves description.

The idea is to thoroughly control the mind and body, letting beauty penetrate into one's inmost nature with a calm and dispassionate frame of mind. It is not the reckless dissipation of the sensualist; there is not the slightest trace of excess anywhere. To draw oneself far away from the mind's surface, where the waves are constantly rising and falling to the clash of selfish propensities and the winds of various needs and wants, and to bury oneself in the depths of beauty—this is the moral of the tea-ceremony.

FROM *Letters from Java*

THE ISLAND OF BALI

Not that all the dancing here is dramatic; there is also the pure dance. We saw that last night at the palace of the Raja of Giyanyar. Two little girls beautifully decorated, with flowers in their tiaras swinging to every movement, danced to the music of the *gamelan*. This music was somewhat different from ours. Our *jaltaranga* has always struck me as a childish musical instrument; but in the gongs of the gamelan the same idea has gained breadth, dignity and variety. The Malayan musical modes have little resemblance to our *ragas* and *raginis*, the only common feature being the drum and cymbal accompaniment. Gongs are a prominent element of their concert music which, however, is neither like our modern attempts at melodic orchestration, nor has it the harmony of the Western symphony. The main melody, rung out by the gongs, is interwoven with the sounds of the other instruments into a kind of tonal mosaic.

In spite of the dissimilarity, it was pleasing to our ears and did not seem to hinder the appreciation of the Europeans.

The grace of the dancing of these two little girls was indeed charming. A marvel of elegance and variety, of delicacy and naturalness, the rhythm played through their limbs and over their bodies. Elsewhere one sees the dancer moving the body, but to see these girls, it seemed that the body itself was a spontaneous fountain of dance. . . .

There was once a multitude of Rajas in this little island, many of whom, with thousands of their kinsmen and followers, committed suicide on the eve of the Dutch conquest. The few that still remain are like old candelabra in which candles are no longer lighted. They have their palace and their pomp, and the locality which they inhabit may still be called their capital, but the differences between these capital towns and the surrounding villages are as much as between brother and sister—they live in the same house, not walled off from each other. In modern India the life of the town is distinct from that of the village, with many special features of government and business activity. The lights of the town, however, do not shed any rays on the villages. It is as if there has been a partition of property between the two, and the share allocated to the villages is not enough to maintain the same style of life. That is why the country as a whole cannot sustain or encourage any branch of learning or art. When the townsman thinks of his country, he looks on it as a town, while the villager has forgotten how to think of it at all. As we motor about from one end of this island to another, we see a deep intimacy between its hills, rivers and cornfields, its towns and villages; whatever wealth it has, permeates the whole people.

This is our last day in Bali. I have taken refuge in a dak-bungalow on the Munduk hill. So far we have been going about amidst inhabited and cultivated localities, villages shaded with thick groves of coconut, betelnut, mango and tamarind trees. Here on the hillsides we see the original forest; it is somewhat like Shillong. The slopes below are terraced into rice fields. Through a gap in the range, one has a glimpse of the sea. Like the old history of the island, the distant views here are mostly misty. We are having moonlit nights, but the moonshine is vague, like some imperfectly known language. . . .

The rays of the sun have fallen on the green forest of the nearer slopes; the distant hills are enveloped in a bluish haze. The sea, seen through the gap to the south, is dulled, like a mirror that has been breathed upon. The fronds of the betelnut palms of the village near by, nestling in its groves on the hillside, are trembling in the cool breeze. The women are carrying vessels of water. On the other side of the valley, habitations can be seen in the distance, peeping out of the dense woods, here and there. Around us the glistening leaves of the coconut trees are drinking draughts of sunlight.

At the moment of departure it occurs to me that beautiful as the island is, fine as are its people, nevertheless my mind would not care to build its nest here. From over the seas the call of India haunts me. Not merely because from infancy my communion with the universe has been through India, but because in its rivers and plains, in its atmosphere and its light, I have received intimations of an immensity that has captivated my mind into adoration forever. It is true that it causes me much suffering, the desolation that is everywhere in the lives of her people; yet, transcending it all, there is always with us the message of supreme liberation that has resounded in her skies from the beginning of time.

FROM *Rural England*[3]

AT A VILLAGE PARSONAGE IN STAFFORDSHIRE

It is August, high summer in England; townsmen are longing to visit the countryside. People rush to parks and open fields; whenever they can get a few more hours they go out of town. Joining the flock of flying townsmen, we also got away. . . .

When we reached the house, our hostess took us to the warm drawing room where a fire had been lit. The house was not an old parsonage but a new one; the garden was also new, perhaps they had themselves cultivated it. Clusters of many colored flowers fringed the deep lawn. I had never seen such profusion, such freshness of

9

foliage. It is unbelievable, unless one has seen it, how richly green and thick the grass can be.

The rooms of the house were neat and tidy, the library full of books on many subjects; there was not the least trace of negligence. Furniture, decoration, and comfort are of a much higher standard than in our country; every object is kept spotlessly clean with vigilant care. Slackness would not be tolerated by these people.

In the late afternoon my host Mr. Outram took us on a walk; the rain had stopped, but there was no gap in the clouds. On all sides was the deep green of undulating meadows divided by low hedges. Though hilly, the landscape had nowhere the roughness of hills; earth's exuberance was held in a beautiful harmony.

While walking, Mr. Outram met an acquaintance and discussed some business. I learned that a rural committee had been appointed for encouraging farmers to do some gardening of their own; some days ago a competition had taken place and this stranger had received the first prize for flowers. Mr. Outram took me to the houses of a few farm-holders. Everyone had a flower garden around their cottage and a kitchen garden, and there was an atmosphere of homely toil leading to happiness and simplicity. After the day's labor in the fields they returned to their homes and did gardening in the evening. . . . I had occasion to see many other proofs of the human fellowship developed through services and welfare work that existed between Mr. Outram and the village people who were under his care.

Institutional religion may occasionally hamper the progress of people but in spite of it the spirit of religion works in this country and there is no doubt that the clergy have kept the inner standards fairly high in the life of the village people. In our country this was the work of the Brahmins but being based on *varna* the system led to inevitable neglect of individual responsibility. I do not believe that all clergymen have accepted the ideal of Christ in their lives, but they are not clergymen by birth, and have to be responsible to society. It would be difficult for them to allow their character or behavior to be debased, and they have on the whole held up the pursuit of pure character as an ideal of religion. . . .

The religious orders have arranged for a generalized provision of religion for the communities. But this is not enough—the great problems of humanity that present themselves to the country from time to time demand spiritual power and inspiration which institutionalism cannot provide. Such problems should be faced by clergy-men with the inner music of Christ's own words in their hearts, by establishing Him in their lives. But how rarely this happens. . . .

FROM *Journey to Persia*

April 11, 1932

So long as our plane was passing over Bengal, it flew low. The villages, clustering around pieces of water overgrown with weeds, appeared to our gaze like tiny islands dotted over an expanse of bare fields. From our height they looked like cosy green nooks, but our hearts could feel the thirst of the parched land suffering at the approach of summer, its inhabitants having no resource except the whimsical favors of the Rain-God.

Men, beasts and birds were all out of sight. No sound, no movement, no sign of vitality—a world seemingly deserted by life lay before us, swathed in a patch-work shroud. As we rose higher, even this remnant of form was reduced to a pattern of scratchy lines, as though some extinct country of a forgotten name had recorded its annals on a drab surface in unknown characters of undecipherable meaning. . . .

Up to this time we had not felt its motion very much, but suffered from the intolerable din of its propellers—there was no possibility of communication between passengers. My ears stuffed with cotton-wool, I could only look about me. In the front row was a Dane, employed in a sugar-cane plantation in Manila, now going home. He had been busy following our route on a partly rolled-up map, occasionally helping himself to bread and cheese, or chocolates. He had brought along with him a pile of newspapers which he perused one after the other. There were also three wireless operators who, taking turns, sat in their corners with the apparatus strapped to their ears, taking notes or writing their reports between intervals of eating and dozing. Together with the pilots these comprised our little community, snatched off the earth into isolation, pursuing a course through infinite solitude. . . .

Look at our four Dutch pilots—immensely built, the personification of energy. Their country has not drained their lives, but has kept them fresh. Their rude but overflowing health, inherited from generations nourished by good food, keeps them from being tied down by dull routine. But India's millions do not have enough to eat and have been exhausted by the toll paid to internal and external enemies. Any worthy achievement depends on the co-operation of man's physical and mental forces. We may have the mind, but where is our physical energy? Our starved bodies cannot help shirking the needed exertion, resulting in perfunctory habits that are killing our people. In the endeavor to solve their food problem, Western governments compete with one another to empty their coffers, not hesitating to perpetrate cruel injustice on outsiders, knowing that its solution depends on both the material and moral advancement of the nation. In our country the remedy has to be sought individually, hampered by the dispensers of our fate. . . .

April 15

Ever since our arrival, all kinds of functions have been held, and are being planned, to do me honor. My heart finds some difficulty in appropriating this honor because its meaning is not clear to me.

Who am I to these Bushire crowds? In my work, thought, and everyday life, I am far out of their world. When I was in Europe, the people there knew something of me as a poet, and so could judge me on materials before them. These people also believe me to be a poet, but solely by force of imagination. To them I am a poet, not of this or that kind, but in the abstract; so that nothing stands in the way of clothing me with their own idea of what a poet should be. Persians have a passion for poetry, a genuine affection for their poets, and I have obtained a share of this affection without having to show anything for it in return.

I am reminded of what happended when I was in Egypt. The leading statesmen who came to welcome me on my arrival told me that parliament had been temporarily suspended because of my visit. Such a thing could be possible only in an oriental country. They evidently looked on me not only as a poet, but an Oriental Poet, and must have felt that their country was sharing in the honor which was being shown to me. . . .

April 16

We should have started for Shiraz at 7 o'clock this morning, and so, though I felt far from strong, I was up as usual at dawn. But the others were still in bed, and it was past nine by the time we were all ready.

Our road is an unmetalled track and its condition does not co-operate with the gait of our motor car, so that we are at every moment kept aware of this disharmony, made to feel it in our bones! Empty plains follow one after another with no sign of trees or human dwellings. The greater part of Persia is on a high plateau, several thousand feet above sea-level, surrounded by hills, with mountain ranges running through. This slopes down toward a large tract of desert land, with a scanty rainfall, clouds being intercepted by the hills. Some of the hill streams reach this tract, making streaks of fertility through it, but fail to cross over it to the sea, being absorbed by the desert. . . .

Arrangements for an alfresco dinner have been made in the garden, but for the present I have to forego the pleasure of sitting out there, I am so utterly tired. They show me into a little carpeted room with a bed, on which I lie down. The breeze is soothing, and the foliage refreshes my eyes through the open window.

After a while I leave my bed and go out into the garden where I find the dinner being cooked in huge pots under the trees—much as it is done on the occasion of a feast in India.

A public holiday had been declared in honor of our expected arrival, but the large gathering, originally waiting for us, was thinned down because of our delay. We eventually sat down to dinner outside under lighted lamps, with those who had waited. Our host, out of consideration for my fatigue, offered to have me served in my own room, but I preferred to join the party. The viands—*pillau, kabab*—were of the style known in Bengal as *moghlai*. Our fellow-guests were all full of praise for their king whose extraordinary genius has changed the face of Persia within the short space of a single decade. . . .

LETTERS

Tagore's letters comprise twelve volumes. Some of them have appeared in Bengali collections published in India, notably *Bhanusinher Patravali, Pathe O Pather Prante,* and the *Chithipatra* series (some of which have been published in translation). Others were written directly in English, notably *Letters to a Friend* (Allen and Unwin, London, 1928). It is obvious that in an anthology such as this, space limitations prohibit a comprehensive collection; the attempt has been made here to choose those few letters which are best representative of both Tagore's personality and ideas current in certain phases of his life.

The letters to his wife are a selection from the first book of the *Chithipatra* series published by the *Visva-Bharati,* consisting of letters dating from 1890–1901 which were written by Tagore to his young wife, Mrinalini Devi,[1] during their short separations. The letters have been translated from Bengali by Lila Majumdar.

The excerpt from Tagore's letter to his niece Indira Devi was translated by herself into English.

The letters to Sturge Moore, W. W. Pearson, C. F. Andrews and Leonard Elmhirst were written by Tagore in English.

The letters to Ranu are a selection from the book *Bhanusinher Patravali,* a collection of letters written to a young girl, Ranu, daughter of Professor P. B. Adhikari of Benares Hindu University. The letters date from 1917 to 1923 and were published in book form in 1930 and dedicated to Ranu (now Lady Ranu Mookerji). They have been translated into English by Lila Majumdar.

The letters to Mrs. Rani Mahalanobis are a selection from the book *Pathe O Pather Prante,* in which are collected a number of letters Rabindranath wrote to Mrs. Rani Mahalanobis dating from November, 1926.

The immediate occasion for starting the correspondence was (according to the poet) to maintain a link with his fellow travelers, P. C. Mahalanobis and his wife, who had accompanied him through the major portion of his European tour (May–November, 1936) and had stayed back while the poet made his return voyage to India. The letters have been translated into English by Somnath Maitra.

All the letters printed here follow a strict chronology according to dates, except for the Pearson letter of October 6, 1918, which precedes the letter to Ranu of April 15, 1918.

The letter to Elmhirst of December 29, 1924, was actually dictated to him by Tagore during their stay in Argentina, but because of its spontaneous nature and its formal epistolary content, it seemed more suitable to include it as a letter rather than as an article.

FROM *Letters to His Wife*

Shelidah
1901

I could not write to you yesterday because of the ceremonies when the tenants pay their New Year's rent. I arrived at Shelidah on the evening before, and the empty house yawned at me. I thought I would enjoy the lonely quiet after all the harassments of many days, but my mind was unwilling to enter alone where we have been accustomed to living together. Especially when I went into the house, tired after my journey and with no one to look after my wants and be glad and show tenderness, it all seemed very empty. I tried to read but I could not.

When I came in after walking through the garden the empty room with its kerosene lamp appeared emptier. The upstairs rooms seemed even more vacant. I came down again, trimmed the lamp and tried to read once more, but it was no use.

We had an early dinner and went to bed; I slept in the west room upstairs and *Rathi*[2] in the east room. It was really cold during the night and I had to cover myself with my woolen rug. The days are also fairly cold.

The rent-collecting was completed yesterday with music and prayers and so on. In the evening a party of *kirtan*-singers came to the courthouse and we listened to them until eleven.

Your herb garden is full now, but the greens have been planted so closely that they have no room to grow. We shall send you some of them with the other things. A number of pumpkins have been put away. The rose-trees that Nitu sent are in full bloom but the greater part of them are the odorless variety. He was cheated badly. The tube roses, the gardenias, the *malati*, the *passiflora*, the *mehedi* are flowering profusely. The lady-of-the-night is also flowering but there is no perfume. I think flowers lose their perfume in the rainy season.

The tank is full to the brim, the sugarcane in front has grown well, the fields all around are heavy with corn—a flawless green carpet. Everybody asks, "When will mother be here?" . . .

Shelidah
June, 1901

When the rent-collecting celebrations were over I set my hand to writing again. Once engrossed in my work I am like a landed fish which has found water again. Now the loneliness of this place gives me complete protection, the little details of life no longer touch me and I can easily forgive those who have been my enemies.

I can understand why you feel oppressed by loneliness; I would be happy if I could share with you my joy in this mood, but it is something which no one can give to another.

When you leave the crowds of Calcutta and find yourself in the midst of the emptiness here, you do not like it in the beginning, and even when you do get used to it you feel a repressed impatience within you. But tell me what else I can do when my life grows barren in Calcutta. That is why I lose my temper, fret about every little thing, cannot sincerely forgive everyone and so preserve my own peace of mind.

Besides, everyone is so restless there, Rathi and the others never can be properly educated. For all these reasons you must resign yourself to a sentence of exile. Perhaps later on, when I can afford it, I shall be able to select a better place, but I shall never be able to bury all my powers in Calcutta.

Now heavy clouds are darkening the sky and rain is beginning to fall. I have shut all the windows of my downstairs room and while I write to you I enjoy the sight of the falling rain. You could never see such a wonderful sight from your first floor room over there. The gentle, dusky, new summer rain over the green fields all around me is beautiful.

I am writing a critical essay on "Meghdut." [3] If I could portray in my essay the deep duskiness of this heavy summer day, if I could give to my readers the greenness of Shelidah's fields in some permanent form, how would it be? In my books I have said so many things in so many ways, but where can I find this array of clouds, this movement of branches, this ceaseless fall of rain, this thick-shadowed embracement of earth and sky?

How naturally this rainy day gathers over the solitude of the fields, over the earth and the water and the sky; how the sunless mid-afternoon of idle cloudy June gathers around me, and yet I can leave no trace of all this in my writings!

No one will ever know I strung these words together in my mind, or when or where, in the long leisurely hours and in this lonely house. The rain has stopped after a particularly heavy shower, so this is the time to send my letter to the post.

Santiniketan
July, 1901

I have just come back after leaving Bela [4] in her new home. It is not what you may imagine from a distance; Bela is quite contented there. There is no doubt that she likes her new way of life. We are now no longer necessary to her.

I have come to the conclusion that at least for a short period immediately after marriage a girl should keep away from her parents and give herself unrestricted opportunity for being with her husband. The presence of her parents in the midst of this union interferes with it because the habits and tastes of her husband's family are not the same as those of her own, and there are bound to be differences of opinion. With her parents near at hand a girl cannot forget her old ways and identify herself wholly with her husband. Since one must give away a daughter why try to retain any influence over her? In such circumstances one must consider the girl's welfare. What is the use of her considering our happiness or misery and adding her paternal attachments to those of her husband's home?

Remember that Bela is quite happy and try to console your own grief at separation. I can say with certainty that if we had clung around them the result would not have been good. Because they are far away, the affection between them and us will always remain the same. When they come to us for the Pujah holidays or when we go to them, we shall all enjoy a deep and fresh delight.

In every kind of love there should be a certain amount of separation and detachment. No good ever comes of completely swamping each other. And even if Rani goes far away after her marriage, it will be good for her. Of course she will be near us for the first couple of years, but after that, as soon as she is old enough, she should be sent entirely away from us for her own good.

The education, tastes, customs, language and way of thinking of our family are different from those of other families in Bengal; that is why it is all the more necessary for our girls to remove themselves from us after marriage. Otherwise every little detail of her new life might be so irksome to the girl that it might influence her respect for and dependence upon her husband. All the faults of Rani's nature will be corrected as soon as she is separated from her parental home, but she will never get rid of her old associations if she keeps in close contact with us.

Think of yourself. If I had lived in Fultala[5] after marrying you, your nature and your behavior would have been quite different. Where one's children are concerned, one should entirely disregard one's own feelings. They were not born for our happiness; our joy should consist in their welfare and in the fulfillment of their lives.

All day yesterday memories of Bela's childhood kept coming back to my mind. How carefully I reared her with my own hands; how naughty she would be, penned in by her pillows; how she would shout and hurl herself on any small child of her own age whom she met; how greedy she was, but how good-natured; how I would bathe her myself in the Park Street house; how I gave her warm milk to drink at night in Darjeeling. I keep remembering the time when my love for her first stirred in my heart, but she does not know of these things and it is better so. Let her bind herself to her new home without pain and fulfill her life with faith and affection and household duties. Let there be no regrets in our hearts.

Arriving in Santiniketan today I am steeped in peacefulness. One cannot imagine how necessary it is to come away like this from time to time. Surrounded by the limitless sky and the wind and the light, I am, as it were, nursed in the arms of the primal mother.

TO *Indira Devi*

London
May 6, 1913

. . . You have alluded to the English translation of *Gitanjali*.[19] To this day I have not been able to imagine how I came to do it and how people came to like it so much. That I cannot write English is such a patent fact, that I never had even the vanity to feel ashamed of it. If anybody wrote an English note asking me to tea, I never felt equal to answering it. Perhaps you think that by now I have gotten over that delusion, but in no way am I deluded that I have composed in English. On the day I was to board the ship, I became ill because of my frantic efforts at leave-taking, and the journey was postponed. Then I went to Shelidah to rest, but unless the mind is active, one does not feel strong enough to relax completely, so the only way to keep myself calm was to do some light work.

It was then the month of Chaitra (March–April), the air was thick with the fragrance of mango-blossoms and all hours of the day were filled with the songs of birds. When a child is full of vigor, he does not think of his mother; it is only when he feels tired that he wants to nestle in her lap. That was exactly my position. With all my heart and all the abandon of leisure I settled myself comfortably in the arms of Chaitra, without missing even a particle of its light, its air, its scent and its song. In such a state one cannot remain idle. When the air strikes one's bones they tend to respond in music; this is an old habit of mine, as you know. Yet I did not have the energy to gird up my loins and sit down to write. So I took up the poems of *Gitanjali* and set myself to translate them one by one. You may wonder why such a crazy ambition should possess one in such a weak state of health. But believe me, I did not undertake this task in a spirit of reckless bravery; I simply felt an urge to recapture, through the medium of another language, the feelings and sentiments which had created such a feast of joy within me in past days. The pages of a small exercise-book came gradually to be filled, and with it in my pocket I boarded the ship. The idea of keeping it in my pocket was that when my mind became restless on the high seas, I could recline on a deck-chair and set myself to translate one or two poems. And that is what actually happened. I passed from one exercise book to another. From an Indian friend, Rothenstein [20] already had an inkling of my reputation as a poet; therefore, when in the course of conversation he expressed a desire to see some of my poems, I handed him my manuscript, with some reluctance. I could hardly believe the opinion he expressed after reading it. He then gave my book to Yeats. The story of what followed is known to you. From this explanation of mine you will see that I was not responsible for the offense, but that it was due mainly to the force of circumstances. . . .

TO *Sturge Moore* [6]

Shilida, Nadia
February 17, 1914

Dear Sturge Moore,

An incident will show you how the award of the Nobel prize has roused up antipathy and suspicion against me in certain quarters. A report has reached me from a barrister friend of mine who was present on the occasion when in a meeting of the leading Mohammedan gentlemen of Bengal, Valentine Chirol [7] told the audience that the English Gitanjali was practically a production of Yeats. It is very likely he did not believe it himself, it being merely a political move on his part to minimize the significance of this Nobel prize affair which our people naturally consider to be a matter for national rejoicing. It is not possible for him to relish the idea of Mohammedans sharing this honour with Hindus. Unfortunately for me there are signs of this feeling of antagonism in England itself which may be partly due to the natural reaction following the chorus of praise that Gitanjali evoked and partly, as you have said in your letter, to the bitterness of disappointment in the minds of the partisans of the candidates for the Nobel prize. You know it had been the source of a rare great pleasure for me while in England to be able to admire your manly power of appreciation which was without a tinge of meanness or jealousy. I could have gladly sacrificed my Nobel prize if I could be left to the enjoyment of this strong friendliness and true-hearted admiration.

I had forgotten to tell you how greatly we all admire your beautiful design on the cover of the *Crescent Moon*.[8] It is perfect in its simplicity and grace.

You must have read in the papers that in Paris they are holding an exhibition of pictures by our modern Indian artists. I hope you will find time to go and see it and realize the stir of new life in Bengal that is breaking out in manifold expressions. The head of this art movement in our country is my nephew Abanindranath who is sure to receive recognition some day in Europe. I hear that Havell[9] will try to exhibit these pictures in the South Kensington Museum some time later on.

I have got a copy of *Chitra*[10] sent to me last week. Its get-up is attractive and I hope it will not be deprived of its due because my books have been coming in too quick succession jostling each other. I am sure my publishers are not giving enough intervals to my readers for their appetite to be revived. However this must be said to my credit that the four poetical works of mine closely following each other are different in their character—and by this time critics must be thinking of modifying their classification of my poems as mystic. All poets have the sense of the infinite in some shape or other but it is their own keen sense of the finite that truly individualizes them. It is not according to what they contemplate but what they definitely see that poets have to be classified.

It was difficult to believe when I saw Miss Cooper that she was dying. She was so serenely radiant that she seemed less mortal than most other human beings. In fact, I felt an impulse of a deeper life in my soul when I met her that evening. I must thank you for giving me the opportunity of knowing this woman in whom life triumphed so beautifully in the face of death.

Kindly remember me to Mrs. Moore.

Ever yours,
Rabindranath Tagore

Santiniketan
Balpur, Bengal
May 1, 1914

My dear Sturge Moore,

Our school is closed, and after a long interval of a busy time a full day has been given to me to spend as I like. I took up your book—*The Sea Is Kind*—finishing it at one sitting. It will be difficult for you to imagine this blazing summer sky of ours with hot blasts of air repeatedly troubling the fresh green leaves of a tree whose name will be of no use to you. This is as unlike the climate and the country where your poems were written as anything could be. I feel your environment in your poems. There is in them the reticence of your sky, the compactness of your indoor life and the general consciousness of strength ready to defy fate. Here in the East the transparent stillness of our dark nights, the glare of the noonday sun melting into a tender haze in the blue distance, the plaintive music of the life that feels itself afloat in the Endless, seem to whisper into our ears some great secret of existence which is incommunicable. All the same, nay, all the more, your literature is precious to us. The untiring hold upon life which you never lose, the definiteness of your aims and positive reliance you have upon things present before you, inspire us with a strong sense of reality which is so much needed both for the purposes of art and of life. Literature of a country is not chiefly for home consumption. Its value lies in the fact that it is imperatively necessary for the lands where it is foreign. I think it has been the good fortune of the West to have the opportunity of absorbing the spirit of the East through the medium of the Bible. It has added to the richness of your life because it is alien to your temperament. In course of time you may discard some of its doctrines and teachings but it has done its work—it has created a bifurcation in your mental system which is so needful for all life growth. The Western literature is doing the same work with us, bringing into our life elements some of which supplement and some contradict our tendencies. This is what we need. It is not enough to charm or to surprise us—we must receive shocks and be hurt. Therefore we seek in your writings not simply what is artistic but what is vivid and forceful. That is why Byron had such immense influence over our youths of the last generation. Shelley, in spite of his vague idealism, roused our minds because of his fanatic impetuosity which is born of a faith in life. What I say here is from the point of view of a foreigner. We cannot but miss a great deal of the purely artistic element of your literature but whatever is broadly human and deeply true can be safely shipped for distant times and remote countries. We look for your literature to bring to us the thundering life flood of the west, even though it carries with it all the debris of the passing moments.

I am getting ready to go off to the hills to spend my vacation there.

Ever yours,
Rabindranath Tagore

FROM *Letters to a Friend*

TO C. F. ANDREWS [11]

Calcutta
July 11, 1915

. . . In India, when the upper classes ruled over the lower, they forged their own chains. Europe is closely following Brahmin India, when she looks upon Asia and Africa as her legitimate fields for exploitation. The problem would be simpler if she could altogether denude other continents of their population; but so long as there are alien races, it will be difficult for Europe to realize her moral responsibility with regard to them. The gravest danger is when Europe deceives herself into thinking that she is helping the cause of humanity by helping herself, that men are essentially different, and what is good for her people is not good for others who are inferior. Thus Europe, gradually and imperceptibly, is losing faith in her own ideals and weakening her own moral supports.

But I must not go on weaving truisms; and on our own side I must equally acknowledge this truth, that weakness is heinous because it is a menace to the strong and the surest cause of downfall for others than those who own it. It is a moral duty for every race to cultivate strength, so as to be able to help the world's balance of power to remain even. We are doing England the greatest disservice possible by making it easy for her to despise us and yet to rule; to feel very little sympathy for us and yet to judge us.

Will Europe never understand the genesis of the present war, and realize that the true cause lies in her own growing skepticism toward her own ideals—those ideals that have helped her to be great? She seems to have exhausted the oil that once lighted her lamp. Now she is feeling a distrust against the oil itself, as if it were not at all necessary for her light.

FROM *Letters to W. W. Pearson* [12]

October 25, 1917

My continuous stay in Calcutta for the last few months was not a particularly exhilarating experience for me. Yet for all I know, it was necessary, not for my peace of mind, but for realizing, rightly or wrongly, that my mission of life was not for exclusively turning out verses difficult of comprehension. I was too long out of touch with our Calcutta people—especially without students. In fact, as far as the Bengali public outside our Santiniketan was concerned, I had been living in a phantom world of a vanished generation. The present generation of our youth merely knows me as a man who has achieved his reputation. But an assured reputation gives a sense of finality to one's career. It no longer appears like a flame but like a splendid snuffer to the candle of life. It was like a railway train which had accomplished its end and reached its terminus, therefore no longer of interest to the passengers who were beginning or continuing their journey. But this time I had the opportunity to prove to them that I was on the running line and that the signal was down. Our students were rather surprised to find that I still had in me most of the properties of solid matter—weight, penetrability and the power of occupying space. So, like Dada of Phalguni, I am in danger of being surrounded by the crowd, made use of and even praised. I am feeling excessively nervous because I am beginning to be flattered by my countrymen, to which experience, you know, I am not at all accustomed. When misunderstanding lands one upon the Alpine height of praise it is more perilous for him than when it hurls him into the depth of calumny. I am waiting every moment for the downward push to roll back again into my normal position of unambiguous revilement.

However, I am tired. I wish I were in some Japanese monastery with you practising Zen. I have come to the conclusion that a poet ought to be a poet and nothing else. The combination of a *setar* and a fishing-rod in one may be convenient but such ingenious monstrosities should be discouraged.

But please do not imagine that my clouds had no gold lining whatever. We staged *Dakghar (Post Office)* [13] in our Vichitra Hall, gave five performances and felt happier each time we did it. I took the part of Thakurda, Gagan [14] that of Madhab, and Aban [15] personated Morhal to perfection. The boy who personated Amal was glorious. He is a new acquisition to our school whom you do not know. We did miss you so much! I know if Andrews were among the audience he would have created a tremendous scene.

I had a letter from Andrews some time ago saying that he was coming back in November. I hope he will not change his plan. The absence of both of you is a sore trial to me.

Dear Pearson,

All through this last session I have been taking classes in the morning, spending the rest of the day writing text books. It is a kind of work apparently unsuitable for a man of my temperament. But I found it not only interesting, but restful. Mind has its own burden, which can be lightened when it is floated on a stream of work. Some engrossing idea also helps us in the same way—but ideas are unreliable—they run according to no timetable whatever—and the hours and days you spend in waiting for them grow heavy. Of all places of rest waiting rooms are the least rest-giving, because you have to put up with a leisure which is unmeaning and undesired. Lately I came to that state of mind when I could not afford to wait for the inspiration of ideas, so I surrendered myself to some work which was not capricious, but had its daily supply of coal to keep it running. However, this teaching work was not a monotonous piece of drudgery for me; for, contrary to the usual practice, I treated my students as living organisms—and dealing with life can never be dull. Unfortunately, poets cannot be expected to enjoy lucid intervals for long, and directly some muse takes possession of their minds they become useless for all decent purposes of life. These are intellectual gypsies, vagrancy is in their blood, and already I feel the call of an irresponsible vagabondage, a kind of passion for an extravagant idleness. The schoolmaster in me is perilously near being lured away by the mischievous imps of truancy. I am going to move away from this place in a day or two, for the ostensible reason of visiting South India from where invitations have been pouring upon me for long, but I tell you in confidence, it is the lapse of reason, my frequent visitor, the spirit of losing way, who is beckoning me, ready to escort me over all lines of prescribed works. I long to discover some fairyland of holidays—not a Lotus Island—not a world where all week days are Sundays, but where Sundays are not at all needed, where all works carry their rest in themselves, where all duties look delightfully undutiful, like clouds bearing rain appearing perfectly inconsequential.

FROM *Letters from Bhanusinha*

TO RANU

Santiniketan
April 15, 1918

You may have read in books that some birds leave their nests at certain times and fly over the sea. I am such a bird. From time to time something calls me from beyond the ocean and my wings flutter. So I have arranged to board a ship at the beginning of May and cross the Pacific Ocean. If nothing prevents me I shall really set out.

Nowadays, with this war on, the western sea-route does not always take one to the farther shore, but to the bottom of the sea. The eastern route is still safe, but perhaps one day the winds of war will arrive here as well. However, please do not imagine that I have forgotten all about your invitation to Benares. You go ahead with your arrangements while I drop in at Australia, Japan, America, and a few other places on my way, until at last I settle down comfortably with you. But a west-province diet will not do for me. I feel sure you have an excellent cook, in spite of which, unless you prepare everything for me with your own hands, from the first small dish of vegetables down to the last sweet milk-rice I shall instantly rebel. I have not yet made up my mind, but I was thinking of going back to Australia at once, without my lunch, only I am not sure if it would be possible to keep such a promise, so I shall not say anything more for the present.

But I suppose you cannot cook? Is that it? You have been doing nothing except your lessons? Well, I will give you one year's grace; meanwhile take lessons from your mother. Let us leave it at that. In the meantime I must go to Calcutta and pack my trunks. I am a wonderful packer, but I have one little fault. I often forget to pack the most important things, and just when I need them most I find I have left them behind!

All this causes a great deal of inconvenience but it makes packing very easy. There is always plenty of room inside my trunks and I have to pay the railway and steam-ship companies much less, the boxes weigh so little!

Besides, there is the other advantage in carrying unnecessary rather than necessary things: one does not have to keep opening one's trunks to get them out, so they remain nicely packed; and even if they get lost or are stolen it does not interfere with one's work or matter one bit!

I must leave by the three o'clock train so I have not much more time to write. I have a wonderful knack of missing trains but it will be of no use today, so I shall just send you my blessings for the New Year and rush off to buy my ticket.

Santiniketan
July 21, 1918

Yesterday evening, layers of dark blue clouds covered the sky while my English friend and I were having tea on the east verandah downstairs. I had finished everything and was starting on the fried parched rice when a whistling wind came up from the west and spread black clouds from one end of the sky to the other.

The sight of those rain clouds after so many days was a pleasure to my eyes. Had I been a Hindustani girl from your Benares I would have gone off to the swing on the *sirish* tree, singing *kajri* songs. But neither Andrews nor I have the appearance, nature or manners of a Hindustani girl, and in addition, he does not know any *kajri* songs and I have forgotten what I knew. So the two of us went upstairs and sat on the verandah before the terrace.

In no time, heavy rain began to fall and the rainwater and the wind made merry in the heavens. They caught hold of the long leaves of the papaya tree in front of our verandah and cuffed its ears. When the rain grew more violent and began to spatter us with drops, we took shelter in my own corner.

Suddenly a thunderbolt fell, dazzling our eyes and making a tremendous noise. We had an idea that it must have fallen in the garden somewhere. As we hurried out, we saw the boys running toward Haricharan Babu's [16] house.

Indeed, the house had been struck by lightning. His eldest daughter had been boiling milk over the oven and she had dropped down, unconscious. From a distance the boys saw smoke issuing from the thatched roof. They climbed up and kept shouting for water which was fetched from the well to put out the fire. Mercifully, no one in the house was injured, except that the daughter's hand was slightly scalded.

What pleased me most was the boys' enterprising spirit. They knew neither fear nor weariness. They tore off the burning thatch with their bare hands, flung it to the ground, ran to the distant well, and falling into line, fetched pitchers of water. If they had not noticed the blaze and rushed to the rescue a terrible fire would have broken out.

In this way, the rain and the storm continued far into the night and it is much cooler today. The sky is still overcast; perhaps there will be another spell of rain this evening.

Santiniketan
July 28, 1918

You seem to be deeply engrossed in your lessons these days, but please do not imagine that I am sitting around doing nothing.

My classes continue as usual. You know that I have to teach three classes every morning. Then I have my bath and lunch, and if any letters must be written, I write them. Then I prepare more lessons for my classes until tea is announced.

Later in the evening I sit quietly on the terrace; sometimes the boys come to hear my poems. When it grows dark and the sky is studded with stars, I can hear the boys learning songs in Dinu's room. At last the singing ends.

Then I hear the sound of singing with the harmonium and flute in the senior boys' rooms. Slowly the singing stops and I can see one or two lights moving along the distant village roads. Afterwards those lights also disappear and only the sky-wide starlight remains. Then I feel sleepy, so I get up and go slowly to bed.

Then at a certain time the sky in front of my eastern door gradually gets lighter and a bird or two begins to twitter; the clouds are touched with a hint of gold. The senior-school bell rings at half-past four and immediately I get up.

I wash my face and say my prayers on the stone seat in my east verandah. The sun slowly climbs up and blesses me with its rays.

Nowadays we have early breakfast because at half-past six all the members of the asrama, old and young, gather together in the open ground in front of the school. We sing a song and commence our school work.

I do not teach any classes during the first hour, but sit in my own corner and go through my books and papers and get ready for lessons. After this, my classes commence.

So here is an account of my whole day and night; how peacefully the days pass. I love to work with the boys because they do not realize that the work we do for them has any value. They accept our service as naturally as they accept the light from the sun, and not as they bargain with and buy things from the shopkeepers in the market.

When these boys grow up and take their place in the business of the world, perhaps they will remember these open fields, this *sal* avenue, the generous light of these skies, these free winds and this obeisance to God every morning and evening, silently, under the open sky.

Santiniketan
November 25, 1918

As yet there is no relief from the pressure of my work. Everyone thinks that I am a poet, that day and night I gaze at the clouds playing in the sky, and listen to the song of the wind. I drown in the moonlight, I am intoxicated with the scent of flowers, I tremble with the murmuring of the leaves, etc. etc. All this is due to jealousy. They wish to boast about the fact that though they may not compose poems they go to the office seven days in the week; they go to court, they run newspapers, give lectures, carry on trades, they are all such terribly busy people.

I wish they would come here and see whether I do any work or not. Well they may do a lot of work, I acknowledge that, but have they the power NOT to do a lot of work? When they have no work to do, they either sleep or play cards or drink or find fault with people; indeed they cannot think how to spend their time. I have this advantage, that when there is work to be done I really do it, but when there is no work then I can do no work with all my heart. Your father's committee meetings are nothing compared to that. I get absolutely emaciated in the crush, due to the pressure of doing nothing. Recently, however, I have had such a lot of work to do that I have not been able to write a single work of that drama. . . .

Santiniketan
May 18, 1919

I have just received the account of your travels and have been wondering how to write a reply that will equal your letter. You move, I am stationary; you are a bird in the sky, I am an *aswath* tree at the edge of the forest; your singing and the rustling of my leaves cannot be the same. At one point we both agree: you have gone for a change of air and so have I. You have gone from Benares to Salon, I have gone from my writing desk to my long chair by the window. A great change indeed. But there is one fundamental difference between your traveling and mine. You move yourself, but I remain stationary while everything before me moves. My travels consist in that kind of movement.

This is traveling worthy of kings. Some one else does the traveling and I do not have to move for the sake of movement. Look, today is Sunday, market day, there is a bullock-cart passing in front of me, and my eyes turn into passengers riding in the cart. Look, there go the Santal girls with bundles of straw on their heads. There goes Santosh Babu's herdsman driving his herd of buffaloes. There go some people from the station toward Goalpara, who and why I have not the least idea. A flat-bottomed coconut-shell for smoking tobacco hangs from somebody's hand, somebody carries a torn umbrella over his head, and somebody a naked baby on his shoulder. See, there come the girls from Bhuvandanga, waterpitchers at their hips, to fetch water from our Santiniketan wells. I let my mind float with the current of all this, and sit here in silence. The clouds pass across the sky, the broken file of last night's storm, looking very damaged. I shall see them again this evening in blue, red, gold and purple uniforms, heralding the storms and marching from the northwest with the deep rolling of drums, all in military parade. They will not look so meek then.

Our school is closed and only the chattering birds keep the asrama alive; many kinds have gathered here—the banyan fruit is ripe and they are uninvited guests. But Mother Nature has set places for everybody.

July 11, 1919

Your letter put me to shame today. Shall I tell you why? I had already received one letter from you and was thinking of answering it, when this other letter arrived. You win.

How am I to compete with all those dangerous travels you have written about? This morning I thought of standing on the railway track before the little wood at night, and then after the passenger train had passed over my chest, if I could still move my hand, I would write a letter to you that could vie with yours! But I have not yet consulted my daughter-in-law about this, or spoken with Mr. Andrews. I suspect they will not agree. Besides, I have a few doubts of my own. Supposing my thumb is injured by the weight of the train, why, I may not be able to write at all! And then your two letters will always remain winners. I give up the idea.

Nothing terrible has happened here in the last few days. We have had a little rain and storm, but not enough to bring our roof down, and no one has been hit by even an ordinary thunderbolt. All over the country there are robberies with guns and daggers but we are so unfortunate that none of them, or even their distant relatives, have cared to visit our asrama!

No, that is not correct. A blood-curdling event did take place a few days ago. A long road passes in front of our asrama, along the edge of the lonely fields, right up to the station at Bolpur. To the west of this road there is a two-storeyed house. A lady from Bengal lives all alone on the ground floor, with only a few maids and servants and a footman and a milkman and a cook; and an Englishman called Mr. Andrews lives upstairs. Besides these, there is not a single person in the whole house. That night, the sky was overcast and the moon shed a few pale moonbeams from behind the clouds. When it was about eleven and the lonely lady was resting with only ten or twelve people about her, who was the man that entered her room? Who was the strange young man? Where did he live, and what did he want? Suddenly he disturbed the silence of the quietly slumbering room and asked, "Where is the school?" The lady who was awakened so abruptly felt her heart thumping furiously. In a choking voice she said, "The school is to our west." Then the young man asked, "Where is the headmaster's room?" The lady said, "I do not know." Here commences the next chapter. In the pale moonlight, in the middle of the night, resounding with the chirp of crickets, ignoring the shrill protests of the asrama dogs, the young man walked along the gravel paths of the asrama and entered the room of a second defenseless woman. At the moment there was not a single other person in the room besides her grown-up husband. He asked the same two questions, and the almost empty room lit by a dim lamp, was silent with panic. Why had the man come here from a far country, in search of the headmaster? What enmity was there between them? That night, the lady who had her husband with her and the other one who had not, both fell asleep with a load of fear in their simple and gentle hearts. I wonder if they were afraid that the remains of the headmaster would be discovered somewhere next morning—the *minus* "master" part of him.

Then follows the third chapter. Next day, the first lady said to me, "Father, at midnight a young man, etc." Whereupon I hope my reader will not be astonished to learn that I did not run away from the asrama, that I did not even bare my sword. Even if I had wished to do so, I did not possess a sword; in fact a pen-knife was all I had. I did not take any infantry or cavalrymen with me when I went out to find the young man who disturbed the sleep of delicate ladies last night in his search for the headmaster.

Then comes the conclusion. The young man was discovered and questioned. From his answers, we learned that he had come here to get a young relative admitted into the school. Finis.

FROM *Letters to a Friend*

TO C. F. ANDREWS

Ardennes
August 21, 1920

Here we are in a most beautiful part of France. But of what avail is the beauty of Nature when you have lost your trunks which contained all your clothes? I could have been in perfect sympathy with the trees surrounding me if, like them, I were not dependent upon tailors for maintaining self-respect. The most important event for me in this world at present is not what is happening in Poland, or Ireland, or Mesopotamia, but the fact that all the trunks belonging to our party have disappeared from the goods-van in their transit from Paris to this place!

And therefore, though the sea is singing its hymns to the rising and setting sun and to the starlit silence of the night, and though the forest around me is standing tiptoe on the rock, like an ancient Druid, raising its arms to the sky, chanting its incantation of primeval life, we have to hasten back to Paris to be restored to respectability at the hands of tailors and washermen!

I have just received your letter, and for some time I have felt myself held tight in the bosom of our Asram. I cannot tell you how I feel about the prolonged separation from it which is before me; but at the same time I know that unless my relationship with the wide world of humanity grows in truth and love, my relationship with the Asram will not be perfect.

Houston, Texas
February 23, 1921 [17]

Tied to the chariot-wheel of karma we flit from one birth to another. What that means to the individual soul I have been made to realize in these last few days. It is my tyrant karma which is dragging me from one hotel to another. Between my two hotel incarnations I usually have my sleep in a Pullman car, the very name of which suggests the agency of death. I am ever dreaming of the day when I shall attain my nirvana, freed from this chain of hotel lives, and reach utter peace in uttarayan.

I have not written to you for some time. For I am tired to the profound depth of my being.

Yet, since coming to Texas, I have felt as it were a sudden coming of spring into my life through a breach in the ice castle of winter. It has come to me like a revelation that all these days my soul had been thirsting for the draught of sunshine poured from the beaker of infinite space. The sky has embraced me, and the warmth of its caress thrills me with joy.

Strasbourg
April 29, 1921

I am writing this from Strasbourg, where I am going to read my lecture at the University this evening.

I miss you very much at this moment; for I feel certain it would overwhelm you with happiness could you be with me now, realizing the great outburst of love for me in the continental countries of Europe which I have visited. I have never asked for it, or striven for it, and I never can believe that I have deserved it. However, if it be more than is due to me, I am in no way responsible for this mistake. For I could have remained perfectly happy in my obscurity to the end of my days, on the banks of the Ganges, with the wild ducks as my only neighbors on the desolate sand islands.

"I have only sown my dreams in the air," for the greater part of my life, and I never turned back to see if they bore any harvest. But the harvest now surprises me, almost obstructs my path, and I cannot make up my mind to claim it for my own. All the same, it is a great good fortune to be accepted by one's fellow-beings from across the distance of geography, history and language, and through this fact we realize how truly One is the mind of Man, and what aberrations are the conflicts of hatred and the competitions of self-interest.

We are going to Switzerland tomorrow, and our next destination will be Germany. I am to spend my birthday this year in Zurich. I have had my second birth in the West, and there is rejoicing at the event. But by nature all men are *dwija* or twice-born, first they are born to their home and then, for their fulfillment, they have to be born to the larger world. Do you not feel yourself that you have had your second birth among us? And with this second birth you have found your true place in the heart of humanity.

It is a beautiful town, this Strasbourg, and today the morning light is beautiful. The sunshine has mingled with my blood and tinged my thoughts with its gold, and I feel ready to sing: "Brothers, let us squander this morning with futile songs."

This is a delightful room where I am sitting now, with its windows looking over the fringe of the Black Forest. Our hostess is a charming lady, with a fascinating little baby, whose plump fingers love to explore the mystery of my eye-glasses.

Stockholm
May 27, 1921

I have been following the track of spring from Switzerland to Denmark, and from Denmark to Sweden, watching everywhere flowers breaking out in a frenzy of colors. And it seems to me like the earth's shouting of victory, and flinging up its colored cap to the sky. My path in the West also has had the same exuberant outburst of welcome.

At first I felt the impulse to describe it to you in detail; for I was sure it would give you great delight. But now I shrink from doing it. For somehow it does not cause exultation in my own mind, but makes me sad. It would be absurd for me to claim what has been offered to me as fully mine. The fact is, there is a rising tide of heart in the West rushing toward the shores of the East, following some mysterious law of attraction. The unbounded pride of the European peoples has suddenly found a check, and their mind appears to be receding from the channel it had cut for itself.

The giant, being weary, is seeking peace; and as the fountain of peace has ever flowed from the East, the face of troubled Europe is instinctively turned today toward the East. Europe is like a child who has been hurt in the midst of her game. She is shunning the crowd and looking out for her mother. And has not the East been the mother of spiritual humanity, giving it life from its own life?

How pitiful it is that we, in India, are unaware of this claim for succor from Europe which has come to our door; that we fail to realize the great honor of the call to serve humanity in her hour of need!

Bewildered at heart by the great demonstrations made in my honor in these countries, I have often tried to find out the real cause. I have been told it was because I loved humanity. I hope that this is true; and all through my writings, my love of man has found its utterance and touched human hearts across all barriers. If it be true, then let that truest note in my writings guide my own life henceforth.

The other day, when I was resting alone in my room in the hotel at Hamburg, timidly there entered two shy and sweet German girls, with a bunch of roses for their offering to me. One of them, who spoke broken English, said to me: "I love India." I asked her: "Why do you love India?" She answered: "Because you love God."

The praise was too great for me to accept with any degree of complaisance. But I hope its meaning was in the expectation from me which it carried, and therefore was a blessing. Or possibly she meant that my country loved God, and therefore she loved India. That also was an expectation whose meaning we should try to appreciate and understand.

The nations love their own countries; and that national love has only given rise to hatred and suspicion of one another. The world is waiting for a country that loves God and not herself. Only that country will have the claim to be loved by men of all countries. . . .

Berlin
June 4, 1921

. . . I saw *Post Office* acted in a Berlin theater. The girl who took the part of Amal was delightful in her acting, and altogether the whole thing was a success. But it was a different interpretation from that of ours in our own acting in Vichitra. I had been trying to define the difference in my mind, when Dr. Otto of Marburg University who was among the audience, hit upon it. He said that the German interpretation was suggestive of a fairy-story, full of elusive beauty whereas the inner significance of this play is spiritual. . . . Do you think that *Post Office* has some meaning at this time for my country in this respect, that her freedom must come direct from the King's Messenger, and not from the British Parliament; and that when her soul awakes nothing will be able to keep her within walls? . . .

TO LEONARD K. ELMHIRST [18]

Miralrio, Argentina
December 29, 1924

. . . whenever some great personality is born, his voice reaches out to challenge the spirit in us and to remind us that we are not just animals, but men. I believe the time has now come when some new warning has to be preached to us in the realm of politics. We all know that there was a time when a difference of religious belief was punished by physical punishment. Heretics were burned to death. Spiritual truth was believed to be almost material in character. But a sin which belongs to the realm of the spirit can never be eradicated by punishment which is merely physical. The very idea that it could be is but an example of the beast in man speaking. To those who automatically hold religious creeds different from our own, we no longer mete out physical punishment. Today religious conflict is carried on through intellectual discussion, a kind of warfare it is true, but at least on a plane higher than the purely physical one.

Gandhi has, I believe, faith in a new kind of political warfare, one which can have a spiritual character of its own. Only by those who have the courage to accept suffering and not inflict it can, says he, such a spiritual war be waged. If a whole nation could be trained not to fear physical death, no power in the world could keep it in bondage. We yield to those who have physical power over us, not because of a difference in degree between our physical strength and theirs, but because of our own lack of moral courage. As long as a people is afraid of physical suffering, machinery for intimidating them will always be invented. Directly as we are able to say we are no longer afraid of physical suffering or of death, arms and armaments lose their significance. If such a faith in our spiritual strength can be inculcated, and Gandhi thinks that a whole people can be brought to accept such an idea, that in itself would be permanent freedom. It is for this idea that he is struggling. It is a great idea.

To convince us that the putting of such an idea into practice is not so difficult and that a great period of peace and of freedom could be imminent and in the realm of the possible, some man of outstanding faith is needed. Jesus Christ had faith in the coming of just such a Kingdom, and in the fact that it was "near at hand." All idealists tell us that some kind of "Kingdom of God" is within our reach and suggest that any obstruction that may exist in our minds to the idea of its realization is but flimsy and unreal. It may be that we are not yet ready to receive such a message or to act upon it, but it is well that such a challenge to adventure in faith should be uttered. Only thus is our belief in it likely to grow, and this, after all, is the first step. . . .

FROM *Pathe O Pather Prante*

TO MRS. RANI MAHALANOBIS

Santiniketan
February 8, 1927

. . . I am past the age for letter writing. When one speaks through his pen, much of the life goes out of what one has to say. When one is in the fullness of power, enough remains even after the inevitable loss in transmission. That is why writing then never seems to lose its natural conversational flow. Now, however, the words do not bubble up naturally into talk, their current at the tip of the pen becomes thin, and one feels disinclined to undergo the pains of composition.

However, let me tell you of something I feel deeply. The times are out of joint, there is much to worry about, much that hurts; there is want and conflict. The shadow of despondency grows deeper every moment, a sense of pain sweeps like a wind across the mind. Then I suddenly remember that the shadow is that of the demon called "I" which has no real substance. The wind then jumps up and asserts loudly that the demon is not there, it has no real existence. Quickly the mind becomes clean and whole again. I pace the red-graveled path outside my house with this tussle in my mind between light and shade. Who, seeing me from outside, will understand that this process of creation goes on within me? Does this creation start and end in my mind? Has it no eternal bond with the creative process of the universe? It certainly has. Something is taking shape throughout the universe and through all eternity. We feel the impact of it in the pain of our hearts. The stage at which man has arrived in the march of civilization has been attained by the creative endeavors of countless millions of unknown individuals, the history of whose personal struggles lies merged in oblivion. Whatever abides in creation is the momentary handiwork of the countless many that have passed away. Those architects of creation, those that are gone, are functioning within me—the thing called "I" only furnishes them with a sort of prop. The scaffolding of a house in construction may be necessary today, but tomorrow when there is no trace left of it, no one will miss it. The completed building never sorrows for its lost scaffolding. The point is that as I pace this path I feel that much of the construction going on within me is being stored in the treasury of Man's creation, with the signature of my name obliterated.

Santiniketan
November 7, 1928

The principal news about me from day to day is that I am drawing pictures.[1] Lines have spread their magic net over my entire mind.

41

This untimely infatuation for an unknown *inamorata* has resulted in my poetry leaving the neighborhood—I have forgotten that I have at any time written poetry. My present occupation is so fascinating because it is so unpremeditated. However indistinctly, at the very beginning the thought of a poem suggests itself to the mind; and then, like the Ganges rushing down from the matted locks of Siva's hair through a chasm in the Himalayas, the poem comes cascading down the tip of the pen, and the rhythms begin to flow. But in the pictures I try to draw, the method of composition is just the reverse. The first faint suggestion of lines come from the pen itself; then, as these lines begin to assume familiar forms, the mind starts to take cognizance of them. The wonder of these fascinates the mind. If I had been an expert artist, I would have first formed the idea, and then worked it out in a picture; the thing within me would thus have found outward expression. There is pleasure in that, too. But when one's whole mind is engrossed in the creation of something that lies outside oneself, the pleasure is still more intoxicating. As a result of this, my other responsibilities have been peeping in at the door and going away after giving me up for lost. If I had been free from the claims of other work as in my younger days, I would have sat on the banks of the Padma, and produced rich harvests of pictures and loaded them in Time's golden boat. But at present, I can only make a little room for them by pushing aside the claims of so many other things. That does not satisfy. They want the whole sky, and I, too, am eager to give it to them, but the planets conspire to place so many obstacles in the way—chief among which is the betterment of the world!

Santiniketan
November 29, 1928

Before saying anything else I want to tell you that the tea you sent was excellent. That I have not written for so long is on account of the peculiarity of my nature. I write letters as I paint pictures. When I feel prompted to write, I put down whatever comes into my head. It has nothing to do with the events of my day-to-day life. It is the same with my pictures; I suddenly see a figure within my mind. It may not have a resemblance or relation to anything around me—there is always a process of creation and destruction, movement and adjustment, going on within us. Now an idea, now an image, rises up in the mind to assume different forms. It is with them that my pen has to do. Formerly my mind used to hear the voice of the sky and the music of the wind; words used to come to it out of the air. Now it has its eyes open to the world of forms and the crowds of lines. When I look at trees and plants I see them intensely and understand that the world is a pageant of forms. My pen seeks to join in the play of those forms. Not emotion, not sentiment, not thought—but an assemblage of forms! The surprising thing is that there is deep joy in this, and an intoxication. Lines have come to possess me; I cannot shake them off. They reveal themselves to me in ever-new gestures; there is no end to their mystery. I have at last come to know how the mind of the Creator-Artist works. The Unmanifest binds Himself by means of lines in ever-new finite forms. In size, the forms He gives Himself may be limited, but in their variety they are infinite. So it comes to this, that fullness of expression can only be achieved through limitation. When the Infinite reveals Himself in the finite, He fulfills Himself. The joy that pictures bring is the joy of definiteness; within the restraint of lines we see the particular with distinctness. Whatever object I perceive, whether it is a piece of stone, a donkey, a prickly shrub, or an old woman, I tell myself that I have seen it exactly as it is. And whenever I see a thing with exactness, I touch the Infinite and feel delighted. But that should not make me forget that I very much enjoyed the tea you sent.

SHORT STORIES

Tagore wrote short stories at every stage of his life. His first story, "*Bhikharini*" ("The Beggar Woman"), was published in 1877 when he was sixteen, and his last few stories, which were outlines rather than finished pieces, were written a few months before his death in 1941. The three volumes of *Galpaguchchha*, in which all but the very last few are collected, contain eighty-four stories. Over half of these were written between 1891 and 1895 during his first great creative period, usually referred to as the *Sadhana* period after the monthly magazine which he edited for some years. The rest were written at intervals, sometimes of several years. The largest later groups, seven in 1914 and three in 1917, belong to the *Sabuj Patra* period when he was contributing a large part every month to the magazine of that name edited by the late Pramatha Chaudhuri.

Tagore's stories reflect his surroundings, currently dominant ideas, and problems which exercised his mind, at different periods of his life. Tagore, himself, liked his earlier stories best because of their freshness and spontaneity. He wrote them when he was managing the family estates and living mostly in the villages—Shilaida, Patisar, Shajadpur, and others. In a letter dated June 25, 1895, he wrote: "As I sit writing bit by bit a story for the *Sadhana*, the lights and shadows and colors of my surroundings mingle with my words. The scenes and characters and events that I am now imagining have this sun and rain and river and the reeds on the river bank, this monsoon sky, this shady village, these rain-nourished happy cornfields to serve as their background and to give them life and reality. . . ."

It is also interesting to note that up to the time that these stories were written, the ordinary man and woman, and especially the poor, had not been written about with any psychological depth in Indian literature.

The Cabuliwallah [1] was first published in the November, 1892, issue of the monthly *Sadhana*; its English translation by Sister Nivedita appeared in the January, 1912, issue of the *Modern Review*.

The Hungry Stones was first published in the August, 1895, issue of the *Sadhana*, and was translated into English by Pannalal Basu and published in the February, 1910, issue of *The Modern Review*.

The Runaway was first published as *Atithi* in the August, 1895, issue of the *Sadhana*. It was translated by Surendranath Tagore for *The Modern Review* of September, 1919, and was later included in *The Runaway and Other Stories* (Visva-Bharati, 1959).

The Cabuliwallah

(The Fruitseller from Cabul)

Mini, my five year old daughter, cannot live without chattering. I really believe that in all her life she has not wasted one minute in silence. Her mother is often vexed at this, and would stop her prattle, but I do not. To see Mini quiet is unnatural and I cannot bear it for long. Because of this, our conversations are always lively.

One morning, for instance, when I was in the midst of the seventeenth chapter of my new novel, Mini stole into the room, and putting her hand into mine, said: "Father! Ramdayal the door-keeper calls a crow a *krow*! He doesn't know anything, does he?"

Before I could explain the language differences in this country, she was on the trace of another subject. "What do you think, Father? Shola says there is an elephant in the clouds, blowing water out of his trunk, and that is why it rains!"

The child had seated herself at my feet near the table, and was playing softly, drumming on her knees. I was hard at work on my seventeenth chapter, where Pratap Singh, the hero, had just caught Kanchanlata, the heroine, in his arms, and was about to escape with her by the third-story window of the castle, when all of a sudden Mini left her play, and ran to the window, crying: "A Cabuliwallah! a Cabuliwallah!" Sure enough, in the street below was a Cabuliwallah passing slowly along. He wore the loose, soiled clothing of his people, and a tall turban; there was a bag on his back, and he carried boxes of grapes in his hand.

I cannot tell what my daughter's feelings were at the sight of this man, but she began to call him loudly. Ah, I thought, he will come in and my seventeenth chapter will never be finished! At this exact moment the Cabuliwallah turned and looked up at the child. When she saw this she was overcome by terror, fled to her mother's protection, and disappeared. She had a blind belief that inside the bag which the big man carried were two or three children like herself. Meanwhile, the pedlar entered my doorway and greeted me with a smiling face.

So precarious was the position of my hero and my heroine that my first impulse was to stop and buy something, especially since Mini had called to the man. I made some small purchases, and a conversation began about Abdurrahman, the Russians, the English, and the Frontier Policy.

As he was about to leave, he asked: "And where is the little girl, sir?"

I, thinking that Mini must get rid of her false fear, had her brought out. She stood by my chair, watching the Cabuliwallah and his bag. He offered her nuts and raisins but she would not be tempted, and only clung closer to me, with all her doubts increased. This was their first meeting.

One morning, however, not many days later, as I was leaving the house I was startled to find Mini seated on a bench near the door, laughing and talking with the great Cabuliwallah at her feet. In all her life, it appeared, my small daughter had never found so patient a listener, except for her father. Already the corner of her little sari was stuffed with almonds and raisins, gifts from her visitor. "Why did you give her those?" I said, and taking out an eight-anna piece, handed it to him. The man accepted the money without delay, and slipped it into his pocket.

Alas, on my return an hour later, I found the unfortunate coin had made twice its own worth of trouble! The Cabuliwallah had given it to Mini, and her mother seeing the bright round object, had pounced on the child with: "Where did you get that eight-anna piece?"

"The Cabuliwallah gave it to me," said Mini cheerfully.

"The Cabuliwallah gave it to you!" cried her mother much shocked. "O Mini! how could you take it from him?"

Entering at this moment, I saved her from impending disaster, and proceeded to make my own inquiries. I found that it was not the first or the second time the two had met. The Cabuliwallah had overcome the child's first terror by a judicious bribery of nuts and almonds, and the two were now great friends.

They had many quaint jokes which afforded them a great deal of amusement. Seated in front of him, and looking with all her tiny dignity on his gigantic frame, Mini would ripple her face with laughter, and begin "O Cabuliwallah! Cabuliwallah! what have you got in your bag?"

He would reply in the nasal accents of a mountaineer: "An elephant!" Not much cause for merriment, perhaps, but how they both enjoyed their joke! And for me, this child's talk with a grown-up man always had in it something strangely fascinating.

Then the Cabuliwallah, not to be caught behind, would take his turn with: "Well, little one, and when are you going to the father-in-law's house?"

Now most small Bengali maidens have heard long ago about the father-in-law's house, but we, being a little modern, had kept these things from our child, and at this question Mini must have been a trifle bewildered. But she would not show it, and with instant composure replied: "Are you going there?"

Among men of the Cabuliwallah's class, however, it is well known that the words "father-in-law's house" have a double meaning. It is a euphemism for jail, the place where we are well cared for at no expense. The sturdy pedlar would take my daughter's question in this sense. "Ah," he would say, shaking his fist at an invisible policeman, "I will thrash my father-in-law!" Hearing this, and picturing the poor, uncomfortable relative, Mini would go into peals of laughter, joined by her formidable friend.

These were autumn mornings, the time of year when kings of old went forth to conquest; and I, never stirring from my little corner in Calcutta, would let my mind wander over the whole world. At the very name of another country, my heart would go out to it, and at the sight of a foreigner in the streets, I would fall to weaving a network of dreams: the mountains, the glens, the forests of his distant homeland with a cottage in its setting, and the free and independent life of far-away wilds. Perhaps these scenes of travel pass in my imagination all the more vividly because I lead a vegetable existence such that a call to travel would fall upon me like a thunderbolt. In the presence of this Cabuliwallah I was immediately transported to the foot of mountains, with narrow defiles twisting in and out amongst their towering, arid peaks. I could see the string of camels bearing merchandise, and the company of turbaned merchants carrying queer old firearms, and some of their spears down toward the plains. I could see—but at this point Mini's mother would intervene, imploring me to "beware of that man."

Unfortunately Mini's mother is a very timid lady. Whenever she hears a noise in the street or sees people coming toward the house, she always jumps to the conclusion that they are either thieves, drunkards, snakes, tigers, malaria, cockroaches, caterpillars, or an English sailor. Even after all these years of experience, she is not able to overcome her terror. Thus she was full of doubts about the Cabuliwallah, and used to beg me to keep a watchful eye on him.

I tried to gently laugh her fear away, but then she would turn on me seriously and ask solemn questions.

Were children never kidnapped?

Was it, then, not true that there was slavery in Cabul?

Was it so very absurd that this big man should be able to carry off a tiny child?

I told her that, though not impossible, it was highly improbable. But this was not enough, and her dread persisted. As her suspicion was unfounded, however, it did not seem right to forbid the man to come to the house, and his familiarity went unchecked.

Once a year, in the middle of January, Rahmun the Cabuliwallah was in the habit of returning to his country, and as the time approached he would be very busy going from house to house collecting his debts. This year, however, he always found time to come and see Mini. It would have seemed to an outsider that there was some conspiracy between them, for when he could not come in the morning, he would appear in the evening.

49

Even to me it was a little startling now and then, to suddenly surprise this tall, loose-garmented man of bags in the corner of a dark room; but when Mini would run in, smiling, with her "O Cabuliwallah! Cabuliwallah!" and the two friends so far apart in age would subside into their old laughter and their old jokes, I felt reassured.

One morning, a few days before he had made up his mind to go, I was correcting my proof sheets in my study. It was chilly weather. Through the window the rays of the sun touched my feet, and the slight warmth was very welcome. It was almost eight o'clock, and the early pedestrians were returning home with their heads covered. All at once I heard an uproar in the street, and, looking out, saw Rahmun bound and being led away between two policemen, followed by a crowd of curious boys. There were blood-stains on the clothes of the Cabuliwallah, and one of the policemen carried a knife. Hurrying out, I stopped them and inquired what it all meant. Partly from one, partly from another, I gathered that a certain neighbor had owed the pedlar something for a Rampuri shawl, but had falsely denied having bought it, and that in the course of the quarrel Rahmun had struck him. Now, in the heat of his excitement, the prisoner began calling his enemy all sorts of names. Suddenly, from a verandah of my house my little Mini appeared, with her usual exclamation: "O Cabuliwallah! Cabuliwallah!" Rahmun's face lighted up as he turned to her. He had no bag under his arm today, so she could not discuss the elephant with him. She at once therefore proceeded to the next question: "Are you going to the father-in-law's house?" Rahmun laughed and said: "Just where I am going, little one!" Then seeing that the reply did not amuse the child, he held up his fettered hands. "Ah," he said, "I would have thrashed that old father-in-law, but my hands are bound!"

On a charge of murderous assault, Rahmun was sentenced to many years of imprisonment.

Time passed and he was forgotten. The accustomed work in the accustomed place was ours, and the thought of the once free mountaineer spending his years in prison seldom occurred to us. Even my light-hearted Mini, I am ashamed to say, forgot her old friend. New companions filled her life. As she grew older she spent more of her

50

time with girls, so much in fact that she came no more to her father's room. I was scarcely on speaking terms with her.

Many years passed. It was autumn once again and we had made arrangements for Mini's marriage; it was to take place during the Puja holidays. With the goddess Durga returning to her seasonal home in Mount Kailas, the light of our home was also to depart, leaving our house in shadows.

The morning was bright. After the rains, there was a sense of cleanness in the air, and the rays of the sun looked like pure gold; so bright that they radiated even to the sordid brick walls of our Calcutta lanes. Since early dawn, the wedding-pipes had been sounding, and at each beat my own heart throbbed. The wailing tune, Bhairavi, seemed to intensify my pain at the approaching separation. My Mini was to be married tonight.

From early morning, noise and bustle pervaded the house. In the courtyard the canopy had to be slung on its bamboo poles; the tinkling chandeliers should be hung in each room and verandah; there was great hurry and excitement. I was sitting in my study, looking through the accounts, when some one entered, saluting respectfully, and stood before me. It was Rahmun the Cabuliwallah, and at first I did not recognize him. He had no bag, nor the long hair, nor the same vigor that he used to have. But he smiled, and I knew him again.

"When did you come, Rahmun?" I asked him.

"Last evening," he said, "I was released from jail."

The words struck harsh upon my ears. I had never talked with anyone who had wounded his fellowman, and my heart shrank when I realized this, for I felt that the day would have been better-omened if had he not turned up.

"There are ceremonies going on," I said, "and I am busy. Could you perhaps come another day?"

At once he turned to go; but as he reached the door he hesitated, and said: "May I not see the little one, sir, for a moment?" It was his belief that Mini was still the same. He had pictured her running to him as she used to do, calling "O Cabuliwallah! Cabuliwallah!" He had imagined that they would laugh and talk together, just as in the past. In fact, in memory of those former days he had

51

brought, carefully wrapped up in paper, a few almonds and raisins and grapes, somehow obtained from a countryman—his own little fund was gone.

I said again: "There is a ceremony in the house, and you will not be able to see any one today."

The man's face fell. He looked wistfully at me for a moment, said "Good morning," and went out.

I felt a little sorry, and would have called him back, but saw that he was returning of his own accord. He came close up to me holding out his offerings, and said: "I brought these few things, sir, for the little one. Will you give them to her?"

I took them and was going to pay him, but he caught my hand and said: "You are very kind, sir! Keep me in your recollection; do not offer me money! You have a little girl; I too have one like her in my own home. I thought of my own, and brought fruits to your child, not to make a profit for myself."

Saying this, he put his hand inside his big loose robe and brought out a small dirty piece of paper. With great care he unfolded this, and smoothed it out with both hands on my table. It bore the impression of a little hand, not a photograph, not a drawing. The impression of an ink-smeared hand laid flat on the paper. This touch of his own little daughter had been always on his heart, as he had come year after year to Calcutta to sell his wares in the streets.

Tears came to my eyes. I forgot that he was a poor Cabuli fruit-seller, while I was—but no, was I more than he? He was also a father.

That impression of the hand of his little Parbati in her distant mountain home reminded me of my own little Mini, and I immediately sent for her from the inner apartment. Many excuses were raised, but I would not listen. Clad in the red silk of her wedding-day, with the sandal paste on her forehead, and adorned as a young bride, Mini came and stood bashfully before me.

The Cabuliwallah was staggered at the sight of her. There was no hope of reviving their old friendship. At last he smiled and said: "Little one, are you going to your father-in-law's house?"

But Mini now understood the meaning of the word "father-in-law," and she could not reply to him as in the past. She flushed at the question and stood before him with her bride's face looking down.

I remembered the day when the Cabuliwallah and my Mini first met, and I felt sad. When she had gone, Rahmun heaved a deep sigh and sat down on the floor. The idea had suddenly come to him that his daughter also must have grown up during this long time, and that he would have to make friends with her all over again. Surely he would not find her as he used to know her; besides, what might have happened to her in these eight years?

The marriage-pipes sounded, and the mild autumn sun streamed around us. But Rahmun sat in the little Calcutta lane, and saw before him the barren mountains of Afghanistan.

I took out a bank-note and gave it to him, saying: "Go back to your own daughter, Rahmun, in your own country, and may the happiness of your meeting bring good fortune to my child!"

After giving this gift, I had to eliminate some of the festivities. I could not have the electric lights, nor the military band, and the ladies of the house were saddened. But to me the wedding-feast was brighter because of the thought that in a distant land a long-lost father met again with his only child.

The Hungry Stones[2]

My kinsman and I were returning to Calcutta from our Puja trip when we met the man in a train. From his dress and bearing we at first took him for an up-country Mohammedan, but were puzzled as we listened to him speak. He talked so confidently on all subjects that you might think the Disposer of All Things consulted him at all times. Hitherto we had been perfectly happy; we did not know that secret forces were at work, that the Russians had advanced close to us, that the English had deep and secret policies, that confusion among the native chiefs had come to a point. But our newly-acquired friend said with a sly smile: "There happen more things in heaven and earth, Horatio, than are reported in your newspapers." As we had never before stirred from our homes, the demeanour of the man struck us with wonder. Even on the most trivial topic he would quote science or comment on the Vedas or repeat quatrains from some Persian poet, and as we had no knowledge of science or the Vedas or Persian, our admiration for him increased, and my kinsman, a theosophist, was convinced that our fellow-passenger must have been supernaturally inspired by some strange magnetism or occult power or astral body. He listened with devotional rapture to even the tritest saying of our extraordinary companion, and secretly took notes of the conversation. I think that the man saw this and was pleased by it.

When the train reached its junction, we stood in the waiting-room for our connection. It was 10 P.M., and since we heard that the train was likely to be quite late, because of something wrong in the lines, I spread my bed on the table and was about to lie down for a comfortable doze, when this extraordinary person began spinning the following yarn. Of course, I got no sleep that night.

"When, owing to a disagreement about some questions of administrative policy, I quit my post at Junagarh and entered the service of the Nizam of Hyderabad, they appointed me at once, as a strong young man, collector of cotton duties at Barich.

"Barich is a lovely place. The Susta chatters over stones and babbles on the pebbles, tripping through the woods like a skillful dancing girl. A flight of 150 steps rises from the river, above which, at the foot of the hills, stands a solitary marble palace. Nobody lives nearby; the village and the cotton market are far away.

"About 250 years ago, Emperor Mahmud Shah II built this lonely palace for his pleasure and luxury. In those days jets of rose-water spurted from its fountains, and on the cold marble floors of its spray-cooled rooms young Persian women sat, their hair dishevelled before bathing, and splashing their soft naked feet in the clear water of the reservoirs, would sing the *ghazals* of their vineyards, to the tune of a guitar.

"The fountains play no longer, the songs have ceased, white feet no longer step gracefully on the snowy marble. It is now the lonely home of men oppressed with solitude and deprived of the society of women. Karim Khan, my old office clerk, repeatedly warned me not to take up my abode there. 'Pass the day there if you like,' said he, 'but never stay the night.' I passed it off with a light laugh. The servants said that they would work till dark and then go away. I gave my assent. The house had such a bad name that even thieves would not venture near it after dark.

"At first the solitude of the deserted palace weighed upon me like a nightmare. I would stay out and work as long as possible, then return home tired at night, go to bed and fall asleep.

"Before a week had passed, the place began to exert a weird fascination upon me. It is difficult to describe or to induce people to believe; but I felt as if the whole house was like a living organism slowly and imperceptibly digesting me by the action of some stupefying gastric juice.

"Perhaps the process had begun as soon as I set my foot in the house, but I distinctly remember the day on which I first was conscious of it. It was the beginning of summer, and the market being dull I had no work to do. A little before sunset I was sitting in an armchair near the water's edge below the steps. The Susta had sunk low; a broad patch of sand on the other side glowed with the hues of evening, and on this side the pebbles at the bottom of the clear shallow waters were glistening. There was not a breath of wind anywhere, and the still air was laden with an oppressive scent from the spicy shrubs growing on the hills close by.

"As the sun sank behind the hilltops a long dark curtain fell upon the stage of day, and the intervening hills cut short the time in which light and shade mingle at sunset. I thought of going out for a ride, and was about to get up when I heard a footfall on the steps behind. I looked back, but there was no one.

"As I sat down again, thinking it an illusion, I heard many footfalls, is if a large number of persons were rushing down the steps. A strange delight, slightly tinged with fear, passed through my body, and although there was no figure before my eyes, I thought I saw a bevy of maidens coming down the steps to bathe in the Susta that summer evening. No sound broke the silence of the valley, the river, or the palace, but I distinctly heard the maidens' gay and mirthful laugh, like the gurgle of a spring gushing forth in a hundred cascades, as they ran past me in playful pursuit toward the river. As they were invisible to me, so I was, as it were, invisible to them. The river was perfectly calm, but I felt that its clear and shallow waters were suddenly stirred by the splashes of arms jingling with bracelets, and that the girls laughed and spattered water at one another, while the feet of those who were swimming tossed up tiny waves in a shower of pearls.

"I felt a thrill at my heart; I cannot say whether it was due to fear or curiosity. I had a strong desire to see them more clearly, but nothing was visible. I thought I could catch all that they said if I only strained my ears, but I heard nothing but the chirping of the cicada in the woods. It seemed as if a dark curtain of 250 years was hanging before me, and I could tremblingly lift a corner of it and peer through, although the other side was completely enveloped in darkness.

"The oppressive closeness of the evening was broken by a sudden gust of wind, the surface of the Susta rippled and curled like the hair of a nymph, and from the woods wrapt in the evening gloom there came a simultaneous murmur as though they were awakening from a black dream. Call it reality or dream, the momentary glimpse of that invisible mirage reflected from a far-off world, 250 years old, vanished in a flash. The mystic forms that brushed past me with their quick, ethereal steps, and loud voiceless laughter, threw themselves into the river and did not return wringing their dripping robes. Like fragrance wafted away by the wind they were dispersed by a single breath of the spring.

"Then I was filled with the fear that it was the Muse that had taken advantage of my solitude, and possessed me—the witch had evidently come to ruin a poor devil like myself making a living by collecting cotton duties. I decided to have a good dinner; it is the empty stomach that all sorts of incurable diseases find an easy prey. I sent for my cook and gave orders for a sumptuous *moghlai* dinner, redolent of spices and *ghi*.

"Next morning the whole affair seemed like a queer fantasy. With a light heart I put on a sola hat like the sahebs, and drove out to my work. I was to have written my quarterly report that day, and expected to return late, but before it was dark I was strangely drawn to my house—by what I could not say. I felt that they were all waiting, and that I should not delay any longer. Leaving my report unfinished, I rose, put on my sola hat, and startling the dark, deserted path with the rattle of my carriage, I reached the palace on the gloomy skirts of the hills.

"On the first floor the stairs led to a spacious hall, its roof stretching over ornamental arches resting on three rows of massive pillars, and groaning day and night under the weight of its own solitude. The day had just come to an end and the lamps had not yet been lighted. As I pushed the door open there was a great bustle, as if a throng of people had broken in confusion and rushed out through doors, windows, corridors, verandas and rooms, to make a hurried escape.

"I saw no one and stood bewildered, my hair on end in a kind of ecstatic delight. A faint scent of attar and unguents effaced by age lingered in my nostrils. Standing in the darkness between the rows of those ancient pillars, I could hear the gurgle of fountains splashing on the marble floor, a strange tune on the guitar, the jingle of ornaments and the tinkle of anklets, the clang of bells tolling the hours, the distant note of *nahabat*, the din of the crystal pendants of chandeliers shaken by the breeze, the song of bulbuls from the cages in the corridors, the cackle of storks in the gardens—all creating a strange, unearthly music.

"Then I came under such a spell that this intangible, inaccessible vision appeared to be the only reality in the world, everything else a mere dream. That I, Srijut So-and-so, the eldest son of So-and-so of blessed memory, should be drawing a monthly salary of 450 rupees as collector of cotton duties, driving in my dog-cart to my office every day in a shirt coat and sola hat, appeared to me to be such an astonishingly ludicrous illusion that I burst into a horse-laugh as I stood in the gloom of that vast, silent hall.

"At that moment my servant entered with a lighted kerosene lamp in his hand. I do not know whether he thought me mad, but it came back to me at once that I was indeed Srijut So-and-so, son of So-and-so of blessed memory, and that, while our poets, great and small, could alone say whether inside or outside the earth there was a region where unseen fountains perpetually played, and fairy guitars struck by invisible fingers sent forth an eternal harmony, at any rate it was certain that I collected duties at the cotton market at Barich, and earned 450 rupees *per mensem* as my salary. As I sat over the newspaper at my camp-table lighted by the kerosene lamp, I laughed in great glee at my curious illusion.

"After I had finished my paper and eaten my *moghlai* dinner, I put out the lamp and lay down on my bed in a small side-room.

Through the open window a star high above the Avalli hills was gazing from millions and millions of miles at Mr. Collector lying on a humble camp-bedstead. I was amused at the idea, and do not know when I fell asleep or how long I slept, but I suddenly awoke, although I heard no sound and saw no intruder. The bright star on the hilltop had disappeared, and the dim light of the new moon was stealthily entering the room through the open window, as if ashamed of its intrusion.

"I saw nobody but felt as if someone was gently pushing me. She said nothing, but beckoned me with her five fingers adorned with rings to follow her cautiously. I got up noiselessly, and though not a soul except myself was there in the apartments of that deserted palace with its slumbering sounds and waking echoes, I feared at every step lest anyone should awake. Most of the rooms were always closed, and I had never entered them.

"Breathlessly and with silent steps I followed my invisible guide —I cannot now say where. What endless dark and narrow passages, what long corridors, what silent and solemn audience-chambers and secret cells!

"Though I could not see my guide, she was not invisible to my mind's eye: an Arab girl, her arms visible through loose sleeves, smooth as marble, a thin veil falling on her face from the fringe of her cap, and a curved dagger at her waist! I thought that one of the thousand and one Arabian Nights had been wafted to me from the world of romance, and that at the dead of night I was wending my way through the narrow alleys of slumbering Bagdad to a trysting-place fraught with peril.

"At last my guide stopped before a deep blue screen, and seemed to point to something below. There was nothing there, but a sudden dread froze the blood in my heart. I thought I saw on the floor at the foot of the screen a terrible Negro eunuch dressed in rich brocade, sitting and dozing with outstretched legs, with a naked sword on his lap. My guide lightly skipped over his legs and held up a fringe of the screen. I could catch a glimpse of a room with a Persian carpet. Some one was sitting on a bed; I could not see her, but caught a glimpse of two exquisite feet in gold-embroidered slippers hanging out from loose saffron-colored pajamas and placed idly on the orange-colored velvet carpet. On one side there was a bluish crystal tray on which a few apples, pears, oranges, bunches of grapes, two small cups, and gold-tinted decanter were evidently awaiting the guest. A fragrant, intoxicating vapor from a strange incense that burned within almost overpowered my senses.

"With a trembling heart I attempted to step across the out-stretched legs of the eunuch, but he suddenly woke with a start and the sword fell from his lap with a sharp clang on the marble floor.

"A terrific scream made me jump, and I saw I was sitting on my camp-bedstead, sweating heavily. The crescent moon was pale in the morning light like a sleepless patient at dawn, and our crazy Meher Ali was crying out, as is his daily custom, 'Stand back! Stand back!' while he went along the lonely road.

"Such was the abrupt close of one of my Arabian Nights, but there were a thousand left.

"Then there followed a great discord between my days and nights. During the day I would go to my work worn and tired, cursing the bewitching night and her empty dreams, but at night my daily life would appear as a petty, false, and ludicrous vanity.

"At darkness I was caught and overwhelmed in the snare of a strange intoxication. I would be transformed into some unknown personage of a bygone age, playing my part in unwritten history, and my short English coat and tight breeches did not suit me in the least. With a red velvet hat, loose pajamas, an embroidered vest, a long flowing silk gown, and colored handkerchiefs scented with attar, I would complete my elaborate toilet, sit on a high-cushioned chair, and replace my cigarette with a many-coiled narghileh filled with rose-water, as if in eager expectation of a strange meeting with a beloved one.

"I have no power to describe the incidents that unfolded as the gloom of the night deepened. I felt as if in the curious apartments of that vast edifice the fragments of a beautiful story, which I could follow for some distance, but of which I could never see the end, flew about in a sudden gust of the vernal breeze. And in pursuit of them I would wander from room to room the whole night long.

"Amid the eddy of these dream-fragments, the smell of henna, the twanging of the guitar, the waves of air charged with fragrant spray, I would catch the momentary glimpse of a fair young woman. It was she who had saffron-colored pajamas, white soft feet in gold-

59

embroidered slippers with curved toes, a close-fitting bodice wrought with gold, and a red cap from which a golden frill fell on her brow and cheeks. She maddened me. In pursuit of her I wandered from room to room, from path to path among the bewildering maze of alleys in the enchanted dreamland of the nether world of sleep.

"Sometimes in the evening, while carefully arraying myself as a prince before a large mirror, a candle burning on either side, I would see a sudden reflection of the Persian beauty by my side. A swift turn of her neck, an eager glance of passion and pain glowing in her large dark eyes, a suspicion of speech on her dainty red lips, her figure, fair and slim, crowned with youth like a blossoming creeper, quickly uplifted in her graceful tilting gait, a dazzling flash of pain and craving and ecstasy, a smile and a glance and a blaze of jewels and silk, and she melted away. A wild gust of wind, laden with all the fragrance of hills and woods, would put out my light, and I would fling aside my array and lie down on my bed, my eyes closed and my body thrilling with delight. There around me in the breeze, amid all the perfume of the woods and hills, caresses, kisses, tender touches, gentle murmurs in my ears, and fragrant breaths on my brow floated through the silent gloom, or a sweetly-perfumed kerchief was wafted again and again on my cheeks. Then slowly a mysterious serpent would twist her stupefying coils about me, and heaving a sigh I would lapse into insensibility, and then into a profound slumber.

"One evening I decided to ride my horse. My English hat and coat were resting on a rack, and I was about to take them down when a sudden whirlwind, crested with the sands of the Susta and the dead leaves of the Avalli hills, caught them up and whirled them around and around while a loud peal of merry laughter rose higher and higher, striking all the chords of mirth till it died away in the land of the sunset. I could not go out for my ride, and the next day I gave up for good my queer English coat and hat.

"Again that day at the dead of night I heard stifled, heart-breaking sobs, as if below the bed, below the floor, below the stony foundation of that gigantic palace, from the depths of a dark damp grave, a voice piteously cried and implored me: 'Oh, rescue me! Break through these doors of illusion, slumber and fruitless dreams, place me by your side on the saddle, press me to your heart, and riding through hills and woods and across the river, take me to the warm radiance of your sunny rooms above!'

"Oh, how can I rescue you? What drowning beauty, what incarnate passion shall I drag to the shore from this wild eddy of dreams? O lovely apparition! Where did you flourish and when? By what cool spring, under the shade of what date-groves were you born; in the lap of what homeless wanderer in the desert? What Bedouin snatched you from your mother's arms, an opening bud plucked from a wild creeper; placed you on a horse swift as lightning; crossed the burning sands; and took you to the slave-market of what royal city? And there, what officer of the Badshah, seeing the glory of your bashful blossoming youth, paid for you in gold, placed you in a golden palanquin and offered you as a present for the seraglio of his master? And O, the history of that place! The music of the *sareng*, the jingle of anklets, the occasional flash of daggers, the glowing wine of Shiraz poison, and the piercing, flashing glance! What grandeur, what servitude! The slave-girls to your right and left waved the *chamar* as diamonds flashed from their bracelets; the Badshah, the king of kings, fell on his knees at your snowy feet in bejewelled shoes, and outside the terrible Abyssinian eunuch, looking like a messenger of death, but clothed like an angel, stood with a naked sword in his hand! Then, flower of the desert, swept away by the blood-stained ocean of grandeur with its foam of jealousy, and rocks and shoals of intrigue, on what shore of cruel death were you cast, or in what other land more splendid and more cruel?

"Suddenly at this moment that crazy Meher Ali screamed out: 'Stand back! Stand back!! All is false! All is false!' I opened by eyes and saw that it was already light. My *chaprasi* came and handed me my letters, and the cook waited with a salam for my orders.

"I said: 'No, I can stay here no longer.' That very day I packed up and moved to my office. Old Karim Khan smiled a little as he saw me. I felt nettled, but said nothing and began my work.

"As evening approached I grew absent-minded; I felt as if I had an appointment to keep, and the work of examining the cotton accounts seemed wholly useless. Even the Nizamat of the Nizam did not appear to be worth much. Whatever belonged to the present, whatever was moving and acting and working for bread seemed trivial, meaningless, and contemptible.

"I threw down my pen, closed my ledgers, got into my dog-cart, and drove away. It stopped by itself at the gate of the marble palace just at the hour of twilight. I quickly climbed the stairs and entered the room.

"A heavy silence was reigning. The dark rooms were sullen, as if they had taken offense. My heart was full of contrition but there was no one to whom I could open it, or of whom I could ask forgiveness. I wandered about the dark rooms with a vacant mind. I wished I had a guitar by which I could sing to the unknown: 'O fire, the poor moth that made a vain effort to fly away has come back to thee! Forgive it but this once, burn its wings and consume it in thy flame!'

"Suddenly two tear-drops fell on my brow from overhead. Dark clouds had overcast the top of the Avalli hills; the gloomy woods and the sooty waters of the Susta were waiting in an ominous calm. Suddenly land, water, and sky shivered, and a wild tempest-blast rushed howling through the distant pathless woods, showing its lightning-teeth like a raving maniac who had broken his chains. The desolate halls of the palace banged their doors, and moaned in the bitterness of anguish.

"The servants were all in the office, and there was no one to light the lamps. The night was cloudy and moonless. In the dense gloom I could distinctly feel that a woman was lying on her face on the carpet below the bed, clasping and tearing her long dishevelled hair with desparate fingers. Blood was trickling down her fair brow, and she was now laughing a hard, mirthless laugh, now bursting into violent wringing sobs, now rending her bodice and striking at her bare bosom, as the wind roared in through the open window and the rain poured in torrents and soaked her through and through.

"All during the night there was no cessation of the storm or of the passionate cry. In sorrow I wandered in the dark from room to room. Whom could I console when no one was here? Whose agony was this? Where did this inconsolable grief come from?

"And the mad man cried out: 'Stand back! Stand back! All is false! All is false!'

"I saw that the day had dawned, and that in that dreadful weather Meher Ali was going around the palace with his usual cry. Suddenly it came to me that perhaps he had once lived in that house, and that although he had gone mad, he came there every day and went around and around, fascinated by the weird spell cast by the marble demon. Despite the storm and rain I ran to him and asked: 'Ho, Meher Ali, what is false?'

"He did not answer, but pushed me aside and went around and around with his frantic cry like a bird flying fascinated about the jaws of a snake, and making a desperate effort to warn himself by repeating: 'Stand back! Stand back! All is false! All is false!' I ran like a mad man through the pelting rain to my office, and asked Karim Khan: 'Tell me the meaning of all this!'

"What I gathered from that old man was this: that at one time unrequited passion and unsatisfied longings and flames of wild pleasure raged within that palace, and the curse of all the heart-aches and blasted hopes had made its every stone thirsty and hungry, eager to swallow up like a famished ogress any living man who might chance to approach. Not one of those who lived there for three consecutive nights could escape these cruel jaws, save Meher Ali, who had escaped at the cost of his reason.

"I asked: 'Is there no means of my release?' The old man said: 'There is only one means, and that is very difficult. I will tell you what it is, but first you must hear the history of a young Persian girl who once lived in that pleasure-dome. A stranger or a more bitterly heart-rending tragedy was never enacted on this earth.'"

Just at this moment the coolies announced that the train was coming. We hurriedly picked up our luggage as the train steamed in. An English gentleman, apparently just aroused from slumber, and endeavoring to read the name of the station was looking out of a first-class carriage. As soon as he caught sight of our fellow-passenger, he cried, "Hello," and invited him into his compartment. As we got into a second-class carriage, we had no chance of discovering who the man was or the end of his story.

I said: "The man evidently took us for fools and imposed upon us out of fun. The story is pure fabrication from start to finish." The discussion that followed ended in a lifelong rupture between my theosophist kinsman and myself.

❦ The Runaway

Moti Babu, Zemindar of Katalia, was on his way home by boat. There had been the usual morning stop alongside a village market on the river, and the cooking of the noon meal was in progress.

A Brahmin boy came up to the boat and asked: "Which way are you going, Sir?" He could not have been older than fifteen or sixteen.

"To Katalia," Moti Babu replied.

"Could you give me a lift to Nandigram, on your way?"

Moti Babu agreed and asked the young fellow his name.

"My name is Tara," said the boy.

With his fair complexion, his large eyes and delicate, finely-cut, smiling lips, the lad was strikingly handsome. All he had on was a dhoti, somewhat tattered, and his bare upper body looked like some sculptor's masterpiece.

"Son," said Moti Babu affectionately, "have your bath and come on board. You can eat with me."

"Just a second, Sir," said Tara, and he jumped on the servants' boat moored astern, and started to help with the cooking. Moti Babu's servant was an up-country man and it was evident that his ideas of preparing fish for the pot were crude. Tara relieved him of his task and finished it easily. Then, with a skill which showed a good deal of practice, he made up one or two vegetable dishes. After finishing this, and after a plunge in the river, Tara took out a fresh dhoti from his bundle, clad himself in spotless white, and with a little wooden comb smoothed back the wavy hair from his forehead into a cluster behind his neck. Then, with his sacred thread glistening over his breast, he presented himself before his host.

Moti Babu took him into the cabin where his wife, Annapurna, and their nine-year-old daughter were sitting. The good lady was pleased with the attractive young boy and her whole heart went out to him. Where could he be coming from; whose child could he be; how could his mother, poor thing, bear to be separated from him, she thought to herself.

Dinner was served and a place set for Tara beside Moti Babu, but

64

the boy seemed to have a poor appetite. Annapurna thought it was bashfulness and repeatedly asked him to try this and that, but he would not be persuaded. He clearly had a will of his own, but he showed it quite simply and naturally, without any appearance of wilfulness or obstinacy.

When they had all finished, Annapurna made Tara sit by her side and answer questions. She could not gather much of a connected story, but it was clear that he had run away from home at the age of ten or eleven.

"Don't you have a mother?" asked Annapurna.

"Yes."

"Doesn't she love you?"

This last question seemed to strike the boy as highly absurd. He laughed as he replied, "Why shouldn't she?"

"Why did you leave her, then?" pursued the mystified lady.

"She has four other boys and three girls."

Annapurna was shocked. "What a thing to say!" she cried. "Could one bear to cut off a finger simply because there are four more?"

2

Tara's history was as brief as his years were few, but still he was a unique boy. He was the fourth son of his parents and had lost his father in his infancy. In spite of the large number of children, Tara had always been the favorite, and was petted by his mother, his brothers and sisters, and the neighbors. Even the schoolmaster usually spared him the rod, and when he did not, the punishment was felt by all the class. So there was no reason for him to leave home. But, curiously enough, although the scamp of the village, whose time was divided between eating fruit stolen from the neighbors' trees and feeling the even more fruitful consequences of his stealing, at the hands of these same neighbors, remained within the village clinging to his scolding mother, the pet of the village ran away to join a band of wandering players.

There was a quick response, and a rescue party hunted him out and brought him back. His distracted mother strained him to her breast and deluged him with tears. A sense of duty forced his elders to make a heroic effort to administer a mild corrective, but they lavished their repentant fondness on him worse than ever. The neighbors' wives redoubled their attentions in the hope of reconciling him to his home life, but all bonds, even those of affection, were irksome to the boy. The star under which he was born must have decreed him homeless.

When, in his wanderings through unknown lands, Tara saw foreign boats being towed along the river, or a *sannyasi* resting under one of the village trees, or a gypsy camp by the river—the gypsies seated by their mat-walled huts, splitting bamboos and weaving baskets—his spirit longed for the freedom of the mysterious outside world, unhampered by ties of affection. After he had repeated his escapade two or three times, his relations and neighbors gave up hope.

When the owner of the band of players which he had joined began to love Tara as a son, and he became the favorite of the whole party, when he found that even the people of the houses at which their performances were given, chiefly the women, would send for him to express their special appreciation, he eluded them all, and his companions could find no trace of him.

Tara was as impatient of bondage as a young deer, and as susceptible to music. It was the songs in the theatrical performances which had drawn him away from home. Their tunes would make corresponding rhythms course through his veins and his whole being swayed. Even when he was a small child, the solemn way in which he would sit out a musical performance, gravely nodding to mark the time, made it difficult for the adults to restrain their laughter. Not only music, but the patter of the heavy July rain on the trees in full foliage, the roll of the thunder, the moaning of the wind through the thickets, like some infant giant strayed from its mother, would make him completely distraught. The distant kites flying high in the midday sky, the croaking of the frogs on a rainy evening, the howling of the jackals at the dead of night—all these stirred him to his depths.

This passion for music led him to join a company of ballad singers. The master took great pains in teaching him to sing and recite ballads composed in alliterative verse and jingling meter, based on stories from the epics, and became as fond of him as if he were a pet singing-bird. But after he had learned several pieces, one morning it was found that the bird had flown.

During June and July in this part of the country, a succession of fairs are held in the different villages, and bands of players and singers and dancing girls, together with hordes of traders of every kind, journey in boats along the rivers from fair to fair. Since the year before, a novel party of acrobats had joined the throng. Tara, after leaving the ballad singers, had been traveling with a trader, helping him to sell his *pan*. His curiosity being roused, he joined the acrobats. He had taught himself to play the flute, and it was his sole function to play jigs, in the Lucknow style, while the acrobats were doing their feats. It was from this troupe that he had just run away. Tara had heard that the Zemindar of Nandigram was promoting some amateur theatricals on a grand scale. He promptly tied up his belongings in a bundle with the intention of going there, when he came across Moti Babu.

Tara's imaginative nature had saved him from acquiring the manners of any of the different companies with whom he had lived. His mind had always remained aloof and free. He had seen and heard many ugly things, but there was no room within him for these; like other bonds, habit also failed to contain him. Swan-like, he swam over the muddy waters of the world, and no matter how often his curiosity impelled him to dive into the mire beneath, his feathers remained unruffled and white. That is why the face of the runaway shone with a youthfulness that made even the middle-aged, worldly Moti Babu accept and welcome him without a question or a doubt.

After dinner was over, the boat cast off. Annapurna, with an affectionate interest, continued asking about Tara's relatives and his home life, but the boy made the shortest possible replies and at last sought refuge by a flight to the deck.

The vast river, swollen by the seasonal rains to the last limit of its banks, seemed to embarrass Mother Nature herself by its boisterous recklessness. As though with a magic wand, the sun, shining out of a break in the clouds, touched the rows of half-submerged reeds at the water's edge, the juicy green of the sugarcane higher up on the bank, and the purple haze of the woodlands on the farther shore against the distant horizon. Everything was gleaming and quickening with life.

Tara mounted the upper deck and stretched himself under the shade of the spreading sail. One after another, sloping meadows, flooded jute fields, deep green waves of *aman* rice, paths winding up to the village from the riverside, villages nestling in dense groves, appeared and passed away. This world, with its far-gazing sky, the whisper in its fields, the tumult in its water, the restless trees, the vast space above and below, was on terms of the closest intimacy with the boy, and yet it never for a moment tried to bind his restless spirit with a jealous embrace.

Calves were gambolling by the riverside; village ponies limped along, grazing on the meadows. Kingfishers perched on bamboo poles put up for spreading the nets took an occasional plunge after fish. Boys were playing in the river. Village girls up to their breasts in the water chattered and laughed as they scrubbed their clothes. Fishwives with baskets, their cloth tucked around their waist, bargained with the fishermen. These scenes never exhausted their novelty for Tara; his eyes were always eager.

Tara then began to talk with the boatmen. He jumped up and took turns with them at the poles whenever the boat hugged the shore too closely, and when the steersman felt he would like a smoke Tara relieved him at the helm, knowing exactly how to work the sail with the changing direction of the breeze and the boat.

A little before evening Annapurna sent for Tara and asked him: "What do you usually have for supper?"

"Whatever I get," was the reply, "and some days I don't get anything at all!"

Annapurna was disappointed at this lack of response. She would have liked to feed and care for this homeless waif until he was happy, but somehow she could not find out what would please him. A little later when the boat was moored for the night, she bustled about and sent servants into the village to get milk and sweetmeats and other dainties, but Tara contented himself with a slight supper and refused the milk altogether. Even Moti Babu, who was a man of few words, tried to press the milk on him, but he simply said: "I don't care for it."

Thus passed two or three days of their life on the river. Tara of his own accord, and with great alacrity, helped in the marketing and the cooking and lent a hand with the boatmen in whatever had to be done. Anything worth seeing never escaped his keen glance. His eyes, his limbs, his mind were always on the alert. Like Nature herself, he was constantly active, yet aloof and undistracted. Every person has some fixed point, but Tara was just a ripple on the current of things rushing across the infinite blue. Nothing bound him to past or future; his part in life was simply to flow onwards.

From the various professionals with whom he had associated he had picked up many entertaining accomplishments. Free from all troubling thoughts, his mind was wonderfully receptive. He had memorized a number of ballads, songs and long passages from dramas. One day as was his custom, Moti Babu was reading from the Ramayana to his wife and daughter. He was about to come to the story of Kusha and Lava, the valiant sons of Rama, when Tara could not contain his excitement any longer. Stepping from the deck into the cabin he exclaimed: "Put away the book, Sir. Let me sing you the story." He then began to recite Dasarathi's version in a flute-like voice, showering and scattering its rhymes and alliterations. The atmosphere became full with laughter and tears. The boatmen hung around the cabin doors to listen, and even the occupants of passing boats strained their ears to get snatches of the melody. When he finished, all the listeners sighed because it ended so soon!

With her eyes filling, Annapurna longed to take Tara into her lap and fold him to her bosom. Moti Babu thought that if only he could persuade the lad to stay on with them he would cease to feel the want of a son. But Charu, their little daughter, felt that she would explode with jealousy.

3

Charu was an only child, the sole claimant to her parents love. There was no end to her whims and caprices. She had her own ideas about dress and grooming, but these changed constantly. So whenever she was invited out, her mother was nervous till the last moment, afraid she would get something impossible into her head. If she did not like the way her hair had been done, taking it down and doing it up again would not do any good—the matter was sure to end in a fit of sulking. It was the same with other things; however, when she was in a good humor, she was reasonableness itself. She would kiss and embrace her mother with gushing affection, and distract her with incessant prattle and laughter. In a word, this little girl was an impossible enigma.

With all the fierceness of her untamed heart Charu began to hate Tara. She started tearfully pushing away her plate at dinner, saying the cooking was poor. She slapped her maid and found fault with her for no reason, and succeeded in making her parents thoroughly uncomfortable. In spite of the fact that her mind refused to admit Tara's merits, she found his accomplishments interesting, and the more he gave proof of those merits, the angrier she became.

When Tara first sang the story of Kusha and Lava, Annapurna had hoped that the music, which could have charmed the beasts of the forests, might soften the temper of her wayward daughter. She asked, "And how did you like it, Charu?" A vigorous shaking of the head was the reply she got, which translated into words must have meant: "I did not like it, and I never will like it, so there!"

Realizing that it was a pure case of jealousy the mother stopped showing any attention to Tara in her daughter's presence. But when Charu had gone off to bed, and Moti Babu was sitting on deck with Tara, Annapurna took her seat near the cabin door and asked Tara to sing to them. As the melody wafted into the evening, enhancing the hush of the villages reposing in the dusk, and filling Annapurna's heart with an ecstasy of love and beauty, Charu left her bed and came up sobbing: "What a noise you are all making, mother! I can't get a wink of sleep!" How could she bear the idea of being sent off to bed alone, and all of them surrounding Tara, revelling in his singing?

Tara found the tantrums of this little girl with the bright black eyes highly diverting. He tried to win her by telling her stories, singing songs, playing on the flute, but with no success. Only when he plunged into the river for his daily swim, with his dhoti lifted short above his knees and tightened round his waist, his supple limbs knifing the water with skillful ease, she could not help being attracted. Every morning she looked forward to his bath-time, but without letting any one guess her fascination. And when the time came, this little actress would start knitting a woolen scarf by the cabin window; now and then her eyes would lift to throw a casual, seemingly contemptuous glance at Tara's performance.

They had passed by Nandigram, but Tara had taken no notice.

70

The big boat swept onwards with a leisurely movement, sometimes under sail, sometimes towed along. The days wore on like streams, with a lazy flow of unexciting hours. No one was in any kind of hurry. They all took plenty of time over their daily bath and meals, and even before it grew dark the boats would be moored near the landing place of some village of sufficient size, against a background lively with the sparkle of fireflies and the chirping of cicadas. In this way it took them over ten days to get to Katalia.

4

Hearing the news of Zemindar Babu's arrival, men, palanquins and ponies were sent out to meet his boat, and the retainers fired off a salvo startling the village crows into misgivings. Impatient because of the delay caused by this formal welcome, Tara quietly slipped off the boat and made a rapid tour of the village. He hailed some as brother or sister, others as uncle or aunt, and in the space of two or three hours had made friends with all sorts of people.

Perhaps it was because Tara acknowledged no bonds that he could win his way so easily into others' affections. Anyhow, in a few days the whole village had unconditionally capitulated. One of the reasons for his easy victory was the quickness with which he could enter into the spirit of every class, as if he were one of themselves. He was not the slave of any custom and could easily adjust to things. With children he became child-like; with his elders, he was mature; with the peasant, he was a peasant without losing his brahminhood. He took part in the work and play of all of them with zest and skill. One day as he was seated by a sweetmeat-shop the proprietor asked him to mind the shop while he went on an errand, and the boy cheerfully sat there for hours, driving off the flies with a *palmyra* leaf. He had some knowledge of how to make sweetmeats, and could also take a hand at the loom or at the potter's wheel.

Although he had made a conquest of the village, he had been unable to overcome the jealousy of one little girl, and it may be that because he felt that this atom of femininity desired his banishment with all her might, he made such a prolonged stay in Katalia.

But little Charu was not long in furnishing fresh proof of the inscrutability of the feminine mind. Sonamani, the daughter of the cook, had been widowed at the early age of five. She was now Charu's age and her closest friend. She was confined to her quarters with some ailment when the family returned home and so could not come to see her companion for some days. When at last she did turn up, the two friends nearly separated for good. This is how it happened.

Charu started on the story of her travels with great circumstance. With the thrilling episode of the abduction of the gem known as Tara, she expected to arouse her friend's curiosity and wonderment. But when she learned that Tara was not unknown to Sonamani, that he called Sonamani's mother aunt, and Sonamani called him *dada*; when she further learned that Tara had not only charmed both mother and daughter by playing *kirtan* tunes on the flute, but had actually made a bamboo flute for Sonamani with his own hand, and plucked fruit for her from tree tops and flowers for her from brambly thickets—she felt as if a red-hot spear had been thrust into her.

That day, Charu vowed eternal enmity to Sonamani. And going into Tara's room she pulled out his favorite flute, threw it on the floor and trampled it into slivers.

While she was furiously busy Tara came into the room. This picture of passion which the girl presented amazed him. "Charu!" he cried. "Why are you smashing my flute?"

"Serves you right. I'd do it again!" she screamed, and with a flushed face and reddened eyes she gave the flute some more kicks and ran crying from the room.

Tara picked up his flute and saw that it was ruined. He could not help laughing when he thought of the sudden fate which had overtaken his innocent instrument. As the days went by, Charu was becoming for him more and more an object of curiosity.

He also found in the house other objects which fully aroused his curiosity. These were the illustrated English books in Moti Babu's library. Though his knowledge of the outside world was considerable, he found it difficult to completely enter this world of pictures. He tried to make up for this deficiency by his imagination, but that was not satisfactory.

One day, finding the books so attractive to Tara, Moti Babu asked him: "Would you like to learn English? Then you could understand all about these pictures."

"I would indeed!" exclaimed Tara.

Moti Babu, delighted, at once arranged with the headmaster of the village school to give Tara English lessons.

5

With his keen memory and undivided attention, Tara worked at his English lessons. He seemed to have embarked on an adventurous quest which left his old life behind. The neighbors saw no more of him, and when in the afternoon, just before it got dark, he would pace rapidly up and down the deserted riverside reading his lessons, his devoted band of boys looked on dejectedly from a distance, not daring to interrupt him.

Even Charu rarely saw him. Tara used to come into the *zenana* for his meals, which he ate leisurely under the kindly eyes of Annapurna. But now he could no longer tolerate the loss of time over all this, and begged Moti Babu's permission to be served in his room outside. Annapurna grieved and protested at the prospect of losing his company, but Moti Babu, glad to find the boy so earnest in his studies, agreed with the idea and so arranged it.

All of a sudden Charu announced that she also would learn English. Her parents at first took it as a great joke and laughed heartily over their little girl's latest caprice. But she washed away the humor with a flood of tears, and her helpless parents had to take the matter seriously. Charu was placed under the same tutor and had her lessons with Tara.

But studiousness did not come naturally to this flighty little creature. Not only did she not learn, but also made it difficult for Tara to do so. She would lag behind by not preparing her lessons, but would fly into a rage or burst into tears if Tara went on to the next one without her. When Tara was through with one book and had to get another, the same had to be procured for her also. Her jealousy would not allow Tara to sit alone in his room to do his exercises. She began stealing in when he was not there, and daubing his exercise book with ink, or taking away his pen. Tara would bear this as long as he could, and then would chastise her, but she would not reform.

At last, by accident, Tara hit upon an effective method. One day,

73

as he tore out an ink-spattered page from his exercise book and was sitting there thoroughly vexed about it, Charu peeped in. "Now I am going to catch it," she thought. But as she came in, she was disappointed; Tara sat quietly without a word. She teasingly skipped near enough for him to cuff her, if he had been so minded. But he remained as still and grave as ever. The little culprit was completely frustrated. She was not used to apologizing, and yet her penitent heart yearned to make it up to Tara. Finding no other way, she took up the torn-out page and sitting near him wrote on it in large round handwriting: "I will never do it again." She then went through a variety of maneuvers to draw Tara's attention to what she had written. Tara could keep his countenance no longer, and burst out laughing. The girl fled from the room in grief and anger. She felt that nothing short of the complete obliteration of that sheet of paper, from eternal time and infinite space, would wipe away her mortification!

Bashful, Sonamani would sometimes come to the schoolroom door, hesitate at the threshold and then leave. She had made it up with Charu, and they were as great friends as ever, but where Tara was concerned Sonamani was cautious. She usually chose the time when Charu was inside the *zenana*, to hover near the schoolroom door. One day Tara caught sight of the retreating figure and called out: "Hullo, Sona, is that you? What's the news: how is my aunt?"

"You haven't been to us for so long," said Sonamani. "Mother has a pain in the back or she would have come to see you herself."

At this point Charu came up. Sonamani was embarrassed. She felt as if she had been caught stealing her friend's property. Charu, with a toss of her head, cried out in a shrill voice: "Shame on you, Sonamani, coming and disturbing lessons! I'll tell mother." To hear this self-constituted guardian of Tara, one would have thought that her sole care in life was to prevent the disturbance of his studies! What brought her here at this time the Lord might have known, but Tara had no idea.

Poor flustered Sonamani sought refuge by making all kinds of excuses, whereupon Charu called her a nasty little storyteller, and she had to slink away in complete defeat.

But the sympathetic Tara shouted after her: "All right, Sona, tell your mother I'll go and see her this evening."

"Oh! Will you?" sneered Charu. "Haven't you got lessons to do? I'll tell *master-mashai*, you see if I don't!"

Undaunted by the threat, Tara went over on the next two evenings. On the third, Charu went further than merely threatening. She fastened the chain outside Tara's door, and taking a small padlock off her mother's spice-box, locked him in for the evening, only letting him out when it was supper time. Tara was so annoyed that he swore he would not touch a morsel of food. The repentant girl, beside herself, begged for forgiveness. "I'll never, never do it again," she pleaded, "I beg of you at your feet, do please have something to eat." Tara was obstinate at first, but when she began to sob as if her heart would break, he sat down to his supper.

Charu often said to herself she would never again tease Tara and would be very, very good to him, but Sonamani, or something or other, would get in the way and spoil her virtuous resolution.

And it came about that whenever Tara found her particularly quiet and good he began to look for an explosion. How or why it happened he could never make out, but sure enough, there it was, a regular storm, followed by showers of tears. Then the bright sun was shining and there was peace.

6

Thus passed two whole years. Tara had never before permitted any one to cage him for so long. Perhaps it was the novelty of his studies; perhaps it was his growth of character, which made his restless spirit welcome the change to a quiet life; perhaps his fellow-student, with her endless variety of teasing, had cast a secret spell over his heart.

Charu reached marriageable age, and Moti Babu was anxiously looking for a suitable bridegroom. But the mother said to her husband, "Why are you hunting for bridegrooms? Tara is a nice boy and our daughter is fond of him."

This took Moti Babu by surprise. "How can you say that?" he exclaimed. "We know nothing of his family history. Our only daughter must make a good marriage."

One day a family came over from the Zemindar of Raydanga to see

75

Charu, with the idea of making a proposal. Annapurna tried to get Charu dressed up and taken to the reception room, but she locked herself in her bedroom and refused to come out. Moti Babu stood by the door and pleaded and scolded in vain; at last he had to go back and make feeble excuses to the would-be bridegroom's party, saying his daughter was indisposed. They came to the conclusion that there was something wrong with the girl which was being concealed and the matter fell through.

Then Moti Babu thought again of Tara, who was handsome and well-behaved, and in every way desirable. He could continue to live with them, and the pain of sending away their only child to another house could be avoided. It also occurred to him that Charu's obstinacies, which seemed so excusable in her father's home, would not be so indulgently tolerated in the home of her husband.

Moti Babu and Annapurna had a long talk about it and finally decided to send to Tara's village with inquiries. When the news came back that the family was respectable but poor, a formal proposal was at once sent off to the mother and the elders. And they, overjoyed at the prospect, lost no time in returning their consent.

Moti Babu discussed the time and place of the wedding with his wife, but with his habitual caution kept the matter secret from everybody else.

Meanwhile Charu would occasionally make stormy raids on Tara's room, sometimes angry, sometimes affectionate, sometimes contemptuous, but always disturbing. And gleams, like lightning flashes, would create a tumult in the once free and open sky of the boy's mind. His life now felt the network of dreamstuff into which it had drifted and become entangled. Some days Tara would leave his lessons and go to the library, where he would remain immersed in the pictures. And the world which his imagination now conjured up was different from the former and less colorful. The boy was happy with this change in himself, and conscious of a new experience.

Moti Babu had fixed upon a day in July for the ceremony, and sent out invitations to Tara's mother and relatives. He also instructed his agent in Calcutta to send down a brass band and other paraphernalia necessary for a wedding. But to Tara, he had not said a word.

In the meantime the monsoon set in. The river had almost dried up, the only sign of water being the pools in the hollows; elsewhere the river bed was deeply scored with the tracks of carts which had recently crossed. The village boats, stranded, were imbedded in the caking mud. Then all of a sudden one day, like a married daughter returning to her father's house, a swift-flowing current, babbling with glee, danced straight into the empty heart and outstretched arms of the village. The boys and girls romped with joy, and never seemed to tire of sporting and splashing in the water, their long lost friend. The village women left their tasks and came out to greet their companion of old. And everywhere fresh life stirred up in the dry, languishing village.

Boats from distant parts, of all shapes and sizes, bringing their freight, were now seen on the river, and the bazaars in the evening resounded with the songs of the foreign boatmen. During the dry season, the villages on either bank had been left in their secluded corners to pass the time with domestic concerns, and now in the rains the great outside world came a-wooing, mounted on a silt-red chariot laden with merchandise, and all pettiness was swept away in the glamour of the courting; all would now be life and gaiety, and festive clamor would fill the skies.

This year the Nag Zemindars, close by, were organizing an especially gorgeous car-festival, and there was to be a grand fair. In the moon-lit evening when Tara went sauntering by the river, he saw all the boats hurrying by, some filled with merry-go-rounds, others bearing theatrical parties singing and playing as they went, and any number carrying traders with their wares. There was one containing a party of strolling players, with a violin vigorously playing a well-known tune, and the usual ha! ha! of encouragement shouted out every time it came back to the refrain. The up-country boatmen of the cargo boats kept clanging their cymbals without any accompanying song or tune. Everywhere there was excitement and bustle.

As Tara looked on, an immense cloud rolled up from the horizon, spreading and bellying out like a great black sail; the moon was overcast; the east wind sprang up, driving cloud after cloud; the river swelled and heaved. In the swaying woods on the river banks the darkness grew tense, frogs croaked and shrill cicadas seemed to be sawing away at the night with their chirp.

All the world was holding a car-festival that evening, with flags

77

flying, wheels whirling and the earth rumbling. Clouds pursued each other, the wind rushed after them, the boats sped on, and songs leapt to the skies. Then the lightning flashed out, rending the sky from end to end; the thunder crackled forth; and out of the depths of the darkness came a scent of moist earth and torrential rain. The sleepy little village of Katalia dozed in a corner, with its doors closed and lights out.

The next day, Tara's mother and brothers landed at Katalia with three boats full of wedding necessities. Sonamani, with great trepidation, took some preserves and pickles to Tara's room, and stood hesitating at his door. But there was no Tara. Before this conspiracy of love and affection had succeeded in completely surrounding him, the free-souled Brahmin boy had fled in the rainy night, carrying with him the heart of the village which he had stolen, and returned to the arms of his great world-mother, who was serene in her unconcern.

# AUTOBIOGRAPHICAL

Although Tagore warned, in the introduction to *Jivansmriti* (*My Reminiscences*), 1912, that to take "my memory pictures . . . as an attempt at autobiography would be a mistake," he also wrote that "It is as literary material that I offer them." On this basis, excerpts from three autobiographical selections are included in this volume.

Tagore was born during a transitional period in Bengali history, and it caused his later achievements to be a matter of public curiosity, and even of public controversy. His originality in art, his pioneering in education, and his unorthodox religion and views of men and public affairs needed explanation. This, together with his own introspective nature, impelled him to search deeply into his personal history.

The original Bengali book, *Jivansmriti*, was published in 1912, and included black and white sketches by Gaganendranath Tagore, his artist nephew. It was translated by Surendranath Tagore and published as *My Reminiscences* (Macmillan & Co., Ltd., London, 1917).

At the invitation of Liang Chi-Chao, president of the University Lecture Association of Peking, Tagore delivered a series of lectures in China during April and May of 1924. As a means of introducing or interpreting himself, many of these lectures were given in an autobiographical style. A paper-bound volume, now out of print, was published by Visva-Bharati (1925) containing lecture notes and a few translations from his earlier writings. From these, *My Life* was compiled by Anthony X. Soares for his book, *Lectures and Addresses by Rabindranath Tagore* (Macmillan & Co., Ltd., London, 1928).

Chhelebela, the Bengali original of *My Boyhood Days*, is a sequence of memories covering the period from Tagore's earliest recollections to his first trip abroad in 1878. *Chhelebela* was published in 1940, and its

79

English translation by Marjorie Sykes was serialized almost simultaneously in the *Visva-Bharati Quarterly*. *My Boyhood Days* was published in book form by Visva-Bharati, Calcutta, in April, 1940.

FROM *My Life*

I was born in 1861, not an important date in world history, but a date belonging to a great period in the history of Bengal. Just as we have our places of pilgrimage where the great rivers meet, symbolizing the spirit of life in nature, and emblematic of the meeting of ideals, we have the currents of three movements in the life of India. These currents met about the time I was born.

One of these movements was religious, introduced by a great-hearted man of gigantic intelligence, Raja Rammohan Roy.[1] He was a revolutionary, and tried to reopen the channel of spiritual life which had been obstructed for many years by the debris of formal and materialistic creeds that were fixed in practices lacking spiritual significance.

A great fight ensued between him and the orthodox who suspected every living idea that was dynamic. People who cling to an ancient past have their pride in the antiquity of their accumulations, and in the sublimity of their high-walled surroundings. They grow nervous and angry when some lover of truth breaks open their enclosure and floods it with the sunshine of thought and life. Ideas cause movement, but they consider all forward movements to be a menace against their warehouse security.

I am proud to say that my father was one of the leaders of that movement, for which he suffered ostracism and social indignities. I was born in this atmosphere of new ideals, but ideals which were older than all the other antiquities of which that age was proud.

But our self-expression must find its freedom not only in spiritual ideas but in literary manifestations, and there was a second movement of equal importance. Bankim Chandra Chatterjee,[2] who lived long enough for me to see him, was the first pioneer in the literary revolution which occurred in Bengal about that time.

Our literature had allowed its creative life to vanish; it lacked movement, and was fettered by a rhetoric as rigid as death. This man was brave enough to challenge the orthodoxy which believed in the security of tombstones and in perfection which can only belong to the dead. He lifted from our language the dead weight of ponderous forms and with a touch of his wand aroused our literature from her age-long sleep. And what beauty she revealed when she awoke in the fullness of her strength and grace.

The third movement which started about this time in my country was national. It was not fully political but began to express our people who were trying to assert their own personality. It was a voice of indignation at the humiliation constantly heaped upon us by those who were not oriental, and who had, especially at that time, the habit of dividing people into good and bad according to what was similar to their life and what was different.

This contemptuous spirit of separateness was causing great damage to our own culture. It generated in the young men of our country distrust of all things that had come to them as an inheritance from their past. Our students, imitating the laughter of their European schoolmasters, laughed at the old Indian pictures and other works of art. The same spirit of rejection, born out of ignorance, was cultivated in other areas of our culture, the result of a hypnotism exercised upon the minds of the younger generation by people who had loud voices and strong arms.

This spirit of revolt had just awakened when I was born, and some people were already trying to suppress it. The movement had leaders from my own family, my brothers and cousins, and they tried to save the people from being insulted and ignored by those who were their fellow men.

We had to find some universal basis, and we had to discover those things which have an everlasting value. The national movement was started to proclaim the fact that we must not be indiscriminate in our rejection of the past. This was not a reactionary movement but a revolutionary one; it set out with great courage to deny and to oppose all pride in mere borrowings.

These three movements had started, and the members of my family took an active part in all three. We were ostracized because of our heterodox opinions about religion; therefore, we enjoyed the freedom of the outcaste. We had to build our world with our own thoughts, we had to build it from the foundation, and therefore had to seek the foundation that was firm.

I was born into a family which had to live its own life, which led me in my young days to seek guidance for my self-expression from my own inner standard of judgment. My medium of expression was Bengali, but the language of the people had to be modulated according to the urging which I as an individual had.

No poet should borrow his medium ready-made from some shop of respectability; he should not only have his own seeds but should prepare his own soil. Each poet has his own language, not because all language is of his own making, but because his individual use transforms it into a special vehicle of his own creation.

All men have poetry in their hearts, and it is necessary for them, as much as possible, to express their feelings. For this they must have a medium, moving and pliant, which can refreshingly become their own, age after age. All great languages undergo change. Those languages which resist the spirit of change are doomed and will never produce great harvests of thought and literature. When forms become fixed, the spirit either weakly accepts its imprisonment or rebels. All revolutions consist of the "within" fighting against invasion from the "without."

Revolution must come, and men must risk revilement and misunderstanding, especially from those who want to be comfortable, who put their faith in materialism and convention, and who belong truly, not to modern times but to the dead past, when physical flesh and size predominated, and not the mind of man.

This kind of physical dominance is mechanical, and modern machines merely exaggerate our bodies, lengthening and multiplying our limbs. The modern child delights in size, representing an inordinate material power, saying, "Let me have the big toy and no sentiment which can disturb it," not realizing that we are returning to that antediluvian age which revelled in the production of gigantic physical frames, leaving no place for the free inner spirit.

All great human movements are related to some great idea. Some say that such a doctrine of spirit has been in its death-throes for over a century and is now moribund, that we have nothing to rely upon but external forces and material foundations. But I say that this doctrine was obsolete long ago. It was exploded in the springtime of life, when mere size was swept off the face of the world and replaced by naked man with his helpless body, but also with his indomitable mind and spirit.

The impertinence of material things is extremely old; the revelation of the spirit in man is truly modern. I am on its side, for I am modern.

When I began my life as a poet, the writers among our educated community took their inspiration from English literature. I suppose it was fortunate for me that I never in my life had what is called an education, that is to say, the kind of school and college training which is considered proper for a boy from a respectable family. Though I cannot say I was altogether free from influences that ruled young minds in those days, my writings were nevertheless saved from imitative forms. I believe it was chiefly because I had the good fortune to escape the school training which could set up for me an artificial standard based upon the prescription of the schoolmaster. In my versification, vocabulary and ideas I yielded myself to the vagaries of an untutored fancy which brought castigation upon me from critics who were learned, and uproarious laughter from the witty. My ignorance combined with my heresy turned me into a literary outlaw.

When I began my career I was ridiculously young; in fact, I was the youngest of the writers of that time who had made themselves articulate. I had neither the protective armor of mature age nor that of a respectable English education, so in my seclusion of contempt and qualified encouragement I had my freedom. Gradually I grew up, and cut my way through derision and occasional patronage into a recognition in which the proportion of praise and blame was much like that of land and water on our earth.

If you ask what gave me boldness when I was young, I should say that one thing was my early acquaintance with the old *Vaishnava* [3] poems of Bengal, full of freedom in meter and expression. I think I was only twelve when these poems first began to be reprinted. I surreptitiously obtained copies from the desks of my elders. For the edification of the young, I must confess that this was not right for a boy of my age; I should have been passing my examinations and not following a path that would lead to failure. I must also admit that the greater part of these lyrics was erotic and not quite suited to a boy just about to reach his teens, but my imagination was completely occupied with the beauty of their forms and the music of their words, and their breath, heavily laden with voluptuousness, passed over my mind without distracting it.

This vagabondage in my literary career had another origin: my father was the leader of a new religious movement, a strict monotheism based upon the teachings of the Upanishads, and my countrymen in Bengal thought him almost as bad as a Christian, if not worse. So we were completely ostracized, which probably saved me from another disaster, that of imitating our own past.

Most of the members of my family had some gift: some were artists, some poets, some musicians, and the atmosphere of our home was permeated with the spirit of creation. I had a deep sense, almost from infancy, of nature, a feeling of intimate companionship with the trees and the clouds, and the touch of the seasons. At the same time I had a peculiar susceptibility to human kindness. These craved for expression, and naturally I wanted to give them my own expression, though I was too immature to give them any perfection of form.

Since then I have achieved a reputation in India, but a strong current of antagonism in a large number of my countrymen still persists. Some say that my poems do not spring from the heart of the national traditions; some complain that they are incomprehensible, others that they are unwholesome. In fact, I have never had complete acceptance from my own people, and that too has been a blessing, for nothing is so demoralizing as unqualified success.

This is the story of my career; I wish I could reveal it through my work in my own language. I hope that will be possible some day or other. Languages are jealous. They do not give up their best treasures to those who try to deal with them through an intermediary belonging to an alien rival. You have to court them in person and dance attendance on them. Poems are not like gold or other substantial things that are transferable, and you cannot receive the smiles and glances of your sweetheart through an attorney, however diligent and dutiful he may be.

I have tried to experience the wealth of beauty in European literature. When I was young I approached Dante, unfortunately through
a translation. I utterly failed, and felt it my pious duty to stop, so
Dante remained closed to me.

I also wanted to know German literature, and by reading Heine
in translation, I thought I had caught a glimpse of the beauty there.
Fortunately I met a lady missionary from Germany, and asked her
help. I worked hard for some months, but being rather quick-witted,
which is not a good quality, I was not persevering. I had the dangerous facility which helps one to guess the meaning too easily. My
teacher thought I had almost mastered the language, which was not
true. I succeeded, however, in getting through Heine, like a sleep-
walker easily crossing unknown paths, and I found immense pleasure.

Then I tried Goethe, but that was too ambitious. With the help
of the little German I had learned, I went through Faust. I believe
I found my entrance to the place, not like one who has keys for all
the doors, but as a casual visitor who is tolerated in some guest room,
comfortable but not intimate. Properly speaking, I do not know my
Goethe; and in the same way many other great luminaries are dark to
me. This is as it should be; man cannot reach the shrine if he does
not make the pilgrimage. I hope that this may make others want to
learn Bengali some day.

In regard to music, I claim to be something of a musician myself.
I have composed many songs which have defied the canons of respectable orthodoxy, and good people are disgusted at the impudence
of a man who is audacious, because he is untrained. But I persist,
and God forgives me because I do not know what I do. Possibly
that is the best way of doing things in the sphere of art, for I find
that people blame me, but also sing my songs, even if not always
correctly. . . .

I have been asked to tell you something of my religion. One of
the reasons why I always feel reluctant to speak about this is that I
have not achieved my religion by passively accepting a particular
creed through some accident of birth. I was born to a family who
were pioneers in the revival of a great religion based upon the utterance of Indian sages in the Upanishads. But owing to my idiosyn-
crasy of temperament, it was impossible for me to accept any religious
teaching on the basis that people in my surroundings believed it

to be true. I could not persuade myself to imagine that I had a religion simply because everybody whom I might trust believed in its value.

Thus, my mind was always free from the dominance of any creed that had its sanction in the definite authority of some scripture or in the teaching of some organized body of worshipers; therefore, when I am questioned about religion, I have no prepared ground on which to stand, no training in a systematic approach to the subject.

Essentially, my religion is a poet's religion. Its touch comes to me through the same trackless channels as the inspiration of my music. My religious life and my poetical life have followed the same mysterious line of growth. Somehow they are wedded to each other, and though their betrothal had a long period of ceremony, it was kept secret from me. Then suddenly a day came when their union was revealed to me.

At that time I was living in a village. The day brought all the drifting trivialities of the commonplace. I finished my morning's work, and before going to take my bath I stood for a moment at my window overlooking a market place on the bank of a dry river bed. Suddenly I became conscious of a stirring within me. My world of experience seemed to become lighted, and facts that were detached and dim found a great unity of meaning. The feeling that I had was like what a man, groping through a fog without knowing his destination, might feel when he suddenly discovers that he stands before his own house.

I remember the day in my childhood when, after the painful process of learning my Bengali alphabet, I unexpectedly came to the first simple combination of letters which gave me the words: "It rains, the leaves tremble." I was thrilled with the picture which these words suggested to me. The fragments lost their individual isolation and my mind revelled in the unity of a vision. In a similar manner, on that morning in the village, the facts of my life suddenly appeared to me in a luminous unity. All things that had seemed like vagrant waves were revealed in relation to a boundless sea, and from that time I have been able to maintain the faith that, in all my experience of nature or man, there is the fundamental truth of spiritual reality.

You will understand me if I tell you how unconsciously I had been traveling toward the realization which I stumbled upon that day. . . . From my infancy I had the sensitiveness which always kept my mind conscious of the world around me.

We had a small garden beside our house; it was a fairyland to me, where miracles of beauty were of everyday occurrence. Every morning at an early hour I would run out from my bed to greet the first pink flush of dawn through the trembling leaves of the coconut trees which stood in a line along the garden boundary. The dewdrops glistened as the grasss caught the first tremor of the morning breeze. The sky seemed to bring a personal companionship, and my whole body drank in the light and peace of those silent hours. I was anxious never to miss a single morning, because each one was more precious to me than gold to the miser.

I had been blessed with that sense of wonder which gives a child his right to enter the treasure-house of mystery in the heart of existence. I neglected my studies because they took me from my friend and companion, the world around me; and when I was thirteen I freed myself from the clutches of an educational system that tried to imprison me with lessons.

Perhaps this will explain the meaning of my religion. The world was alive, intimately close to my life. I still remember my repulsion when a medical student brought me a piece of human windpipe and tried to excite my admiration for its structure. He tried to convince me that it was the source of the beautiful human voice, but I rejected that information with disgust. I did not admire the skill of the workman, but rather the artist who concealed the machinery and revealed his unified creation.

God does not care to expose His power written in geological inscriptions, but He is proud of the beauty in green grass, in flowers, in the play of color on the clouds, in the music of running water.

It was good for me that my consciousness was never dulled to the surrounding world. That the cloud was the cloud, that a flower was a flower, was enough, because they spoke directly to me, and I could not be indifferent to them. I still remember the moment, one afternoon, when coming home from school I jumped from the carriage and suddenly saw in the sky, behind the upper terrace of our house, deep dark rain-clouds lavishing cool shadows on the atmosphere. The marvel of it, the generosity of its presence, gave me a joy which was freedom, the kind of freedom we feel in the love of a dear friend.

That which merely gives information can be explained in terms of measurement, but that which gives joy cannot be explained by the grouping of atoms and molecules. Somewhere in the arrangement of this world there seems to be a great concern with giving delight, showing that in addition to the meaning of matter and force there is a message conveyed through the magic touch of personality. This touch cannot be analyzed, it can only be felt.

Is it merely because the rose is round and red that it gives me more satisfaction than the gold which could buy the necessities of life, or any number of slaves? You may deny the claim that a rose gives more delight than a piece of gold, but you must remember that I am not speaking about artificial values. If we had to cross a desert whose sand was made of gold, the glitter of those dead particles would become a terror for us, and the sight of a rose would bring us the music of paradise.

The final meaning of the delight which we find in a rose can never be in the roundness of its petals, just as the final meaning of the joy of music cannot be in a phonograph record. Somehow we feel that through a rose the language of love reaches our heart. Do we not carry a rose to our beloved because it has already embodied a message which unlike our language of words cannot be analyzed? Through this gift we utilize a universal language of joy for our own purposes of expression.

Facts and power belong to the outer, not to the inner soul of things. Gladness is the one criterion of truth, and we know we have touched it by the music truth gives, by the joy it sends to the truth in us. It is not as ether waves that we receive our light; the morning does not wait for a scientist to introduce it. In the same way, we touch the reality within us only when we receive love or goodness, not through the erudite discussion of ethical doctrines.

All that I feel about my religion is from vision and not from knowledge. I cannot satisfactorily answer questions about evil, or about what happens after death, and yet I am sure that there have been moments when my soul has become intensely conscious of the infinite. It has been said in our Upanishads that the mind comes away, baffled, from the supreme truth, and he who knows that truth is saved from all doubts and fears.

In the night we stumble over things and become acutely conscious of their separateness, but the day reveals the unity which embraces them. And the man whose inner vision is bathed in consciousness at once realizes the spiritual unity which reigns over all racial differences, and his mind no longer stumbles over individual facts, accepting them as final. He realizes that peace is an inner harmony and not an outer adjustment, that beauty carries the assurance of our relationship to reality, which waits for its perfection in the response of our love.

FROM *My Reminiscences*

. . . Some years ago, when questioned about the events of my past life, I had occasion to pry into this picture-chamber. I expected to be content with selecting a few materials for my life's story, but discovered, as I opened the door, that life's memories are not life's history. Memories are the original work of an unseen artist. The variegated colors are not reflections of outside lights, but belong to the painter himself, and come passion-tinged from his heart, thereby disqualifying the canvas as evidence in a court of law.

But though the attempt to gather precise history from memory's storehouse may be fruitless, there is a fascination in looking over the pictures. This fascination cast its spell on me.

The road and the wayside shelter are not pictures while we travel; they are too necessary, too obvious. When, however, before turning into the evening resthouse, we look back upon the cities, fields, rivers and hills where we have traveled in the morning of our life, they are pictures indeed. Thus, when my opportunity came, I looked back, and was engrossed.

Was this interest only a natural affection for my own past? There must have been some personal feeling, of course, but the pictures also had an artistic value of their own. No event in my reminiscences is worthy of being preserved for all time, but the quality of the subject is not the only justification for a record. What one has truly felt, if only it can be made sensible ,to others, is always of importance to one's fellow men. If pictures which have taken shape in memory can be brought out in words, they are worth a place in literature.

It is as literary material that I offer my memory pictures; to take them as an attempt at autobiography would be a mistake. In such a view these reminiscences would appear useless as well as incomplete.

Going out of the house was forbidden to us, in fact we did not have even the freedom of all of its rooms. So we peeped at nature behind barriers. This limitless thing called the Outside was beyond my reach, flashes and sounds and scents of which used to come momentarily and touch me through its interstices. With so many gestures it seemed to want to play with me through the bars, but it was free and I was bound, and there was no way of meeting. So the attraction was all the stronger. The chalk line has been wiped away today, but the confining ring is still there. The distant is just as distant, the outside is still beyond me. . . .

The parapets of our terraced roofs were higher than my head. When I had grown taller, when the tyranny of the servants had relaxed, when, with the coming of a new bride into the house I had achieved some recognition as a companion of her leisure, then I sometimes went up to the terrace in the middle of the day. By that time everybody in the house would have finished their meal, there would be an interval in the business of the household, and over the inner apartments there rested the quiet of the midday. . . .

There was still another place in our house which I have not yet succeeded in discovering. A little girl playmate of my own age called this the "King's palace." [4] "I have just been there," she would sometimes tell me, but somehow the moment never arrived when she could take me with her. That was a wonderful place, and its playthings were as wonderful as the games that were played there. It seemed to me that it must be somewhere very near, perhaps in the first or second story; the only thing was that I never seemed to get there. How often I asked her, "Only tell me, is it really inside the house or outside?" And she would always reply, "No, no, it's in this very house." I would sit and wonder: "Where then can it be? Don't I know all the rooms of the house?" Who the king might be I never inquired; where his palace was still remains a mystery; but this much was clear, the King's palace was within our house.

Looking back on the days of childhood, the thing that recurs most often is the mystery which filled life and the world. Something undreamed of was lurking everywhere, and the most important question every day was: "When, oh! when would we come across it?" It was as if nature held something in closed hands and was smilingly asking us: "What do you think I have?" The impossible was the thing we had no idea of.

I remember the custard apple seed which I planted in a corner of the south verandah, and watered every day. The thought that the seed might grow into a tree kept me in a state of fluttering wonder. Custard apple seeds still have the habit of sprouting, but no longer to the accompaniment of that feeling of wonder. The fault is not in the custard apple but in the mind.

We once stole some rocks from an elder cousin's rockery and started a little rockery of our own. The plants which we sowed in its interstices were cared for so excessively that it was only because of their vegetable nature that they managed to put up with it until their untimely death. Words cannot recount the joy and wonder which this miniature mountaintop held for us. We had no doubt that our creation would be also wonderful to our elders. The day that we tested this, however, the hillock in the corner of our room, with all its rocks and vegetation, vanished. The knowledge that the schoolroom floor was not a proper foundation for the erection of a mountain was imparted so rudely, and with such suddenness, that it gave us a considerable shock. The weight from the stones, of which the floor was relieved, settled on our minds when we realized the gulf between our fancies and the will of our elders. . . .

PRACTICING POETRY

That blue manuscript book was soon filled, like the hive of some insect, with a network of variously slanting lines and the strokes of letters. The eager pressure of the boy writer got frayed, and twisted up claw-like as if to hold fast the writing within, till at last, down what river *Baitarani* I know not, its pages were swept away by merciful oblivion. Anyhow, they escaped the pangs of a passage through the printing press and need fear no birth into this vale of woe.

I cannot claim to have been a passive witness of the spread of my reputation as a poet. Though Satkari Babu was not a teacher of our class, he was very fond of me. He had written a book on natural history —I hope no unkind humorist will try to find a reason for such fondness. He sent for me one day and asked: "So you write poetry, do you?" I did not conceal the fact. From that time on, he would occasionally ask me to complete his quatrain by adding a couplet of my own.

Gobinda Babu of our school was dark, short and fat; he was the superintendent. He sat in his black suit with his account books in an office room on the second floor. We were all afraid of him because he was the rod-bearing judge. On one occasion I escaped from some bullies, five or six older boys, into his room. I had no witnesses on my side except my tears. I won my case, and from then on Govinda Babu had a soft corner in his heart for me.

One day he called me into his room during recess. I went in fear and trembling but had no sooner stepped before him than he also accosted me with the question: "So you write poetry?" I admitted it, and he commissioned me to write a poem on some high moral precept which I forget. The amount of condescension and affability implied can only be appreciated by those who were his pupils. When I handed him the verses next day, he took me to the highest class and made me stand before the boys. "Recite," he demanded. And I recited loudly.

The only praiseworthy thing about this moral poem was that it soon got lost. Its moral effect on the class was far from encouraging; the sentiment it aroused was not admiration for its author. Most of the boys were certain that it was not my own composition. One said he could produce the book from which it was copied, but was not pressed to do so; the process of proving is such a nuisance to those who want to believe. Also, the number of seekers after poetic fame began to increase, alarmingly, and their methods were not those which are recognized as roads to moral improvement.

Nowadays there is nothing strange in a youngster writing verses.

The glamour of poesy is gone. I remember how the few women who wrote poetry in those days were looked upon as miraculous creations of the Deity. If one hears today that a young lady does not write poems one feels skeptical. Poetry now appears many years before the highest Bengali class is reached, and no modern Gobinda Babu would have taken any notice of the poetic exploit I have just recalled.

BEREAVEMENTS

. . . When my mother died I was quite a child. She had been ailing for a long time, and we did not even know when her malady had taken a fatal turn. She used to sleep on a separate bed in the same room with us. Then she was taken for a boat trip on the river, and on her return a room on the third floor of the inner apartments was set apart for her.

On the night she died we were asleep in our room downstairs. Suddenly, our old nurse ran in weeping and crying: "O my little ones, you have lost your all!" My sister-in-law rebuked her and led her away in order to save us the sudden shock in the middle of the night. Half awakened by her words, I felt my heart sink, but could not tell what had happened. When, in the morning, we were told of her death, I could not realize all that it meant for me.

As we went out to the verandah we saw my mother laid on a bedstead in the courtyard; there was nothing in her appearance which showed death to be terrible. The aspect which death wore in that morning light was as lovely as a calm and peaceful sleep, and the gulf between life and its absence was not evident to us.

Only when her body was taken out by the main gateway, and we followed the procession to the cremation ground, did a storm of grief pass through me at the thought that mother would never return by this door and take again her accustomed place in the affairs of her household. As the day wore on, and we returned from the cremation, we turned into our lane and I looked up toward my father's room on the third floor. He was still in the front verandah sitting motionless in prayer. . . .

CHAPTER II

(Editor's note. The palanquin is a conveyance, usually for one person, consisting of an enclosed litter borne on the shoulders of men by means of poles.)

The palanquin belonged to the days of my grandmother. Lordly in appearance, it was large enough to have eight bearers for each pole, but when the wealth and glory of the family faded like the clouds at sunset, the palanquin bearers, with their gold bracelets, thick earrings, and sleeveless red tunics, disappeared along with it. The body of the palanquin was decorated with colored line drawings, some of which were not defaced; the surface was stained and discolored, and the stuffing was coming out of the upholstery. It lay in a corner of the countinghouse verandah as though it were a piece of commonplace lumber. I was seven or eight years old.

I was not yet, therefore, old enough to do any serious work, and the old palanquin had been dismissed from any useful service. Perhaps it was this mutual inactivity that attracted me to it. It was an island in the midst of the ocean, and on holidays I became Robinson Crusoe. There I sat within its closed doors, delightfully safe from prying eyes.

Outside my retreat, our house was full of relatives and other people. From all parts of the house I could hear the shouts of servants at work: Pari the maid returning from the bazaar through the front courtyard, her vegetables in a basket on her hip; Dukhon the bearer carrying Ganges water in a yoke across his shoulder; the weaver woman going into the inner apartments to trade the newest style of sari; Dinu the goldsmith, who received a monthly wage, sitting in the room next to the lane, blowing his bellows and carrying out the orders of the family, now coming to the countinghouse to present his bill to Kailash Mukherjee, who has a quill pen stuck behind his ear. The carder sits on the courtyard cleaning the mattress-stuffing on his twanging bow. Mukundalal the *durwan* is outside rolling on the ground with the one-eyed wrestler, trying out a new wrestling fall. He slaps his thighs loudly, and repeats his movements twenty or thirty times, dropping on all fours. There sits a crowd of beggars waiting for their regular dole.

The day wears on, the heat grows intense, the clock in the gate-house strikes the hour. Inside the palanquin, however, the day does not acknowledge the authority of clocks. Our noontime is that of former days, when the drum at the great door of the king's palace would announce the breaking up of the court, and the king would go to bathe in sandal-scented water. On holiday noons, those in charge of me eat their meal and go to sleep. I sit alone; my palanquin travels on imaginary journeys. My bearers, sprung from the air at my bidding, eating the salt of my imagination, carry me wherever my fancy leads. We pass through strange lands, and I name each country from books I have read. My imagination cuts a road through a deep forest. Tiger eyes blaze from the thickets, my flesh creeps and tingles. With me is Biswanath the hunter; his gun speaks— Crack! Crack!—and then all is still. Sometimes my palanquin becomes a peacock-boat, floating on the ocean until the shore is out of sight. The oars dip into the water with a gentle plash, the waves swing and swell around us. The sailors cry to us to beware, a storm is coming. By the tiller stands Abdul the sailor, with his pointed head, shaven moustache and close-cropped hair. I know him, for he brings *hilsa* fish and turtle eggs from the Padma for my elder brother.

CHAPTER VII

. . . Through the morning all kinds of studies were heaped upon me, but as the burden grew greater, my mind contrived to get rid of the fragments. Making a hole in the enveloping net, my parrot-learning slipped through its meshes and escaped, and the opinion that Master Nilkamal expressed about his pupil's intelligence was not the kind to be made public.

In another part of the verandah is the old tailor, his thick-lensed spectacles on his nose, bent over his sewing, and at the prescribed hours going through the ritual of his *Namāz*. I watch him and think what a lucky fellow Niāmut is. Then, with my head whirling from doing sums, shade my eyes with my slate, look down and see in front of the entrance porch, Chandrabhān the *durwan*, combing his long beard with a wooden comb, dividing it in two and looping it around each ear. The assistant *durwan*, a slender boy, is sitting near by, a bracelet on his arm, cutting tobacco. The horse has already finished his morning allowance of gram, and the crows are hopping around, pecking at the scattered grains. Our dog's (Johnny's) sense of duty is aroused and he barks them away.

I had planted a custard-apple seed in the dust which continual sweeping had piled in one corner of the verandah. I watched excitedly for the sprouting of the new leaves, and as soon as Master Nilkamal had gone, I ran to examine and water it. In the end my hopes went unfulfilled; the same broom that gathered the dust together dispersed it again to the four winds.

Now the sun climbs higher, and the slanting shadows cover only half the courtyard. The clock strikes nine. Govinda, short and dark, with a dirty yellow towel slung over his shoulder, takes me off for a bath. Promptly at half past nine comes our monotonous, unvarying meal: the daily ration of rice, *dāl* and fish curry—it was not much to my taste.

The clock strikes ten. From the main street comes the hawker's cry of "Green mangoes!" and awakens wistful dreams. Farther and farther in the distance resounds the clanging of the brass-peddler. The lady of the neighboring house is drying her hair on the roof, and her two little girls are playing with shells. They have plenty of leisure, for girls are not yet obliged to go to school, and I think "How fine to be born a girl." As it is, the old horse draws me in the rickety carriage to my Andamans, and from ten to four I am doomed to exile.

At half past four I return from school. The gymnastic master has come, and for about an hour I exercise on the parallel bars. He has no sooner gone than the drawing master arrives.

Gradually, the rusty daylight fades, the blurred noises of the evening sound like a dreamy hum resounding over the demon city of brick and mortar. In the study an oil lamp is burning; Master Aghor has come and the English lesson begins. The black-covered reader is lying in wait for me on the table. The cover is loose; the pages are stained and a little torn; I have tried writing my name in English in it, in the wrong places, and all in capital letters. As I read I nod, then jerk myself awake with a start, but miss far more than I read. When finally I tumble into bed I have at last a little time for myself, and there I listen for endless stories of the king's son traveling over an endless, trackless plain.

CONVERSATIONS

Tagore came into close contact, both in India and abroad, with practically all the eminent thinkers, intellectuals, and artists of his day—men like Henri Bergson, George Bernard Shaw, Thomas Mann, and Robert Frost. Fortunately, some of these interviews, or rather exchanges of views on matters of mutual interest, were recorded and published. The four conversations published here took place during Tagore's world tour of 1930.

The meeting with H. G. Wells occurred in Geneva early in June, 1930, and was recorded by Dr. Sudhin Ghose and this editor.

Tagore and Einstein met through a common friend, Dr. Mendel. Tagore visited Einstein at his residence at Kaputh in the suburbs of Berlin on July 14, 1930, and Einstein returned the call and visited Tagore at the Mendel home. Both conversations were recorded by this editor.

Tagore's contact with Rolland dated from 1919 when Rolland wrote to compliment Tagore on his condemnation of narrow nationalism. At Rolland's request, Tagore signed his name to *La Déclaration pour l'indépendance de l'esprit*, which was probably the first organized attempt to mobilize intellectual opinion all over the world against war. Their first meeting took place in April, 1921, in Paris. The conversation reproduced here took place in August, 1930, in Geneva.

Except for the July 14 conversation with Einstein, which was published in *The Religion of Man* (George Allen & Unwin, Ltd., London), Appendix II, pp. 222–225, the other conversations were published in *Asia* (March, 1937), pp. 151–154.

99

〰〰 Tagore and Einstein

TAGORE: I was discussing with Dr. Mendel today the new mathematical discoveries which tell us that in the realm of infinitesimal atoms chance has its play; the drama of existence is not absolutely predestined in character.

EINSTEIN: The facts that make science tend toward this view do not say good-by to causality.

TAGORE: Maybe not, yet it appears that the idea of causality is not in the elements, but that some other force builds up with them an organized universe.

EINSTEIN: One tries to understand in the higher plane how the order is. The order is there, where the big elements combine and guide existence, but in the minute elements this order is not perceptible.

TAGORE: Thus duality is in the depths of existence, the contradiction of free impulse and the directive will which works upon it and evolves an orderly scheme of things.

EINSTEIN: Modern physics would not say they are contradictory. Clouds look as one from a distance, but if you see them near by, they show themselves as disorderly drops of water.

TAGORE: I find a parallel in human psychology. Our passions and desires are unruly, but our character subdues these elements into a harmonious whole. Does something similar to this happen in the physical world? Are the elements rebellious, dynamic with individual impulse? And is there a principle in the physical world which dominates them and puts them into an orderly organization?

EINSTEIN: Even the elements are not without statistical order; elements of radium will always maintain their specific order, now and ever onward, just as they have done all along. There is, then, a statistical order in the elements.

TAGORE: Otherwise the drama of existence would be too desultory. It is the constant harmony of chance and determination which makes it eternally new and living.

EINSTEIN: I believe that whatever we do or live for has its causality; it is good, however, that we cannot see through to it.

TAGORE: There is in human affairs an element of elasticity also, some freedom within a small range which is for the expression of our personality. It is like the musical system in India, which is not so rigidly fixed as western music. Our composers give a certain definite outline, a system of melody and rhythmic arrangement, and within a certain limit the player can improvise upon it. He must be one with the law of that particular melody, and then he can give spontaneous expression to his musical feeling within the prescribed regulation. We praise the composer for his genius in creating a foundation along with a superstructure of melodies, but we expect from the player his own skill in the creation of variations of melodic flourish and ornamentation. In creation we follow the central law of existence, but if we do not cut ourselves adrift from it, we can have sufficient freedom within the limits of our personality for the fullest self-expression.

EINSTEIN: That is only possible where there is a strong artistic tradition in music to guide the people's mind. In Europe, music has come too far away from popular art and popular feeling and has become something like a secret art with conventions and traditions of its own.

TAGORE: You have to be absolutely obedient to this too complicated music. In India the measure of a singer's freedom is in his own creative personality. He can sing the composer's song as his own, if he has the power creatively to assert himself in his interpretation of the general law of the melody which he is given to interpret.

EINSTEIN: It requires a very high standard of art to realize fully the great idea in the original music, so that one can make variations upon it. In our country the variations are often prescribed.

TAGORE: If in our conduct we can follow the law of goodness, we can have real liberty of self-expression. The principle of conduct is there, but the character which makes it true and individual is our own creation. In our music there is a duality of freedom and prescribed order.

EINSTEIN: Are the words of a song also free? I mean to say, is the singer at liberty to add his own words to the song which he is singing?

TAGORE: Yes. In Bengal we have a kind of song—*kirtan*, we call it— which gives freedom to the singer to introduce parenthetical comments, phrases not in the original song. This occasions great enthusiasm, since the audience is constantly thrilled by some beautiful, spontaneous sentiment added by the singer.

EINSTEIN: Is the metrical form quite severe?

TAGORE: Yes, quite. You cannot exceed the limits of versification; the singer in all his variations must keep the rhythm and the time, which is fixed. In European music you have a comparative liberty with time, but not with melody.

EINSTEIN: Can the Indian music be sung without words? Can one understand a song without words?

TAGORE: Yes, we have songs with unmeaning words, sounds which just help to act as carriers of the notes. In North India music is an independent art, not the interpretation of words and thoughts, as in Bengal. The music is very intricate and subtle and is a complete world of melody by itself.

EINSTEIN: It is not polyphonic?

TAGORE: Instruments are used, not for harmony, but for keeping time and for adding to the volume and depth. Has melody suffered in your music by the imposition of harmony?

EINSTEIN: Sometimes it does suffer very much. Sometimes the harmony swallows up the melody altogether.

TAGORE: Melody and harmony are like lines and colors in pictures. A simple linear picture may be completely beautiful; the introduction of color may make it vague and insignificant. Yet color may, by combination with lines, create great pictures, so long as it does not smother and destroy their value.

EINSTEIN: It is a beautiful comparison; line is also much older than color. It seems that your melody is much richer in structure than ours. Japanese music also seems to be so.

TAGORE: It is difficult to analyze the effect of eastern and western music on our minds. I am deeply moved by the western music; I feel that it is great, that it is vast in its structure and grand in its composition. Our own music touches me more deeply by its fundamental lyrical appeal. European music is epic in character; it has a broad background and is Gothic in its structure.

EINSTEIN: This is a question we Europeans cannot properly answer, we are so used to our own music. We want to know whether our own music is a conventional or a fundamental human feeling, whether to feel consonance and dissonance is natural or a convention which we accept.

TAGORE: Somehow the piano confounds me. The violin pleases me much more.

EINSTEIN: It would be interesting to study the effects of European music on an Indian who had never heard it when he was young.

TAGORE: Once I asked an English musician to analyze for me some classical music and explain to me what elements make for the beauty of a piece.

EINSTEIN: The difficulty is that the really good music, whether of the East or of the West, cannot be analyzed.

TAGORE: Yes, and what deeply affects the hearer is beyond himself.

EINSTEIN: The same uncertainty will always be there about everything fundamental in our experience, in our reaction to art, whether in Europe or in Asia. Even the red flower I see before me on your table may not be the same to you and me.

TAGORE: And yet there is always going on the process of reconciliation between them, the individual taste conforming to the universal standard.

Tagore and Rolland

TAGORE: Do you think that Geneva is likely to play an important role in the world of international relationship?

ROLLAND: It may, but a good deal depends on factors over which Geneva has no control.

TAGORE: The League of Nations seems to me to be but one of the various forces which are at work here. At the present moment it is by no means the most instrumental for the readjustment of international relationships. It may or may not develop into a power for bringing greater harmony in the political world. I have much faith in the various international groups and societies and the individuals working in this place, and my hope is that they will eventually create in Geneva a genuine center of international activities which will shape the politics of the future.

ROLLAND: We find a large number of people eagerly looking for a message from the East. India, they think—and I may add, rightly —is the country that can in this epoch give that message to the world.

TAGORE: It is curious to note how India has furnished probably the first internationally minded man of the nineteenth century. I mean Raja Rammohun Roy; he had a passion for truth. He came from an orthodox Brahmin family, but he broke all bonds of superstition and formalism. He wanted to understand Buddhism, went to Tibet, studied Hebrew, Greek, Arabic, Persian, English, French; he traveled widely in Europe, and died in Bristol. Spiritual truth for him did not mean a sort of ecclesiasticism confined within sectarian sanctuaries; nor did he think that it could be inflicted upon people outside the sect by men who have professional rights to preach it as a doctrine. He realized that a bond of spiritual unity links the whole of mankind and that it is the purpose of religion to reach down to that fundamental unity of human relationship, of human efforts and achievements.

ROLLAND: I have often wondered at the spirit of religious toleration in India; it is unlike anything we have known in the West. The cosmic nature of your religion and the composite character of your civilization make this possible. India has allowed all kinds of religious faith and practice to flourish side by side.

TAGORE: Perhaps that has also been our weakness, and it is due to an indiscriminate spirit of toleration that all forms of religious creeds and crudities have run riot in India, making it difficult for us to realize the true foundation of our spiritual faith. The practice of animal sacrifice, for instance, has nothing to do with our religion, yet many people sanction it on the ground of tradition. Similar aberrations of religion can be found in every country. Our concern in India today is to remove them and intensify the larger beliefs which are our true spiritual heritage.

ROLLAND: In Christian scriptures, too, this theme of animal sacrifice dominates. Take the opening chapters: God gave preference to Abel because he had offered a lamb for sacrifice.

TAGORE: I have never been able to love the God of the Old Testament.

ROLLAND: . . . The emphasis is wrongly placed, and the attitude is not spiritual in the larger sense.

TAGORE: We should stress always the "larger sense." Truth cannot afford to be tolerant where it faces positive evil; it is like sunlight, which makes the existence of evil germs impossible. As a matter of fact, Indian religious life suffers today from the lack of a wholesome spirit of intolerance, which is characteristic of creative religion. Even a vogue of atheism may do good to India today, even though my country will never accept atheism as her permanent faith. It will sweep away all noxious undergrowths in the forest, and the tall trees will remain intact. At the present moment even a gift of negation from the West will be of value to a large section of the Indian people.

ROLLAND: I believe that scientific rationalism will help to solve India's question.

TAGORE: I know that India can never believe in mere intellectual determination for any long period of time; balance and harmony will certainly be restored. That is why a temporary swing in one direction may help us to arrive at the central adjustment of spiritual life. Science should come to our aid to be humanized by us at the end.

ROLLAND: Science is probably the most international element in the modern world; that is, the spirit of cooperation in scientific research. But we have today poison gas at the disposal of politicians. It is tragic that scientists are at the disposal of military powers who are not in the least interested in the progress of human thought and culture. . . . The problem today is not so much the antagonism of nations as the clash between different classes in the body of a nation itself. This does not, of course, justify or minimize to any degree the real curse of aggressive nationalism and the spirit of war.

TAGORE: Words are too conscious; lines are not. Ideas have their form and color, which wait for their incarnation in pictorial art. Just now painting has become a mania with me. My morning began with songs and poems; now, in the evening of my life, my mind is filled with forms and colors.

❧ Tagore and Wells

TAGORE: The tendency in modern civilization is to make the world uniform. Calcutta, Bombay, Hong Kong and other cities are more or less alike, wearing big masks which represent no country in particular.

WELLS: Yet don't you think this very fact is an indication that we are reaching out for a new world-wide human order which refuses to be localized?

TAGORE: Our individual physiognomy need not be the same. Let the mind be universal. The individual should not be sacrificed.

WELLS: We are gradually thinking now of one human civilization on the foundation of which individualities will have great chance of fulfillment. The individual, as we take him, has suffered from the fact that civilization has been split up into separate units, instead of being merged into a universal whole, which seems to be the natural destiny of humankind.

TAGORE: I believe the unity of human civilization can be better maintained by the linking up in fellowship and cooperation of the different civilizations of the world. Do you think there is a tendency to have one common language for humanity?

WELLS: One common language will probably be forced on mankind whether we like it or not. Previously a community of fine minds created a new dialect. Now it is necessity that will compel us to accept a universal language.

TAGORE: I quite agree. The time for five-mile dialects is fast vanishing. Rapid communication makes for a common language. Yet this common language probably would not exclude national languages. There is again the curious fact that just now, along with the growing unities of the human mind, the development of national self-consciousness is leading to the formation or rather revival of national languages everywhere. Don't you think that in America, in spite of constant touch between America and England, the English language is tending toward a definite modification and change?

WELLS: I wonder if that is the case now. Forty or fifty years ago this would have been the case, but now in literature and in common speech it becomes increasingly difficult to distinguish between English and American. There seems to be much more repercussion in the other direction. Today we are elaborating and perfecting physical methods of transmitting words. Translation is a bother. Take your poems—do they not lose much by that process? If you had a method of making them intelligible to all people at the same time, it would be really wonderful.

TAGORE: Music of different nations has a common psychological foundation, and yet that does not mean that national music should not exist. The same thing is, in my opinion, probably true for literature.

WELLS: Modern music is going from one country to another without loss—from Purcell to Bach, then Brahms, then Russian music, then oriental. Music is of all things in the world the most international.

TAGORE: May I add something? I have composed more than three hundred pieces of music. They are all sealed from the West because they cannot properly be given to you in your own notation. Perhaps they would not be intelligible to your people even if I could get them written down in European notation.

WELLS: The West may get used to your music.

TAGORE: Certain forms of tunes and melodies which move us profoundly seem to baffle western listeners; yet, as you say, perhaps closer acquaintance with them may gradually lead to their appreciation in the West.

WELLS: Artistic expression in the future will probably be quite different from what it is today; the medium will be the same and comprehensible to all. Take radio, which links together the world. And we cannot prevent further invention. Perhaps in the future, when the present clamor for dialects and national languages in broadcasting subsides and new discoveries in science are made, we shall be conversing with one another through a common medium of speech yet undreamt of.

TAGORE: We have to create the new psychology needed for this age. We have to adjust ourselves to the new necessities and conditions of civilization.

WELLS: Adjustments, terrible adjustments!

TAGORE: Do you think there are any fundamental racial difficulties?

WELLS: No. New races are appearing and reappearing, perpetual fluctuations. There have been race mixtures from the earliest historical times; India is the supreme example of this. In Bengal, for instance, there has been an amazing mixture of races in spite of castes and other barriers.

TAGORE: There is the question of race pride. Can the West fully acknowledge the East? If mutual acceptance is not possible, then I shall be very sorry for that country which rejects another's culture. Study can bring no harm, though men like Dr. Haas and Henri Matisse seem to think that the eastern mind should not go outside eastern countries, and then everything will be all right.

WELLS: I hope you disagree. So do I!

TAGORE: It is regrettable that any race or nation should claim divine favoritism and assume inherent superiority to all others in the scheme of creation.

WELLS: The supremacy of the West is only a question of probably the past hundred years. Before the battle of Lepanto the Turks were dominating the West; the voyage of Columbus was undertaken to avoid the Turks. Elizabethan writers and even their successors were struck by the wealth and the high material standards of the East. The history of western ascendancy is very brief indeed.

TAGORE: Physical science of the nineteenth century probably has created this spirit of race superiority in the West. When the East assimilates this physical science, the tide may turn and take a normal course.

WELLS: Modern science is not exactly European. A series of accidents and peculiar circumstances prevented some of the eastern countries from applying the discoveries made by humanists in other parts of the world. They themselves had once originated and developed a great many of the sciences that were later on taken up by the West and given greater perfection. Today, Japanese, Chinese and Indian names in the world of science are gaining due recognition.

TAGORE: India has been in a bad situation.

WELLS: When Macaulay imposed a third-rate literature and a poor system of education on India, Indians naturally resented it. No human being can live on Scott's poetry. I believe that things are now changing. But, remain assured, we English were not better off. We were no less badly educated than the average Indian, probably even worse.

TAGORE: Our difficulty is that our contact with the great civilization of the West has not been a natural one. Japan has absorbed more of the western culture because she has been free to accept or reject according to her needs.

WELLS: It is a very bad story indeed, because there have been such great opportunities for knowing each other.

TAGORE: And then, the channels of education have become dry river beds, the current of our resources having systematically been diverted along other directions.

WELLS: I also am a member of a subject race. I am taxed enormously. I have to send my check—so much for military aviation, so much for the diplomatic machinery of government! You see, we suffer from the same evils. In India the tradition of officialdom is, of course, more unnatural and has been going on for a long time. The Moguls, before the English came, seem to have been as indiscriminate as our own people.

TAGORE: And yet there is a difference. The Mogul government was not scientifically efficient and mechanical to a degree. The Moguls wanted money, and so long as they could live in luxury they did not wish to interfere with the progressive village communities in India. The Muslim emperors did not dictate terms and force the hands of Indian educators and villagers. Now, for instance, the ancient educational systems of India are completely disorganized, and all indigenous educational effort has to depend on official recognition.

WELLS: "Recognition" by the state, and good-by to education!

TAGORE: I have often been asked what my plans are. My reply is that I have no scheme. My country, like every other, will evolve its own constitution; it will pass through its experimental phase and settle down into something probably quite different from what you or I expect.

❧ *Note on the Nature of Reality*

EINSTEIN: Do you believe in the Divine as isolated from the world?

TAGORE: Not isolated. The infinite personality of man comprehends the universe. There cannot be anything that cannot be subsumed by the human personality, and this proves that the truth of the universe is human truth. I have taken a scientific fact to illustrate this—Matter is composed of protons and electrons, with gaps between them; but matter may seem to be solid. Similarly, humanity is composed of individuals, yet they have their interconnection of human relationship, which gives living solidarity to man's world. The entire universe is linked up with us in a similar manner, it is a human universe. I have pursued this thought through art, literature and the religious consciousness of man.

EINSTEIN: There are two different conceptions about the nature of the universe: (1) The world as a unity dependent on humanity. (2) The world as a reality independent of the human factor.

TAGORE: When our universe is in harmony with man, the eternal, we know it as truth, we feel it as beauty.

EINSTEIN: This is a purely human conception of the universe.

TAGORE: There can be no other conception. This world is a human world—the scientific view of it is also that of the scientific man. There is some standard of reason and enjoyment which gives it truth, the standard of eternal man, whose experiences are through our experiences.

EINSTEIN: This is a realization of the human entity.

TAGORE: Yes, one eternal entity. We have to realize it through our emotions and activities. We realize the supreme man who has no individual limitations through our limitations. Science is concerned with that which is not confined to individuals; it is the impersonal human world of truths. Religion realizes these truths and links them up with our deeper needs; our individual consciousness of truth gains universal significance. Religion applies values to truth, and we know truth as good through our own harmony with it.

EINSTEIN: Truth, then, or beauty, is not independent of man?

TAGORE. No.

EINSTEIN: If there would be no human beings any more, the Apollo of Belvedere would no longer be beautiful?

TAGORE: No.

EINSTEIN: I agree with regard to this conception of beauty, but not with regard to truth.

TAGORE: Why not? Truth is realized through man.

EINSTEIN: I cannot prove that my conception is right, but that is my religion.

TAGORE: Beauty is in the ideal of perfect harmony which is in the universal being; truth the perfect comprehension of the universal mind. We individuals approach it through our own mistakes and blunders, through our accumulated experience, through our illumined consciousness—how, otherwise, can we know truth?

EINSTEIN: I cannot prove scientifically that truth must be conceived as a truth that is valid independent of humanity; but I believe it firmly. I believe, for instance, that the Pythagorean theorem in geometry states something that is approximately true, independent of the existence of man. Anyway, if there is a reality independent of man there is also a truth relative to this reality; and in the same way the negation of the first engenders a negation of the existence of the latter.

TAGORE: Truth, which is one with the universal being, must essentially be human, otherwise whatever we individuals realize as true can never be called truth—at least the truth which is described as scientific and can only be reached through the process of logic; in other words, by an organ of thoughts which is human. According to Indian philosophy there is Brahman the absolute truth, which cannot be conceived by the isolation of the individual mind or described by words, but can only be realized by completely merging the individual in its infinity. But such a truth cannot belong to science. The nature of truth which we are discussing is an appearance—that is to say what appears to be true to the human mind and therefore is human, may be called *maya*, or part illusion.

EINSTEIN: So according to your conception, which may be the Indian conception, it is not the illusion of the individual, but of humanity as a whole.

TAGORE: In science we go through the discipline of eliminating the personal limitations of our individual minds and thus reach that comprehesion of truth which is in the mind of the universal man.

EINSTEIN: The problem begins, whether truth is independent of our consciousness.

TAGORE: What we call truth lies in the rational harmony between the subjective and objective aspects of reality, both of which belong to the super-personal man.

EINSTEIN: Even in our everyday life we feel compelled to ascribe a reality independent of man to the objects we use. We do this to connect the experiences of our senses in a reasonable way. For instance, if nobody is in this house, yet that table remains where it is.

TAGORE: Yes, it remains outside the individual mind, but not outside the universal mind. The table which I perceive is perceptible by the same kind of consciousness which I possess.

EINSTEIN: Our natural point of view in regard to the existence of truth apart from humanity cannot be explained or proved, but it is a belief which nobody can lack—no primitive beings even. We attribute to truth a super-human objectivity; it is indispensable for us, this reality which is independent of our existence and our experience and our mind—though we cannot say what it means.

TAGORE: Science has proved that the table as a solid object is an appearance, and therefore that which the human mind perceives as a table would not exist if that mind were naught. At the same time it must be admitted that the fact that the ultimate physical reality of the table is nothing but a multitude of separate revolving centers of electric forces also belongs to the human mind.

In the apprehension of truth there is conflict between the universal human mind and the same mind confined in the individual. The perpetual process of reconciliation is being carried on in our science and philosophy and in our ethics. In any case, if there be any truth absolutely unrelated to humanity then for us it is absolutely non-existing.

It is not difficult to imagine a mind to which the sequence of things happens not in space, but only in time like the sequence of notes in music. For such a mind its conception of reality is akin to the musical reality in which Pythagorean geometry can have no meaning. There is the reality of paper, infinitely different from the reality of literature. For the kind of mind possessed by the moth, which eats that paper, literature is absolutely non-existent, yet for man's mind literature has a greater value of truth than the paper itself. In a similar manner, if there be some truth which has no sensuous or rational relation to the human mind it will ever remain as nothing so long as we remain human beings.

EINSTEIN: Then I am more religious than you are!

TAGORE: My religion is in the reconciliation of the super-personal man, the universal human spirit, in my own individual being. This has been the subject of my Hibbert Lectures, which I have called "The Religion of Man."

FABLES

To non-Bengali readers, Tagore's fame as a mystical poet, and his interest in education and public affairs, have contributed to the idea that when he did not sing, he preached. In reality, however, there is something in Tagore which is less intense and less formal, but just as exacting—his wit. In his humorous fables and sketches, an intellectual detachment and irony mingle with deep human feeling, and although any translation can only remotely suggest the flavor of the original, two are included in this volume as examples of an art form in which Tagore revealed an important part of himself and his concerns.

The Trial of the Horse is really the trial of man, whose cupidity and craftiness are perversions of nature's design. The gods frown at man's treatment of the horse, but man, in the Imperial tradition, protests that the harness is fitted for equestrian prosperity. This sketch *(Ghoda)* was originally composed in 1918, and later published in a book of sketches called *Lipika* (1922). Translated by Surendranath Tagore, it was included in *The Parrot's Training and Other Stories* (Visva-Bharati, Calcutta, 1944).

Big News, a parable of today, expresses the imminent conflict between the oars that labor and the sail that claims to direct the boat while doing so little. Though the boatman wants them both, the account has to be settled. And that is the big news: the need for a drastic readjustment. This sketch *(Bado Khabar)* is a portion of a dialogue taken from *Galpa-Salpa*, a collection of tales and fancies, disguised as grandfatherly prattle, which Tagore dictated in 1941, shortly before his death. It was translated into English by this editor, and included in *The Parrot's Training and Other Stories*.

🌿 The Trial of the Horse

BRAHMA, the creator, was nearing the end of his task of creation when a new idea struck him.

He sent for the Storekeeper and said: "O keeper of the stores, bring to my factory a quantity of each of the five elements. For I am ready to create another creature."

"Lord of the universe," the Storekeeper replied, "when in the first flush of creative extravagance you began to turn out such exaggerations as elephants and whales and pythons and tigers, you took no count of the stock. Now, all the elements that have density and force are nearly used up. The supply of earth and water and fire has become inconveniently scanty, while of air and ether there is as much as is good for us and a good deal more."

The four-headed deity looked perplexed and pulled at his four pairs of moustaches. At last he said: "The limitedness of material gives all the more scope to originality. Send me whatever you have left."

This time BRAHMA was excessively sparing with earth, water and fire. The new creature was not given either horns or claws, and his teeth were only meant for chewing, not for biting. The prudent care with which fire was used, made him a necessity in war without making him warlike.

This animal was the Horse.

The reckless expenditure of air and ether in his composition was amazing. And, in consequence, he perpetually struggled to outreach the wind, to outrun space itself. Other animals ran only when they had a reason, but the horse would run for no reason whatever, as if to run out of his own skin. He had no desire to chase, or to kill, but only to fly on and on until he dwindled into a dot, melted into a swoon, blurred into a shadow, and vanished into vacancy.

The CREATOR was glad. He had given habitations to his other creatures, forests to some, caves to others, but because of his enjoyment of the disinterested spirit of energy in the Horse, he gave him an open meadow under the eye of heaven.

By the side of this meadow lived Man.

Man has his delight in pillaging and piling things, and is never happy until they grow into a burden. When he saw this new creature pursuing the wind and kicking at the sky, he said to himself: "If only I could bind and secure this Horse, I could use his broad back for carrying my loads."

So one day he caught the Horse.

Man then put a saddle on the Horse's back and a spiky bit in his mouth. The horse regularly had hard rubbing and scrubbing to keep him fit, and there were the whip and spurs to remind him that it was wrong to have his own will.

Man also put high walls around the Horse, lest the creature might escape if left at large.

So it came to pass, that while the Tiger who had his forest remained in the forest, the Lion who had his cave remained in the cave, the Horse who once had his open meadow came to spend his days in a stable. Air and atmosphere had roused in the horse longings for deliverance, but Man swiftly delivered him into bondage.

When he felt that bondage did not suit him, the Horse kicked at the stable walls.

This hurt his hoofs more than it hurt the wall, yet some of the plaster came off and the wall lost its beauty.

Man felt aggrieved.

"What ingratitude!" he cried. "Do I not give him food and drink? Do I not keep highly-paid men-servants to watch over him day and night? Indeed, he is difficult to please."

In their desperate attempts to please the Horse, the men-servants fell upon him and so vigorously applied all their winning methods that he lost his power to kick, and a great deal more besides.

Then Man called his friends and neighbors together, and said to them exultingly: "Friends, did you ever see so devoted a steed as mine?"

"Never!" they replied. "He seems as still as ditch water and as mild as the religion you profess."

The Horse, as is well known, had no horns, no claws, no adequate teeth, at his birth. When on top of this, all kicking at the walls and even into emptiness had been stopped, the only way to give vent to his feelings was to neigh.

But that disturbed Man's sleep.

Moreover, this neighing was not likely to impress the neighbors as devotion and thankfulness. So Man invented devices to shut the Horse's mouth.

But the voice cannot be completely suppressed as long as the mistake is made of leaving any breath in the body; therefore a spasmodic moaning now and then came from his throat.

One day this noise reached BRAHMA's ears.

The CREATOR woke from his meditation. It gave him a start when he glanced at the meadow and saw no sign of the Horse.

"This is all your doing," cried BRAHMA, in anger to Yama, the god of death: "You have taken away the Horse!"

"Lord of all creatures!" Death replied: "All your worst suspicions you keep only for me. But most of the calamities in your beautiful world will be explained if you turn your eyes in the direction of Man."

BRAHMA looked below. He saw a small enclosure, walled in, from which came the dolorous moaning of his Horse.

BRAHMA frowned in anger.

"Unless you set free my Horse," he said, "I shall take care that he grows teeth and claws like the Tiger."

"It would be ungodly," cried Man "to encourage ferocity. All the same, if I may speak the plain truth about a creature of your own making, this Horse is not fit to be set free. It was for his eternal good that I built him this stable—this marvel of architecture."

BRAHMA was persistent.

"I bow to your wisdom," said Man, "but if, after seven days, you still think that your meadow is better for him than my stable, I will humbly admit defeat."

After this, Man set to work.

He let the Horse go free, but hobbled his front legs, and the result was so diverting that it was enough to make even a frog burst his sides with laughter.

BRAHMA, from the height of heaven, could see the comic gait of his Horse, but not the tragic rope which hobbled him. He was mortified to find an earthly creature openly exposing his divine maker to ridicule.

"It was an absurd blunder of mine," he cried, "closely touching the sublime."

"Grandsire," said Man with a pathetic show of sympathy, "what can I do for this unfortunate creature? If there is a meadow in your heaven, I am willing to take the trouble to transport him thither."

"Take him back to your stable!" cried BRAHMA in dismay.

"Merciful God!" cried Man, "what a great burden it will be for mankind!"

"It is the burden of humanity," muttered BRAHMA.

Big News

Said Kusmi: "You will give me all the big news; you promised to didn't you, Dadamashay? How else could I get educated?"

Answered Dadamashay: "But there would be such a sack of big news to carry, and so much rubbish in it."

"Why not leave those out."

"Then little else would remain, and you would regard that remainder as small news. But that would be the real news."

"Give it to me—the real news."

"So I will."

"Well, Dadamashay, let me see what skill you have. Tell me the big news of these days, making it ever so small."

"Listen."

"Work was proceeding in peace.

In a *mahajani* boat a row started between the sail and the oars.

The oars came clattering to the court of the Boatman, and said: "This cannot be endured any longer. That braggart sail of yours, swelling himself, calls us *chhoto lok* because, tied night and day to the lower planks, we must toil, pushing the waters as we proceed, while he moves by whim, not caring for the push of anyone's hand. And so he is a *bara lok*. You must decide who is more worthy. If we are *chhoto lok*, the inferior ones, we shall resign in a body. Let us see how you make your boat move."

The Boatman, seeing danger ahead, called the oars aside and whispered secretly: "Do not give ear to his words, brothers. That sail speaks an empty language. If you strong fellows did not work away, staking life and death, the boat would lie altogether inert. And that sail sits there in hollow luxury, perched on the top. At the slightest touch of stormy wind he flops, folds himself up, lies low on the boat's thatch. Then all his vain flutterings are silenced, not a word from him at all. But in weal and woe, in danger and in crisis, on the way to the market and the *ghat*, you are my constant support. It is a pity that you have to carry that useless burden of luxury to and fro. Who says you are *chhoto lok*?"

But the Boatman was afraid, lest these words be overheard by the sail. So he came to him and whispered into his ear: "Mr. Sail, none can ever be compared with you. Who says that you drive the boat? That is the work of laborers. You move at your own pleasure, and your pals and comrades follow you at your slightest gesture. Whenever you feel out of breath, you flop down easefully, and rest. Do not lend your ear, friend, to the parleying of those low-bred oars; so firmly have I tied them up, that splutter as they may, they cannot but work as slaves."

Hearing this, the sail stretched himself, and yawned mightily.

But the signs were not good. Those oars are hard-boned fellows; they now lie aslant, but who knows when they will stand up straight, slap at the sail and shatter his pride into shreds. Then the world will know that it is the oars who make the boat move, come storm or tornado, whether it be upstream or at ebb tide.

Asked Kusmi: "Your big news, is it so small as this? You are joking."

Said Dadamashay: "Joking it seems to be, but soon this news will become big indeed."

"And then?"

"Then your Dadamashay will practice keeping time with the strokes of those oars."

"And I?"

"Where the oars creak too much, you will pour a drop of oil."

Dadamashay continued: "True news appears small, like the seeds. And then comes the tree with its branches and foliage. Do you understand now?"

"So I do," said Kusmi. Her face showed that she had not understood. But Kusmi had one virtue: she would not admit to her Dadamashay that she did not understand. That she is less clever than Iru Mashi is better kept concealed.

DRAMA

Tagore was sixteen when he made his first appearance on the stage; his brother Jyotirindranath had written a comedy based on Molière's *Le Bourgeois gentilhomme*, and Rabindranath was given the leading role. When he was twenty, his first play, *Valmiki Pratibha (The Genius of Valmiki)*, was staged in the family residence at Calcutta. From that time on, Tagore independently wrote and produced plays which were quite distinct from the main body of Bengali drama. His plays achieved a kind of lyrical action, a rhythmic treatment of emotions which moved around one idea. He was impressed more with music than action, more with idea than story. He said himself that the main principle in his plays was "the play of feeling and not of action." It is important to state this because it is precisely this lyricism and this music, in addition to the many dance scenes, which, at the same time that they constitute the genius of the writing, defy translation.

Tagore's early plays reach their highest dramatic point in *Visarjan*, 1890. The English translation which Tagore approved but slightly revised in 1917 as *Sacrifice* shows several departures from the original Bengali. Different scenes are amalgamated, subplots are omitted, and long declamations are severely cut. It is interesting to note that Edward Thompson, after seeing Tagore himself act the part of Raghupati, wrote: "How moving he can be as an actor only *this* generation can realize."

With *Dakghar (Post Office)* in 1912, Tagore's plays became more philosophical-symbolical. The original Bengali version was performed late in 1917 before an audience which included the then less known Mahatma Gandhi. It is probably the only Tagore play which was successfully performed abroad before it was staged in India. (The Irish Theatre staged it in London in 1914.) Yeats said of *Post Office* that, "on the stage, the little play shows that it is very perfectly constructed and conveys to the right audience an emotion of gentleness and peace." The play was also popular in Berlin and Paris. *Dakghar* was translated into English in 1914, at least in its first drafts, by Devavrata Mookerjee, but was slightly revised by Tagore.

Chandalika represents Tagore's later drama (1933). It is based on a Buddhist legend in which Ananda, the Buddha's famous disciple, stopped one hot day and asked for some water from a *chandalika*, a girl belonging to the lowest ("untouchable") caste.[1] The girl gave him water and in so doing fell in love; she induced her mother, who practiced primitive magic, to work a spell on the monk. It was successful, and Ananda came to the girl's house at night, but as the girl prepared the bed, he was overcome with shame and prayed to the Buddha who answered by breaking the magic spell, thus allowing Ananda to leave the house. Tagore transformed the legend into a drama of intense spiritual conflict in which a very sensitive girl who has been condemned by birth to a despised caste is suddenly awakened to the consciousness of her destiny as a woman. By asking her for water, the Buddhist monk teaches her to judge herself, not by the artificial standards of society, but by her capacity for love and service. Since her own self is the most she can give, and since no one is more worthy of her gift, she yearns to offer herself to the monk. But when the mother works her primitive spell and Ananda appears, degraded and shamed, at her door, Prakriti throws herself at his feet and asks forgiveness. The mother revokes the spell, but dies in the process, and the *chandalika* who learns that love does not claim possession, but gives freedom, is redeemed a second time.

Krishna Kripalani prepared an English translation of *Chandalika* in 1938 for the *Visva-Bharati Quarterly*, and Marjorie Sykes translated it into English in 1950 for her edition of *Three Plays by Rabindranath Tagore* (Geoffrey Cumberlege: Oxford University Press). The translation offered here, for the first time in print, is based on the two previous translations, with some changes by Robert Steele and Donald Junkins, of Boston University. Some of the metaphors in Tagore's Bengali text have been omitted in order that the clarity of the original might be preserved. Likewise, some words have been added, not to inject new or different meaning, but to preserve the force of the Bengali text. Omissions which occur both here and in the other English translations are explained in the Notes, page 385.

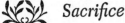 *Sacrifice*

A Temple in Tippera

(Enters Gunavati, the Queen)

GUNAVATI: Have I offended thee, dread Mother? Thou grantest children to the beggar woman, who sells them to live, and to the adulteress, who kills them to save herself from infamy, and here am I, the Queen, with all the world lying at my feet, hankering in vain for the baby-touch at my bosom, to feel the stir of a dearer life within my life. What sin have I committed, Mother, to merit this,—to be banished from the mothers' heaven?

(Enters Raghupati, the priest)

O Master, have I ever been remiss in my worship? And my husband, is he not godlike in his purity? Then why has the Goddess who weaves the web of this world-illusion assigned my place in the barren waste of childlessness?

RAGHUPATI: Our Mother is all caprice, she knows no law, our sorrows and joys are mere freaks of her mind. Have patience, daughter, today we shall offer special sacrifice in your name to please her.

GUNAVATI: Accept my grateful obeisance, father. My offerings are already on their way to the temple,—the red bunches of hibiscus and beasts of sacrifice.   [*They go out*

(Enter Govinda, the King; Jaising, the servant of the temple; and Aparna, the beggar girl)

JAISING: What is your wish, Sire?

GOVINDA: Is it true that this poor girl's pet goat has been brought by force to the temple to be killed? Will Mother accept such a gift with grace?

JAISING: King, how are we to know from whence the servants collect our daily offerings of worship? But, my child, why is this weeping? Is it worthy of you to shed tears for that which Mother herself has taken?

APARNA: Mother! I am his mother. If I return late to my hut, he refuses his grass, and bleats, with his eyes on the road. I take him up in my arms when I come, and share my food with him. He knows no other mother but me.

JAISING: Sire, could I make the goat live again, by giving up a portion of my life, gladly would I do it. But how can I restore that which Mother herself has taken?

APARNA: Mother has taken? It is a lie. Not mother, but demon.

JAISING: Oh, the blasphemy!

APARNA: Mother, art thou there to rob a poor girl of her love? Then where is the throne before which to condemn thee? Tell me, King.

GOVINDA: I am silent, my child. I have no answer.

APARNA: This blood-streak running down the steps, is it his? Oh, my darling, when you trembled and cried for dear life, why did your call not reach my heart through the whole deaf world?

JAISING (to the image): I have served thee from my infancy, Mother Kali, yet I understand thee not. Does pity only belong to weak mortals, and not to gods? Come with me, my child, let me do for you what I can. Help must come from man when it is denied by the gods.   [Jaising and Aparna go out

(Enter Raghupati; Nakshatra, who is the King's
brother; and the courtiers)

ALL: Victory be to the King!

GOVINDA: Know you all, that I forbid shedding of blood in the temple from today for ever.

MINISTER: You forbid sacrifice to the Goddess?

GENERAL NAYAN RAI: Forbid sacrifice?

NAKSHATRA: How terrible! Forbid sacrifice?

RAGHUPATI: Is it a dream?

GOVINDA: No dream, father. It is awakening. Mother came to me, in a girl's disguise, and told me that she cannot suffer blood.

RAGHUPATI: She has been drinking blood for ages. Whence comes this loathing all of a sudden?

GOVINDA: No, she never drank blood, she kept her face averted.

RAGHUPATI: I warn you, think and consider. You have no power to alter laws laid down in scriptures.

GOVINDA: God's words are above all laws.

RAGHUPATI: Do not add pride to your folly. Do you have the effrontery to say that you alone have heard God's words, and not I?

NAKSHATRA: It is strange that the King should have heard from gods and not the priest.

GOVINDA: God's words are ever ringing in the world, and he who is wilfully deaf cannot hear them.

RAGHUPATI: Atheist! Apostate!

GOVINDA: Father, go to your morning service, and declare to all worshipers that from hence they will be punished with banishment who shed creatures' blood in their worship of the Mother of all creatures.

RAGHUPATI: Is this your last word?

GOVINDA: Yes.

RAGHUPATI: Then curse upon you! Do you, in your enormous pride, imagine that the Goddess, dwelling in your land, is your subject? Do you presume to bind her with your laws and rob her of her dues? You shall never do it. I declare it,—I who am her servant.

[Goes

NAYAN RAI: Pardon me, Sire, but have you the right?

MINISTER: Sin can never have such a long lease of life. Could they be sinful,—the rites that have grown old at the feet of the Goddess?

(The King is silent)

NAKSHATRA: Indeed they could not be.

MINISTER: Our ancestors have performed these rites with reverence; can you have the heart to insult them?

(The King remains silent)

NAYAN RAI: That which has the sanction of ages, have you the right to remove it?

GOVINDA: No more doubts and disputes. Go and spread my order in all my lands.

MINISTER: But, Sire, the Queen has offered her sacrifice for this morning's worship; it is come near the temple gate.

GOVINDA: Send it back.   [He goes

MINISTER: What is this?

127

NAKSHATRA: Are we, then, to come down to the level of Buddhists, and treat animals as if they have their right to live? Preposterous! [*They all go out*

(Enters Raghupati,—Jaising following him with a jar of water to wash his feet)

JAISING: Father.

RAGHUPATI: Go!

JAISING: Here is some water.

RAGHUPATI: No need of it!

JAISING: Your clothes.

RAGHUPATI: Take them away!

JAISING: Have I done anything to offend you?

RAGHUPATI: Leave me alone. The shadows of evil have thickened. The King's throne is raising its insolent head above the temple altar. Ye gods of these degenerate days, are ye ready to obey the King's laws with bowed heads, fawning upon him like his courtiers? Have only men and demons combined to usurp gods' dominions in this world, and is Heaven powerless to defend its honor? But there remain the Brahmins, though the gods be absent; and the King's throne will supply fuel to the sacrificial fire of their anger. My child, my mind is distracted.

JAISING: Whatever has happened, father?

RAGHUPATI: I cannot find words to say. Ask the Mother Goddess who has been defied.

JAISING: Defied? By whom?

RAGHUPATI: By King Govinda.

JAISING: King Govinda defied Mother Kali?

RAGHUPATI: Defied you and me, all scriptures, all countries, all time, defied Mahākāli, the Goddess of the endless stream of time,— sitting upon that puny little throne of his.

JAISING: King Govinda?

RAGHUPATI: Yes, yes, your King Govinda, the darling of your heart. Ungrateful! I have given all my love to bring you up, and yet King Govinda is dearer to you than I am.

JAISING: The child raises its arms to the full moon, sitting upon his father's lap. You are my father, and my full moon is King Govinda. Then it is true, what I hear from people, that our King forbids all sacrifice in the temple? But in this we cannot obey him.

RAGHUPATI: Banishment is for him who does not obey.

JAISING: It is no calamity to be banished from a land where Mother's worship remains incomplete. No, so long as I live, the service of the temple shall be fully performed. [*They go out*

(Enter Gunavati and her attendant)

GUNAVATI: What is it you say? The Queen's sacrifice turned away from the temple gate? Is there a man in this land who carries more than one head on his shoulders, that he could dare think of it? Who is that doomed creature?

ATTENDANT: I am afraid to name him.

GUNAVATI: Afraid to name him, when I ask you? Whom do you fear more than me?

ATTENDANT: Pardon me.

GUNAVATI: Only last evening court minstrels came to sing my praise, Brahmins blessed me, the servants silently took their orders from my mouth. What can have happened in the meantime that things have become completely upset,—the Goddess refused her worship, and the Queen her authority? Was Tripura a dreamland? Give my salutation to the priest, and ask him to come. [*Attendant goes out*

(Enters Govinda)

GUNAVATI: Have you heard, King? My offerings have been sent back from Mother's temple.

GOVINDA: I know it.

GUNAVATI: You know it, and and yet bear the insult?

GOVINDA: I beg to ask your pardon for the culprit.

GUNAVATI: I know, King, your heart is merciful, but this is no mercy. It is feebleness. If your kindness hampers you, leave the punishment in my hand. Only, tell me, who is he?

GOVINDA: It is I, my Queen. My crime was in nothing else but having given you pain.

GUNAVATI: I do not understand you.

GOVINDA: From today shedding of blood in gods' temples is forbidden in my land.

GUNAVATI: Who forbids it?

GOVINDA: Mother herself.

GUNAVATI: Who heard it?

GOVINDA: I.

GUNAVATI: You! That makes me laugh. The Queen of all the world comes to the gate of Tripura's King with her petition.

GOVINDA: Not with her petition, but with her sorrow.

GUNAVATI: Your dominion is outside the temple limit. Do not send your commands there, where they are impertinent.

GOVINDA: The command is not mine, it is Mother's.

GUNAVATI: If you have no doubt in your decision, do not cross my faith. Let me perform my worship according to my light.

GOVINDA: I promised my Goddess to prevent sacrifice of life in her temple, and I must carry it out.

GUNAVATI: I also promised my Goddess the blood of three hundred kids and one hundred buffaloes, and I will carry it out. You may leave me now.

GOVINDA: As you wish.   [He goes out

(Enters Raghupati)

GUNAVATI: My offerings have been turned back from the temple, father.

RAGHUPATI: The worship offered by the most ragged of all beggars is not less precious than yours, Queen. But the misfortune is that Mother has been deprived. The misfortune is that the King's pride is growing into a bloated monster, obstructing divine grace, fixing its angry red eyes upon all worshipers.

GUNAVATI: What will come of all this, father?

RAGHUPATI: That is only known to her, who fashions this world with her dreams. But this is certain, that the throne which casts its shadow upon Mother's shrine will burst like a bubble, vanishing in the void.

GUNAVATI: Have mercy and save us, father.

RAGHUPATI: Ha, ha! I am to save you,—you, the consort of a King who boasts of his kingdom in the earth and in heaven as well, before whom the gods and the Brahmins must—Oh, shame! Oh, the evil age, when the Brahmin's futile curse recoils upon himself, to sting him into madness.

(About to tear his sacrificial thread)

GUNAVATI *(preventing him)*: Have mercy upon me.

RAGHUPATI: Then give back to Brahmins what are theirs by right.

GUNAVATI: Yes, I will. Go, master, to your worship and nothing will hinder you.

RAGHUPATI: Indeed your favor overwhelms me. At the merest glance of your eyes gods are saved from ignominy and the Brahmin is restored to his sacred offices. Thrive and grow fat and sleek till the dire day of judgment comes.   *[Goes out*

(Re-enters King Govinda)

GOVINDA: My Queen, the shadow of your angry brows hides all light from my heart.

GUNAVATI: Go! Do not bring curse upon this house.

GOVINDA: Woman's smile removes all curse from the house, her love is God's grace.

GUNAVATI: Go, and never show your face to me again.

GOVINDA: I shall come back, my Queen, when you remember me.

GUNAVATI *(clinging to the King's feet)*: Pardon me, King. Have you become so hard that you forget to respect woman's pride? Do you not know, beloved, that thwarted love takes the disguise of anger?

GOVINDA: I would die, if I lost my trust in you. I know, my love, that clouds are for moments only, and the sun is for all days.

GUNAVATI: Yes, the clouds will pass by, God's thunder will return to his armory, and the sun of all days will shine upon the traditions of all time. Yes, my King, order it so, that Brahmins be restored to their rights, the Goddess to her offerings, and the King's authority to its earthly limits.

GOVINDA: It is not the Brahmin's right to violate the eternal good. The creature's blood is not the offering for gods. And it is within the rights of the King and the peasant alike to maintain truth and righteousness.

GUNAVATI: I prostrate myself on the ground before you; I beg at your feet. The custom that comes through all ages is not the King's own. Like heaven's air, it belongs to all men. Yet your Queen begs it of you, with clasped hands, in the name of your people.

Can you still remain silent, proud man, refusing entreaties of love in favor of duty which is doubtful? Then go, go, go from me. [*They go*

(*Enter Raghupati, Jaising, and Nayan Rai*)

RAGHUPATI: General, your devotion to Mother is well known.

NAYAN RAI: It runs through generations of my ancestors.

RAGHUPATI: Let this sacred love give you indomitable courage. Let it make your sword-blade mighty as God's thunder, and win its place above all powers and positions of this world.

NAYAN RAI: The Brahmin's blessings will never be in vain.

RAGHUPATI: Then I bid you collect your soldiers and strike Mother's enemy down to the dust.

NAYAN RAI: Tell me, father, who is the enemy?

RAGHUPATI: Govinda.

NAYAN RAI: Our King?

RAGHUPATI: Yes, attack him with all your force.

NAYAN RAI: It is evil advice. Father, is this to try me?

RAGHUPATI: Yes, it is to try you, to know for certain whose servant you are. Give up all hesitation. Know that the Goddess calls, and all earthly bonds must be severed.

NAYAN RAI: I have no hesitation in my mind. I stand firm in my post, where my Goddess has placed me.

RAGHUPATI: You are brave.

NAYAN RAI: Am I the basest of Mother's servants, that the order should come for me to turn traitor? She herself stands upon the faith of man's heart. Can she ask me to break it? Then today comes to dust the King, and tomorrow the Goddess herself.

JAISING: Noble words!

RAGHUPATI: The King, who has turned traitor to Mother, has lost all claims to your allegiance.

NAYAN RAI: Drive me not, father, into a wilderness of debates. I know only one path,—the straight path of faith and truth. This stupid servant of Mother shall never swerve from that highway of honor. [*Goes out*

JAISING: Let us be strong in our faith as he is, Master. Why ask the aid of soldiers? We have the strength within ourselves for the task given to us from above. Open the temple gate wide, father.

Sound the drum. Come, come, O citizens, to worship her who takes all fear away from our hearts. Come, Mother's children.

(Citizens come)

FIRST CITIZEN: Come, come, we are called.
ALL: Victory to Mother!

(They sing and dance)

The dread Mother dances in the battlefield,
Her lolling tongue burns like a red flame of fire,
Her dark tresses fly in the sky, sweeping away the sun and stars,
Red streams of blood run from her cloud-black limbs,
And the world trembles and cracks under her tread.

JAISING: Do you see the beasts of sacrifice coming toward the temple, driven by the Queen's attendants?

(They cry)

Victory to Mother! Victory to our Queen!
RAGHUPATI: Jaising, make haste and get ready for the worship.
JAISING: Everything is ready, father.
RAGHUPATI: Send a man to call Prince Nakshatra in my name.
[Jaising goes. Citizens sing and dance
GOVINDA: Silence, Raghupati! Do you dare to disregard my order?
RAGHUPATI: Yes, I do.
GOVINDA: Then you are not for my land.
RAGHUPATI: No, my land is there, where the King's crown kisses the dust. No! Citizens! Let Mother's offerings be brought in here.

(They beat drums)

GOVINDA: Silence! *(To his attendants.)* Ask my General to come. Raghupati, you drive me to call soldiers to defend God's right. I feel the shame of it; for the force of arms only reveals man's weakness.
RAGHUPATI: Skeptic, are you so certain in your mind that Brahmins have lost the ancient fire of their sacred wrath? No, its flame will burst out from my heart to burn your throne into ashes. If it does not, then I shall throw into the fire the scriptures, and my

133

Brahmin pride, and all the arrant lies that fill our temple shrines in the guise of the divine.

(Enter General Nayan Rai and Chandpal, who is the second in command of the army)

GOVINDA: Stand here with your soldiers to prevent the sacrifice of life in the temple.

NAYAN RAI: Pardon me, Sire. The King's servant is powerless in the temple of God.

GOVINDA: General, it is not for you to question my order. You are to carry out my words. Their merits and demerits belong only to me.

NAYAN RAI: I am your servant, my King, but I am a man above all. I have reason and my religion. I have my King,—and also my God.

GOVINDA: Then surrender your sword to Chandpal. He will protect the temple from the pollution of blood.

NAYAN RAI: Why to Chandpal? This sword was given to my forefather by your royal ancestors. If you want it back, I will give it up to you. Be witness, my fathers, who are in the heroes' paradise—the sword that you made sacred with your loyal faith and bravery, I surrender to my King.   [*Goes out*

RAGHUPATI: The Brahmin's curse has begun its work already.

(Enters Jaising)

JAISING: The beasts have been made ready for the sacrifice.

GOVINDA: Sacrifice?

JAISING: King, listen to my earnest entreaties. Do not stand in the way, hiding the Goddess, man as you are.

RAGHUPATI: Shame, Jaising! Rise up and ask my pardon. I am your Master. Your place is at my feet, not the King's. Fool! Do you ask the King's sanction to do God's service? Leave alone the worship and the sacrifice. Let us wait and see how his pride prevails in the end. Come away.   [*They go out*

(Enters Aparna)

APARNA: Where is Jaising? He is not here, but only you,—the image whom nothing can move. You rob us of all our best without uttering a word. We pine for love, and die beggars for want of it. Yet it comes to you unasked, though you need it not. Like a grave, you hoard it under your miserly stone, keeping it from the use of the yearning world. Jaising, what happiness do you find from her? What can she speak to you? O my heart, my famished heart!

(Enters Raghupati)

RAGHUPATI: Who are you?

APARNA: I am a beggar girl. Where is Jaising?

RAGHUPATI: Leave this place at once. I know you are haunting this temple to steal Jaising's heart from the Goddess.

APARNA: Has the Goddess anything to fear from me? I fear her.

[*She goes out*

(Enter Jaising and Prince Nakshatra)

NAKSHATRA: Why have you called me?

RAGHUPATI: Last night the Goddess told me in a dream that you shall become king within a week.

NAKSHATRA: Ha, ha, this is news indeed.

RAGHUPATI: Yes, you shall be king.

NAKSHATRA: I cannot believe it.

RAGHUPATI: You doubt my words?

NAKSHATRA: I do not want to doubt them. But suppose, by chance, it never comes to pass.

RAGHUPATI: No, it shall be true.

NAKSHATRA: But, tell me, how can it ever become true?

RAGHUPATI: The Goddess thirsts for the King's blood.

NAKSHATRA: The King's blood?

RAGHUPATI: You must offer it to her before you can be king.

NAKSHATRA: I know not where to get it.

RAGHUPATI: There is King Govinda.—Jaising, keep still.—Do you understand? Kill him in secret. Bring his blood, while warm, to the altar.—Jaising, leave this place if you cannot remain still—

NAKSHATRA: But he is my brother, and I love him.

RAGHUPATI: Your sacrifice will be all the more precious.

NAKSHATRA: But, father, I am content to remain as I am. I do not want the kingdom.

RAGHUPATI: There is no escape for you, because the Goddess commands it. She is thirsting for blood from the King's house. If your brother is to live, then you must die.

NAKSHATRA: Have pity on me, father.

RAGHUPATI: You shall never be free in life, or in death, until her bidding is done.

NAKSHATRA: Advise me, then, how to do it.

RAGHUPATI: Wait in silence. I will tell you what to do when the time comes. And now, go.   [*Nakshatra goes*

JAISING: What is it that I heard? Merciful Mother, is it your bidding? To ask brother to kill brother? Master, how could you say that it was Mother's own wish?

RAGHUPATI: There was no other means but this to serve my Goddess.

JAISING: Means? Why means? Mother, have you not your own sword to wield with your own hand? Must your wish burrow underground, like a thief, to steal in secret? Oh, the sin!

RAGHUPATI: What do you know about sin?

JAISING: What I have learnt from you.

RAGHUPATI: Then come and learn your lesson once again from me. Sin has no meaning in reality. To kill is but to kill—it is neither sin nor anything else. Do you not know that the dust of this earth is made of countless killings? Old Time is ever writing the chronicle of the transient life of creatures in letters of blood. Killing is in the wilderness, in the habitations of man, in birds' nests, in insects' holes, in the sea, in the sky; there is killing for life, for sport, for nothing whatever. The world is ceaselessly killing; and the great Goddess Kali, the spirit of ever-changing time, is standing with her thirsty tongue hanging down from her mouth, with her cup in hand, into which is running the red lifeblood of the world, like juice from the crushed cluster of grapes.

JAISING: Stop, Master. Is, then, love a falsehood and mercy a mockery, and the one thing true, from beginning of time, the lust for destruction? Would it not have destroyed itself long ago? You are playing with my heart, my Master. Look there, she is gazing at me with her sweet mocking smile. My bloodthirsty Mother, wilt thou accept my blood? Shall I plunge this knife into my breast and make an end to my life, as thy child, for evermore? The lifeblood flowing in these veins, is it so delicious to thee?

O my Mother, my bloodthirsty Mother!—Master, did you call
me? I know you wanted my heart to break its bounds in pain overflowing my Mother's fee. This is the true sacrifice. But the King's
blood! The Mother, who is thirsting for our love, you accuse of
bloodthirstiness!

RAGHUPATI: Then let the sacrifice be stopped in the temple.

JAISING: Yes, let it be stopped.—No, no, Master, you know what is
right and what is wrong. The heart's laws are not the laws of
scripture. Eyes cannot see with their own light—the light must
come from the outside. Pardon me, Master, pardon my ignorance.
Tell me, father, is it true that the Goddess seeks the King's blood?

RAGHUPATI: Alas, child, have you lost your faith in me?

JAISING: My world stands upon my faith in you. If the Goddess must
have the King's blood, let me bring it to her. I will never allow a
brother to kill his brother.

RAGHUPATI: But there can be no evil in carrying out God's wishes.

JAISING: No, it must be good, and I will earn the merit of it.

RAGHUPATI: But, my boy, I have reared you from your childhood,
and you have grown close to my heart. I can never bear to lose
you, by any chance.

JAISING: I will not let your love for me be soiled with sin. Release
Prince Nakshatra from his promise.

RAGHUPATI: I shall think, and decide tomorrow.   [He goes

JAISING: Deeds are better, however cruel they may be, than the hell
of thinking and doubting. You are right, my Master; truth is in
your words. To kill is no sin, to kill brother is no sin, to kill the
king is no sin.—Where do you go, my brothers? To the fair at
Nishipur? There the women are to dance? Oh, this world is
pleasant! And the dancing limbs of the girls are beautiful. In
what careless merriment the crowds flew through the roads, making the sky ring with their laughter and song. I will follow them.

(Enters Raghupati)

RAGHUPATI: Jaising.

JAISING: I do not know you. I drift with the crowd. Why ask me to
stop? Go your own way.

RAGHUPATI: Jaising.

JAISING: The road is straight before me. With an alms-bowl in hand

and the beggar girl as my sweetheart I shall walk on. Who says that the world's ways are difficult? Anyhow we reach the end— the end where all laws and rules are no more, where the errors and hurts of life are forgotten, where is rest, eternal rest. What is the use of scriptures, and the teacher and his instructions?— My Master, my father, what wild words are these of mine? I was living in a dream. There stands the temple, cruel and immovable as truth. What was your order, my teacher? I have not forgotten it. *(Bringing out the knife.)* I am sharpening your words in my mind, till they become one with this knife in keenness. Have you any other order to give me?

RAGHUPATI: My boy, my darling, how can I tell you how deep is my love for you?

JAISING: No, Master, do not tell me of love. Let me think only of duty. Love, like the green grass, and the trees, and life's music, is only for the surface of the world. It comes and vanishes like a dream. But underneath is duty, like the rude layers of stone, like a huge load that nothing can move.   [*They go out*

(Enter Govinda and Chandpal)

CHANDPAL: Sire, I warn you to be careful.

GOVINDA: Why? What do you mean?

CHANDPAL: I have overheard a conspiracy to take away your life.

GOVINDA: Who wants my life?

CHANDPAL: I am afraid to tell you, lest the news become to you more deadly than the knife itself. It was Prince Nakshatra, who—

GOVINDA: Nakshatra?

CHANDPAL: He has promised to Raghupati to bring your blood to the Goddess.

GOVINDA: To the Goddess? Then I cannot blame him. For a man loses his humanity when it concerns his gods. You go to your work and leave me alone.   [*Chandpal goes out*
(Addressing the image.) Accept these flowers, Goddess, and let your creatures live in peace. Mother, those who are weak in this world are so helpless, and those who are strong are so cruel. Greed is pitiless, ignorance blind, and pride takes no heed when it crushes the small under its foot. Mother, do not raise your sword and lick your lips for blood; do not set brother against

138

brother, and woman against man. If it is your desire to strike me by the hand of one I love, then let it be fulfilled. For the sin has to ripen to its ugliest limits before it can burst and die a hideous death; and when the King's blood is shed by a brother's hand, then lust for blood will disclose its demon face, leaving its disguise as a goddess. If such be your wish I bow my head to it.

(Jaising rushes in)

JAISING: Tell me, Goddess, dost thou truly want the King's blood? Ask it in thine own voice, and thou shalt have it.
A VOICE: I want King's blood.
JAISING: King, say your last prayer, for your time has come.
GOVINDA: What makes you say it, Jaising?
JAISING: Did you not hear what the Goddess said?
GOVINDA: It was not the Goddess. I heard the familiar voice of Raghupati.
JAISING: The voice of Raghupati? No, no! Drive me not from doubt to doubt. It is all the same, whether the voice comes from the Goddess, or from my Master.—

(He unsheathes his knife, and then throws it away)

Listen to the cry of thy children, Mother. Let there be only flowers, the beautiful flowers for thy offerings—no more blood. They are red even as blood—these bunches of hibiscus. They have come out of the heart-burst of the earth, pained at the slaughter of her children. Accept this. Thou must accept this. I defy thy anger. Blood thou shalt never have. Redden thine eyes. Raise thy sword. Bring thy furies of destruction. I do not fear thee.—King, leave this temple to its Goddess, and go to your men.   [*Govinda goes*
Alas, alas, in a moment I gave up all that I had, my Master, my Goddess.

(Raghupati comes)

RAGHUPATI: I have heard all. Traitor, you have betrayed your master.
JAISING: Punish me, father.
RAGHUPATI: What punishment will you have?
JAISING: Punish me with my life.

RACHUPATI: No, that is nothing. Take your oath touching the feet of the Goddess.

JAISING: I touch her feet.

RACHUPATI: Say, I will bring kingly blood to the ãltar of the Goddess before it is midnight.

JAISING: I will bring kingly blood to the altar of the Goddess before it is midnight.   [*They go out*

(Enters Gunavati)

GUNAVATI: I failed. I had hoped that if I remained hard and cold for some days he would surrender. Such faith I had in my power, vain woman that I am. I showed my sullen anger, and remained away from him; but it was fruitless. Woman's anger is like a diamond's glitter; it only shines, but cannot burn. I wish it were like thunder, bursting upon the King's house, startling him from his sleep, and dashing his pride to the ground.

(Enters the boy Druva)

GUNAVATI: Where are you going?

DRUVA: I am called by the King.   [*Goes out*

GUNAVATI: There goes the darling of the King's heart. He has robbed my unborn children of their father's love, usurped their right to the first place in the King's breast. O Mother Kali, your creation is infinite and full of wonders, only send a child to my arms in merest whim, a tiny little warm living flesh to fill my lap, and I shall offer you whatever you wish. (*Enters Nakshatra.*) Prince Nakshatra, why do you turn back? I am a mere woman, weak and without weapon; am I so fearful?

NAKSHATRA: No, do not call me.

GUNAVATI: Why? What harm is in that?

NAKSHATRA: I do not want to be a king.

GUNAVATI: But why are you so excited?

NAKSHATRA: May the King live long, and may I die as I am—a prince.

GUNAVATI: Die as quick as you can; have I ever said anything against it?

NAKSHATRA: Then tell me what you want of me.

GUNAVATI: The thief that steals the crown is awaiting you—remove him. Do you understand?

NAKSHATRA: Yes, except who the thief is.

GUNAVATI: That boy, Druva. Do you not see how he is growing in the King's lap, till one day he reaches the crown?

NAKSHATRA: Yes, I have often thought of it. I have seen my brother putting his crown on the boy's head in play.

GUNAVATI: Playing with the crown is a dangerous game. If you do not remove the player, he will make a game of you.

NAKSHATRA: Yes, I do not like it.

GUNAVATI: Offer him to Kali. Have you not heard that Mother is thirsting for blood?

NAKSHATRA: But, sister, this is not my business.

GUNAVATI: Fool, can you feel yourself safe, so long as Mother is not appeased? Blood she must have; save your own, if you can.

NAKSHATRA: But she wants the King's blood.

GUNAVATI: Who told you that?

NAKSHATRA: I know it from one to whom the Goddess herself sends her dreams.

GUNAVATI: Then that boy must die for the King. His blood is more precious to your brother than his own, and the King can only be saved by paying the price, which is more than his life.

NAKSHATRA: I understand.

GUNAVATI: Then lose no time. Run after him. He is not gone far. But remember. Offer him in my name.

NAKSHATRA: Yes, I will.

GUNAVATI: The Queen's offerings have been turned back from Mother's gate. Pray to her that she may forgive me. [*They go out*

(Enters Jaising)

JAISING: Goddess, is there any little thing that yet remains out of the wreck of thee? If there be but a faintest spark of thy light in the remotest of the stars of evening, answer my cry, though thy voice be the feeblest. Say to me, "Child, here I am."—No, she is nowhere. She is naught. But take pity upon Jaising, O Illusion, and for him become true. Art thou so irredeemably false, that not even my love can send the slightest tremor of life through thy nothingness? O fool, for whom have you upturned your cup of life, emptying it to the last drop?—for this unanswering void—truthless, merciless, and motherless?

141

Aparna, they drive you away from the temple: yet you come back over and over again. For you are true, and truth cannot be banished. We enshrine falsehood in our temple, with all devotion; yet she is never there. Leave me not, Aparna. Sit here by my side. Why are you so sad, my darling? Do you miss some god, who is god no longer? But is there any need of god in this little world of ours? Let us be fearlessly godless and come closer to each other. They want our blood. And for this they have come down to the dust of our earth, leaving their magnificence of heaven. For in their heaven there are no men, no creatures, who can suffer. No, my girl, there is no Goddess.

APARNA: Then leave this temple, and come away with me.

JAISING: Leave this temple? Yes, I will leave. Alas, Aparna, I must leave. Yet I cannot leave it, before I have paid my last dues to the—But let that be. Come closer to me, my love. Whisper something to my ears which will overflow this life with sweetness, flooding death itself.

APARNA: Words do not flow when the heart is full.

JAISING: Then lean your head on my breast. Let the silence of two eternities, life and death, touch each other. But no more of this. I must go.

APARNA: Jaising, do not be cruel. Can you not feel what I have suffered?

JAISING: Am I cruel? Is this your last word to me? Cruel as that block of stone, whom I called Goddess? Aparna, my beloved, if you were the Goddess, you would know what fire is this that burns my heart. But you *are* my Goddess. Do you know how I know it?

APARNA: Tell me.

JAISING: You bring to me your sacrifice every moment, as a mother does to her child. God must be all sacrifice, pouring out his life in all creation.

APARNA: Jaising, come, let us leave this temple and go away together.

JAISING: Save me, Aparna, have mercy upon me and leave me. I have only one object in my life. Do not usurp its place.

[*Rushes out*

APARNA: Again and again I have suffered. But my strength is gone. My heart breaks. *[She goes out*

(*Enter Raghupati and Prince Nakshatra*)

RAGHUPATI: Prince, where have you kept the boy?

NAKSHATRA: He is in the room where the vessels for worship are kept. He has cried himself to sleep. I think I shall never be able to bear it when he wakes up again.

RAGHUPATI: Jaising was of the same age when he came to me. And I remember how he cried till he slept at the feet of the Goddess —the temple lamp dimly shining on his tear-stained child-face. It was a stormy evening like this.

NAKSHATRA: Father, delay not. I wish to finish it all while he is sleeping. His cry pierces my heart like a knife.

RAGHUPATI: I will drug him to sleep if he wakes up.

NAKSHATRA: The King will soon find it out, if you are not quick. For, in the evening, he leaves the care of his kingdom to come to this boy.

RAGHUPATI: Have more faith in the Goddess. The victim is now in her own hands and it shall never escape.

NAKSHATRA: But Chandpal is so watchful.

RAGHUPATI: Not more so than our Mother.

NAKSHATRA: I thought I saw a shadow pass by.

RAGHUPATI: The shadow of your own fear.

NAKSHATRA: Do we not hear the sound of a cry?

RAGHUPATI: The sound of your own heart. Shake off your despondency, Prince. Let us drink this wine duly consecrated. So long as the purpose remains in the mind it looms large and fearful. In action it becomes small. The vapor is dark and diffused. It dissolves into water-drops that are small and sparkling. Prince, it is nothing. It takes only a moment,—not more than it does to snuff a candle. That life's light will die in a flash, like lightning in the stormy night of July, leaving its thunderbolt for ever deep in the King's pride. But, Prince, why are you so silent?

NAKSHATRA: I think we should not be too rash. Leave this work till tomorrow night.

RAGHUPATI: Tonight is as good as tomorrow night, perhaps better.

NAKSHATRA: Listen to the sound of footsteps.

RAGHUPATI: I do not hear it.

NAKSHATRA: See there—the light.

RAGHUPATI: The King comes. I fear we have delayed too long.

(King comes with attendants)

GOVINDA: Make them prisoners. (To Raghupati.) Have you anything to say?

RAGHUPATI: Nothing.

GOVINDA: Do you admit your crime?

RAGHUPATI: Crime? Yes, my crime was that, in my weakness, I delayed in carrying out Mother's service. The punishment comes from the Goddess. You are merely her instrument.

GOVINDA: According to my law, my soldiers shall escort you to exile, Raghupati, where you shall spend eight years of your life.

RAGHUPATI: King, I never bent my knees to any mortal in my life. I am a Brahmin. Your caste is lower than mine. Yet, in all humility, I pray to you, give me only one day's time.

GOVINDA: I grant it.

RAGHUPATI (mockingly): You are the King of all kings. Your majesty and mercy are alike immeasurable. Whereas I am a mere worm, hiding in the dust.   [He goes out

GOVINDA: Nakshatra, admit your guilt.

NAKSHATRA: I am guilty, Sire, and I dare not ask for your pardon.

GOVINDA: Prince, I know you are tender of heart. Tell me, who beguiled you with evil counsel?

NAKSHATRA: I will not take other names, King. My guilt is my own. You have pardoned your foolish brother more than once, and once more he begs to be pardoned.

GOVINDA: Nakshatra, leave my feet. The judge is still more bound by his laws than his prisoner.

ATTENDANTS: Sire, remember that he is your brother, and pardon him.

GOVINDA: Let me remember that I am a king. Nakshatra shall remain in exile for eight years, in the house we have built, by the sacred river, outside the limits of Tripura. (Taking Nakshatra's hands.) The punishment is not yours only, brother, but also mine—the more so because I cannot share it bodily. The vacancy that you leave in the palace will prick my heart every day with a thousand needles. May the gods be more friendly to you, while you are away from us.   [They all go out

144

(Enter Raghupati and Jaising)

RAGHUPATI: My pride wallows in the mire. I have shamed my Brahminhood. I am no longer your master, my child. Yesterday I had the authority to command you. Today I can only beg your favor. That light is extinct in me, which gave me the right to defy King's power. The earthen lamp can be replenished and lighted again and again, but the star once extinguished is lost for ever. I am that lost star. Life's days are mere tinsel, most trifling of God's gifts, and I had to beg for one of those days from the King with bent knees. Let that one day be not in vain. Let its infamous black brows be red with the King's blood before it dies. Why do you not speak, my boy? Though I forsake my place as your master, yet have I not the right to claim your obedience as your father,—I who am more than a father to you, because father to an orphan? But that man is the most miserable of all beggars who has to beg for love. You are still silent, my child? Then let my knees bend to you, who were smaller than my knees when you first came to my arms.

JAISING: Father, do not torture the heart that is already broken. If the Goddess thirsts for kingly blood, I will bring it to her before tonight. I will pay all my debts, yes, every farthing. Keep ready for my return. I will delay not.   [*Goes out*

(Storm outside)

RAGHUPATI: She is awake at last, the Terrible. Her curses go shrieking through the town. The hungry Furies are shaking the cracking branches of the world-tree with all their might, for the stars to break and drop. My Mother, why didst thou keep thine own people in doubt and dishonor so long? Leave it not for thy servant to raise thy sword. Let thy mighty arm do its own work! —I hear steps.

(Enters Aparna)

APARNA: Where is Jaising?

RAGHUPATI: Away, evil omen. *(Aparna goes out.)* But if Jaising never comes back? No, he will not break his promise. Victory to thee, Great Kali, the giver of all success!—But if he meet with obstruction? If he be caught and lose his life at the guards' hands?

145

—Victory to thee, watchful Goddess, Mother invincible! Do not allow thy repute to be lost, and thine enemies to laugh at thee. If thy children must lose their pride and faith in their Mother, and bow down their heads in shame before the rebels, who then will remain in this orphaned world to carry thy banner?—I hear his steps. But so soon? Is he coming back foiled in his purpose? No, that cannot be. Thy miracle needs not time, O Mistress of all time, terrible with thy necklace of human skulls.

(Jaising rushes in)

Jaising, where is the blood?

JAISING: It is with me. Let go my hands. Let me offer it myself *(entering the temple)*. Must thou have kingly blood, Great Mother, who nourishest the world at thy breast with life?—I am of the royal caste, a Kshatriya. My ancestors have sat upon thrones, and there are rulers of men in my mother's line. I have kingly blood in my veins. Take it, and quench thy thirst for ever.

(Stabs himself, and falls)

RAGHUPATI: Jaising! O cruel, ungrateful! You have done the blackest crime. You kill your father!—Jaising, forgive me, my darling. Come back to my heart, my heart's one treasure! Let me die in your place.

(Enters Aparna)

APARNA: It will madden me. Where is Jaising? Where is he?

RAGHUPATI: Come, Aparna, come, my child, call him with all your love. Call him back to life. Take him to you, away from me, only let him live.

(Aparna enters the temple and swoons)

(Beating his forehead on the temple floor.) Give him, give him, give him!—Give him back to me! *(Stands up addressing the image.)* Look how she stands there, the silly stone—deaf, dumb, blind—the whole sorrowing world weeping at her door—the noblest hearts wrecking themselves at her stony feet! Give me back my Jaising! Oh, it is all in vain. Our bitterest cries wander in emptiness—the emptiness that we vainly try to fill with these stony images of delusion. Away with them! Away with these

146

our impotent dreams, that harden into stones, burdening our world!

(He throws away the image, and comes out into the courtyard.
Enters Gunavati)

GUNAVATI: Victory to thee, great Goddess!—But where is the Goddess?

RAGHUPATI: Goddess there is none.

GUNAVATI: Bring her back, Father. I have brought her my offerings. I have come at last, to appease her anger with my own heart's blood. Let her know that the Queen is true to her promise. Have pity on me, and bring back the Goddess only for this night. Tell me—where is she?

RAGHUPATI: She is nowhere—neither above nor below.

GUNAVATI: Master, was not the Goddess here in the temple?

RAGHUPATI: Goddess?—If there were any true Goddess anywhere in the world, could she bear this thing to usurp her name?

GUNAVATI: Do not torture me. Tell me truly. Is there no Goddess?

RAGHUPATI: No, there is none.

GUNAVATI: Then who was here?

RAGHUPATI: Nothing, nothing.

(Aparna comes out from the temple)

APARNA: Father!

RAGHUPATI: My sweet child! "Father," did you say? Do you rebuke me with that name? My son, whom I have killed, has left that one dear call behind him in your sweet voice.

APARNA: Father, leave this temple. Let us go away from here.

(Enters the King)

GOVINDA: Where is the Goddess?

RAGHUPATI: The Goddess is nowhere.

GOVINDA: But what blood-stream is this?

RAGHUPATI: Jaising, who loved you so dearly, has killed himself.

GOVINDA: Killed himself? Why?

RAGHUPATI: To kill the falsehood that sucks the lifeblood of man.

GOVINDA: Jaising is great. He has conquered death. My flowers are for him.

GUNAVATI: My King!

GOVINDA: Yes, my love.

GUNAVATI: The Goddess is no more.

GOVINDA: She has burst her cruel prison of stone, and come back to the woman's heart.

APARNA: Father, come away.

RAGHUPATI: Come, child. Come, Mother. I have found thee. Thou art the last gift of Jaising.

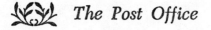 *The Post Office*

ACT I

(Madhav's House)

MADHAV: What a state I am in! Before he came, nothing mattered; I felt so free. But now that he has come, goodness knows from where, my heart is filled with his dear self, and my home will be no home to me when he leaves. Doctor, do you think he—

PHYSICIAN: If there's life in his fate, then he will live long. But what the medical scriptures say, it seems—

MADHAV: Great heavens, what?

PHYSICIAN: The scriptures have it: "Bile or palsy, cold or gout spring all alike."

MADHAV: Oh, get along, don't fling your scriptures at me; you only make me more anxious; tell me what I can do.

PHYSICIAN *(taking snuff)*: The patient needs the most scrupulous care.

MADHAV: That's true; but tell me how.

PHYSICIAN: I have already mentioned, on no account must he be let out of doors.

MADHAV: Poor child, it is very hard to keep him indoors all day long.

PHYSICIAN: What else can you do? The autumn sun and the damp are both very bad for the little fellow—for the scriptures have it:
"In wheezing, swooning, or in nervous fret,
In jaundice or leaden eyes—"

MADHAV: Never mind the scriptures, please. Eh, then we must shut the poor thing up. Is there no other method?

PHYSICIAN: None at all: for "In the wind and in the sun—"

MADHAV: What will your "in this and in that" do for me now? Why don't you let them alone and come straight to the point? What's to be done, then? Your system is very, very hard for the poor boy; and he is so quiet too with all his pain and sickness. It tears my heart to see him wince, as he takes your medicine.

PHYSICIAN: The more he winces, the surer is the effect. That's why the sage Chyabana observes: "In medicine as in good advice, the least palatable is the truest." Ah, well! I must be trotting now.

[Exit

(Gaffer enters)

MADHAV: Well, I'm jiggered, there's Gaffer now.

GAFFER: Why, why, I won't bite you.

MADHAV: No, but you are a devil to send children off their heads.

GAFFER: But you aren't a child, and you've no child in the house; why worry then?

MADHAV: Oh, but I have brought a child into the house.

GAFFER: Indeed, how so?

MADHAV: You remember how my wife was dying to adopt a child?

GAFFER: Yes, but that's an old story; you didn't like the idea.

MADHAV: You know, brother, how hard all this getting money has been. That somebody else's child would sail in and waste all this money earned with so much trouble—Oh, I hated the idea. But this boy clings to my heart in such a queer sort of way—

GAFFER: So that's the trouble! and your money goes all for him and feels jolly lucky it does go at all.

MADHAV: Formerly, earning was a sort of passion with me; I simply couldn't help working for money. Now, I make money, and as I know it is all for this dear boy, earning becomes a joy to me.

GAFFER: Ah, well, and where did you pick him up?

MADHAV: He is the son of a man who was a brother to my wife by village ties. He has had no mother since infancy; and now the other day he lost his father as well.

GAFFER: Poor thing: and so he needs me all the more.

MADHAV: The doctor says all the organs of his little body are at loggerheads with each other, and there isn't much hope for his life. There is only one way to save him and that is to keep him out of this autumn wind and sun. But you are such a terror! What with this game of yours at your age, too, to get children out of doors!

GAFFER: God bless my soul! So I'm already as bad as autumn wind and sun, eh! But, friend, I know something, too, of the game of keeping them indoors. When my day's work is over I am coming in to make friends with this child of yours.   [Exit

(Amal enters)

AMAL: Uncle, I say, Uncle!

MADHAV: Hullo! Is that you, Amal?

AMAL: Mayn't I be out of the courtyard at all?

MADHAV: No, my dear, no.

AMAL: See there, where Auntie grinds lentils in the quern, the squirrel is sitting with his tail up and with his wee hands he's picking up the broken grains of lentils and crunching them. Can't I run up there?

MADHAV: No, my darling, no.

AMAL: Wish I were a squirrel!—it would be lovely. Uncle, why won't you let me go about?

MADHAV: The doctor says it's bad for you to be out.

AMAL: How can the doctor know?

MADHAV: What a thing to say! The doctor can't know and he reads such huge books!

AMAL: Does his book-learning tell him everything?

MADHAV: Of course, don't you know!

AMAL *(with a sigh)*: Ah, I am so stupid! I don't read books.

MADHAV: Now, think of it; very, very learned people are all like you; they are never out of doors.

AMAL: Aren't they really?

MADHAV: No, how can they? Early and late they toil and moil at their books, and they've eyes for nothing else. Now, my little man, you are going to be learned when you grow up; and then you will stay at home and read such big books, and people will notice you and say, "He's a wonder."

AMAL: No, no Uncle; I beg of you, by your dear feet—I don't want to be learned; I won't.

MADHAV: Dear, dear; it would have been my saving if I could have been learned.

AMAL: No, I would rather go about and see everything that there is.

MADHAV: Listen to that! See! What will you see, what is there so much to see?

AMAL: See that far-away hill from our window—I often long to go beyond those hills and right away.

MADHAV: Oh, you silly! As if there's nothing more to be done but just get up to the top of that hill and away! Eh! You don't talk sense, my boy. Now listen, since that hill stands there upright as a barrier, it means you can't get beyond it. Else, what was the use in heaping up so many large stones to make such a big affair of it, eh!

AMAL: Uncle, do you think it is meant to prevent us crossing over? It seems to me because the earth can't speak it raises its hands into the sky and beckons. And those who live far off and sit alone by their windows can see the signal. But I suppose the learned people—

MADHAV: No, they don't have time for that sort of nonsense. They are not crazy like you.

AMAL: Do you know, yesterday I met some one quite as crazy as I am.

MADHAV: Gracious me, really, how so?

AMAL: He had a bamboo staff on his shoulder with a small bundle at the top, and a brass pot in his left hand, and an old pair of shoes on; he was making for those hills straight across that meadow there. I called out to him and asked, "Where are you going?" He answered, "I don't know; anywhere!" I asked again, "Why are you going?" He said, "I'm going out to seek work." Say, Uncle, have you to seek work?

MADHAV: Of course I have to. There are many about looking for jobs.

AMAL: How lovely! I'll go about like them too, finding things to do.

MADHAV: Suppose you seek and don't find. Then—

AMAL: Wouldn't that be jolly? Then I should go farther! I watched that man slowly walking on with his pair of worn-out shoes. And when he got to where the water flows under the fig tree, he stopped and washed his feet in the stream. Then he took out from his bundle some gram-flour, moistened it with water and began to eat. Then he tied up his bundle and shouldered it again; tucked up his cloth above his knees and crossed the stream. I've asked Auntie to let me go up to the stream, and eat my gram-flour just like him.

MADHAV: And what did your Auntie say to that?

AMAL: Auntie said, "Get well and then I'll take you over there." Please, Uncle, when shall I get well?

MADHAV: It won't be long, dear.

AMAL: Really, but then I shall go right away the moment I'm well again.

MADHAV: And where will you go?

AMAL: Oh, I will walk on, crossing so many streams, wading through water. Everybody will be asleep with their doors shut in the heat of the day and I will tramp on and on seeking work far, very far.

MADHAV: I see! I think you had better be getting well first; then—

AMAL: But then you won't want me to be learned, will you, Uncle?

MADHAV: What would you rather be, then?

AMAL: I can't think of anything just now; but I'll tell you later on.

MADHAV: Very well. But mind you, you aren't to call out and talk to strangers again.

AMAL: But I love to talk to strangers!

MADHAV: Suppose they had kidnaped you?

AMAL: That would have been splendid! But no one ever takes me away. They all want me to stay in here.

MADHAV: I am off to my work—but, darling, you won't go out, will you?

AMAL: No, I won't. But, Uncle, you'll let me be in this room by the roadside. [Exit Madhav

DAIRYMAN: Curds, curds, good nice curds.

AMAL: Curdseller, I say, Curdseller.

DAIRYMAN: Why do you call me? Will you buy some curds?

AMAL: How can I buy? I have no money.

DAIRYMAN: What a boy! Why call out then? Ugh! What a waste of time!

AMAL: I would go with you if I could.

152

DAIRYMAN: With me?

AMAL: Yes, I seem to feel homesick when I hear you call from far down the road.

DAIRYMAN (*lowering his yoke-pole*): Whatever are you doing here, my child?

AMAL: The doctor says I'm not to be out, so I sit here all day long.

DAIRYMAN: My poor child, whatever has happened to you?

AMAL: I can't tell. You see, I am not learned, so I don't know what's the matter with me. Say, Dairyman, where do you come from?

DAIRYMAN: From our village.

AMAL: Your village? Is it very far?

DAIRYMAN: Our village lies on the river Shamli at the foot of the Panch-mura hills.

AMAL: Panch-mura hills! Shamli river! I wonder. I may have seen your village. I can't think when, though!

DAIRYMAN: Have you seen it? Been to the foot of those hills?

AMAL: Never. But I seem to remember having seen it. Your village is under some very old big trees, just by the side of the road—isn't that so?

DAIRYMAN: That's right, child.

AMAL: And on the slope of the hill cattle grazing.

DAIRYMAN: How wonderful! Cattle grazing in our village! Indeed there are!

AMAL: And your women with red saris fill their pitchers from the river and carry them on their heads.

DAIRYMAN: Good, that's right! Women from our dairy village do come and draw their water from the river; but then it isn't everyone who has a red sari to put on. But, my dear child, surely you must have been there for a walk some time.

AMAL: Really, Dairyman, never been there at all. But the first day the doctor lets me go out, you are going to take me to your village.

DAIRYMAN: I will, my child, with pleasure.

AMAL: And you'll teach me to cry curds and shoulder the yoke like you and walk the long, long road?

DAIRYMAN: Dear, dear, did you ever? Why should you sell curds? No, you will read big books and be learned.

AMAL: No, I never want to be learned—I'll be like you and take my

153

curds from the village by the red road near the old banyan tree, and I will hawk it from cottage to cottage. Oh, how do you cry —"Curds, curds, fine curds"? Teach me the tune, will you?

DAIRYMAN: Dear, dear, teach you the tune; what a notion!

AMAL: Please do. I love to hear it. I can't tell you how queer I feel when I hear you cry out from the bend of that road, through the line of those trees! Do you know I feel like that when I hear the shrill cry of kites from almost the end of the sky?

DAIRYMAN: Dear child, will you have some curds? Yes, do.

AMAL: But I have no money.

DAIRYMAN: No, no, no, don't talk of money! You'll make me so happy if you take some curds from me.

AMAL: Say, have I kept you too long?

DAIRYMAN: Not a bit; it has been no loss to me at all; you have taught me how to be happy selling curds.   [Exit

AMAL (intoning): Curds, curds, fine curds—from the dairy village—from the country of the Panch-mura hills by the Shamli bank. Curds, good curds; in the early morning the women make the cows stand in a row under the trees and milk them, and in the evening they turn the milk into curds. Curds, good curds. Hello, there's the watchman on his rounds. Watchman, I say, come and have a word with me.

WATCHMAN: What's all this row about? Aren't you afraid of the likes of me?

AMAL: No, why should I be?

WATCHMAN: Suppose I march you off, then?

AMAL: Where will you take me to? Is it very far, right beyond the hills?

WATCHMAN: Suppose I march you straight to the King?

AMAL: To the King! Do, will you? But the doctor won't let me go out. No one can ever take me away. I've got to stay here all day long.

WATCHMAN: The doctor won't let you, poor fellow! So I see! Your face is pale and there are dark rings round your eyes. Your veins stick out from your poor thin hands.

AMAL: Won't you sound the gong, Watchman?

WATCHMAN: The time has not yet come.

AMAL: How curious! Some say the time has not yet come, and some say the time has gone by! But surely your time will come the moment you strike the gong!

WATCHMAN: That's not possible; I strike up the gong only when it is time.

AMAL: Yes, I love to hear your gong. When it is midday and our meal is over, Uncle goes off to his work and Auntie falls asleep reading her Ramayana, and in the courtyard under the shadow of the wall our doggie sleeps with his nose in his curled-up tail; then your gong strikes out, "Dong, dong, dong!" Tell me, why does your gong sound?

WATCHMAN: My gong sounds to tell the people, Time waits for none, but goes on for ever.

AMAL: Where, to what land?

WATCHMAN: That none knows.

AMAL: Then I suppose no one has ever been there! Oh, I do wish to fly with the time to that land of which no one knows anything.

WATCHMAN: All of us have to get there one day, my child.

AMAL: Have I too?

WATCHMAN: Yes, you too!

AMAL: But the doctor won't let me out.

WATCHMAN: One day the doctor himself may take you there by the hand.

AMAL: He won't; you don't know him. He only keeps me in.

WATCHMAN: One greater than he comes and lets us free.

AMAL: When will this great doctor come for me? I can't stick in here any more.

WATCHMAN: Shouldn't talk like that, my child.

AMAL: No. I am here where they have left me—I never move a bit. But, when your gong goes off, dong, dong, dong, it goes to my heart. Say, Watchman?

WATCHMAN: Yes, my dear.

AMAL: Say, what's going on there in that big house on the other side, where there is a flag flying high up and the people are always going in and out?

WATCHMAN: Oh, there? That's our new Post Office.

AMAL: Post Office? Whose?

WATCHMAN: Whose? Why, the King's, surely!

AMAL: Do letters come from the King to his office here?

WATCHMAN: Of course. One fine day there may be a letter for you in there.

AMAL: A letter for me? But I am only a little boy.

WATCHMAN: The King sends tiny notes to little boys.

AMAL: Oh, how splendid! When shall I have my letter? How do you know he'll write to me?

WATCHMAN: Otherwise why should he set his Post Office here right in front of your open window, with the golden flag flying?

AMAL: But who will fetch me my King's letter when it comes?

WATCHMAN: The King has many postmen. Don't you see them run about with round gilt badges on their chests?

AMAL: Well, where do they go?

WATCHMAN: Oh, from door to door, all through the country.

AMAL: I'll be the King's postman when I grow up.

WATCHMAN: Ha! ha! Postman, indeed! Rain or shine, rich or poor, from house to house delivering letters—that's very great work!

AMAL: That's what I'd like best. What makes you smile so? Oh, yes, your work is great too. When it is silent everywhere in the heat of the noonday, your gong sounds, Dong, dong, dong,— and sometimes when I wake up at night all of a sudden and find our lamp blown out, I can hear through the darkness your gong slowly sounding, Dong, dong, dong!

WATCHMAN: There's the village headman! I must be off. If he catches me gossiping there'll be a great to-do.

AMAL: The headman? Whereabouts is he?

WATCHMAN: Right down the road there; see that huge palm-leaf umbrella hopping along? That's him!

AMAL: I suppose the King's made him our headman here?

WATCHMAN: Made him? Oh, no! A fussy busybody! He knows so many ways of making himself unpleasant that everybody is afraid of him. It's just a game for the likes of him; making trouble for everybody. I must be off now! Mustn't keep work waiting, you know! I'll drop in again tomorrow morning and tell you all the news of the town. [*Exit*

AMAL: It would be splendid to have a letter from the King every day. I'll read them at the window. But, oh! I can't read writing. Who'll read them out to me, I wonder! Auntie reads her *Ramayana*; she may know the King's writing. If no one will, then I must keep them carefully and read them when I'm grown up. But if the postman can't find me? Headman, Mr. Headman, may I have a word with you?

HEADMAN: Who is yelling after me on the highway? Oh, it's you, is it, you wretched monkey?

AMAL: You're the headman. Everybody minds you.

HEADMAN *(looking pleased)*: Yes, oh yes, they do! They must!

AMAL: Do the King's postmen listen to you?

HEADMAN: They've got to. By Jove, I'd like to see—

AMAL: Will you tell the postman it's Amal who sits by the window here?

HEADMAN: What's the good of that?

AMAL: In case there's a letter for me.

HEADMAN: A letter for you! Whoever's going to write you?

AMAL: If the King does.

HEADMAN: Ha! ha! what an uncommon little fellow you are! Ha! ha! the King, indeed; aren't you his bosom friend, eh! You haven't met for a long while and the King is pining for you, I am sure. Wait till tomorrow and you'll have your letter.

AMAL: Say, Headman, why do you speak to me in that tone of voice? Are you cross?

HEADMAN: Upon my word! Cross, indeed! You write to the King! Madhav is a devilish swell nowadays. He's made a little pile; and so kings and padishahs are everyday talk with his people. Let me find him once and I'll make him dance. Oh, you—you snipper-snapper! I'll get the King's letter sent to your house— indeed I will!

AMAL: No, no, please don't trouble yourself about it.

HEADMAN: And why not, pray! I'll tell the King about you and he won't be long. One of his footmen will come presently for news of you. Madhav's impudence staggers me. If the King hears of this, that'll take some of his nonsense out of him.   [*Exit*

AMAL: Who are you walking there? How your anklets tinkle! Do stop a while, won't you?

(A girl enters)

GIRL: I haven't a moment to spare; it is already late!

AMAL: I see, you don't wish to stop; I don't care to stay on here either.

GIRL: You make me think of some late star of the morning! Whatever's the matter with you?

AMAL: I don't know; the doctor won't let me out.

GIRL: Ah me! Don't go, then! Should listen to the doctor. People will be cross with you if you're naughty. I know, always looking out and watching must make you feel tired. Let me close the window a bit for you.

AMAL: No, don't, only this one's open! All the others are shut. But will you tell me who you are? I don't seem to know you.

GIRL: I am Sudha.

AMAL: What Sudha?

SUDHA: Don't you know? Daughter of the flower-seller here.

AMAL: What do *you* do?

SUDHA: I gather flowers in my basket.

AMAL: Oh, flower-gathering! That is why your feet seem so glad and your anklets jingle so merrily as you walk. Wish I could be out too. Then I would pick some flowers for you from the very topmost branches right out of sight.

SUDHA: Would you really? Do you know as much about flowers as I?

AMAL: Yes, I *do*, quite as much. I know all about Champa of the fairy tale and his six brothers. If only they let me, I'll go right into the dense forest where you can't find your way. And where the honey-sipping humming-bird rocks himself on the end of the thinnest branch, I will blossom into a *champa*. Would you be my sister *parul*?

SUDHA: You are silly! How can I be sister *parul* when I am Sudha and my mother is Sasi, the flower-seller? I have to weave so many garlands a day. It would be jolly if I could lounge here like you!

AMAL: What would you do then, all the day long?

SUDHA: I could have great times with my doll Benay the bride, and Meni the pussy-cat, and—but I say, it is getting late and I mustn't stop, or I won't find a single flower.

AMAL: Oh, wait a little longer; I do like it so!

SUDHA: Ah, well—now don't be naughty. Be good and sit still,

and on my way back home with the flowers I'll come and talk
with you.

AMAL: And you'll let me have a flower, then?

SUDHA: No, how can I? It has to be paid for.

AMAL: I'll pay when I grow up—before I leave to look for work on
the other side of that stream.

SUDHA: Very well, then.

AMAL: And you'll come back when you have your flowers?

SUDHA: I will.

AMAL: You will, really?

SUDHA: Yes, I will.

AMAL: You won't forget me? I am Amal, remember that.

SUDHA: I won't forget you, you'll see.   [Exit

(A troop of boys enter)

AMAL: Say, brothers, where are you all off to? Stop here a little.

A BOY: We're off to play.

AMAL: What will you play at, brothers?

A BOY: We'll play at being plowmen.

ANOTHER BOY *(showing a stick)*: This is our plowshare.

ANOTHER BOY: We two are the pair of oxen.

AMAL: And you're going to play the whole day?

A BOY: Yes, all day long.

AMAL: And you will come home in the evening by the road along
the river bank?

A BOY: Yes.

AMAL: Do you pass our house on your way home?

A BOY: Come out and play with us; yes, do.

AMAL: The doctor won't let me out.

A BOY: The doctor! Do you mean to say you mind what the doctor
says? Let's be off; it is getting late.

AMAL: Don't go. Play on the road near this window. I could watch
you, then.

A BOY: What can we play at here?

AMAL: With all these toys of mine that are lying about. Here you
are; have them. I can't play alone. They are getting dirty and
are of no use to me.

BOYS: How jolly! What fine toys! Look, here's a ship. There's old mother Jatai. Isn't this a gorgeous *sepoy*? And you'll let us have them all? You don't really mind?

AMAL: No, not a bit; have them by all means.

A BOY: You don't want them back?

AMAL: Oh, no, I shan't want them.

A BOY: Say, won't you get a scolding for this?

AMAL: No one will scold me. But will you play with them in front of our door for a while every morning? I'll get you new ones when these are old.

A BOY: Oh, yes, we will. I say, put these *sepoys* into a line. We'll play at war; where can we get a musket? Oh, look here, this bit of reed will do nicely. Say, but you're off to sleep already.

AMAL: I'm afraid I'm sleepy. I don't know, I feel like it at times. I have been sitting a long while and I'm tired; my back aches.

A BOY: It's hardly midday now. How is it you're sleepy? Listen! The gong's sounding the first watch.

AMAL: Yes, Dong, dong, dong; it tolls me to sleep.

A BOY: We had better go, then. We'll come in again tomorrow morning.

AMAL: I want to ask you something before you go. You are always out—do you know of the King's postmen?

BOYS: Yes, quite well.

AMAL: Who are they? Tell me their names.

A BOY: One's Badal.

ANOTHER BOY: Another's Sarat.

ANOTHER BOY: There's so many of them.

AMAL: Do you think they will know me if there's a letter for me?

A BOY: Surely, if your name's on the letter they will find you out.

AMAL: When you call in tomorrow morning, will you bring one of them along so that he'll know me?

A BOY: Yes, if you like.

CURTAIN

ACT II

(Amal in bed)

AMAL: Can't I go near the window today, Uncle? Would the doctor mind that too?

MADHAV: Yes, darling; you see you've made yourself worse squatting there day after day.

AMAL: Oh, no, I don't know if it's made me more ill, but I always feel well when I'm there.

MADHAV: No, you don't; you squat there and make friends with the whole lot of people round here, old and young, as if they are holding a fair right under my eaves—flesh and blood won't stand that strain. Just see—your face is quite pale.

AMAL: Uncle, I fear my fakir will pass and not see me by the window.

MADHAV: Your fakir; whoever's that?

AMAL: He comes and chats to me of the many lands where he's been. I love to hear him.

MADHAV: How's that? I don't know of any fakirs.

AMAL: This is about the time he comes in. I beg of you, by your dear feet, ask him in for a moment to talk to me here.

(Gaffer enters in a fakir's guise)

AMAL: There you are. Come here, Fakir, by my bedside.

MADHAV: Upon my word, but this is—

GAFFER *(winking hard)*: I am the Fakir.

MADHAV: It beats my reckoning what you're not.

AMAL: Where have you been this time, Fakir?

GAFFER: To the Isle of Parrots. I am just back.

MADHAV: The Parrots' Isle!

GAFFER: Is it so very astonishing? I am not like you. A journey doesn't cost a thing. I tramp just where I like.

AMAL *(clapping)*: How jolly for you! Remember your promise to take me with you as your follower when I'm well.

GAFFER: Of course, and I'll teach you so many travelers' secrets that nothing in sea or forest or mountain can bar your way.

MADHAV: What's all this rigmarole?

GAFFER: Amal, my dear, I bow to nothing in sea or mountain; but if the doctor joins in with this uncle of yours, then I with all my magic must own myself beaten.

AMAL: No. Uncle won't tell the doctor. And I promise to lie quiet; but the day I am well, off I go with the Fakir, and nothing in sea or mountain or torrent shall stand in my way.

MADHAV: Fie, dear child, don't keep on harping upon going! It makes me so sad to hear you talk so.

AMAL: Tell me, Fakir, what the Parrots' Isle is like.

GAFFER: It's a land of wonders; it's a haunt of birds. No men are there; and they neither speak nor walk, they simply sing and they fly.

AMAL: How glorious! And it's by some sea?

GAFFER: Of course. It's on the sea.

AMAL: And green hills are there?

GAFFER: Indeed, they live among the green hills; and in the time of the sunset when there is a red glow on the hillside, all the birds with their green wings go flocking to their nests.

AMAL: And there are waterfalls!

GAFFER: Dear me, of course; you don't have a hill without its water-falls. Oh, it's like molten diamonds; and, my dear, what dances they have! Don't they make the pebbles sing as they rush over them to the sea! No devil of a doctor can stop them for a moment. The birds looked upon me as nothing but a man, merely a trifling creature without wings—and they would have nothing to do with me. Were it not so I would build a small cabin for myself among their crowd of nests and pass my days counting the sea-waves.

AMAL: How I wish I were a bird! Then—

GAFFER: But that would have been a bit of a job; I hear you've fixed up with the dairyman to be a hawker of curds when you grow up; I'm afraid such business won't flourish among birds; you might land yourself into serious loss.

MADHAV: Really this is too much. Between you two I shall turn crazy. Now, I'm off.

AMAL: Has the dairyman been, Uncle?

MADHAV: And why shouldn't he? He won't bother his head running errands for your pet fakir, in and out among the nests in his

162

Parrots' Isle. But he has left a jar of curds for you saying that he is busy with his niece's wedding in the village, and has to order a band at Kamlipara.

AMAL: But he is going to marry me to his little niece.

GAFFER: Dear me, we are in a fix now.

AMAL: He said she would be my lovely little bride with a pair of pearl drops in her ears and dressed in a lovely red sari and in the morning she would milk with her own hands the black cow and feed me with warm milk with foam on it from a brand-new earthen cruse; and in the evenings she would carry the lamp round the cow-house, and then come and sit by me to tell me tales of Champa and his six brothers.

GAFFER: How charming! It would even tempt me, a hermit! But never mind, dear, about this wedding. Let it be. I tell you that when you marry there'll be no lack of nieces in his household.

MADHAV: Shut up! This is more than I can stand.   [*Exit*

AMAL: Fakir, now that Uncle's off, just tell me, has the King sent me a letter to the Post Office?

GAFFER: I gather that his letter has already started; it is on the way here.

AMAL: On the way? Where is it? Is it on that road winding through the trees which you can follow to the end of the forest when the sky is quite clear after rain?

GAFFER: That is where it is. You know all about it already.

AMAL: I do, everything.

GAFFER: So I see, but how?

AMAL: I can't say; but it's quite clear to me. I fancy I've seen it often in days long gone by. How long ago I can't tell. Do you know when? I can see it all: there, the King's postman coming down the hillside alone, a lantern in his left hand and on his back a bag of letters; climbing down for ever so long, for days and nights, and where at the foot of the mountain the waterfall becomes a stream he takes to the footpath on the bank and walks on through the rye; then comes the sugar-cane field and he disappears into the narrow lane cutting through the tall stems of sugar-canes; then he reaches the open meadow where the cricket chirps and where there is not a single man to be seen, only the snipe wagging their tails and poking at the mud with their bills. I can feel him coming nearer and nearer and my heart becomes glad.

GAFFER: My eyes are not young; but you make me see all the same.

AMAL: Say, Fakir, do you know the King who has this Post Office?

GAFFER: I do; I go to him for my alms every day.

AMAL: Good! When I get well I must have my alms too from him, mayn't I?

GAFFER: You won't need to ask, my dear; he'll give it to you of his own accord.

AMAL: No, I will go to his gate and cry, "Victory to thee, O King!" and dancing to the tabor's sound, ask for alms. Won't it be nice?

GAFFER: It will be splendid, and if you're with me I shall have my full share. But what will you ask?

AMAL: I shall say, "Make me your postman, that I may go about, lantern in hand, delivering your letters from door to door. Don't let me stay at home all day!"

GAFFER: What is there to be sad for, my child, even were you to stay at home?

AMAL: It isn't sad. When they shut me in here first I felt the day was so long. Since the King's Post Office was put there I like more and more being indoors, and as I think I shall get a letter one day, I feel quite happy and then I don't mind being quiet and alone. I wonder if I shall make out what'll be in the King's letter?

GAFFER: Even if you didn't, wouldn't it be enough if it just bore your name?

(Madhav enters)

MADHAV: Have you any idea of the trouble you've got me into, between you two?

GAFFER: What's the matter?

MADHAV: I hear you've let it get rumored about that the King has planted his office here to send messages to both of you.

GAFFER: Well, what about it?

MADHAV: Our headman Panchanan has had it told to the King anonymously.

GAFFER: Aren't we aware that everything reaches the King's ears?

MADHAV: Then why don't you look out? Why take the King's name in vain? You'll bring me to ruin if you do.

AMAL: Say, Fakir, will the King be cross?

GAFFER: Cross, nonsense! And with a child like you and a fakir such as I am? Let's see if the King be angry, and then won't I give him a piece of my mind!

AMAL: Say, Fakir, I've been feeling a sort of darkness coming over my eyes since the morning. Everything seems like a dream. I long to be quiet. I don't feel like talking at all. Won't the King's letter come? Suppose this room melts away all on a sudden, suppose—

GAFFER (*fanning Amal*): The letter's sure to come today, my boy.

(*Doctor enters*)

DOCTOR: And how do you feel today?

AMAL: Feel awfully well today, Doctor. All pain seems to have left me.

DOCTOR (*aside to Madhav*): Don't quite like the look of that smile. Bad sign, his feeling well! Chakradhan has observed—

MADHAV: For goodness' sake, Doctor, leave Chakradhan alone. Tell me what's going to happen?

DOCTOR: Can't hold him in much longer, I fear! I warned you before —this looks like a fresh exposure.

MADHAV: No, I've used the utmost care, never let him out of doors; and the windows have been shut almost all the time.

DOCTOR: There's a peculiar quality in the air today. As I came in I found a fearful draught through your front door. That's most hurtful. Better lock it at once. Would it matter if this kept your visitors off for two or three days? If some one happens to call unexpectedly—there's the back door. You had better shut this window as well, it's letting in the sunset rays only to keep the patient awake.

MADHAV: Amal has shut his eyes. I expect he is sleeping. His face tells me—Oh, Doctor, I bring in a child who is a stranger and love him as my own, and now I suppose I must lose him!

DOCTOR: What's that? There's your headman sailing in!—What a bother! I must be going, brother. You had better stir about and see to the doors being properly fastened. I will send on a strong dose directly I get home. Try it on him—it may save him at last, if he can be saved at all. [*Exeunt Madhav and Doctor*

(The Headman enters)

HEADMAN: Hello, urchin!—

GAFFER (*rising hastily*): 'Sh, be quiet.

AMAL: No, Fakir, did you think I was asleep? I wasn't. I can hear everything; yes, and voices far away. I feel that mother and father are sitting by my pillow and speaking to me.

(Madhav enters)

HEADMAN: I say, Madhav, I hear you hobnob with bigwigs nowadays.

MADHAV: Spare me your jokes, Headman; we are but common people.

HEADMAN: But your child here is expecting a letter from the King.

MADHAV: Don't you take any notice of him, a mere foolish boy!

HEADMAN: Indeed, why not! It'll beat the King hard to find a better family! Don't you see why the King plants his new Post Office right before your window? Why, there's a letter for you from the King, urchin.

AMAL (*starting up*): Indeed, really!

HEADMAN: How can it be false? You're the King's chum. Here's your letter (*showing a blank slip of paper*). Ha, ha, ha! This is the letter.

AMAL: Please don't mock me. Say, Fakir, is it so?

GAFFER: Yes, my dear. I as Fakir tell you it is his letter.

AMAL: How is it I can't see? It all looks so blank to me. What is there in the letter, Mr. Headman?

HEADMAN: The King says, "I am calling on you shortly; you had better have puffed rice for me.—Palace fare is quite tasteless to me now." Ha! ha! ha!

MADHAV (*with folded palms*): I beseech you, Headman, don't you joke about these things—

GAFFER: Joking indeed! He would not dare.

MADHAV: Are you out of your mind too, Gaffer?

GAFFER: Out of my mind; well then, I am; I can read plainly that the King writes he will come himself to see Amal, with the State Physician.

AMAL: Fakir, Fakir, shh, his trumpet! Can't you hear?

HEADMAN: Ha! ha! ha! I fear he won't until he's a bit more off his head.

AMAL: Mr. Headman, I thought you were cross with me and didn't love me. I never could have believed you would fetch me the King's letter. Let me wipe the dust off your feet.

HEADMAN: This little child does have an instinct of reverence. Though a little silly, he has a good heart.

AMAL: It's hard on the fourth watch now, I suppose. Hark, the gong, "Dong, dong, ding—Dong, dong, ding." Is the evening star up? How is it I can't see—

GAFFER: Oh, the windows are all shut; I'll open them.

(A knocking outside)

MADHAV: What's that?—Who is it?—What a bother!

VOICE *(from outside)*: Open the door.

MADHAV: Headman—I hope they're not robbers.

HEADMAN: Who's there?—It is Panchanan, the headman, who calls.— Aren't you afraid to make that noise? Fancy! The noise has ceased! Panchanan's voice carries far.—Yes, show me the biggest robbers!—

MADHAV *(peering out of the window)*: No wonder the noise has ceased. They've smashed the outer door.

(The King's Herald enters)

HERALD: Our Sovereign King comes tonight!

HEADMAN: My God!

AMAL: At what hour of the night, Herald?

HERALD: On the second watch.

AMAL: When my friend the watchman will strike his gong from the city gates, "Ding dong ding, ding dong ding"—then?

HERALD: Yes, then. The King sends his greatest physician to attend on his young friend.

(State Physician enters)

STATE PHYSICIAN: What's this? How close it is here! Open wide all the doors and windows. *(Feeling Amal's body)* How do you feel, my child?

AMAL: I feel very well, Doctor, very well. All pain is gone. How fresh and open! I can see all the stars now twinkling from the other side of the dark.

PHYSICIAN: Will you feel well enough to leave your bed when the King comes in the middle watches of the night?

AMAL: Of course, I'm dying to be about for ever so long. I'll ask the King to find me the polar star.—I must have seen it often, but I don't know exactly which it is.

PHYSICIAN: He will tell you everything. (*To Madhav*) Arrange flowers through the room for the King's visit. (*Indicating the Headman*) We can't have that person in here.

AMAL: No, let him be, Doctor. He is a friend. It was he who brought me the King's letter.

PHYSICIAN: Very well, my child. He may remain if he is a friend of yours.

MADHAV (*whispering into Amal's ear*): My child, the King loves you. He is coming himself. Beg for a gift from him. You know our humble circumstances.

AMAL: Don't you worry, Uncle.—I've made up my mind about it.

MADHAV: What is it, my child?

AMAL: I shall ask him to make me one of his postmen that I may wander far and wide, delivering his message from door to door.

MADHAV (*slapping his forehead*): Alas, is that all?

AMAL: What'll be our offerings to the King, Uncle, when he comes?

HERALD: He has commanded puffed rice.

AMAL: Puffed rice. Say, Headman, you're right. You said so. You knew all we didn't.

HEADMAN: If you would send word to my house I could manage for the King's advent really nice—

PHYSICIAN: No need at all. Now be quiet, all of you. Sleep is coming over him. I'll sit by his pillow; he's dropping asleep. Blow out the oil-lamp. Only let the starlight stream in. Hush, he sleeps.

MADHAV (*addressing Gaffer*): What are you standing there for like a statue, folding your palms?—I am nervous.—Say, are there good omens? Why are they darkening the room? How will starlight help?

GAFFER: Silence, unbeliever!

(Sudha enters)

SUDHA: Amal!

PHYSICIAN: He's alseep.

SUDHA: I have some flowers for him. Mayn't I give them into his own hand?

PHYSICIAN: Yes, you may.

SUDHA: When will he be awake?

PHYSICIAN: Directly the King comes and calls him.

SUDHA: Will you whisper a word for me in his ear?

PHYSICIAN: What shall I say?

SUDHA: Tell him Sudha has not forgotten him.

CURTAIN

 Chandalika[2]

ACT I

(The setting can be in front of a village house, in a courtyard, or on a path. When the play opens the mother is on stage.)

MOTHER: Prakriti! Prakriti! *(There is no answer)* Where could she have gone? She is never to be found at home!

PRAKRITI *(from a distance)*: Here I am, Mother, I'm here.

MOTHER: Where?

PRAKRITI: Here, at the well.

MOTHER *(calling)*: Come here. I must talk with you. *(To herself)* At the well at this time of the day when the earth is burning like a furnace, and water for the day already brought from the well! *(Prakriti enters)* All the other girls of the village have gotten on with their work, and you sit and melt in the sun for no reason —unless you wish to repeat Uma's[3] penance. Is that why you sit there?

PRAKRITI: Yes, Mother.

169

MOTHER: Good Heavens! And for whom?

PRAKRITI: He who has called me.[4]

MOTHER: Who has called you?

PRAKRITI: His words are ringing in my mind: "Give me water."

MOTHER: "Give me water!" God grant it was not some one outside our caste!

PRAKRITI: He said he was one of us.

MOTHER: Did you tell him you are a *chandalini*?

PRAKRITI: Yes, but he said, "Do not deceive yourself with names. If you call the black cloud a *chandal*, does it cease to be what it is? Does the water it carries lose its value for our earth? Do not degrade yourself, for self-degradation is a greater sin than suicide." I can remember every word he spoke to me. He spoke so beautifully to me.

MOTHER: What nonsense are you saying? Or are you remembering a story from some former birth?

PRAKRITI: I am telling you the story of my new birth.

MOTHER: Your new birth? You are no more my daughter, Prakriti? Tell me. When did this happen?

PRAKRITI: That noontime while I was washing the motherless calf at the well a yellow-robed monk [5] came and stood before me and said, "Give me water." I sprang up and did obeisance. When I found my voice I said, "I am a daughter of the *chandals* and the water of this well is polluted by my family's use." He said, "You and I are of the same family. All water that quenches thirst and relieves need is pure." I never heard such words before, and with these *chandal* hands, which never before would have dared touch the dust of his feet, I poured water for him.

MOTHER: You silly girl, how could you dare such an act? Do you forget who you are and the destiny of your birth?

PRAKRITI: No, but the cup of water he took from my hands seemed to become an infinite ocean in which all the seven seas flowed together. They drowned my family, my caste, and my birth.

MOTHER: How strange! How strange you are! Even your language is changed. It's not your own. You are under some one's spell. What are you saying? Do you understand your own words?

PRAKRITI: Was there no water to be had anywhere else in this whole village? [6] Why did he come to this particular well? Why did he come, Mother, if not to bless me with a new life? Surely, he was seeking an occasion for such a deed. In a holy place he could not have found water that would give him the opportunity to further the mission of his life. He said, "So Seeta bathed in water such as this, which was fetched by a *chandal*, Guhak, at the beginning of her exile in the forest."

MOTHER: Child, listen to me. I do not like this. These monks have a way of changing other people's minds by words. Today I can hardly understand you. Tomorrow your very face may seem foreign to me. I am frightened.

PRAKRITI: You have never really known me, Mother. But he knows me. Every day I watch for him at the well, long after the other girls have gone home with their water.

MOTHER: Watch for whom?

PRAKRITI: For the monk.

MOTHER: What monk will come to you, you sick girl?

PRAKRITI: That one monk, Mother, the only one. Without saying a word he told me he would come. Why then does he not keep his word? My heart is burning dry and there is no water to quench it. Day after day I have waited, and he has not come. Oh, why has he not come? (*Prakriti seems to be talking to herself in near delirium.*)

MOTHER: Prakriti, you talk like someone drunk. Come into the house at once.

PRAKRITI: (*Prakriti continues as if not hearing*) I want him, who came unknown and revealed to me that I, too, am acceptable. He has lifted me up from dust and placed me by his heart.

MOTHER: Don't forget, Prakriti, that pleasant words are not necessarily true. Because of some unknown sin you have been born in a caste whose barrier no one can break. You are untouchable. This is the truth. Accept it. Believe it. The sun has made you ill. Come in I say.

PRAKRITI: (*Sings*)

> Blessed am I says the flower who belongs to the earth,[1]
> For I serve you my God in my lowly home.
> Make me forget that I am born of dust,
> For my spirit is free.
> When you bend your eyes down to me my petals tremble;

> Let the touch of your feet fill this dust with heavenliness,
> For the earth offers worship through me.

MOTHER: I begin to follow you a little. Worship where you love and find there your kingdom of freedom. Caste does not bind a woman if fortune blinds a man to her caste. Such good fortune did come to you once, Prakriti, when the prince had strayed here, deer-hunting, and offered to take you. Do you remember?

PRAKRITI: Yes, I remember.

MOTHER: Then why did you refuse to go with him? He was blind with love. He would have taken you away.

PRAKRITI: Blind! Yes, he was blind to me! He was hunting an animal and could only see the animal in me.

MOTHER: Even though it was a hunt, he saw the beauty of your form. But this monk, how do you know he has seen you as more than just a woman?

PRAKRITI: Hush, Mother! You won't understand, Mother, you won't! [8] I know that it was he who first loved me. And it is he I love and shall always love. I will take to him the worship of my life and offer it at his feet. And his feet shall not be polluted. I yearn to tell him with pride, "If I am not to stay in the dust as everybody's servant, I must be devoted to you."

MOTHER: Do not get so excited, Prakriti. We are servants by birth. We cannot wipe out what providence has ordained.

PRAKRITI: No, no, Mother. Do not wrong yourself by self-degradation. A princess may be a slave, a Brahmin a *chandal*. I am Prakriti— neither slave nor *chandal*.

MOTHER: I am no match for you today. Your tongue is new. I myself will go to him and beg him that even if he goes to other houses for food, he will come to ours for a cup of water.

PRAKRITI: [*Not hearing her mother and deeply disturbed*] (Sings)
> No, I will not call him with my voice,
> I will call him with my heart and bring him near.
> My heart aches to give to him
> But I know not where he goes, he who will receive me.
> How can this union come about?
>
> Can my pain touch his pain, and mingle
> As the Ganges mingles with the dark Jamuna?

172

The music comes and goes
But leaves its word of hope behind.

Mother, when the earth is parched with drought, what good is one cup of water? Won't the clouds be drawn by this thirst, and won't the rain then fall to the dry earth?

MOTHER: This talk is futile. If the clouds do not come of their own accord and the fields burn up, what else can we do but gaze helplessly at the sky?

PRAKRITI: No! Mother, please listen to me and help me. You know the art of magic. You can cast a spell and bring him here.

MOTHER: Hush, Prakriti! My magic is not for play, and this is playing with fire. These monks are not ordinary men. One does not risk spells on them. You frighten me with your madness.

PRAKRITI: Who dared to think of casting a spell on the king's son?

MOTHER: I do not fear the king. The worst he can do is put me on the gallows.

PRAKRITI: I fear nothing, or only one thing: a falling back into the body of the dead Prakriti, losing my new self and again being lost in the darkness. That would be worse than the gallows or any death. Drag him here, Mother, you must! I must have him. Is not this desire of mine a miracle in itself? He worked one miracle and will work a greater one when he comes here to be at my side.

MOTHER: I am frightened and I may be doing you and him a great wrong. It may be I can draw him here, but can you stand the ordeal? Another of the monk's miracles, and nothing of you may remain.

PRAKRITI: No, nothing shall remain. That is my one wish—that I have the chance to give, to pour out my being and be fulfilled. That is the consummation I have been waiting for. The world has conspired to make me forget what I *can* give. Now I know and I *shall* give—everything that I have! I will wait for him. Please bring him, Mother, at once.

MOTHER: Do you fear God?

PRAKRITI: I do not fear what does not fear me.[9] A god that insults, debases, and blinds is no god. Men have conspired to make my god evil. Now I see and am not afraid. Begin your chant and make the monk sit by me. I will exalt him.

MOTHER: Do you fear no curse?

PRAKRITI: The real curse has clung to me by my birth, the monk shall redeem me. I will listen to no delays, Mother. Begin your chant!

MOTHER: I do this for you. Tell me his name.

PRAKRITI: Ananda! His name is Ananda.

MOTHER: Ananda? The Buddha's close companion?

PRAKRITI: Yes, that is he.

MOTHER: It is a sin to work a spell on him.

PRAKRITI: Why a sin?

MOTHER: The Buddha and his companions attract with virtue; I force by magic, as a hunter ambushes game. It is like churning mud.

PRAKRITI: Then churn mud. How else can mud be purified?

MOTHER: Only because I love you, Prakriti. Oh, Ananda, you who art great in soul, forgive my sin. Your power to forgive is greater than my strength to wrong. Accept my adoration as I begin my sacrilege.

PRAKRITI: Do not be so afraid, Mother.[10] It is I who work the spell through you. If to drag him by the anguish of my yearning is wrong, then I do that wrong.

MOTHER: You are daring, Prakriti.

PRAKRITI: Daring? Consider him daring when he said so simply what no one had dared to say before, "Give me water." These simple words illumined my whole life. If you had seen him, you would know your fear is baseless. He had finished begging in the city, and still he walked across the wasteland, past the cremation ground, then he crossed the river, all in the scorching sun, for what? Just to say to me, "Give me water." Such tenderness and grace to shower on a worthless creature! "Give me water!" Water has welled up within me and I must pour it out. "Give me water!" In an instant I knew of a reservoir within me. Now I must give it. That is why I call him night and day. Chant your spell. He will hear it.

(From a distance come the sounds of a Buddhist chant) [11]

MOTHER: Look, Prakriti! There go some monks.

PRAKRITI: See, Mother, see! He is at the head of the procession! *(Both look for what seems like a long time)* He did not look back at

174

the well. He did not look this way once! He might have come and said, "Give me water." How could he pass me up like this? I who am his own creation? *(She falls to the ground weeping)* This earth, this earth, this earth alone is mine. For an instant he raised me up in light, miserable creature that I am! Could this be grace? To let me sink back into my mud and be mixed with it forever, and to be trampled upon by everyone.

MOTHER: Quiet, child. Forget him. It's best that your moment's illusion is shattered. Let what cannot endure vanish as soon as it may.

PRAKRITI: Illusion? This longing from day to day, this insult from year to year, this bird's imprisonment beating wings forever against a cage, do you call this all an illusion? Do you call something which strains every nerve in my body only a dream? Those who have no earthly burdens, no joys or sorrows, who float along like autumn clouds—are they the only ones without illusion? No, I know what is real for me.

MOTHER: I can't see you suffer like this. Get up. Dress your hair. I will drag him here with a spell. I will break his vow of "I desire not" and I will make him moan and crave, "I want, I want, I want."

PRAKRITI: Mother, your spell is as ancient as life itself; thin *mantras* are merely crude and recent words. They cannot match your power.

MOTHER: Where are they going?

PRAKRITI: They are going nowhere. During the rains they fast and do penance for four months, and then they are off again to who knows where. They call this being enlightened.

MOTHER: Then why talk about spells, you crazy girl? If he is going so far away, how can I bring him back? [12]

PRAKRITI: Your spells can overcome distance. He showed no pity for me; I'll show none for him. Work your spell, Mother. Wrap him in a coil he can never escape from.

MOTHER: Hold this mirror in your hand and dance; it will reflect what happens to him.

PRAKRITI: *(Looks into the mirror and dances)* The clouds, Mother, are gathering in the west. They are storm clouds. The spell will work. His dry meditations will be swept away like dry leaves, his

vow extinguished, his path turned toward me. He will be blown
here as a bird which falls into a dark courtyard when its wing
is broken. I see the lightning flash and the sea pound.

MOTHER: It is not too late, Prakriti to stop. Consider. Shall I go on?
Will you be able to bear it? This spell will not subside until it
has burnt his vow to ashes. To undo this spell may cost me my
life.[13]

PRAKRITI: Let him pass through the whole fire. I see his end approaching, and our stormy union will make destruction a bliss.
He will give himself to save me, and I will save you.

ACT II

(A few days have elapsed)

PRAKRITI: (She is dancing) I can bear no more. (Her steps falter) I am
choking. I cannot look into the mirror anymore. What a whirlwind of agony is raging in that noble man.

MOTHER: Speak to me Prakriti. It is not too late to revoke the spell.
Though my own life be extinguished, let me spare this great soul.

PRAKRITI: All right, Mother, stop the spell. . . . No, no, don't. I must
have him. Try a little longer. Let him come a bit nearer. Let
him go through with it and come to me. When he enters my
house, I shall wash away his suffering. My surrender will comfort
and heal him. The fire in me will illumine the darkness of his
fall, and the fountain of my life will bathe and refresh his tortured soul. Once more he shall say, "Give me water." Until that
moment let the spell work.[14]

MOTHER: Oh, it takes so long! Wait! The spell is triumphing. I think
I have won. But I cannot breathe.

PRAKRITI: Go on with it, Mother. I beg you, a little more.

MOTHER: The rainy season is coming, and their fast is at hand.

PRAKRITI: They have gone to the monastery at Vaisali.

MOTHER: But that is so far away. You have no pity, Prakriti.

PRAKRITI: It is only seven days' journey. Fifteen days have already
gone. His meditation has been shaken—he is coming! And that
which was so many million miles away is coming with him.

176

MOTHER: Prakriti, I have worked the spell to its utmost. Such force would have brought down Indra, wielder of the thunderbolt. And still he had not come! What a struggle! You could not have told me all you saw in the mirror.

PRAKRITI: I saw the heavens covered over with mist which here and there was pierced by lightning. I saw gods as they lay exhausted after the war with the demons. That passed. Then I saw black clouds gathering. There was terrifying lightning. And then I saw my life-giving monk. He looked as if he were on fire. Flames were searing him from every direction. I looked and I froze. I rushed to tell you to break the spell and found you unconscious. I came back to look into the mirror and saw only intolerable agony on his face.

MOTHER: It did not kill you? His suffering burned into me until I couldn't stand it any longer.

PRAKRITI: The suffering I saw was of us both. My own suffering mingled with his like copper and gold in a furnace.

MOTHER: Now, finally, you have known fear.

PRAKRITI: I knew something greater than fear.[15] I felt like a witness to creation, something mightier than destruction. It all seemed to be for some purpose. Was it life or death? A feeling of release came over me, and I could not contain myself. My whole being leapt up like a joyous flame.

MOTHER: And the monk?

PRAKRITI: He gazed into the distance. He was as steadfast as the sun in its orbit.

MOTHER: Did he look as if he felt your presence?

PRAKRITI: I shudder when I think of it. His eyes went red with anger, as though he was about to curse. Then he stamped out his flaming passion and like a javelin it seemed to re-enter his soul and become fixed there.

MOTHER: And you endured it?

PRAKRITI: I was amazed at myself. A nobody from nowhere—and his suffering and mine were one.

MOTHER: How long will this horror drag on?

PRAKRITI: Until my suffering is soothed. How can he be freed when I am not?

MOTHER: When did you look into the mirror last?

PRAKRITI: Yesterday evening. Some days before, in darkness, he had passed the lion-gate of Vaisali. After that I saw him, sometimes crossing rivers or mountain passes, sometimes trudging along forest paths, alone in the night. At times he seemed more and more in a dream, forgetful of everything, even of the conflict raging in him. His face looked like death, his eyes were fixed on nothing, and his body seemed old and shrunken.

MOTHER: Where is he now?

PRAKRITI: Yesterday at sunset he was at the village Patal on the Upali River, and it was overflowing with the rains. On the bank was an old peepul tree, glimmering with fireflies, beneath which an altar was overgrown with moss. He looked stunned when he reached that spot, recognizing it as the one where the Buddha had preached to the King Suprabhas. He turned his face away. I could not look a moment longer. I threw away the mirror. *(Prakriti hears the nightwatchman pounding with his stick.)* Now the watchman is calling. It must be past midnight. This night may be wasted. Mother, he may be near. Hurry and cast the spell more powerfully. He must find me.

MOTHER: I am no longer able to. My strength is weakening.

PRAKRITI: No, you cannot weaken, Mother! Keep trying. Don't give up.[16] He may have turned backwards and the chain holding may snap and I will lose him forever. I could not endure it. I beg you, Mother, repeat your earth chant and make the steadfastness of my monk tremble.

MOTHER: Are you prepared for the ending?

PRAKRITI: I am.

MOTHER: Then begin your dance of welcome while I repeat my chant. *(Prakriti dances.)* Prakriti, find your mirror. Look into it again. Tell me when a shadow descends on the altar. Can you see it?

PRAKRITI: No, I will not look. I will only listen and wait. I shall look only when I can look at him.

MOTHER: I can stand it no longer. Something stops my breath, I. . . .

PRAKRITI: Carry on a little longer, Mother! Pull him here. He will come, I know! See? There comes the storm announcing his approach. I feel the earth trembling.

MOTHER *(gasping)*: . . . Coming to curse you, you wretched girl. I am nearly done. My veins are snapping. I can't. . . .

PRAKRITI: Not to curse, no, not to curse! My beloved comes with lightning to smash down the gate of death and to give me a new life. The darkness is breaking. The walls of my prison are giving way, and the great delusion of my life is exposed. I am trembling with fear, but my heart is pounding with joy. Oh my destroyer, you have come! I will seat you on the summit of my degradation and will fashion your throne from my shame, my fear, and my joy!

MOTHER: Look into the mirror. Quick. My time is up.

PRAKRITI: I am afraid to, Mother.[17] His path is nearing the end. How will he look at me? Will I be able to make up for his long torture?

MOTHER: Don't delay, Prakriti, look into the mirror. I want to know. Quick, I can bear it no longer.

PRAKRITI: (*Picks up the mirror, looks in it as if transfixed, and then flings it away.*) Break the spell, Mother, break it. Undo your spell. Revoke it. Immediately! How wicked of me to have dragged him down to this! That heavenly light on his face! Where has it all gone? He comes with his head bowed, his face pale, his body bearing the load of the soul's defeat. What have I done to him (*She kicks away the apparatus of magic.*) I am a wretch, a *chandalini*—how else could I have desecrated my lover? (*Ananda enters. Prakriti falls at his feet.*) You have come, my master, to redeem me. I have caused you much suffering for which I ask forgiveness. Forgive me. I have dragged you down to my earth. But how else could you have raised me? Oh, pure one, the earth under your feet is made pure. You are blessed.

MOTHER: (*Lifting her head and attempting to kneel.*) You are blessed and ever victorious, O Lord. At your feet my sin and my life are both at an end. (*She dies*)

ANANDA: (*Chants*) I honor the Enlightened One, most pure, an ocean of mercy, the Buddha, endowed with the vision of pure and supreme knowledge, who destroys all sin and suffering in this world.

ON INDIA

In 1912, Tagore wrote, "I love India, not because I cultivate the idolatry of geography, not because I have had the chance to be born in her soil, but because she has saved through tumultuous ages the living words that have issued from the illuminated consciousness of her great sons. . . ." This reverence for ideas and ideals, at the same time that it rejects foreign encroachment and exploitation, condemns any kind of nationalism which is pompous or aggressive, and advocates an India which is growing both in self-insight and world consciousness. From a knowledge of the words of the ages comes the wisdom for the decisions of the present.

In Tagore's view, the problems that confronted ancient India were not so much political as cultural and social. Indian society, since the olden days, has had two conflicting forces at work, the progressive Kshatriyas and the conservative Brahmins. Out of this interaction, India's history was shaped. Tagore expressed this view in a written lecture, *Bharatvarsher Itihaser Dhara*, which he delivered to the Calcutta public in 1912. Out of the controversy it created came an English translation by the historian Sri Jadunath Sarkar, who approved of it, and it was published in the August–September issue of the *Modern Review*, 1913. Tagore later enlarged it for the *Visva-Bharati Quarterly* in 1923, and it came out in booklet form in 1951 (Visva-Bharati).

On July 22, 1904, because of a proposal by the British Government for the partitioning of Bengal, Tagore gave a public lecture in Calcutta, *Swadeshi Samaj*, in which he spoke for the cultural integrity of Bengal and advocated a comprehensive program for the reorganization of rural Bengal on the basis of self-help. Tagore attempted in his own family estates to organize a society according to the proposals in his lecture, and drafted a set of rules for the guidance of its members. The English translation of the lecture was made by Surendranath Tagore and it appeared in the book, *Greater India* (S. Ganesan, Madras, 1921).

A few months after the partition of Bengal was proposed, there was a further announcement for implementing reforms in primary education. A commission was appointed which advocated that instruction in the primary grades should be imparted through regional languages, some of which were dialects. There was now further agitation in Calcutta and a public protest was organized for the General Assemblies Hall at Scottish Church College on March 11, 1905. Tagore, among others, addressed this meeting, and his written lecture, *Saphalatar Sadupay*, was published in the Bangadarshan in April, 1905. Surendranath Tagore translated it into English and it was published as *The Way to Get It Done* in the May, 1921, issue of the *Modern Review*.

During his lecture tour of Japan and the United States in 1916–1917, Tagore made no attempt to conceal his views on chauvinistic and aggressive nationalism, and when both of these countries were on the verge of World War I, his ideas brought him many enemies in administrative and military circles. But it also brought him friends like Romain Rolland, and other avowed internationalists. *Nationalism* (Macmillan & Co., Ltd., 1917) contains the lectures given on this tour, including the essay "Nationalism in India," which was also later incorporated in Anthony X. Soares's edition of *Lectures and Addresses of Rabindranath Tagore* (Macmillan & Co., Ltd., 1928).

After Tagore's China tour of 1924, a group of orientalist scholars of Calcutta, including Prabodh C. Bagchi, Suniti Kumar Chatterji, and Kalidas Nag, formed a society to promote cultural exchanges with Southeast Asian countries with which India had close Buddhist associations. At a meeting held in Calcutta University, sponsored by the society, on the eve of his Southeast Asian tour of July, 1927, Tagore gave a lecture, parts of which were published in the July, 1927, issue of *Prabasi*. The English translation (*Greater India*) by Kalidas Nag appeared in the summer, 1943 issue of *The Visva-Bharati Quarterly*.

❧ A Vision of India's History

When communities which differ from each other in race and culture come and settle in the same vicinity, the first attempts at unity become too obviously mechanical. Some system of adjustment is needed, but to be successful, it must submit to a higher principle — life itself.

The history of India has been the history of a struggle between the mechanical spirit of cadence and conformity in social organization, and the creative spirit of man, which seeks freedom and love in self-expression. We must watch and see if the latter is still alive in India, and if the former can offer service and hospitality to man.

We do not know the heroes of the times when racial strife between Aryan and non-Aryan was at its height, and it is significant that the names of such conquerors have not been sung in Indian epics. It may be that an episode of that race war lies enshrouded in the mythical version of King Janamejaya's ruthless serpent sacrifice —the attempted extermination of the entire Naga race; there is, however, no special glorification of the king on this account. Yet, he who strove to bring about the reconciliation between Aryan and non-Aryan is worshiped to this day as an Avatar.

As the leading figures of the movement which sought to embrace both Aryan and non-Aryan in a larger synthesis, we find the names of three Kshatriyas most prominent in the story of the Ramayana: Janaka, Visvamitra and Rama-chandra; they are related not merely by kinship and affection, but by the same ideal. What if, as a matter of historical fact, Janaka, Visvamitra and Rama may not have been contemporaries? That does not diminish their nearness in idea. From the standpoint of space, the distance between the earth and the moon may appear large, but there are many double stars in the firmament of history whose distance from each other does not affect their brotherhood. We know from the epic Ramayana that Janaka, Visvamitra and Rama, even if actually separated by time, were nevertheless members of such a triple system.

In the history of an idea, a hero often represents the ideal of his race, and in Aryan history, Janaka and Visvamitra, as well as Rama, have become historical symbols; they are composite pictures of numerous personalities having a common purpose. Just as King Arthur, out of the Christendom of the Dark Ages, represents the Christian Knight, the valiant champion of Faith, so in India we get glimpses of the Kshatriya ideal gathering champions for a prolonged crusade. There is proof that these opponents were often Brahmins.

The idea behind the neo-Kshatriya movement cannot be known

today in its full meaning, but it is possible to discern the lines of divergence between Brahmin and Kshatriya.

The four-headed god Brahma represents the four Vedas with all their hymns and regulations of sacrifice. The Brahmin Bhrigu, one of the most renowned priests of the ancient days, is said to have sprung from the heart of Brahma, thereby showing that he occupied a prominent part in the cult of Vedic ceremonialism. In the Bhagavata Purana it says that the Kshatriya king, Kartavirya, stole a sacrificial cow from Yamadagni, a priest of the same Bhrigu clan, and caused the class war led by Parasu-rama, the son of Yamadagni, against the whole Kshatriya community. Unless the stealing of the sacrificial cow stands for an idea, such a Brahmin crusade against the entire Kshatriya class fails to have meaning; it really indicates that among a great body of Kshatriyas there arose a spirit of resistance against sacrificial rites, and this gave rise to a fierce conflict between the two communities.

It has to be noted that the series of battles begun by Parasu-rama, the descendant of Bhrigu, at last came to their end with his defeat at the hands of Rama-chandra. This Kshatriya hero, as we all know, is accepted and adored as an incarnation of Vishnu, the deity of the monotheistic sect of Bhagavatas, meaning that this fight was one of ideals, terminating in the triumph of the religion in which, at a later date, Ramachandra occupied a central place. . . .

Those institutions which are static in their nature raise walls of division; this is why, in the history of religions, priesthood has always maintained dissensions and hindered the freedom of man. But the principle of life unites, it deals with the varied, and seeks unity. The Brahmins, who incorporated the static ideals of society, inaugurated different forms of ritualism and set up sectarian barriers between clans and classes. Of the two original deities of the Indo-Aryan tribe, the Sun and the Fire, the latter especially represented the Brahmin cult. Different forms of sacrifice gathered around it and were accompanied by strict rules of incantation; it came to be intimately associated with the pluralism of divinity, since fire had always been the vehicle of oblation to numerous gods.

The Kshatriyas, on the other hand, as they rallied against all obstacles, developed in their life the principles of expansion and inclusion. Born and nourished amid the clash of forces, the complexities of the external forms of religious worship could have no special significance for them. However, the Sun-god seems to have a special status; from him, Manu, the lawgiver who was a Kshatriya, and also the great kingly line of Raghu, to which Rama-chandra belonged, are said to have sprung. This Sun-god, in the course of time, developed into the personal god of the Bhagavata sect, Vishnu, who belonged principally to the Kshatriyas.

From Brahma's four mouths had issued the four Vedas, revealed for all time, and jealously sealed against outsiders—as unchanging as the passive features of Brahma rapt in meditation. This was the symbol of Brahmanism, placid and immutable, filled with the mystery of knowledge. But the four active arms of Vishnu were busy proclaiming the way of the Good, expanding the cycle of unity, maintaining the reign of law, and supporting the spirit of beauty and plenitude. All the symbols carried by Vishnu contain the different aspects of Kshatriya life. . . .

That there was naturally a period of struggle between the cult of ritualism supported by the Brahmins, and the religion of love, is evident. The mark of the Brahmin Bhrigu's kick, which Vishnu carries on his breast, is a myth-relic of the original conflict. The fact that Krishna, a Kshatriya, was not only at the head of the Vaishnava cult, but also the object of its worship, and that in his teaching, as inculcated in the Bhagavad-Gita, there are hints of detraction against Vedic verses, seems to prove that this cult was developed by the Kshatriyas. Another proof is found in the fact that the two nonmythical human avatars of Vishnu, Krishna and Rama-chandra, were both Kshatriyas, and the Vaishnava religion of love was spread by the teaching of the one and the life of the other. . . .

It is significant to note that the lives of great Brahmins of olden times, like Yajnavalkya, are associated with intellectual profundity and spiritual achievement, while those of great Kshatriyas represent an ethical magnanimity which has love for its guiding principle; it is also significant that the people of India, though entertaining a deep veneration for the Brahmin sages, instinctively ascribe divine inspiration to the Kshatriya heroes who actively realized high moral ideals in their personalities. Parasu-rama, the only historical personage belonging to the Brahmin caste who has been given a place in the list of avatars, has never found a place in the hearts of the people. This shows that, as far as India is concerned, divine power should be used for the reconciliation of different races, not for acquiring dominance over others through physical prowess and military skill. . . .

The religion represented by the third human avatar of Vishnu, who is Buddha, has in it the same moral quality which we find in the life and teaching of Rama and Krishna. It clearly shows the Kshatriya ideal: its freedom, courage of intellect, and self-sacrificing heart.

Foreign critics are too often anxious to misunderstand the conservative spirit of India, attributing it to the trade artifice of an interested priestcraft. But they forget that there was no racial difference between Brahmin and Kshatriya; these merely represented two different functions of the body politic, which, though appearing antagonistic, have as a matter of fact cooperated in the evolution of Indian history. Sowing seed in one's own land and reaping the harvest for distant markets are apparently contradictory. The seed-sowers naturally cling to the soil which they cultivate, while the distributors of the harvest develop a different mentality. The Brahmins were the guardians of the seed of culture in ancient India and the Kshatriyas strove to harvest its wisdom. The principle of stability and the principle of movement, though they depend upon each other for truth, are apt to lose their balance and come into fierce conflict. Yet these conflicts, as meteorology shows us on the physical plane, have the effect of purifying the atmosphere and restoring equilibrium; in fact, perfect balance in these opposing forces would lead to a deadlock in creation. Life moves in the cadence of constant adjustment of opposites; it is a perpetual process of the reconciliation of contradictions. . . .

It is evident that the sun, the one source of light and life, had led the thoughts of the Indo-Aryan sages toward the monotheistic ideal. The following prayer addressed to the sun, concludes the Ishopanishad. "O Sun, nourisher of the world, Truth's face lies hidden in thy golden vessel. Take away thy cover for the eyes of him who is a devotee of Truth."

According to the Chandogya Upanishad, the teacher Ghora, after having explained to his disciple Krishna, who had become *apipasa*, free from desire, the consecration ceremony which leads to giving oneself a new spiritual birth, and in which austerity, almsgiving, and truthfulness are one's gifts for the priests, ends his teaching with these words: "In the final hour one should take refuge in three thoughts: You are the Indestructible; you are the Unshaken, you are the very Essence of Life." On this point there are these two Rig verses:

> Proceeding from primeval seed,
> The early morning light they see,
> That gleameth higher than the heaven,
> From out of darkness all around,
> We, gazing on the higher light—
> Yea, gazing on the higher light—
> To Surya, god among the gods,
> We have attained the highest light!
>   Yes, the highest light!

We find a hint here on the teaching that was developed by Krishna into a great religious movement which preached freedom from desire and absolute devotion to God, and which spiritualized the meaning of ceremonies. That this religion had some association with the sun can be inferred from the legend of Krishna finding an inexhaustible store of food in her vessel after worshiping the sun; also the piercing of the target by Arjuna, which was very likely the mystic disc of the sun, the golden vessel that holds Truth which can be attained only by piercing the cover.

In connection with this we should note that the spiritual religion which Krishna preached must have ignored the exclusiveness of priestly creeds and extended its invitation to peoples of all classes, Aryans and non-Aryans alike. The legend of his intimate relationship with shepherd tribes supports this view, and we still find the religion, of which Krishna is the center, to be the great refuge of the lower castes and outcastes of the present Indian population. The most significant fact of Indian history is that all the human avatars of Vishnu had, by their life and teaching, broken the barriers of priestcraft by acknowledging the fellowship between the privileged and the despised.

One day Rama-chandra, the Kshatriya of royal descent, embraced as his friend the untouchable *chandala*, Guhaka, an incident which even today is quoted as proof of the largeness of his soul. During the succeeding period of conservative reaction, an attempt was made to suppress this evidence of Rama-chandra's liberality of heart in a supplemental canto of the epic which is an obvious interpolation, which stated that Rama beheaded with his own hands an ambitious Sudra for presuming to claim equal status in the attainment of spiritual excellence. It is like the ministers of the Christian religion, in the late war, invoking Christ's name and justifying the massacre of men.

Nevertheless, India has never forgotten that Rama-chandra was the beloved comrade of a *chandala*, that he seemed divine to the primitive tribes, some of whom had the totem of monkey, some that of bear. His name is remembered with reverence because he won over his antagonists and built a bridge of love between Aryan and non-Aryan.

This is one swing of the pendulum during Aryan times. We shall never know India truly unless we study the manner in which she reacted to the pull of these two opposite principles: self-preservation, represented by the Brahmin, and self-expansion, represented by the Kshatriya.

When the first overtures toward social union were being made, it became necessary for the Aryans to understand the non-Aryan religion. In the beginning, there was a state of war between the followers of Siva and the worshipers of the Vedic gods. The fortune of arms sometimes favored one side, sometimes the other. Even Krishna's valiant comrade, Arjuna, once had to acknowledge defeat at the hands of Siva of the Kiratas, a hunter tribe. There is also the well known record of a refusal to give Siva a place in a great Vedic sacrifice, which led to the cessation of the ceremony by the non-Aryans. At last, by the identification of Siva with the Vedic Rudra, an attempt had to be made to bring this constant religious antagonism to an end. And yet in the Mahabharata we find the later story of a battle between Rudra and Vishnu, which ended in the former acknowledging the latter's superiority. Even in Krishna worship we find the same struggle, and therefore in the popular recitation of Krishna legends we often hear of Brahma's attempt to ignore Krishna, until the ancestor god of the Aryans is compelled to pay homage to the later divinity of the populace. These stories reveal the persisting self-consciousness of the new arrivals, even after they had been admitted to the privileges of the old, established pantheon.

The advent of the two great Kshatriya founders of religion, Buddha and Mahavira, in the same eastern part of India where once Janaka had his seat, brought a spirit of simplification. They exercised a great force against the maze of religions and doctrines which had bewildered the country. Amid the ceremonial intricacies on one hand, and the subtleties of metaphysical speculation on the other, the simple truth was overlooked that creeds and rites have no value in themselves, and that human welfare is the one object toward which religious enthusiasm must be directed. These two Kshatriya *sannyasins* refused to admit that any distinctions between men were inherent and perpetual; according to their teaching, man could be saved by realizing truth, and not by social conformity or amoral practices. These teachings rapidly overcame the obstacles of tradition and habit, and swept over the whole country.

Long before the flood of the Buddhistic influence had subsided, most of the protecting walls were broken down, and the banks of discipline through which the forces of unification had been flowing in a regulated stream were obliterated. In fact, Buddhism, in departing, left all the aboriginal diversities in India to rear their heads unchecked, because one of the two guiding forces of Indian history had been enfeebled, and its spirit of resistance had been enhancing the process of assimilation.

In the midst of the Buddhistic revolution only the Brahmins were able to keep themselves intact, because the maintaining of exclusiveness had all along been their function; but the Kshatriyas had merged with the rest of the people, and in the succeeding age most of the kings had ceased to belong to Kshatriya dynasties. Then came the Sakas and the Hunas, whose hordes repeatedly flowed into India and mixed with the elder inhabitants. The Aryan civilization, thus stricken, summoned all its forces in a supreme attempt at recovery, and its first effort was directed at regaining its race consciousness.

During this long social and religious revolution, which had the effect of erasing individual features of the traditional Aryan culture, the question of identity became paramount, and the chief endeavor became the rescue of a racial personality from the prevailing chaos. Aroused by a destructive opposition, for the first time, India sought to define her individuality. When she now tried to know and name herself, she recalled the empire of Bharata, a legendary suzerain of by-gone days, and defining her boundaries accordingly, she called herself Bharata-varsha. In order to restore the fabric of her original civilization, she tried to tie together the lost threads of earlier achievements. Thus, collection and compilation, rather than any new creation, were characteristics of this age. The great sage of this epoch, Vyasa, who is reported to have performed this function, may not have been a real person, but he was, at any rate, the personification of the spirit of the times.

The movement began with the compilation of the Vedas. Now that it became necessary to have a unifying agent, the Vedas, as the oldest part of Aryan lore, had to be elevated in order to serve as a center of reference around which the distracted community could rally. Another task undertaken by this age was the gathering and arranging of historical material. In this process, spread over a long period of time, all the scattered myths and legends were assimilated, along with all the beliefs and discussions which lingered in the racial memory. This literary image of old Aryan India was called the Mahabharata—the great Bharata. Even the name shows an awakened consciousness of unity in a people struggling to find expression in a permanent record.

This eagerness to gather all drifting fragments from the wreckage resulted in an indiscriminate overloading of the central narrative of the epic. The artists's natural desire to impart an aesthetic relevancy to the story was swamped by the exigency of the time, for the age needed an immortal epic, a majestic ship fit to cross the sea of time, to carry materials for the building of a permanent shelter for the racial mind.

Therefore, though the Mahabharata may not be history in the modern western definition of the term, it is, nevertheless, a receptacle of historical records which had been written in the living memory of a people. Had any competent person attempted to sift and sort and analyze this material into an ordered array of facts, we would have lost the picture of a changing Aryan society, one in which the lines are vivid or dim, connected or confusing and conflicting, according to the lapses of memory, changes of ideal, and variations of light and shade incident to time's perspective. In this great work, self-recording annals of history, as they are imprinted on the living tablet of time, are bared to our sight.

The genius of that extraordinary age did not stop at the discovery of a unity in the various historical materials; it also searched out a unified spiritual philosophy running through all contradictions that are found in the metaphysical speculations of the Vedas. The outline presentation of this philosophy was made by the same Vyasa, who had not only the industry to gather and assimilate the details, but also the power to visualize the whole. His compilation is a creative synthesis.

One thing which remains significant is the fact that this age of compilation has insisted upon the sacredness of the Brahmins and of Brahminic lore by means of constant reiteration and exaggerated language. It proves that there was a militant spirit fighting great opposition, and that a complete loss of faith in the freedom of intellect and conscience had occurred among the people. An analogy can be found in the occasional distrust of democracy which we observe among some modern intellectuals of Europe.

The main reason for this was that, during the period of alternating ascendancy of Brahmin and Kshatriya, the resulting synthesis had an Aryan character, but during the Buddhist period, when not only non-Aryans but also non-Indians from outside gained free access, it became difficult to maintain organic coherence. A strong undercurrent of race-mingling and religious compromise set in, and as the mixture of races and beliefs began to make itself felt, the Aryan forces of self-preservation struggled to put up a series of walls in order to prevent further encroachments. Only those intrusions which could not be resisted found a place within the barriers.

Let no one imagine, however, that the non-Aryan contributors were received only because of circumstance, and that they had no value of their own. As a matter of fact, the old Dravidian culture should in no way be underrated; the result of its combination with the Aryan was the Hindu civilization, which acquired both richness and depth from the Dravidians. They may not have been introspective or metaphysical, but they were artists, and they could sing, design and build. The transcendental mind of the Aryan, by its marriage with the emotional and creative art of the Dravidian, gave birth to an offspring which was neither fully Aryan, nor Dravidian, but Hindu.

With its Hindu civilization, India was able to realize the universal in the commonplaceness of life; but on the other hand, because of the mixed strain in its blood, whenever Hinduism has failed to attempt the reconciliation of opposites, which is its essence, it has fallen prey to incongruous folly and blind superstition. This is the predicament in which Hindu India has been placed by its birthright. Where a harmony between the differences has been organically effected, beauty has blossomed; so long as it remains wanting, there is no end to deformities. Moreover, we must remember that not only the Dravidian civilization, but also things pertaining to primitive non-Aryan tribes, found entrance into the Aryan polity, and the torment of these unassimilable intrusions has been a darkly cruel legacy left to the succeeding Hindu society.

When the non-Aryan gods found a place in the Aryan pantheon, their inclusion was symbolized by the trinity of Brahma, Vishnu and Siva—Brahma representing the ancient tradition of exclusive externalism, Vishnu representing the transition when the original Vedic Sun-god became humanized and emerged from the rigid scriptural texts into the world of the pulsing heart, and Siva representing the period when the non-Aryan found entrance into the social organization of the Aryan; but though the Aryan and non-Aryan thus met, they did not merge completely. Like the Ganges and the Jumna at their confluence, they flowed on together in two distinguishable streams.

In spite of Siva's entry amongst the Aryan gods, his Aryan and non-Aryan aspects remained different. In the former, he is the lord of ascetics, who, having conquered desire, is enraptured in the bliss of nirvana, as bare of raiment as of worldly ties; in the latter, he is terrible, clad in raw, bleeding elephant hide, intoxicated by the hemp decoction. In the former, he is the replica of Buddha, and as such has adorned many a Buddhist shrine; in the latter, he is the overlord of demons, spirits and other dreadful beings, who haunt the places of the dead, and as such has appropriated to himself the worshipers of the phallus, snakes, trees and other totems. In the former, he is worshiped in the quietude of meditation; in the latter, in frenzied orgies of self-torture.

Similarly in the Vaishnava cult, Krishna, who became the mythological god of the non-Aryan religious legends, did not have the same character as the brave and sagacious ruler of Dvaraka who acted as the guide, philosopher and friend of the valiant Arjuna. Alongside the heights of the Celestial Song ranged the popular religious stories of the cowherd tribes.

In spite of all that was achieved, however, it was quite impossible, even for the Aryan genius, to harmonize and assimilate all the practices, beliefs and myths of innumerable non-Aryan tribes. As the non-Aryan element became increasingly predominant in the race mixture, more and more of what was non-Aryan came to be not merely tolerated, but welcomed in spite of incongruities. This led to the formulation of the principle that any religion which satisfied the needs of a particular sect was enough for its salvation; but as a consequence, the organizing force was reduced to the mere compulsion of some common customs, some repetition of external practices, which barely served to hold together these heterogeneous elements. For the mind which has lost its vigor, all external habits become tyrannical; the result for India was that extraneous custom has become rigid, leaving little freedom, even in insignificant details of life. This has developed in the people an excessively strong sense of responsibility to the claims of the class tradition which divides, but not the conviction of that inner moral responsibility which unites.

We have seen how, after the decline of Buddhism, a path had to be cleared through the jungle of undergrowth which had been allowed to grow unchecked during the long inaction of the Brahminic hierarchy. Near the end of its career in India the mighty stream of Buddhism grew sluggish and lost itself in morasses of primitive superstitions and promiscuous creeds and practices, which had their root in non-Aryan crudities; it lost its philosophic depth and its feeling for humanity, which had their origin in the Aryan mind.

The time came for the Brahmins to assert themselves and bring back into all this incongruity some unity of ideal, and it was now a difficult task because of the various racial strains which had become part of the constitution of the Indian people. In order to save their ideals from this wild exuberance of heterogeneous life, they fixed them in a permanent rigidity. This had the reactionary effect of making their own ideals inert, and unfit for adaptation to changes of time; while it left to all elements of the different races in India a kind of freedom that was not guided by the dictates of reason. The result has been a huge medley of customs, ceremonials and creeds, some of which are old ruins, and some merely the anomalies of living outgrowths which continue to cling and smother.

Yet, the genius of India continued in spite of the shackled mind of the people. In Vedic times, as we have seen, it was mainly the Kshatriyas who brought storms of fresh thought into the atmosphere of the people's life whenever it showed signs of stagnation; in later ages, when the Kshatriyas had lost their individuality, the message of spiritual freedom and unity in man sprang mainly from the obscure strata of the community: the castes that were despised. Though it has to be admitted that in the medieval age the Brahmin Ramananda was the first to give voice to the cry of unity, and consequently lost his privileges as a Brahmin *guru*, yet it is still true that most of our great saints of that time, who took up this cry in their life and teaching and songs, came from the lower classes: one of them a Mohammedan weaver, one a cobbler, and several coming from the ranks of society whose touch would pollute the drinking water of respectable Hindus. Thus, the living voice of India found its words even in the darkest days of our decline, proclaiming that he knows truth who knows the unity of all beings in the spirit.

We cannot see clearly the age in which we now live, yet we feel that the India of today has aroused herself once more to find her truth, her harmony, and her oneness, not only among her own people, but with the world. The current of her life, which had been dammed up in stagnation, has found a breach in the wall and can now feel the waves of humanity outside. We shall learn that we can reach the world, not through an effacement, but through an expansion of our own individuality. We shall know that just as it is futile mendicancy to covet the wealth of others, so it means utter destitution to keep ourselves segregated and starved by refusing a gift which is the common heritage of man because it is brought to us by a foreign messenger.

Our western critics, whose own people, whenever confronted by a close contact with non-western races find no solution to the problem except extermination or expulsion by physical force, and whose caste feeling against darker races is aggressive and contemptuous, are ready to judge us with a sense of superiority when comparing India's history with their own. They do not consider the difficult burden which Indian civilization has taken upon itself from its beginning. India is the one country in the world where the Aryan colonizers had to make constant social adjustments with peoples who vastly outnumbered them, who were physically and mentally alien to their own race, and who were for the most part distinctly inferior to the invaders. Europe, on the other hand, is one in thought; her dress, custom, culture, and with small variations her habits, are one. Yet her inhabitants, although only politically divided, are perpetually making preparations for deadly combats, wherein entire populations indulge in ferocity unparalleled in the history of the barbarian. It is not merely these periodic eruptions that characterize the relationship between the countries of Europe, even after centuries of close contact and intellectual cooperation, but there is also a feeling of mutual suspicion which generates diplomatic deceitfulness and moral obloquy.

India's problem has been far more complex than that of the West, and our rigid system of social regulation has not solved it; to bring order and peace at the cost of life is terribly wasteful, whether in the policy of government or of society. But we can be proud of the fact that for a long series of centuries beset with vicissitudes of stupendous proportions, crowded with things that are incongruous and facts that are irrelevant, India still keeps alive the inner principle of her own civilization against the cyclonic fury of contradictions and the gravitational pull of the dust.

That has been the great function of the Brahmins of this land, to keep the lamp lighted when the storm has been raging on all sides; they endeavored to permeate the mass of obstructive material with some quickening ideal of their own that would transmute it into the life-stuff of a composite civilization. They tried to discover some ultimate meaning in the inarticulate primitive forms struggling for expression, and to give it a voice. In a word, it was the mission of the Brahmin to comprehend by the light of his own mature understanding the undeveloped minds of the people.

It would be wrong for us, when we judge the historical career of

India, to put all the stress upon the accumulated heap that has not yet been assimilated in one consistent cultural body. Our great hope lies in our realization that something positively precious in our achievements still persists in spite of circumstances that are inclement. The best of us still have our aspirations for the supreme goals of life, which is so often mocked by prosperous people who now control the world. We still believe that the world has a deeper meaning than what is apparent, and that therein the human soul finds its ultimate harmony and peace. We still know that only in spiritual wealth does civilization attain its end, not in a prolific production of materials, and not in the competition of intemperate power with power.

It has certainly been unfortunate for us that we have neglected the cult of Anna Brahma, the infinite as manifested in the material world of utility, and we are dearly paying for it. We have for so long set our mind upon realizing the eternal in the intensity of spiritual consciousness, that we have overlooked the importance of realizing the infinite in the world of extension. In this great field of adventure the West has attained a success for which humanity has to be immensely grateful.

Nevertheless, true happiness and peace are awaiting the children of the West in that *tapasya*, which is realizing Brahma in spirit, acquiring the inner vision before which the sphere of immortality reveals itself.

I love India, not because I cultivate the idolatry of geography, not because I have had the chance to be born in her soil, but because she has saved through tumultuous ages the living words that have issued from the illuminated consciousness of her great sons: Brahma is truth, Brahma is wisdom, Brahma is infinite; peace is in Brahma, goodness is in Brahma, and the unity of all beings is in Brahma.

We have come to know that what India seeks is not the peace of negation or of some mechanical adjustment, but that which is in goodness, and in the truth of perfect union; that India does not enjoin her children to cease from *karma*, but to perform *karma* in the presence of the Eternal, with the knowledge of the spiritual meaning of existence, and that the true prayer of Mother India is:

> He who is one, who is above all color
> distinctions, who dispenses the needs

of men of all colors, who comprehends
all things from their beginning to the
end, let Him unite us to one another
with that wisdom which is the wisdom
of goodness.

FROM *Greater India*

In early life I began reading the so-called history of India, and
from day to day a torture was inflicted upon me: cramming the names
and dates of the dismal chronicle of India's repeated defeats and
humiliations in her political competition with foreigners from Alex-
ander to Clive. In that historical desert of indignities, we tried des-
perately to satisfy our hunger for national glorification in the oasis of
Rajput Chivalry. Everyone knows with what feverish excitement we
tried in those days to use Todd's *Annals of Rajasthan* to enrich our
Bengali poetry, drama and romance, showing how we had starved in
not discovering the true greatness of our country, which was not a
mere geographical expression but a continent of human characters
and human aspirations. The geography of a country no doubt helps
to build bodies, but character develops by the inspiration one derives
from the world of human aspirations, and if we know that world to
be petty and low then we cannot develop strength to deal with our
depressed spirits by merely reading the history of heroic foreign
nations. . . .

When a man is hungry he dreams of food. Today, the hunger for
political self-assertion is for many reasons the most powerful, and
our dreams likewise have taken the form of a political feast. Thus,
the voices of higher realities are rejected as irrelevant.

If we follow the course of our modern political self-assertion we
touch foreign history at its starting point. In a feverish political urge
we had to imagine ourselves to be dream-made Mazzinis, Garibaldis
and Washingtons; in our economic life we were caught in the laby-
rinth of imaginary Bolshevism, Syndicalism or Socialism. These mi-

rage-like manifestations are not the natural outgrowths of Indian history, but are fantasies born of our recent misfortune and hunger. As the film of this dream-cinema is being unrolled before our eyes, we see the trade-mark "Made in Europe" flashed in the corners, betraying the address of the factory where the film originated.

When we thus ramble over unknown roads after unrealities, we lose our identity in sentimental distractions. Our success, however, can only be achieved through the identification of our own personality. If we could realize that above the sphere of politics and economics there is a world of glory, then we could try to build a real future. But if we lose faith and disdain inner truth, we shall continue, futilely, to build castles in the air.

The real wealth of India was never hidden like an old deed in an iron safe; the only true expression of India was in that which she gave openly and freely. The surplus of her cultural life, which she scattered everywhere, was the core of her personality. Through the capacity to give our assets to others, we earn the right to call the "outsider" our own. Anyone who could discard the bonds of his ego could easily transcend the barriers of external geography. So if we want to know what the true wealth of India consisted of, we should cross oceanic barriers to reach the far-off fields of her self-dedication. From India abroad we may glimpse that eternal grace of India which we often fail to grasp, enveloped as we are by the dust storm of modern history.

When I was in China I found the people there quite different from us; we have little similarity with the Chinese in nose or ears, language or manners. But I felt a kinship with them that I have felt with few of our own people. It was not the result of political power or of conquest; the relationship between China and India was built not through the infliction of suffering, but through the acceptance of sacrifice, and our countries were united through that truth which enables us to feel those who are distant and different to be near and meaningful to us. Foreign political history has not mentioned that truth, and we lack the courage to believe in it, but even today we have the convincing evidence scattered in many places far from India.

In the history of our own middle ages, there was a religious conflict between the Hindus and the conquering Muslims. We also find at that time a succession of saints and devotees—many Muslims were among that galaxy—who bridged the gulf of religious differences by personal relationships. They were not politicians and could not even dream of accepting as a reality the so-called political union which was based on opportunism. They went where mankind finds its common and unchanging basis of unity, and they accepted, as their motto, that great truth which teaches us to see *all* as part of *ourselves*. There were many heroes whose names and faces have been recorded in our histories based on foreign models, and those heroes are now almost lost among the dust heap which summarized their glories. But the deathless messages of those saints and devotees are still running in the life-blood of the Indian people. If we could draw our inspiration from that source, we would see an improvement in our politics and economics and also a strengthening in our general plan of action. Whenever our life is stirred by truth, it expresses energy and comes to be filled, as it were, with a creative ardor. This consciousness of the creative urge is evidence of the force of truth on our mind. . . .

FROM *Nationalism*

Neither the colorless vagueness of cosmopolitanism, nor the fierce self-idolatry of nation-worship is the goal of human history. And India has been trying to accomplish her task through social regulations of differences, on the one hand, and the spiritual recognition of unity, on the other. She had made grave errors in setting up the boundary walls too rigidly between races, in perpetuating the results of inferiority in her classification; often she has crippled her children's minds and narrowed their lives in order to fit them into her social forms; but for centuries new experiments have been made and adjustments carried out.

Her mission has been like that of a hostess to provide proper accommodation to her numerous guests whose habits and requirements are different from one another. It is giving rise to infinite complexities whose solution depends not merely upon tactfulness but sympathy and true realization of the unity of man. Toward this realization have worked from the early time of the Upanishads up to the present moment, a series of great spiritual teachers, whose one object has been to set at naught all differences of man by the overflow of our consciousness of God. In fact, our history has not been of the rise and fall of kingdoms, of fights for political supremacy. In our country, records of these days have been despised and forgotten. For they in no way represent the true history of our people. Our history is that of our social life and attainment of spiritual ideals.

But we feel that our task is not yet done. The world-flood swept over our country, new elements have been introduced, and wider adjustments are waiting to be made. . . .

FROM *Nationalism in India*

India has never had a real sense of nationalism. Even though from childhood I had been taught that idolatry of the nation is almost better than reverence for God and humanity, I believe I have out-grown that teaching, and it is my conviction that my countrymen will truly gain their India by fighting against the education which teaches them that a country is greater than the ideals of human-ity. . . .

We must recognize that it is providential that the West has come to India. And yet some one must show the East to the West, and convince the West that the East has her contribution to make to the history of civilization. India is no beggar of the West. And yet even though the West may think she is, I am not for thrusting off Western civilization and becoming segregated in our independence. Let us have a deep association. If providence wants England to be the channel of that communication, of that deeper association, I am will-ing to accept it with all humility. I have great faith in human nature, and I think the West will find its true mission. I speak bitterly of Western civilization when I am conscious that it is betraying its trust and thwarting its own purpose. The West must not make herself a curse to the world by using her power for her own selfish needs, but by teaching the ignorant and helping the weak, she should save herself from the worst danger that the strong is liable to incur, by making the feeble acquire power enough to resist her intrusion. And also she must not make her materialism to be the final thing, but must realize that she is doing a service in freeing the spiritual being from the tyranny of matter. . . .

. . . It was my conviction that what India most needed was constructive work coming from within herself. In this work we must take all risks and go on doing the duties which by right are ours, though in the teeth of persecution; winning moral victory at every step, by our failure and suffering. We must show those who are over us that we have in ourselves the strength of moral power, the power to suffer for truth. Where we have nothing to show, we have only to beg. It would be mischievous if the gifts we wish for were granted to us at once, and I have told my countrymen, time and again, to combine for the work of creating opportunities to give vent to our spirit of self-sacrifice, and not for the purpose of begging. . . .

Once again I draw your attention to the difficulties India has had to encounter and her struggle to overcome them. Her problem was the problem of the world in miniature. India is too vast in its area and too diverse in its races. It is many countries packed in one geographical receptacle. It is just the opposite of what Europe truly is, namely, one country made into many. Thus, Europe in its culture and growth has had the advantage of the strength of the many as well as the strength of the one. India, on the contrary, being naturally many, yet adventitiously one, has all along suffered from the looseness of its diversity and the feebleness of its unity. A true unity is like a round globe, it rolls on, carrying its burden easily; but diversity is a many-cornered thing which has to be dragged and pushed with all force. Be it said to the credit of India that this diversity was not her own creation; she has had to accept it as a fact from the beginning of her history. . . .

. . . In her caste regulations India recognized differences, but not the mutability which is the law of life. In trying to avoid collisions she set up boundaries of immovable walls, thus giving to her numerous races the negative benefit of peace and order but not the positive opportunity of expansion and movement. She accepted nature where it produces diversity, but ignored it where it uses that diversity for its world-game of infinite permutations and combinations. She treated life in all truth where it is manifold, but insulted it where it is ever moving. Therefore life departed from her social system and in its place she is worshiping with all ceremony the magnificent cage of countless compartments that she has manufactured. . . .

FROM *Our Swadeshi Samaj*

Our countrymen are mainly villagers, and whenever they have desired to feel in their own veins the throbbing life of the outside world, they have done so through the mela, an invitation from the village for the world to enter its cottage home. On such festive occasions the village forgets its narrowness by means of this hospitable expansion of heart. Just as in the rainy season when the water-courses are filled from the sky, so in mela time the village heart is filled with the spirit of the Universal.

These melas are a natural growth in our country. If you call people to a formal meeting they come with doubt and suspicion, and it takes time for their hearts to open; but those who come to a mela are already in the holiday mood, for they have left plows and hoes and all their cares behind. That is the place and the time to come and sit by the people and talk with them. There is not a district in Bengal where melas are not held at different times in the year. We should make a list of these times and places, and then take the trouble to make the acquaintance of our own people.

If the leaders of the country will abjure empty politics, and make it their business to give new life and objective to these melas, putting their own heart into the work and bringing together the hearts of Hindu and Muslim, and then confer about the real wants of the people—schools, roads, water reservoirs, grazing commons and the like—then the country will soon awaken.

It is my belief that if a band of workers go from district to district, organizing these Bengal melas, and furnishing them with new compositions by way of *jatras, kirtans*, recitations, bioscope and lantern shows, gymnastics legerdemain, then the money question will solve itself. In fact, if they undertake to pay the *zamindars* their usual fees, on being allowed to make the collections, they will stand to make considerable profit, and if this profit be used for national work, it would result in uniting the organizers of the mela with the people, and would enable them to get acquainted with every detail of the country life. The valuable functions they could then perform in connection with national awakening would be too numerous to count.

Religious and literary education has always been imparted in our country in the midst of the joy of festivity. These days, for one reason or another, the *zamindars* have been drawn to the metropolis, and the festivities at the time of weddings are limited to the dinners and nautches given for their rich town-friends, the poor tenants often being called upon to pay extra impositions for the purpose. Thus, the villages are losing all their joy, and the religious and literary culture, which was a feature of all festivity, and used to be the solace of man, woman and child alike, is getting to be more and more beyond the means of ordinary people. If these organizers can return this current of festivity to the villages, they will reclaim the desert into which the heart of the nation is fast lapsing.

FROM *The Way to Get It Done*

And yet self-government lies at our very door, waiting for us. No one has tried, nor is it possible for any one even if he does try, to deprive us of it. We can do everything we like for our villages—for their education, their sanitation, and the improvement of their communications—if only we make up our minds to set to work, if only we can act in unison. For this work we do not need the sanction of a government badge. . . . But what if we cannot make up our minds? What if we will not be united? Then are there ropes and stones enough for us to go and drown ourselves?

I repeat that our education is the thing which we should first of all take into our own hands.

Considering one's own responsibilities as light and others' responsibilities as heavy is not a legitimate moral code. When sitting in judgment on British behavior toward ourselves, it is well to note their human fallibility and the difficulties which they face; but when searching out our own lapses, there must be no excuses or palliations, no lowering of standards on the basis of expediency. The rousing of indignation against the British government may be an easy political method, but it will not lead us to our goal; rather, the cheap pleasure of giving tit for tat, of dealing shrewd blows, will detract from the efficient pursuit of our own path of duty. When a litigant is aroused to a state of frenzy, he thinks nothing of gambling and losing everything. If anger be the basis of our political activities, the excitement tends to become an end in itself, at the expense of the object to be achieved. Side issues then assume an exaggerated importance, and all gravity of thought and action is lost; such excitement is not an exercise of strength, but a display of weakness.

ON EDUCATION

After Tagore's second visit to England, in 1890, he decided to forego the family hopes for his living the life of a gentleman, and dedicated himself to a more creative existence, but because of increasing social responsibilities and continual inward searchings, Tagore recognized his need to help in the process of nation-building. Literary life, in itself, would not suffice for him in an age of crises. While in rural Bengal, where his father had sent him to look after the family estates, and where he had been writing and making occasional public appearances in Calcutta, Tagore turned to education as another creative opportunity, and decided to establish a school of his own.

In a place called Santiniketan, about one hundred miles from Calcutta, his father had already inaugurated a center for retreat and meditation, and when his youngest son, Rabindranath, approached him with the idea of adding a creative educational center, he agreed. Tagore, with his wife and children, and with a few friends and their families, started an experimental school where he hoped to provide children, not only with modern ideas and proper textbooks, but with the inspiration of nature and the fellowship of young growing minds. Tagore was particularly enthusiastic about bringing children into contact with creative artists and thinkers who would provide an incentive for children to express themselves in poetry, music, and other arts.

In addition to the personal contact with, and experience of nature, Tagore's school provided the following opportunities: fellowship in an all-Indian community; relationships with international representatives; co-educational learning; the absence of sectarian or any other barriers.

When World War I erupted, Tagore's main reaction was to expand his original school and make it, as he called it, "The Guest House of

India." The word "Visva-Bharati," which was used for this new academic unit of Santiniketan, means "world university," and its purpose was to provide young and old with the climate of mutual acceptance in a world torn by hatred and suspicion. This international center, with its academic, artistic, and scientific departments, soon acquired a world-wide reputation and attracted scholars from practically every major nation of the East and the West.

Since Tagore's death, Santiniketan has become one of the major universities of India, receiving its charter from Prime Minister Jawaharlal Nehru, Chancellor of the University. By common agreement, it has been selected as the place where Tagore's concepts of creative education will be continued.

Santiniketan is discussed in the selection, "My School," a chapter from *Personality* (Macmillan & Co., Ltd., 1917), which is a collection of lectures Tagore delivered during his coast-to-coast lecture tour of the United States in 1916–1917.

During his China visit of 1924 (April 12–May 29), Tagore gave many talks, some of which were delivered informally and extemporaneously. Leonard Elmhirst, who accompanied him and acted as his private secretary, took notes in longhand at these talks, and later transcribed them for the Chinese press. These transcriptions were published in 1925, with a minimum of editing and revision, as *Talks in China* (Visva-Bharati), a paperback volume long out of print.

FROM *Talks in China*

TO STUDENTS

I

When I was very young I gave up learning and ran away from my lessons. That saved me, and I owe all that I possess today to that courageous step. I fled the classes which instructed, but which did not inspire me, and I gained a sensitivity toward life and nature.

It is a great world to which we have been born, and if I had cultivated a callous mind, and smothered this sensitivity under a pile of books, I would have lost this world. We can ignore what is scattered in the blue sky, in the seasonal flowers, in the delicate relationships of love and sympathy and mutual friendship, only if we have deadened the thrill of touching the reality which is everywhere—in man, in nature, in everything. I kept this sensitiveness.

If mother Nature could do it, she would bless and kiss me, and would say, "You have loved me." I have lived not as a member of a society or group, but as a scamp and a vagabond, free in a world which I have seen face to face. I have experienced the mystery of its being: its heart and soul. You may call me uneducated and uncultured, just a foolish poet; you may become great scholars and philosophers; and yet I think I would still retain the right to laugh at pedantic scholarship.

I know, really, that you do not dislike me because I know less mathematics than you; for you believe that I have attained the secret of existence in some other way—not through analysis, but as a child who enters his mother's chamber. I have kept the child spirit, and have found entrance to my mother's chamber; it was from her that the symphony of awakening light sang to me from the distant horizon, and I sing now in response to it. Because of this I am close to you, the young hearts of a foreign country whom my heart recognizes as fellow voyagers along the path of dreamland.

II

You who are young do not need for the guidance of your conscience the props of ready-made maxims, or the pruning hooks of prohibition, or the doctrines from dead leaves of books. Your soul has a natural yearning for the inspiration of the sunlight and spring, and for everything that secretly helps the seed to sprout and the bud to blossom.

You are here with the gift of young life which, like the morning star, shines with hope for the unborn day of your country's future. I am here to sing the hymn of praise to youth, I who am the poet of youth, your poet.

You know that fairy tale, the eternal story of youth, which is popular in almost all parts of the world. It is about the beautiful princess taken captive by a cruel giant and the young prince who starts out to free her from his dungeon. When we heard that story in our boyhood, do you remember how our enthusiasm was stirred, how we felt ourselves setting out as that prince to rescue the princess, overcoming all obstacles and dangers, and at last succeeding in bringing her back to freedom. Today the human soul is lying captive in the dungeon of a Giant Machine, and I ask you, my young princes, to feel this enthusiasm in your hearts and be willing to rescue the human soul from the chains of greed.

We traveled here from Shanghai along your great river, Yang Tse. During the night I often came out to watch the scene on the banks, the sleeping cottages with their solitary lamps, the silence spreading over the hills, dim with mist. When morning broke I found great delight in the fleets of boats coming down the river, their sails high in the air—a picture of perfect grace and freedom. It moved my heart deeply; I felt that my own sail had caught the wind, and was carrying me from my captivity, from the sleeping past, bringing me out into the great world of man. . . .

This age to which we belong, does it not still represent night in the human world, a world sleeping while individual races are shut up within their own limits, calling themselves nations, barricading themselves, as these sleeping cottages were barricaded, with closed doors, bolts and bars, and prohibitions of all kinds? Does not all this represent the dark age of civilization, and have we not begun to realize that it is the robbers who are out and awake? The torches which these men hold high are not the lights of civilization, but only pointings to the path of exploitation.

This age must be described as the darkest age in human civilization, but I do not despair. As the first bird, when the dawn is still dark, proclaims the rising of the sun, so my heart sings the coming of a great future which is near. We must be ready to welcome this new age. There are some people, who are proud and wise and practical, who say that it is not in human nature to be generous, that men will always fight one another, that the strong will conquer the weak, and that there can be no real moral foundation for man's civilization. We cannot deny the facts of their assertion that the strong have power in the human world, but I refuse to accept this as a revelation of truth. . . .

We in the East once tried to muzzle the brute in man and control its ferocity, but today the forces of intellect have overwhelmed our belief in spiritual and moral strength. Power in animals was at least in harmony with life, but not bombs, poison gases, and murderous airplanes—the weapons supplied by science.

We should know that truth, any truth that man acquires, is for everyone. Money and property belong to individuals, to each of you, but you must never exploit truth for your personal aggrandizement; that would be selling God's blessing for a profit. However, science is also truth; it has its place in the healing of the sick, and in giving more food and leisure for life. When it helps the strong crush the weak, and rob those who are asleep, it is using truth for impious ends. Those who are thus sacrilegious will suffer and be punished, for their own weapons will be turned against them.

The time has come to discover another great power, that which gives us the power of sacrifice, the strength to suffer, not merely to cause suffering. This will help us to defeat brute greed and egotism, as in the prehistoric age when intelligence overcame the power of mere muscle.

Let the morning of this new age dawn in the East, from which great streams of idealism have sprung in the past, making the fields of life fertile with their influence. I appeal to you to make a trial of this moral power through martyrdom. Prove how, through the heroism of suffering and sacrifice, not weak submission, we can demonstrate our wealth and strength. Know that no organization, however large, can help you, no league of prudence or of power, but only individual faith in the infinite, the invisible, the incorruptible, the fearless.

The great human societies are the creation not of profiteers, but of dreamers. The millionaires who produce bales of merchandise in enormous quantities have never yet built a great civilization; it is they who are about to destroy what others have built. Come to the rescue and free the human soul from the dungeon of the machine. Proclaim the spirit of man and prove that it lies not in machine-guns and cleverness, but in a simple faith.

III

My friends, from across the distance of age I gaze at your young faces beaming with intelligence and eager interest. I am approaching the shore of the sunset-land; you stand over there with the rising sun. My heart reaches out to your hearts and blesses them.

I envy you. When I was a boy, in the dusk of the waning night, we did not fully know to what a great age we had been born; its meaning and message have become clear. I believe there are individuals all over the world who have heard its call.

What a delight it may be for you, and what a responsibility, belonging to a period which is one of the greatest in the whole history of man! We dimly realize the greatness of this age in the light of the pain and suffering that has come upon us, a suffering that is worldwide; we do not even know what form it is going to take.

Now that I am in China, I ask you, I ask myself, what have you got, what out of your own house can you offer in homage to this new age? You must answer this question. Do you know your own mind? Your own culture? What is best and most permanent in your own history? You must know that if you are to save yourselves from the greatest of insults: obscurity and rejection. Bring your light and add it to this great festival of lamps: world culture.

I have heard it said (some among your own people say it) that you are pragmatic and materialistic, that you cling to this life and this world, that you do not send out your dreams to search the heavens for a life beyond.

I cannot, however, bring myself to believe that any nation in this world can be great and yet be materialistic. I have a belief that no people in Asia can be wholly given to materialism. There is something in the blue vault of the sky, in the golden rays of the sun, in the wide expanse of the starlit night, in the procession of the seasons, each bringing its own basket of flowers which somehow gives to us an understanding of the inner music of existence, and I can see that you are not deaf to it.

Materialism is exclusive, and those who are materialistic claim individual rights of possessing and storing. You are not individualists in China; your society is itself the creation of your communal soul. It is not the outcome of a materialistic, of an egoistic mind, a medley of unrestricted competition, which refuses to recognize its obligations to others.

I see that you in China have not developed the prevailing world malady, the meaningless multiplication of millions, and the production of those strange creatures called multi-millionaires. I have heard that, unlike others, you do not give great value to the brute power of militarism. All this could not be possible if you were really materialists.

Is it true that you love this world and the material things about you with an intense attachment, but not by enclosing your possessions within exclusive walls? You share your wealth, you make distant relatives your guests, and you are not inordinately rich. This is only possible because you are not materialistic.

I have traveled through your country and I have seen with what immense care you have made the earth fruitful, with what a perfection you have endowed the articles of everyday use. How could this have been possible through a greedy attachment to material things?

If you had acknowledged greed as your patron, then, at a touch, mere utility would have withered all the beauty and grace of your environment. Have you not seen this? In Shanghai, in Tientsin,—huge demons of ugliness that stalk over the world—in New York, London, Calcutta, Singapore and Hongkong, all huge with ugliness? Everything they touch becomes dead, denuded of grace as if God's blessing had been withdrawn. Peking shows no sign of this, but reveals a marvellous beauty of human association. Even the most ordinary shops have a simple decoration; this shows that you have loved your life. Love gives beauty to everything it touches. Not greed and utility; they produce offices, but not dwelling houses.

To be able to love material things, to clothe them with tender grace, and yet not be attached to them, this is a great service. Providence expects that we should make this world our own, and not live in it as though it were a rented tenement. We can only make it our own through some service, and that service is to lend it love and beauty from our soul. Your own experience shows you the difference between the beautiful, the tender, the hospitable, and the mechanically neat and monotonously useful.

Gross utility kills beauty. We now have all over the world huge productions of things, huge organizations, huge administrations of empire—all obstructing the path of life. Civilization is waiting for a great consummation, for an expression of its soul in beauty. This must be your contribution to the world.

What is it that you have done by beautifying things? You have made, for me who comes from a distant country, even things hospitable by touching them with beauty. Instead of finding them obstacles, I acknowledge them as my own because my soul delights in their beauty. With its piles of things, life in other countries has become like some royal grave of ancient Egypt; these things darkly shout "Keep away." When I find this attractiveness in your every day artifacts they send out their invitation: "Come and accept us."

Are you going to forget the obligations of your great gift, and let this genius for turning everything into beauty go to waste, to kill it by letting in a flood of maleficence?

Deformity has already made its bed in your markets; it is fast encroaching upon your heart and your admiration. Suppose you accept it as your permanent guest, suppose you succeed in doing this violence to yourselves, then in a generation or two you will destroy this great gift. What will remain? What will you offer humanity in return for the privilege to exist? However, it is impossible for me to believe that you have the temperament that will enable you to maintain ugliness.

You may say: "We want progress." Well, you made wonderful progress in your past ages; you devised great inventions that were borrowed and copied by other peoples. You did not lie idle, and yet all that progress never encumbered your life with non-essentials.

Why should there forever remain a gulf between progress and perfection? If you can bridge this gulf with the gift of beauty, you will do a great service to humanity. Your mission is proving that a love for the earth, and for the things of the earth, is possible without materialism, a love without greed. . . .

I am old and tired; this is perhaps my last meeting with you. With all my heart I take this occasion to entreat you not to be turned by the call of vulgar strength, of stupendous size, by the spirit of storage, by the multiplication of millions, without meaning and without end.

Cherish the ideal of perfection, and to that, relate all your work and all your movements. Though you love the material things of earth, they will not hurt you and you will bring heaven to earth and soul into things.

TO TEACHERS

I

I have been told that you would like to hear about the educational crusade I have undertaken, but it will be difficult for me to give you a distinct idea of my institution of learning, which has grown gradually during the last twenty-four years. My own mind has grown with it, and my own ideal of education has reached its fullness so slowly and so naturally, that I find it difficult to analyze and place it before you.

The first question you may all ask is: what urged me to take up education. Until I was forty or more, I had spent most of my time in literary pursuits. I had never any desire to participate in practical work because I had a conviction that I did not have the gift. Perhaps you know the truth, or shall I make a confession? When I was thirteen I finished going to school. I do not want to boast about it, I merely give it to you as a historical fact.

So long as I was forced to attend school, I felt an unbearable torture. I often counted the years before I would have my freedom. My elder brothers had finished their academic career and were engaged in life, each in his own way. How I envied them when, after a hurried meal in the morning, I found the inevitable carriage that took us to school, ready at the gate. How I wished that, by some magic spell, I could cross the intervening fifteen or twenty years and suddenly become a grown-up man. I afterwards realized that what then weighed on my mind was the unnatural pressure of a system of education which prevailed everywhere.

Children's minds are sensitive to the influences of the world. Their subconscious minds are active, always imbibing some lesson, and realizing the joy of knowing. This sensitive receptivity helps them, without any strain, to master language, which is the most complex and difficult instrument of expression, full of indefinable ideas and abstract symbols. Through their natural ability to guess they learn the meaning of words which we cannot explain. It may be easy for a child to know what the word "water" means, but how difficult it must be for him to know what idea is associated with the simple word "yesterday." Yet how easily they overcome such innumerable difficulties because of the extraordinary sensitiveness of their subconscious mind. Because of this their introduction to the world of reality is easy and joyful.

In this critical period, the child's life is subjected to the education factory, lifeless, colorless, dissociated from the context of the universe, within bare white walls staring like eyeballs of the dead. We are born with that God-given gift of taking delight in the world, but such delightful activity is fettered and imprisoned, muted by a force called discipline which kills the sensitiveness of the child mind which is always on the alert, restless and eager to receive first-hand knowledge from mother nature. We sit inert, like dead specimens of some museum, while lessons are pelted at us from on high, like hail stones on flowers.

In childhood we learn our lessons with the aid of both body and mind, with all the senses active and eager. When we are sent to school, the doors of natural information are closed to us; our eyes see the letters, our ears hear the abstract lessons, but our mind misses the perpetual stream of ideas from nature, because the teachers, in their wisdom, think these bring distraction, and have no purpose behind them.

When we accept any discipline for ourselves, we try to avoid everything except that which is necessary for our purpose; it is this purposefulness, which belongs to the adult mind, that we force upon school children. We say, "Never keep your mind alert, attend to what is before you, what has been given you." This tortures the child because it contradicts nature's purpose, and nature, the greatest of all teachers, is thwarted at every step by the human teacher who believes in machine-made lessons rather than life lessons, so that the growth of the child's mind is not only injured, but forcibly spoiled.

Children should be surrounded with the things of nature which have their own educational value. Their minds should be allowed to stumble upon and be surprised at everything that happens in today's life; the new tomorrow will stimulate their attention with new facts of life. What happens in a school is that every day, at the same hour, the same book is brought and poured out for him. His attention is never alerted by random surprises from nature.

Our adult mind is always full of things we have to arrange and deal with, and therefore the things that happen around us, such as the coming of morning, leave no mark upon us. We do not allow them to because our minds are already crowded; the stream of lessons perpetually flowing from the heart of nature does not touch us, we merely choose those which are useful, rejecting the rest as undesirable because we want the shortest path to success.

Children have no such distractions. With them every new fact or event comes to a mind that is always open with an abundant hospitality, and through this exuberant, indiscriminate acceptance, they learn innumerable facts within an amazingly short time, compared with our own slowness. These are the most important lessons in life, and what is still more wonderful is that the greater part of them are abstract truths.

The child learns so easily because he has a natural gift, but adults, because they are tyrants, ignore natural gifts and say that children must learn through the same process that they learned by. We insist upon forced mental feeding and our lessons become a form of torture. This is one of man's most cruel and wasteful mistakes.

Because I underwent this process when I was young, and remembered the torture of it, I tried to establish a school where boys might be free in spite of the school. Knowing something of the natural school which Nature supplies to all her creatures, I established my institution in a beautiful spot, far away from town, where the children had the greatest freedom possible, especially in my not forcing upon them lessons for which their mind was unfitted. I do not wish to exaggerate, however, and I must admit that I have not been able to follow my own plan in every way. Forced as we are to live in a society which is itself tyrannical, and which cannot always be gainsaid, I was often obliged to concede to what I did not believe in, but what the others around me insisted on. Yet I always had it in my mind to create an atmosphere; I felt this was more important than classroom teaching.

The atmosphere was there; how could I create it? The birds sang to the awakening light of the morning, the evening came with its own silence, and the stars brought the peace of night.

We had the open beauty of the sky, and the seasons in all their magnificent color. Through this intimacy with nature we took the opportunity of instituting festivals. I wrote songs to celebrate the coming of spring and the rainy season which follows the long months of drought; we had dramatic performances with decorations appropriate to the seasons.

I invited artists from the city to live at the school, and left them free to produce their own work. If the boys and girls felt inclined to watch, I allowed them to do so. The same was true with my own work; I was composing songs and poems, and would often invite the teachers to sing or read with them. This helped to create an atmosphere in which they could imbibe something intangible, but life-giving. . . .

When races come togther, as in the present age, it should not be merely the gathering of a crowd; there must be a bond of relation, or they will collide with each other.

Education must enable every child to understand and fulfill this purpose of the age, not defeat it by acquiring the habit of creating divisions and cherishing national prejudices. There are of course natural differences in human races which should be preserved and respected, and the task of our education should be to realize unity in spite of them, to discover truth through the wilderness of their contradictions.

We have tried to do this in Visva-Bharati. Our endeavor has been to include this ideal of unity in all the activities in our institution, some educational, some that comprise different kinds of artistic expression, some in the shape of service to our neighbors by helping the reconstruction of village life.

The children began to serve our neighbors, to help them in various ways and to be in constant touch with the life around them. They also had the freedom to grow, which is the greatest possible gift to a child. We aimed at another kind of freedom; a sympathy with all humanity, free from all racial and national prejudices.

The minds of children are usually shut inside prison houses, so that they become incapable of understanding people who have different languages and customs. This causes us to grope after each other in darkness, to hurt each other in ignorance, to suffer from the worst form of blindness. Religious missionaries themselves have contributed to this evil; in the name òf brotherhood and in the arrogance of sectarian pride they have created misunderstanding. They make this permanent in their textbooks, and poison the minds of children.

I have tried to save children from the vicious methods which alienate their minds, and from other prejudices which are fostered through histories, geographies and lessons full of national prejudices. In the East there is a great deal of bitterness against other races, and in our own homes we are often brought up with feelings of hatred. I have tried to save the children from such feelings, with the help of friends from the West, who, with their understanding and their human sympathy and love, have done us a great service.

We are building our institution upon the ideal of the spiritual unity of all races. I want to use the help of all other races, and when I was in Europe I appealed to the great scholars of the West, and was fortunate enough to receive their help. They left their own schools to come to our institution, which is poor in material things, and they helped us develop it.

I have in my mind not merely a University, for that is only one aspect of our Visva-Bharati, but the idea of a great meeting place for individuals from all countries where men who believe in spiritual unity can come in touch with their neighbors. There are such idealists, and when I traveled in the West, even in remote places, many persons without any special reputation wanted to join this work.

It will be a great future, when base passions are no longer stimulated within us, when human races come closer to one another, and when through their meeting new truths are revealed.

There will be a sunrise of truth and love through insignificant people who have suffered martyrdom for humanity, like the great personality who had only a handful of disciples from among the fisherfolk and who at the end of his career seemingly presented a picture of failure at a time when Rome was at the zenith of her glory. He was reviled by those in power, ignored by the crowd, and he was crucified; yet through that symbol he lives forever.

There are martyrs of today who are sent to prison and persecuted, who are not men of power, but who belong to a deathless future.

MY SCHOOL

. . . childhood should be given its full measure of life's draught, for which it has an endless thirst. The young mind should be saturated with the idea that it has been born in a human world which is in harmony with the world around it. And this is what our regular type of school ignores with an air of superior wisdom, severe and disdainful. It forcibly snatches away children from a world full of the mystery of God's own handiwork, full of the suggestiveness of personality. It is a mere method of discipline which refuses to take into account the individual. It is a manufactory specially designed for grinding out uniform results. It follows an imaginary straight line of the average in digging its channel of education. But life's line is not the straight line, for it is fond of playing the seesaw with the line of the average, bringing upon its head the rebuke of the school. For according to the school life is perfect when it allows itself to be treated as dead, to be cut into symmetrical conveniences. And this was the cause of my suffering when I was sent to school. For all of a sudden I found my world vanishing from around me, giving place to wooden benches and straight walls staring at me with the blank stare of the blind.

But the legend is that eating of the fruit of knowledge is not consonant with dwelling in paradise. Therefore men's children have to be banished from their paradise into a realm of death, dominated by the decency of a tailoring department. So my mind had to accept the tight-fitting encasement of the school which, being like the shoes of a mandarin woman, pinched and bruised my nature on all sides and at every movement. I was fortunate enough in extricating myself before insensibility set in.

Though I did not have to serve the full penal term which men of my position have to undergo to find their entrance into cultured society, I am glad that I did not altogether escape from its molestation. For it has given me knowledge of the wrong from which the children of men suffer.

The cause of it is this, that man's intention is going against God's intention as to how children should grow into knowledge. How we should conduct our business is our own affair, and therefore in our offices we are free to create in the measure of our special purposes. But such office arrangement does not suit God's creation. And children are God's own creation.

We have come to this world to accept it, not merely to know it. We may become powerful by knowledge, but we attain fullness by sympathy. The highest education is that which does not merely give us information but makes our life in harmony with all existence. But we find that this education of sympathy is not only systematically ignored in schools, but it is severely repressed. From our very childhood habits are formed and knowledge is imparted in such a manner that our life is weaned away from nature and our mind and the world are set in opposition from the beginning of our days. Thus the greatest of educations for which we came prepared is neglected, and we are made to lose our world to find a bagful of information instead. We rob the child of his earth to teach him geography, of language to teach him grammar. His hunger is for the Epic, but he is supplied with chronicles of facts and dates. He was born in the human world, but is banished into the world of living gramophones, to expiate for the original sin of being born in ignorance. Child-nature protests against such calamity with all its power of suffering, subdued at last into silence by punishment.

We all know children are lovers of the dust; their whole body and mind thirst for sunlight and air as flowers do. They are never in a mood to refuse the constant invitations to establish direct communication coming to their senses from the universe.

But unfortunately for children their parents, in the pursuit of their profession, in conformity to their social traditions, live in their own peculiar world of habits. Much of this cannot be helped. For men have to specialize, driven by circumstances and by need of social uniformity.

But our childhood is the period when we have or ought to have more freedom—freedom from the necessity of specialization into the narrow bounds of social and professional conventionalism. . . .

There are men who think that by the simplicity of living introduced in my school I preach the idealization of poverty which prevailed in the medieval age. The full discussion of this subject is outside the scope of my paper, but seen from the point of view of education, should we not admit that poverty is the school in which man had his first lessons and his best training? Even a millionaire's son has to be born helplessly poor and to begin his lesson of life from the beginning. He has to learn to walk like the poorest of children, though he has means to afford to be without the appendage of legs. Poverty brings us into complete touch with life and the world, for living richly is living mostly by proxy, thus living in a lesser world of reality. This may be good for one's pleasure and pride, but not for one's education. Wealth is a golden cage in which the children of the rich are bred into artificial deadening of their powers. Therefore in my school, much to the disgust of the people of expensive habits, I had to provide for this great teacher—this bareness of furniture and materials—not because it is poverty, but because it leads to personal experience of the world. . . .

. . . What tortured me in my school days was the fact that the school had not the completeness of the world. It was a special arrangement for giving lessons. It could only be suitable for grown-up people who were conscious of the special need of such places and therefore ready to accept their teaching at the cost of dissociation from life. But children are in love with life, and it is their first love. All its color and movement attract their eager attention. And are we quite sure of our wisdom in stifling this love? Children are not born ascetics, fit to enter at once into the monastic discipline of acquiring knowledge. At first they must gather knowledge through their love of life, and then they will renounce their lives to gain knowledge, and then again they will come back to their fuller lives with ripened wisdom.

But society has made its own arrangements for manipulating men's minds to fit its special patterns. These arrangements are so closely organized that it is difficult to find gaps through which to bring in nature. There is a serial adjustment of penalties which follows to the end one who ventures to take liberty with some part of the arrangements, even to save his soul. Therefore it is one thing to realize truth and another to bring it into practice where the whole current of the prevailing system goes against you. This is why when I had to face the problem of my own son's education I was at a loss to give it a practical solution. The first thing that I did was to take him away from the town surroundings into a village and allow him the freedom of primeval nature as far as it is available in modern days. He had a river, noted for its danger, where he swam and rowed without check from the anxiety of his elders. He spent his time in the fields and on the trackless sand banks, coming late for his meals without being questioned. He had none of those luxuries that are not only customary but are held as proper for boys of his circumstance. For which privations, I am sure, he was pitied and his parents blamed by the people for whom society has blotted out the whole world. But I was certain that luxuries are burdens to boys. They are the burdens of other people's habits, the burdens of the vicarious pride and pleasure which parents enjoy through their children.

Yet, being an individual of limited resources, I could do very little for my son in the way of educating him according to my plan. But he had freedom of movement, he had very few of the screens of wealth and respectability between himself and the world of nature. Thus he had a better opportunity for a real experience of this universe than I ever had. But one thing exercised my mind more than anything else as the most important.

The object of education is to give man the unity of truth. Formerly, when life was simple, all the different elements of man were in complete harmony. But when there came the separation of the intellect from the spiritual and the physical, the school education put entire emphasis on the intellect and on the physical side of man. We devote our sole attention to giving children information, not knowing that by this emphasis we are accentuating a break between the intellectual, the physical and the spiritual life.

I believe in a spiritual world—not as anything separate from this world—but as its innermost truth. With the breath we draw we must always feel this truth, that we are living in God. Born in this great world, full of the mystery of the infinite, we cannot accept our existence as a momentary outburst of chance drifting on the current of matter toward an eternal nowhere. We cannot look upon our lives as dreams of a dreamer who has no awakening in all time. We have a personality to which matter and force are unmeaning unless related to something infinitely personal, whose nature we have discovered, in some measure, in human love, in the greatness of the good, in the martyrdom of heroic souls, in the ineffable beauty of nature which can never be a mere physical fact nor anything but an expression of personality.

In India we still cherish in our memory the tradition of the forest colonies of great teachers. These places were neither schools nor monasteries, in the modern sense of the word. They consisted of homes where with their families lived men whose object was to see the world in God and to realize their own life in him. Though they lived outside society, yet they were to society what the sun is to the planets, the center from which it received its life and light. And here boys grew up in an intimate vision of eternal life before they were thought fit to enter the state of the householder.

Thus in the ancient India the school was where life itself was. There the students were brought up, not in the academic atmosphere of scholarship and learning, or in the maimed life of monastic seclusion, but in the atmosphere of living aspiration. They took the cattle to pasture, collected firewood, gathered fruit, cultivated kindness to all creatures and grew in their spirit with their own teachers' spiritual growth. This was possible because the primary object of these places was not teaching but giving shelter to those who lived their life in God.

That this traditional relationship of the masters and disciples is not a mere romantic fiction is proved by the relic we still possess of the indigenous system of education which has preserved its independence for centuries to be about to succumb at last to the hand of the foreign bureaucratic control. These *chatus-pathis*, which is the Sanskrit name for the university, have not the savor of the school about them. The students live in their master's home like the children of the house, without having to pay for their board and lodging or tuition. The teacher prosecutes his own study, living a life of simplicity, and helping the students in their lessons as a part of his life and not of his profession.

This ideal of education through sharing a life of high aspiration with one's master took possession of my mind.

All round our ashram is a vast open country, bare up to the line of the horizon except for sparsely growing stunted date palms and

222

prickly shrubs struggling with ant-hills. Below the level of the field there extend numberless mounds and tiny hillocks of red gravel and pebbles of all shapes and colors, intersected by narrow channels of rainwater. Not far away toward the south near the village can be seen through the intervals of a row of palm trees the gleaming surface of steel-blue water, collected in a hollow of the ground. A road used by the village people for their marketing in the town goes meandering through the lonely fields, with its red dust staring in the sun. Travellers coming up this road can see from a distance on the summit of the undulating ground the spire of a temple and the top of a building, indicating the Santiniketan ashram, among its *amalaki* groves and its avenue of stately *sal* trees.

 ART AND
LITERARY CRITICISM

His own paintings and experiments with design made Tagore
confront, in an unexpected manner, the meaning and purpose of art.
The creative impulse, as he had emphasized in his early essays, was rooted
in man's desire to express and enhance the experience of life; man shared
the divinity of the universal Creator by shaping the material world, the
community, and his own personality according to the implicit laws of
being. Art was socially valuable not only because it served the immediate
purpose of bringing the spirit of harmony into individual or group existence, but also because it revealed the richness and relational beauty of
life itself. In his theory of poetics, expressed in a brilliant series of dia-
logues, *Panchabhuter Diary* ("The Diary of Five Elements" written in
Bengali in 1897–1898; translated in the *Visva-Bharati Quarterly* in 1937),
he had already interpreted art both as otherness, or transcendence, and as
an added intimacy with the nature of daily reality. But toward the end of
his life we find him increasingly concerned with art as form, with the
genesis and organization of artistic inspiration in terms of wood, paint,
stone, or musical structure. Seasoned words, metrical innovations, and
conscious artistry gave a new richness and tone to his poems. Art, as he
knew through his own creation of "pure form," that is to say of non-
representational and yet vivid composition in color or line, was for him
man's response to the msytery of design, to the essential form of life. The
old battle of ethics and aesthetics could be transcended, as it were, by
involvement in the completeness of the art experience.

Mainly, he found in art, even more than in creative science, man's
answer to the total reality. An artist responds through reverence, understanding and delight to the invitation of life; no part of his personality is

ignored in a total response. Whether a poet uses modern images, or an ancient myth, or transcripts drawn straight from the city street or a children's toyshop, a crowded market or a lonely terrace with a slanted view of the evening sky or river, he is answering, in Tagore's words, the call of the real. In so doing he has to use his immediate or previous experiences, he is guided by the collective experience of human societies preserved in the form of traditions—and of course, he is inspired by masterpieces of other artists—but his personality as an artist is centrally related to the divine nature of reality. An artist, therefore, is aroused not by knowledge or emotion alone, but by the wholeness of his perception and imagination; the many-sided and contingent factors of experience are unified in the light of a supreme encounter. The spectacle and meaning of life mold the metrical form when an artist surrenders to his revelation and makes it his own.

It will be seen that Tagore's essays draw distinctions between true and meretricious originality, discuss contemporary trends of representational as well as abstract art, and enter into controversies on modernism in poetry. It may be contended that though he himself was a link between many decades of literature, he also favored the literary trends as he knew them in his formative years. But even when he disagreed with modern realism in poetry he sought to understand what he believed was an over-compensation, rather than a fullness of expression, in an era of self-dividedness and doubt. He sought the early Chinese poetry for its subtle clarity and balance, he found amplitude in the simple lyrics of the Elizabethans, and though he had reached a complex brevity in his own highly modernistic painting and had introduced skeletal *vers libre* forms into his impassioned new poetry, he remained true to his main thesis that art is a largely self-unconscious process, the wealth and overflow of an inner radiance.

In old Sanskrit texts Tagore found an affirmation of his theory that art is abundance, that it comes from a surplus of experience. The art instinct cannot be confined to intellectual purpose, social values, or a moral judgment. Man is born with the capacity to transcend himself and his surroundings; in art he reveals this quality of transcendence. For Tagore this was not a matter of ontological thought but of everyday observation. The color that goes into a child's dress, the flowers arranged in a vase, the music in a festival revealed the surplus that reached beyond man's immediate purpose. It is evident that such an interpretation of art does not rule out the spiritual or religious insight, neither does it exclude the validity of scientific exploration; in fact, Tagore's use of the word "real," as applied to art, demands an integral view of man's creative personality.

In this chapter, selections are included from lectures, articles, and letters. "What Is Art?" is from one of the lectures delivered by Tagore during his United States tour of 1916–1917.

"The Religion of an Artist," a lecture which was first published in the Visva-Bharati Quarterly under the title of "The Meaning of Art," and was also issued as the Dacca University Bulletin XII in 1926. The original address was given by Tagore at Curzon Hall, University of Dacca, February 10, 1926. Before it was incorporated in its present form in Contemporary Indian Philosophy (edited by Sarvapalli Radhakrishnan, George Allen & Unwin, Ltd., London, 1936), it was considerably revised by Tagore.

"Modern Poetry" (Adhunik Kavya) was written at the request of the Parichay group of progressive writers of Bengal who asked Tagore to publish his ideas on the "modern versus Victorian" controversy which was current in the thirties. It was first published in the May, 1933, issue of Parichay, and later included in the book, Sahityer Pathe, a collection of literary essays published by Visva-Bharati in 1936. The English translation made by Indira Devi was published in the Spring, 1946 issue of the Visva-Bharati Quarterly.

The short selection on Japanese poetry is an excerpt from On the Way to Japan, a collection of letters written during his world tour of 1916.

What Is Art?

I shall not define art, but question myself about the reason for its existence, and try to find out whether it owes its origin to some social purpose, or to the need of catering to our aesthetic enjoyment, or whether it has come out of some impulse of expression which is the impulse of our being itself.

A fight has been going on for a long time around the saying, "Art for Art's sake," which seems to have fallen into disrepute among a section of Western critics. It is a sign of the recurrence of the ascetic ideal of the puritanic age, when enjoyment as an end in itself was held to be sinful. But all puritanism is a reaction. It does not represent truth in its normal aspect. When enjoyment loses its direct touch with life, growing fastidious and fantastic in its world of elaborate conventions, then comes the call for renunciation which rejects happiness itself as a snare. I am not going into the history of modern art, which I am not at all competent to discuss, yet I can assert, as a general truth, that when a man tries to thwart himself in his desire for delight, converting it merely into his desire to know, or to do good, then the cause must be that his power of feeling delight has lost its natural bloom and healthiness.

The rhetoricians in old India had no hesitation in saying that enjoyment is the soul of literature—the enjoyment which is disinterested. But the word "enjoyment" has to be used with caution. When analyzed, its spectrum shows an endless series of rays of different colors and intensity throughout its different world of stars. The art world contains elements which are distinctly its own and which emit lights that have their special range and property. It is our duty to distinguish and arrive at their origin and growth. . . .

For man, as well as for animals, it is necessary to give expression to feelings of pleasure and displeasure, fear, anger and love. In animals, these emotional expressions have gone little beyond their bounds of usefulness. But in man, though they still have roots in their original purposes, they have spread their branches far and wide in the infinite sky high above their soil. Man has a fund of emotional energy which is not all occupied with his self-preservation. This surplus seeks its outlet in the creation of art, for man's civilization is built upon his surplus. . . .

It has to be conceded that man cannot help revealing his personality also in the world of use. But there self-expression is not his primary object. In everyday life, when we are mostly moved by our habits, we are economical in our expression, for then our soul-consciousness is at its low level—it has just volume enough to glide on in accustomed grooves. But when our heart is fully awakened in love, or in other great emotions, our personality is in its flood-tide. Then it feels the longing to express itself for the very sake of expression. Then comes art, and we forget the claims of necessity, the thrift of usefulness; the spires of our temples try to kiss the stars and the notes of our music to fathom the depth of the ineffable. . . .

Therefore we find all abstract ideas are out of place in true art, where, in order to gain admission, they must come under the disguise of personification. This is the reason why poetry tries to select words that have vital qualities—words that are not for mere information, but have become naturalized in our hearts and have not been worn out of their shapes by too constant use in the market. For instance, the English word "consciousness" has not yet outgrown the cocoon stage of its scholastic inertia, therefore it is seldom used in poetry; whereas its Indian synonym "*chetana*" is a vital word and is of constant poetical use. On the other hand, the English word "feeling" is fluid with life, but its Bengali synonym "*anubhuti*" is refused in poetry, because it merely has meaning and no flavor. And likewise there are some truths coming from science and philosophy which have acquired life's color and taste, and some which have not. . . .

If you ask me to draw some particular tree—and I am no artist—I try to copy every detail, lest I should otherwise lose the peculiarity if not the personality. But when the true artist comes, he overlooks all details and gets into the essential characterization. He looks on that tree as unique, not as the botanist who generalizes and classifies. It is the function of the artist to particularize that one tree. . . .

In India, the greater part of our literature is religious because God with us is not a distant God. He belongs to our homes as well as to our temples. We feel His nearness to us in all the human relationships of love and affection, and in our festivities. He is the chief guest whom we honor. In seasons of flowers and fruits, in the coming of the rain, in the fullness of the autumn, we see the hem of His mantle and hear His footsteps. We worship Him in all the true objects of our worship and love Him wherever our love is true. In the woman who is good we feel Him, in the man who is true we know Him, in our children He is born again and again, the Eternal Child. Therefore religious songs are our love songs, and our domestic occurrences, such as the birth of a son or the coming of the daughter from her husband's house to her parents and her departure again, are woven in our literature as a drama whose counterpart is in the divine. . . .

So we find that our world of expression does not accurately coincide with the world of facts, because personality surpasses facts on every side. It is conscious of its infinity and creates from its abundance, and because, in art, things are challenged from the standpoint of the immortal Person, those things which are important in our customary life of facts become unreal when placed on the pedestal of art. A newspaper account of domestic incident in the life of a commercial magnate may create agitation in society, yet would lose all its significance if placed by the side of great works of art. We can well imagine how it would hide its face in shame, if by some cruel accident it found itself in the neighborhood of Keats's "Ode on a Grecian Urn."

Yet the very same incident, if treated deeply, divested of its conventional superficiality, might have a better claim in art than the negotiation for raising a big loan for China, or the defeat of British diplomacy in Turkey. A mere household event of a husband's jealousy of his wife, as depicted in one of Shakespeare's tragedies, has greater value in the realm of art than the code of caste regulations in Manu's scripture or the law prohibiting inhabitants of one part of the world from receiving human treatment in another. For when facts are looked upon as mere facts, having their chain of consequences in the world of facts, they are rejected by art. . . .

Everywhere in man's world the Supreme Person is suffering from the killing of the human reality by the imposition of the abstract. In our schools the idea of the class hides the reality of the school children; they become students and not individuals. Therefore it does not hurt us to see children's lives crushed in their classes like flowers pressed between book leaves. In government, the bureaucracy deals with generalizations, and not with men. And therefore it costs it nothing to indulge in wholesale cruelties. Once we accept as truth such a scientific maxim as "Survival of the Fittest" it immediately transforms the whole world of human personality into a monotonous desert of abstraction, where things become dreadfully simple because robbed of their mystery of life. . . .

FROM *"The Religion of an Artist"*

II

The renowned Vedic commentator, Sayanacharya, says:

The food offering which is left over after the completion of sacrificial rites is praised because it is symbolical of Brahma, the original source of the universe.

According to this explanation, Brahma is boundless in his super-fluity, which inevitably finds its expression in the eternal world process. Here we have the doctrine of the genesis of creation, and therefore of the origin of art. Of all living creatures in the world, man has his vital and mental energy vastly in excess of his need which urges him to work in various lines of creation for its own sake. Like Brahma himself, he takes joy in productions that are unnecessary to him, and therefore representing his extravagance and not his hand-to-mouth penury. The voice that is just enough can speak and cry to the extent needed for everyday use, but that which is abundant sings, and in it we find our joy. Art reveals man's wealth of life, which seeks its freedom in forms of perfection which are an end in themselves.

All that is inert and inanimate is limited to the bare fact of existence. Life is perpetually creative because it contains in itself that surplus which ever overflows the boundaries of the immediate time and space, restlessly pursuing its adventure of expression in the varied forms of self-realization. Our living body has its vital organs that are important in maintaining its efficiency, but this body is not a mere convenient sac for the purpose of holding stomach, heart, lungs and brains; it is an image—its highest value is in the fact that it communicates its personality. It has color, shape and movement, most of which belong to the superfluous, that are needed only for self-expression and not for self-preservation.

This living atmosphere of superfluity in man is dominated by his imagination, as the earth's atmosphere by the light. It helps us to integrate desultory facts in a vision of harmony and then to translate it into our activities for the very joy of its perfection; it invokes in us the Universal Man who is the seer and the doer of all times and countries. The immediate consciousness of reality in its purest form unobscured by the shadow of self-interest, irrespective of moral or utilitarian recommendation, gives us joy as does the self-revealing personality of our own. What in common language we call beauty, which is in harmony of lines, colors, sounds, or in grouping of words or thoughts, delights us only because we cannot help admitting a truth in it that is ultimate. "Love is enough," the poet has said; it carried its own explanation, the joy of which can only be expressed in a form of art which also has that finality. Love gives evidence to something which is outside us but which intensely exists and thus stimulates the sense of our own existence. It radiantly reveals the

231

reality of its objects, though these may lack qualities that are valuable or brilliant.

The "I am" in me realizes its own extension, its own infinity whenever it truly realizes something else. Unfortunately, owing to our limitations and a thousand and one preoccupations, a great part of our world, though closely surrounding us, is far away from the lamppost of our attention; it is dim, it passes by us, a caravan of shadows, like the landscape seen in the night from the window of an illuminated railway compartment; the passenger knows that the outside world exists, that it is important, but for the time being the railway carriage for him is far more significant. If among the innumerable objects in this world there be a few that come under the full illumination of our soul and thus assume reality for us, they constantly cry to our creative mind for a permanent representation. They belong to the same domain as the desire of ours which represents the longing for the permanence of our own self.

I do not mean to say that things to which we are bound by the tie of self-interest have the inspiration of reality; on the contrary, these are eclipsed by the shadow of our own self. The servant is not more real to us than the beloved. The narrow emphasis of utility diverts our attention from the complete man to the merely useful man. The thick label of market price obliterates the ultimate value of reality.

That fact that we exist has its truth in the fact that everything else does exist, and the "I am" in me crosses its finitude whenever it deeply realizes itself in the "Thou art." This crossing of the limit produces joy, the joy that we have in beauty, in love, in greatness. Self-forgetting, and in a higher degree, self-sacrifice, is our acknowledgment of our experience of the infinite. This is the philosophy which explains our joy in all arts, the arts that in their creation intensify the sense of the unity which is the unity of truth we carry within ourselves. The personality in me is a self-conscious principle of a living unity; it at once comprehends and yet transcends all the details of facts that are individually mine, my knowledge, feeling, wish and will, memory, my hope, my love, my activities, and all my belongings. This personality which has the sense of the One in its nature, realizes it in things, thoughts and facts made into units. The principle of unity which it contains is more or less perfectly satisfied in a beautiful face or a picture, a poem, a song, a character or a harmony of interrelated ideas or facts and then for it these things become intensely real, and therefore joyful. Its standard of reality, the reality that has its perfect revelation in a perfection of harmony, is hurt when there is a consciousness of discord, because discord is against the fundamental unity which is in its center.

All other facts have come to us through the gradual course of our experience, and our knowledge of them is constantly undergoing contradictory changes through the discovery of new data. We can never be sure that we have come to know the final character of anything that there is. But such a knowledge has come to us immediately with a conviction which needs no arguments to support it. It is this, that all my activities have their sources in this personality of mine, which is indefinable and yet about the truth of which I am more certain than anything in this world. Though all the direct evidence that can be weighed and measured supports the fact that only my fingers are producing marks on the paper, yet no sane man ever can doubt that it is not these mechanical movements that are the true origin of my writings but some entity that can never be known, unless known through sympathy. Thus we have come to realize in our own person the two aspects of activities, one of which is the aspect of law represented in the medium, and the other the aspect of will residing in the personality.

Limitation of the unlimited is personality; God is personal where he creates.

He accepts the limits of his own law and the play goes on, which is this world whose reality is in its relation to the person. Things are distinct not in their essence but in their appearance; in other words, in their relation to one to whom they appear. This is art, the truth of which is not in substance or logic, but in expression. Abstract truth may belong to science and metaphysics, but the world of reality belongs to art.

The world as an art is the play of the Supreme Person reveling in image making. Try to find out the ingredients of the image, they elude you, they never reveal to you the eternal secret of appearance. In your effort to capture life as expressed in living tissue, you will find carbon, nitrogen and many other things utterly unlike life but never life itself. The appearance does not offer any commentary of itself through its material. You may call it *maya* and pretend to disbelieve it, but the great artist,*mayavin*, is not hurt. For art is *maya*, it has no other explanation but that it seems to be what it is. It never tries to conceal its evasiveness, it mocks even its own definition and plays the game of hide-and-seek through its constant flight in changes.

And thus life, which is an incessant explosion of freedom, finds its meter in a continual falling back in death. Every day is a death, every moment even. If not, there would be an amorphous desert of deathlessness eternally dumb and still. So life is *maya*, as moralists love to say, it is and is not. All that we find in it is the rhythm through which it shows itself. Are rocks and minerals any better? Has not science shown us one fact, that the ultimate difference between one element and another is only that of rhythm? The fundamental distinction of gold from mercury lies merely in the difference of rhythm in their respective atomic constitutions like the distinction of the king from his subject which is not in their different constituents, but in their different meters of their situations and circumstances. There you find behind the scene the artist, the magician of rhythm, who imparts an appearance of substance to the unsubstantial.

What is rhythm? It is the movement generated and regulated by harmonious restriction. This is the creative force in the hand of the artist. So long as words remain in uncadenced prose form they do not give any lasting feeling of reality. The moment they are taken and put into rhythm they vibrate into a radiance. It is the same with the rose. In the pulp of its petals you may find everything that went to make the rose, but the rose which is *maya*, an image, is lost; its finality which has the touch of the infinite is gone. The rose appears to me to be still, but because of its meter of composition it has a lyric of movement within that stillness, which is the same as the dynamic quality of a picture that has a perfect harmony. It produces a music in our consciousness by giving it a swing of motion synchronous with its own. Had the picture consisted of a disharmonious aggregate of colors and lines, it would be deadly still.

In perfect rhythm, the art form becomes like the stars which in their seeming stillness are never still, like a motionless flame that is nothing but movement. A great picture is always speaking, but news from a newspaper, even of some tragic happening, is still-born. Some news may be a mere commonplace in the obscurity of a journal, but give it a proper rhythm and it will never cease to shine. That is art. It has the magic wand which gives undying reality to all things it touches, and relates them to the personal being in us. We stand before its productions and say: I know you as I know myself, you are real. . . .

This sensitiveness to the touch of things, such abundant delight in the recognition of them, is obstructed when insistent purposes become innumerable and intricate in our society, when problems crowd in our path clamoring for attention, and life's movement is impeded with things and thoughts too difficult for a harmonious assimilation.

This has been growing evident every day in the modern age, which gives more time to the acquisition of life's equipment than to the enjoyment of it. In fact, life itself is made secondary to life's materials, even like a garden buried under the bricks gathered for the garden wall. Somehow the mania for bricks and mortar grows, the kingdom of rubbish dominates, the days of spring are made futile and the flowers never come.

Our modern mind, a hasty tourist in its rush over the miscellaneous, ransacks cheap markets of curios which mostly are delusions. This happens because its natural sensibility for simple aspects of existence is dulled by constant preoccupations that divert it. The literature that it produces seems always to be poking her nose into out-of-the-way places for things and effects that are out of the common. She racks her resources in order to be striking. She elaborates inconstant changes in style, as in modern millinery, and the product suggests more the polish of steel than the bloom of life.

Fashions in literature that rapidly tire of themselves seldom come from the depth. They belong to the frothy rush of the surface, with its boisterous clamor for recognition of the moment. Such literature, by its very strain, exhausts its inner development and quickly passes through outer changes like autumn leaves, produces with the help of paints and patches an up-to-dateness, shaming its own appearance of the immediately preceding date. Its expressions are often grimaces, like the cactus of the desert which lacks modesty in its distortions and peace in its thorns, in whose attitude an aggressive discourtesy bristles up suggesting a forced pride of poverty. We often come across its analogy in some of the modern writings which are difficult to ignore because of their prickly surprises and paradoxical gesticulations.

Wisdom is not rare in these works, but it is a wisdom that has lost confidence in its serene dignity, afraid of being ignored by crowds which are attracted by the extravagant and the unusual. It is sad to see wisdom struggling to be clever, a prophet arrayed in caps and bells before an admiring multitude.

But in all great arts, literary or otherwise, man has expressed his feelings that are usual in a form that is unique and yet not abnormal. When Wordsworth described in his poem a life deserted by love, he invoked for his art the usual pathos expected by all normal minds in connection with such a subject. But the picture in which he incarnated the sentiment was unexpected and yet every sane reader acknowledges it with joy when the image is held before him of

> —a forsaken bird's nest filled with snow
> Mid its own bush of leafless eglantine.[1]

On the other hand, I have read some modern writing in which the coming out of the stars in the evening is described as the sudden eruption of disease in the bloated body of darkness. The writer seems afraid to own the feeling of a cool purity in the star-sprinkled night, which is usual, lest he should be found out as commonplace. From the point of view of realism the image may not be wholly inappropriate and may be considered as outrageously virile in its unshrinking incivility. But this is not art; this is a jerky shriek, something like the convulsive advertisement of the modern market that exploits mob psychology against its inattention. To be tempted to create an illusion of forcefulness through an over-emphasis of abnormality is a sign of anesthesia. It is the waning vigor of imagination which employs desperate dexterity in the present-day art for producing shocks in order to poke out into a glare the sensation of the unaccustomed. When we find that the literature of any period is laborious in the pursuit of a spurious novelty in its manner and matter, we must know that it is the symptom of old age, of anemic sensibility which seeks to stimulate its palsied taste with the pungency of indecency and the tingling touch of intemperance. It has been explained to me that these symptoms mostly are the outcome of a reaction against the last-century literature which developed a mannerism too daintily saccharine, unmanly in the luxury of its toilet and over-delicate in its expressions. It seemed to have reached an extreme limit of refinement which almost codified its conventions, making it easy for the timid talents to reach a comfortable level of literary respectability. This explanation may be true; but unfortunately reactions seldom have the repose of spontaneity, they often represent the obverse of the mintage which they try to repudiate as false. A reaction against a particular mannerism is liable to produce its own mannerism in a militant fashion. Tired of the elaborately planned flower-beds, the gardener proceeds with grim determination to set up everywhere artificial rocks, avoiding the natural inspiration of rhythm in deference to a fashion of tyranny which itself is a tyranny of fashion. The same herd instinct is followed in a cult of rebellion as it was in the cult of conformity and the defiance, which is a mere counteraction of obedience, also shows obedience in a defiant fashion. Fanaticism of virility produces a brawny athleticism meant for a circus and not the natural chivalry which is modest but invincible, claiming its sovereign seat of honor in all arts.

It has often been said by its advocates that this show of the rudely loud and cheaply lurid in art has its justification in the unbiased recognition of facts as such; and according to them realism must not be shunned even if it be ragged and evil-smelling. But when it does not concern science but concerns the arts we must draw a distinction between realism and reality. In its own wide perspective of normal environment, disease is a reality which has to be acknowledged in literature. But disease in a hospital is realism fit for the use of science. It is an abstraction which, if allowed to haunt literature, may assume a startling appearance because of its unreality. Such vagrant specters do not have a proper modulation in a normal surrounding; and they offer false proportions in their features because the proportion of their environment is tampered with. Such a curtailment of the essential is not art, but a trick which exploits mutilation in order to assert a false claim to reality. Unfortunately men are not rare who believe that what forcibly startles them allows them to see more than the facts which are balanced and restrained, which they have to woo and win. Very likely, owing to the lack of leisure, such persons are growing in number, and the dark cellars of sex-psychology and drugstores of moral virulence are burgled to give them the stimulus which they wish to believe to be the stimulus of aesthetic reality.

I know a simple line sung by some primitive folk in our neighborhood which I translate thus: "My heart is like a pebble bed hiding a foolish stream." The psychoanalyst may classify it as an instance of repressed desire and thus at once degrade it to a mere specimen advertising a supposed fact, as it does a piece of coal suspected of having smuggled within its dark the flaming wine of the sun of a forgotten age. But it is literature, and what might have been the original stimulus that star-led this thought into a song, the significant fact about it is that it has taken the shape of an image, a creation of a uniquely personal and yet universal character. The facts of the repression of a desire are numerously common, but this particular expression is singularly uncommon. The listener's mind is touched because it is an individual poem, representing a personal reality belonging to all time and place in the human world.

But this is not all. This poem no doubt owed its form to the touch of the person who produced it, but at the same time with a gesture of utter detachment, it has transcended its material—the emotional mood of the author. It has gained its freedom from any biographical bondage by taking a rhythmic perfection which is precious in its own exclusive merit. There is a poem which confesses by its title its origin in a mood of dejection. Nobody can say that to a lucid mind the feeling of despondency has anything pleasantly memorable. Yet these verses are not allowed to be forgotten, because directly a poem is fashioned, it is eternally freed from its genesis, it minimizes its history and emphasizes its independence. The sorrow which was solely personal in an emperor was liberated as soon as it took the form of verse in stone, it became a triumph of lament, an overflow of delight, hiding the black boulder of its suffering source. The same thing is true of all creation. A dewdrop is a perfect integrity that has no filial memory of its parentage.

When I use the word "creation," I mean that through it some imponderable abstractions have assumed a concrete unity in its relation to us. Its substance can be analyzed, but not this unity which is in its self-introduction. Literature as an art offers us the mystery which is in its unity.

We read the poem:

Never seek to tell thy love
   Love that never told can be;
For the gentle wind does move
   Silently, invisibly.

I told my love, I told my love,
   I told her all my heart,
Trembling, cold, in ghastly fears
   Ah! she did depart.

Soon as she was gone from me,
   A traveller came by,
Silently, invisibly:
   He took her with a sigh.[2]

It has its grammar, its vocabulary. When we divide them part by part and try to torture out a confession from them, the poem which is one departs like the gentle wind, silently, invisibly. No one knows how it exceeds all its parts, transcends all its laws, and communicates with the person. The significance which is in unity is an eternal wonder.

As for the definite meaning of the poem, we may have our doubts. If it were told in ordinary prose, we might feel impatient and be roused to contradict it. We would certainly have asked for an explanation as to who the traveler was and why he took away love without any reasonable provocation. But in this poem we need not ask for an explanation unless we are hopelessly addicted to meaning-collection which is like the collection mania for dead butterflies. The poem as a creation, which is something more than as an idea, inevitably conquers our attention, and any meaning which we feel in its words is like the feeling in a beautiful face of a smile that is inscrutable, elusive and profoundly satisfactory.

The unity as a poem introduces itself in a rhythmic language in a gesture of character. Rhythm is not merely in some measured blending of words, but in a significant adjustment of ideas, in a music of thought produced by a subtle principle of distribution, which is not primarily logical but evidential. The meaning which the word "character" contains is difficult to define. It is comprehended in a special grouping of aspects which gives it an irresistible impetus. The combination it represents may be uncouth in its totality which claims recognition, often against our wishes, for the assent of our reason. An avalanche has a character, which even a heavier pile of snow has not; its character is in its massive movement, its incalculable possibilities.

It is for the artist to remind the world that with the truth of our expression we grow in truth. When the man-made world is less an expression of man's creative soul than a mechanical device for some purpose of power, then it hardens itself, acquiring proficiency at the cost of the subtle suggestiveness of living growth. In his creative activities man makes nature one with his own life and love. But with his utilitarian energies he fights nature, banishes her from his world, deforms and defiles her with the ugliness of his ambitions.

The world of man's own manufacture, with its discordant shrieks and swagger, impresses on him the scheme of a universe which has no touch of the person and therefore no ultimate significance. All the great civilizations that have become extinct must have come to their end through such wrong expression of humanity; through parasitism on a gigantic scale bred by wealth, by man's clinging reliance on material resources; through a scoffing spirit of denial, of negation, robbing us of our means of sustenance in the path of truth.

It is for the artist to proclaim his faith in the everlasting Yes—to say: "I believe that there is an ideal hovering over and permeating the earth, an ideal of that paradise which is not the mere outcome of fancy, but the ultimate reality in which all things dwell and move."

I believe that the vision of paradise is to be seen in the sunlight and the green of the earth, in the beauty of the human face and the wealth of human life, even in objects that are seemingly insignificant and unprepossessing. Everywhere in this earth the spirit of paradise is awake and sending forth its voice. It reaches our inner ear without our knowing it. It tunes our harp of life which sends our aspiration in music beyond the finite, not only in prayers and hopes, but also in temples which are flames of fire in stone, in pictures which are dreams made everlasting, in the dance which is ecstatic meditation in the still center of movement.

◈ Modern Poetry

Writing about modern English poets is by no means an easy task, for who defines the limit of the modern age in terms of the almanac? It is not so much a question of time as of spirit.

After flowing straight for a while, most rivers take a sudden turn. Likewise, literature does not always follow the straight path; when it takes a turn, that turn must be called modern. We call it *adhunik* in Bengali. This modernity depends not upon time but upon temperament.

The poetry to which I was introduced in my boyhood might have been classed as modern in those days. Poetry had taken a new turn, beginning from Robert Burns, and the same movement brought forth many other great poets, such as Wordsworth, Coleridge, Shelley, and Keats.

The manners and customs of a society are shown in social usage. In countries where these social customs suppress all freedom and individual taste, man becomes a puppet, and his conduct conforms meticulously to social etiquette. Society appreciates this traditional and habitual way of life. Sometimes literature remains in this groove for long periods of time, and whosoever wears the sacred marks of perfect literary style is looked upon as a saintly person. During the age of English poetry that followed Burns, the barriers of style were broken down, and temperament made its debut. "The lake adorned with lotus and the lily" becomes a lake seen through the special view of official blinkers fashioned in the classic workshop. When a daring writer removes those blinkers and catch phrases, and looks upon the lake with open eyes, he also opens up a view through which the lake assumes different aspects and various fancies. But classic judgment cries "fie for shame" on him.

When we began to read English poetry, this unconventionally individualistic mood had already been acknowledged in literature, and the clamor raised by the *Edinburgh Review* had died down. Even so, that period of our life was a new era in modernism.

In those days, the sign of modernism in poetry was an individual's measure of delight. Wordsworth expressed in his own style the spirit of delight that he realized in nature. Shelley's was a Platonic contemplation accompanied by a spirit of revolt against every kind of obstacle, political, religious or otherwise. Keats's poetry was wrought out of the meditation and creation of beauty. In that age, the stream of poetry took a turn from outwardness to inwardness.

A poet's deepest feelings strive for immortality by assuming a form in language. Love adorns itself; it seeks to prove inward joy by outward beauty. There was a time when humanity in its moments of leisure sought to beautify that portion of the universe with which it came into contact, and this outer adornment was the expression of its inner love, and with this love, there could be no indifference. In those days, in the exuberance of his sense of beauty man began to decorate the common articles of daily use; his inspiration lent creative power to his fingers. In every land and village, household utensils and the adornment of the home and person bound man, in color and form, to these outward insignia of life. Many ceremonies were evolved for adding zest to social life, many new melodies, arts and crafts in wood and metal, clay and stone, silk, wool and cotton. In those days, the husband called his wife: "beloved disciple in the fine arts." The bank balance did not constitute the principal asset of the married couple in the work of setting up house; the arts were a more necessary item. Flower garlands were woven, the art of dancing was taught, accompanied by lessons in the vina, the flute and singing, and young women knew how to paint the ends of their saris of China silk. Then, there was beauty in human relationships.

The English poets with whom we came into contact in my early youth saw the universe with their own eyes; it had become their personal property. Not only did their own imaginations, opinions and tastes humanize and intellectualize the universe, but they molded it according to their individual desires. The universe of Wordsworth was specially "Wordsworthian," of Shelley, "Shelleyan," of Byron, "Byronic." By creative magic it also became the reader's universe. The joy that we felt in the poet's world was the joy of enjoying the delight of a particular world aroma. The flower sent its invitation to the bee through a distinctive smell and color, and the note of invitation was sweet. The poet's invitation possessed a spontaneous charm. In the days when the chief bond between man and the universe was individuality, the personal touch in the invitation had to be fostered with care, a sort of competition had to be set up in dress and ornament and manners, in order to show oneself off to the best advantage.

Thus, we find that in the beginning of the nineteenth century the tradition which held priority in the English poetry of the previous age had given place to self-expression. This was called modernism.

But now that modernism is dubbed mid-Victorian senility and made to recline on an easy chair in the next room. Now is the day of the modernism of lopped skirts and lopped hair. Powder is applied to the cheeks and rouge to the lips, and it is proclaimed that the days of illusion are over. But there is always illusion at every step of the creation, and it is only the variety of that illusion which plays so many tunes in so many forms. Science has thoroughly examined every pulse beat, and declares that at the root of things there is no illusion; there is carbon and nitrogen, there is physiology and psychology. We old-fashioned poets thought the illusion was the main thing and carbon and physiology the by-products. Therefore, we must confess that we had striven to compete with the Creator in spreading the snare of illusion through rhyme and rhythm, language and style. In our metaphors and nuances there was some hide-and-seek; we were unable to lift aside that veil of modesty which adorns but does not contradict truth. In the colored light that filtered through the haze, the dawns and evenings appeared in a beauty as tender as a new bride. The modern, Duhshashan,[3] engaged in publicly disrobing Draupadi is a sight we are not accustomed to. Is it merely habit that makes us uncomfortable; is there no truth in this sense of shame; does not Beauty become bankrupt when divested of the veil which reveals rather than conceals?

But the modern age is in a hurry, and livelihood is more important. Man races through his work and rushes through his pleasures in a crowd of accelerating machines. The human being who used to create his own intimate world at leisure now delegates his duties to a factory and rigs up some sort of provisional affair to suit his needs according to some official standard. Feasts are out of fashion; only meals remain. There is no desire to consider whether life is in harmony with the intellect, for the mind of man is also engaged in pulling the rope of the huge car of livelihood. Instead of music, we hear hoarse shouts of "Push, boys, push!" He has to spend most of his time with the crowd, not in the company of his friends; his mentality is the mentality of the hustler. In the midst of all this bustle he has no will power to bypass unadorned ugliness.

Which path must poetry now follow, then, and what is her destination? It is not possible these days to follow one's own taste, to select, to arrange. Science does not select, it accepts whatever is; it does not appraise by the standard of personal taste nor embellish with the eagerness of personal involvement. The chief delight of the scientific mind consists in curiosity, not in forming ties of relationship. It does not regard what "I" want as the main consideration, but rather what the thing in itself exactly is, leaving "me" out of the question; and without "me," the preparation of illusion is unneccesary.

Therefore, in the process of economizing that is being carried out in the poetry of this scientific age, it is adornment that has suffered the biggest loss. A fastidious selectivity in the matter of rhyme, rhythm and words has become almost obsolete. The change is not taking place smoothly, but in order to break the spell of the past, it has become the fashion to repudiate it aggressively, like trying to arrange bits of broken glass in an ugly manner, lest the selective faculty should enter the house by jumping over the garden wall. A poet writes, "I am the greatest laugher of all, greater than the sun, than the oak tree, than the frog and Apollo." "Than the frog and Apollo" is where the bits of broken glass come in, out of fear that someone will think that the poet is arranging his words sweetly and prettily. If the word "sea" were used instead of "frog," the modernists might object to it as regular poetizing. That may be so, but mentioning the frog is a more regular poetizing of the opposite kind. That is to say, it is not introduced naturally, but is like intentionally walking on your toes; that would be modern.

But the fact of the matter is, the days are gone for the frog to be admitted into poetry with the same respect as other creatures. In the category of reality, the frog now belongs to a higher class than Apollo. I do not wish to regard the frog with contempt; rather, in an appropriate context, the croaking laugh of the frog might be juxtaposed with the laugh of the poet's beloved, even if she objected. But even according to the most ultra-scientific theory of equality, the laugh of the sun, of the oak tree, of Apollo, is not that of the frog. It has been dragged in by force in order to destroy the illusion.

Today, this veil of illusion must be removed and the thing must be seen exactly as it is. The illusive dye which colored the nineteenth century has now faded, and the mere suggestion of sweetness is not enough to satisfy one's hunger—something tangible is required. When we say that smelling is half the eating, we exaggerate by nearly three quarters. Let me quote a few lines from a poem addressed to a beauty of bygone days.

> You are beautiful and faded
> Like and old opera tune
> Played upon a harpsichord;
> Or like the sun-flooded silks
> Of an eighteenth-century boudoir.
> In your eyes
> Smoulder the fallen roses of outlived minutes,
> And the perfume of your soul
> Is vague and suffusing,
> With the pungence of sealed spice-jars.
> Your half-tones delight me,
> And I grow mad with gazing
> At your blent colors.
>
> My vigor is a new-minted penny,
> Which I cast at your feet.
> Gather it up from the dust,
> That its sparkle may amuse you.[4]

This kind of modern coinage is cheaper but stronger, and very definite; it clearly sounds the modern note. Old-fashioned charm had an intoxicating effect, but this poem has insolence; and there is nothing misty about it.

The subject matter of modern poetry does not seek to attract the mind by its charm. Its strength consists in firm self-reliance, that which is called "character" in English. It calls out: Ho there! behold me, here am I. The same poetess, whose name is Amy Lowell, has written a poem on a shop of red slippers. The theme is that in the evening snowflakes are whirling outside in the wind; inside, behind polished glass widows, rows of red slippers hang like garlands, "like stalactites of blood, flooding the eyes of passers-by with dripping color, jamming their crimson reflections against the windows of cabs and tram-cars, screaming their claret and salmon into the teeth of the sleet, plopping their little round maroon lights upon the tops of umbrellas. The row of white, sparkling shop-fronts is gashed and bleeding, it bleeds red slippers." [5] The whole poem deals with slippers.

This is called impersonal. There is no ground for being particularly attached to these garlands of slippers, either as a buyer or a seller, but one has to stop and look; as soon as the character of the picture as a whole becomes apparent, it no longer remains trifling. Those concerned with meaning will ask, "What does it all mean, sir? Why so much bother about slippers, even if they are red?" To which one replies—"Just look at them yourself." But the questioner asks, "What's the good of looking?" To which there is no reply.

Let us take another example. There is a poem by Ezra Pound called "A Study in Aesthetics," [6] in which a girl walks along the street, and a boy in patched clothes cries out in uncontrollable excitement, "Oh! look, look, how beautiful!" Three years later, the poet meets the boy again during a great haul of sardines. The father and uncles box the fish in order to send them to the market at Breschia. The boy jumps about, handling the fish, and his elders scold him to be quiet. The boy strokes the neatly-arranged fish, and mutters to himself in a tone of satisfaction "How beautiful!" On hearing this the poet says, "I was mildly abashed."

The pretty girl and the sardines elicit the same comment, "How beautiful!" This observation is impersonal, pure and simple; even the slipper-shop is not outside its purview.

In the nineteenth century poetry was subjective in character; in the twentieth it is objective. Hence, emphasis is now laid on the realism of the subject-matter, not on its adornment; for adornment expresses individual taste, whereas the power of reality consists in expressing the subject itself.

Before making its appearance in literature, this modernism exposed itself in painting. By creating disturbances, it sought to contradict the idea that painting was one of the fine arts. The function of art is not to charm but to conquer the mind, it argued; its sign is not beauty but truth. It did not acknowledge the illusion of form but rather the advertisement of the whole. This form has no other introduction to offer; it only wants to proclaim the fact that it is worth observing. This strong case for being observed is not made by appeals of gesture and posture, nor by copying nature, but by its own inherent truth, which is neither religious, moral, nor ideal—it is natural. That is to say, it must be acknowledged simply because it exists, just as we acknowledge the peacock and the vulture, just as we cannot deny the existence of either the pig or the deer.

Some are beautiful, others are ugly; some are useful, others harmful; but there is no possible pretext for discarding any from the sphere of creation. It is the same with literature and art. If any beauty has been created, it needs no apology; but if it possesses no innate strength of being, only sweetness, then it must be rejected.

Hence, present-day literature that has accepted the creed of modernity, scorns to keep caste by carefully adjusting itself to bygone standards of aristocracy: it does not pick and choose. Eliot's poetry is modern in this sense, but not Bridges'. Eliot writes:

> The winter evening settles down
> With smell of steaks in passageways.
> Six o'clock.
> The burnt out ends of smoky days.
> And now a gusty shower wraps
> The grimy scraps
> Of withered leaves about your feet
> And newspapers from vacant lots;
> The showers beat
> On broken blinds and chimney-pots.
> And at the corner of the street
> A lonely cab-horse steams and stamps.
> And then the lighting of the lamps.

Then comes a description of a muddy morning filled with the smell of stale beer. On such a morning, the following words are addressed to a girl:

> You tossed a blanket from the bed,
> You lay upon your back, and waited;
> You dozed, and watched the night revealing

The thousand sordid images
Of which your soul was constituted;

And this is the account given of the man:

His soul stretched tight across the skies
That fade behind a city block,
Or trampled by insistent feet
At four and five and six o'clock;
And short square fingers stuffing pipes,
And evening newspapers, and eyes
Assured of certain certainties,
The conscience of a blackened street
Impatient to assume the world.

In the midst of this smoky, this muddy, this altogether dingy morning and evening, full of many stale odors, and waste papers, the opposite picture is evoked in the poet's mind. He says:

I am moved by fancies that are curled
Around these images, and cling:
The notion of some infinitely gentle
Infinitely suffering thing.

Here the link between Apollo and the frog is broken. Here the croaking of the frog in the well hurts the laughter of Apollo. It is clearly evident that the poet is not absolutely and scientifically impersonal. His loathing for this tawdry world is expressed through the very description he gives of it. Hence the bitter words with which he ends the poem:

Wipe your hand across your mouth, and laugh;
The worlds revolve like ancient women
Gathering fuel in vacant lots.[7]

The poet's distaste for this gathering world is evident. The difference from the past consists in there being no desire to delude oneself with an imaginary world of rosy dreams. The poet makes his poetry trudge through this mire regardless of his laundered clothes; not because he is fond of mud, but because in this muddy world one must look at mud with open eyes, and accept it. If Apollo's laugh reaches one's ears in the mud, well and good; if not, then one need not despise the loud, leaping laughter of the frog. One can look at it for a moment in the context of the universe; there is something to be said for this. The frog will seem out of place in the cultured language of the drawing-room; but then most of the world lies outside the drawing-room. . . .

But if modernism has any philosophy, and if that philosophy is to be called impersonal, then one must admit that this attitude of aggressive disbelief and calumny toward the universe, is also a personal mental aberration owing to the sudden revolution. This also is an illusion, in which there is no serious attempt to accept reality naturally in a calm and dispassionate frame of mind. Many people think that this aggressiveness, this wantonly destructive challenging is what is called modernity.

I myself don't think so. Even though thousands of people are attacked by influenza today, I shall not say that influenza is the natural condition of the body in modern times. The natural bodily state exists behind influenza.

Pure modernism, then, consists in looking upon the universe, not in a personal and self-regarding manner, but in an impersonal and matter-of-fact manner. This point of view is bright and pure, and there is real delight in this unclouded vision. In the same dispassionate way that modern science analyzes reality, modern poetry looks upon the universe as a whole; this is what is eternally modern.

But, actually, it is nonsense to call this modern. The joy of a natural and detached way of looking at things belongs to no particular age; it belongs to everyone whose eyes know how to wander over the naked earth. It is over a thousand years since the Chinese poet Li-Po wrote his verses, but he was a modern; he looked upon the universe with freshly-opened eyes. In a verse of four lines he writes simply:

Why do I live among the green mountains?
I laugh and answer not, my soul is serene;
It dwells in another heaven and earth belonging to no man,
The peach trees are in flower, and the water flows on. . . .[8]

Another picture:

> Blue water . . . a clear moon . . .
> In the moonlight the white herons are flying.
> Listen! Do you hear the girls who gather water-chestnuts?
> They are going home in the night, singing.[9]

Another:

> Naked I lie in the green forest of summer . . .
> Too lazy to wave my white-feathered fan.
> I hang my cap on a crag,
> And bare my head to the wind that comes
> Blowing through the pine trees.[10]

A river merchant's wife writes:

> I would play, plucking flowers by the gate;
> My hair scarcely covered my forehead, then.
> You would come, riding on your bamboo horse,
> And loiter about the bench with green plums for toys.
> So we both dwelt in Chang-kan town,
> We were two children, suspecting nothing.
>
> At fourteen I became your wife,
> And so bashful I could never bare my face,
> But hung my head, and turned to the dark wall;
> You would call me a thousand times,
> But I could not look back even once.
>
> At fifteen I was able to compose my eyebrows,
> And beg you to love me till we were dust and ashes.
>
> I was sixteen when you went on a long journey.
> Traveling beyond the Ken-Tang gorge,
> Where the giant rocks heap up the swift river,
> And the rapids are not passable in May.

Did you hear the monkeys wailing
Up on the skyey height of the crags?

Do you know your footmarks by our gate are old,
And each and every one is filled up with green moss?
The mosses are too deep for me to sweep away;
And already in the autumn wind the leaves are falling.

The yellow butterflies of October
Flutter in pairs over the grass of the west garden
My heart aches at seeing them . . .
I sit sorrowing alone, and alas!
The vermillion of my face is fading.

Some day when you return down the river,
If you will write me a letter beforehand,
I will come to meet you—the way is not long—
I will come as far as the Long Wind Bench instantly.[11]

In this poem the sentiment is neither maudlin nor ridiculous.
The subject is familiar, and there is feeling. If the tone were sarcastic
and there was ridicule, then the poem would be modern, because the
moderns scorn to acknowledge in poetry that which everybody acknowledges naturally. Most probably a modern poet would have
added at the end of this poem that the husband went his way after
wiping his eyes and looking back repeatedly, and the girl at once
set about frying dried prawn fish-balls. For whom? In reply there
are a line-and-a-half of asterisks. The old-fashioned reader would ask,
"What does this mean?" The modern poet would answer "Things
happen like this." The reader would say, "but they also happen otherwise." And the modern would answer, "Yes, they do, but that is too
respectable. Unless it sheds its refinement, it does not become modern. . . ."

Edwin Arlington Robinson has described an aristocrat thus:

Whenever Richard Cory went down town,
We people on the pavement looked at him:

He was a gentleman from sole to crown,
Clean favored, and imperially slim.

And he was always quietly arrayed,
And he was always human when he talked;
But still he fluttered pulses when he said,
"Good morning," and he glittered when he walked.

And he was rich—yes, richer than a king—
And admirably schooled in every grace:
In fine, we thought that he was everything
To make us wish that we were in his place.

So on we worked, and waited for the light,
And went without the meat, and cursed the bread;
And Richard Cory, one calm summer night,
Went home and put a bullet through his head.[13]

There is no modern sarcasm or loud laughter in this poem; on the contrary, there is pathos, which consists in the fact that there may be some fatal disease lurking inside the apparently healthy and beautiful.

He whom we consider rich has a hidden personality. The anchorites spoke in the same way. They remind the living that one day they would go to the burning-ground slung on bamboo-poles. European monks have described how the decomposed body beneath the soil is eaten by worms. In dissertations on morality we have seen attempts to destroy our illusion by reminding us that the body which seems beautiful is a repulsive compound of bones and flesh and blood and fluids. The best way of cultivating detachment is repeatedly to instil into our minds a contempt for the reality which we perceive. But the poet is not a disciple of detachment, he has come to cultivate attachment. Is the modern age so very degenerate that even the poet is infected with the atmosphere of cremation, that he begins to take pleasure in saying that which we consider great is decayed, that which we admire as beautiful is untouchable at the core? . . .

The mid-Victorian age felt a respect for reality and wished to accord it a place of honor; the modern age thinks it part of its program to insult reality and tear aside all the veils of decency.

If you call a reverence for universal things sentimentalism, then you must also call a rebellion against them by the same name. If the mind becomes bitter, for whatever reason, the vision can never be natural. Hence, if the mid-Victorian age is to be ridiculed as being the leader of ultra-respectability, then the Edwardian age must also be ridiculed with the opposite adjectives. The thing is not natural and therefore not perennial. As for science, so for art, the detached mind is the best vehicle. Europe has gained that mind in science, but not in literature.

✺ Japanese Poetry

. . . This continual curtailment of one's self-expression is to be found in their verse also. Often a poem consists of no more than three lines, but these are sufficient both for poets and readers. That is why I have never heard anyone singing in the streets since I have been here. The hearts of these people are not resonant like a waterfall, but silent like a lake. All their poems which I have heard are picture-poems, not song-poems. When the heart aches and burns, then life is spent; the Japanese spend very little in this direction. Their inner self finds complete expression in their sense of beauty, which is independent of self-interest. We do not have to break our hearts over flowers and birds or the moon. Our only connection with them is the enjoyment of beauty; they do not hurt us anywhere, or deprive us of anything; our lives are in no wise maimed by them. That is why three lines are enough.

Two old Japanese poems will serve to illustrate my meaning:

> Ancient pool,
> Frogs leaping,
> Splash of water.

253

Finished! No more is necessary. The mind of the Japanese reader is all eyes. An ancient pool, dark, silent, deserted by man. As soon as a frog leaps into it, sound is heard, showing how silent the pool is. The picture of this old pool must be sketched in the mind; consequently, only that much has been suggested by the poet; anything more would be unnecessary.

Another poem:

> Rotten bough,
> A crow,
> Autumn.

No more! In autumn there are no leaves on the trees, one or two branches are rotting, on one of them sits a crow. In cold countries, autumn is the season of falling leaves, fading flowers, skies leaden-hued with mist; this season brings to mind a sense of death. That a black crow is sitting on a rotten bough is enough to call up before the mind's eye of the reader all the emptiness and desolation of autumn. The poet introduces the subject, then steps aside. The reason why he has to retire so quickly is because the Japanese reader's power of mental vision is great.

Here is another example of a poem, in which it seems to me that India and Japan have met.

> Heaven and earth are flowers,
> The gods and Buddha are flowers,
> The heart of man is the soul of the flower.

Japan looks upon heaven and earth as full-blown flowers; India says these two flowers have blossomed on the same stalk: heaven and earth, gods and Buddha. Had there been no human heart, then this flowering would have been only an external thing, but this beauty lies within the heart of man.

However that may be, there is not only brevity of wording in these poems, there is also brevity of feeling which is not disturbed by the heart's emotion; it may be called the heart's economy. I think there is something deeply symbolical of Japan in this.

PHILOSOPHICAL
MEDITATIONS

Tagore did not claim to have a philosophical system, nor was he a theologian with organized religious beliefs or affiliations. That is why he often chose to describe his intuitional faith as a poet's religion, tracing his poetry and thoughts to encounters with "experiential reality." It is evident that he was a believer in the deepest and even traditional sense, and was a man of prayer, but he used his freedom as an artist in seeking the newness and wonder of creation through every avenue of the mind, the senses, and the processes of his own spiritual growth.

In this section of "Philosophical Meditations," a wide range of his religious, philosophical, and esthetic writings has been included. It will be seen that he did not feel or accept any break between the highest levels of science or of creative art, nor did he think that religion excluded any of the fundamental areas of man's personal and interpersonal experience. He believed in what he called "the processes of self-creation." To the extent that we are using our resources, which he would call "divine" in the sense that all our powers and potentialities are not demonstrable, and that they are "given" to us by an authority greater than ourselves, we are able to grow into an awareness of and establish a conscious relationship with God's purpose in creation.

Increasingly, in his later years, particularly in the Hibbert Lectures at Oxford, 1930, and in his addresses on "Man" at the Andhra University in 1933, he stressed man's need to know the ground of diverse, authentic religious experiences which have come to human society through the great traditions of religion. He did not believe in a merger of religions as such, or in any syncretistic attempt to evolve one religion out of many, but he did urge his fellow beings to discover and connect the basic and continuous history of man's underlying divinity (or divine humanity), which holds together the entire fabric of civilization.

The Religion of Man (Allen & Unwin, London, 1931) comprises the Hibbert Lectures delivered in Oxford at Manchester College during May, 1930, and includes gleanings from Tagore's thoughts on religion which were harvested from earlier lectures, addresses, and conversations. The chapter reproduced here, "The Artist," was one of the Hibbert Lectures.

Personality (Macmillan & Co., Ltd., 1917) is one of the collections of lectures delivered during Tagore's 1916–1917 lecture tour of the United States.

"Mahatma Gandhi" is a speech given by Tagore on October 2, 1937. Gandhi and Tagore, whom C. F. Andrews brought together, remained lifelong friends in spite of their differences of opinion on certain major issues. Their relationship began in 1915 when Gandhi and his Phoenix party of followers from Durban, South Africa, found shelter for a short time in Tagore's Santiniketan, before Gandhi established his own ashram at Sabarmati. Santiniketan kept Gandhi's birthday (October 2) as a red-letter day in its calendar, and whenever Tagore was present he would preside over the celebration. The speech printed here was translated into English by Surendranath Tagore, and published in the Winter, 1937, issue of the *Visva-Bharati Quarterly*.

Creative Unity (Macmillan & Co., Ltd., 1922) is a book of essays and lectures delivered during Tagore's 1920–1921 tour of Europe and the United States.

Our Universe is the English title of *Visvaparichaya*, a treatise on astronomy that Tagore wrote in 1937 when he was seventy-six. It was translated into English by Indu Dutt for Meridian Books (London, 1958). The excerpt printed here is from the chapter called "The World of Stars."

"Thoughts from Tagore" are excerpts taken from Tagore's English works, published and unpublished, compiled and edited by C. F. Andrews.

"Thought Relics" are Tagore's own translations of passages from his weekly discourses entitled *Santiniketan* delivered during 1906–1909 at the prayer hall at Santiniketan. Tagore started translating them for use in his Sādhanā lectures in the United States, published in *Sādhanā* (The Macmillan Company, New York, 1913), and he added fresh translations while on his way to the West in 1920.

CHAPTER IX: THE ARTIST

The fundamental desire of life is the desire to exist. It claims from us a vast amount of training and experience about the necessaries of livelihood. Yet it does not cost me much to confess that the food that I have taken, the dress that I wear, the house where I have my lodging, represent a stupendous knowledge, practice and organization which I helplessly lack; for I find that I am not altogether despised for such ignorance and inefficiency. Those who read me seem fairly satisfied that I am nothing better than a poet or perhaps a philosopher —which latter reputation I do not claim and dare not hold through the precarious help of misinformation.

It is quite evident in spite of my deficiency that in human society I represent a vocation, which though superfluous has yet been held worthy of commendation. In fact, I am encouraged in my rhythmic futility by being offered moral and material incentives for its cultivation. If a foolish blackbird did not know how to seek its food, to build its nest, or to avoid its enemies, but specialized in singing, its fellow creatures, urged by their own science of genetics, would dutifully allow it to starve and perish. That I am not treated in a similar fashion is the evidence of an immense difference between the animal existence and the civilization of man. His great distinction dwells in the indefinite margin of life in him which affords a boundless background for his dreams and creations. And it is in this realm of freedom that he realizes his divine dignity, his great human truth, and is pleased when I as a poet sing victory to him, to man the self-revealer, who goes on exploring ages of creation to find himself in perfection.

Reality, in all its manifestations, reveals itself in the emotional and imaginative background of our mind. We know it, not because we can think of it, but because we directly feel it. And therefore, even if rejected by the logical mind, it is not banished from our consciousness. As an incident it may be beneficial or injurious, but as a revelation its value lies in the fact that it offers us an experience through emotion or imagination; we feel ourselves in a special field of realization. This feeling itself is delightful when it is not accompanied by any great physical or moral risk; we love to feel even fear or sorrow if it is detached from all practical consequences. This is the reason of our enjoyment of tragic dramas, in which the feeling of pain rouses our consciousness to a white heat of intensity.

The reality of my own self is immediate and indubitable to me. Whatever else affects me in a like manner is real for myself, and it inevitably attracts and occupies my attention for its own sake, blends itself with my personality, making it richer and larger and causing it delight. My friend may not be beautiful, useful, rich or great, but he is real to me; in him I feel my own extension and my joy.

The consciousness of the real within me seeks for its own corroboration the touch of the real outside me. When it fails, the self in me is depressed. When our surroundings are monotonous and insignificant, having no emotional reaction upon our mind, we become vague to ourselves. For we are like pictures, whose reality is helped by the background if it is sympathetic. The punishment we suffer in solitary confinement consists in the obstruction to the relationship between the world of reality and the real in ourselves, causing the latter to become indistinct in a haze of inactive imagination: our personality is blurred, we miss the companionship of our own being through the diminution of our self. The world of our knowledge is enlarged for us through the extension of our information; the world of our personality grows in its area with a large and deeper experience of our personal self in our own universe through sympathy and imagination.

As this world, that can be known through knowledge, is limited to us owing to our ignorance, so the world of personality, that can be realized by our own personal self, is also restricted by the limit of our sympathy and imagination. In the dim twilight of insensitiveness a large part of our world remains to us like a procession of nomadic shadows. According to the stages of our consciousness we have more or less been able to identify ourselves with this world, if not as a whole, at least in fragments; and our enjoyment dwells in that wherein we feel ourselves thus united. In art we express the delight of this unity by which this world is realized as humanly significant to us. I have my physical, chemical and biological self; my knowledge of it extends through the extension of my knowledge of the physical, chemical and biological world. I have my personal self, which has its communication with our feelings, sentiments and imaginations, which lends itself to be colored by our desires and shaped by our imageries.

Science urges us to occupy by our mind the immensity of the knowable world; our spiritual teacher enjoins us to comprehend by our soul the infinite spirit which is in the depth of the moving and changing facts of the world; the urging of our artistic nature is to realize the manifestation of personality in the world of appearance, the reality of existence which is in harmony with the real within us. Where this harmony is not deeply felt, there we are aliens and perpetually homesick. For man by nature is an artist; he never receives passively and accurately in his mind a physical representation of things around him. There goes on a continual adaptation, a transformation of facts into human imagery, through constant touches of his sentiments and imagination. The animal has the geography of its birthplace; man has his country, the geography of his personal self. The vision of it is not merely physical; it has its artistic unity, it is a perpetual creation. In his country, his consciousness being unobstructed, man extends his relationship, which is of his own creative personality. In order to live efficiently man must know facts and their laws. In order to be happy he must establish harmonious relationship with all things with which he has dealings. Our creation is the modification of relationship.

The great men who appear in our history remain in our mind not as a static fact but as a living historical image. The sublime suggestions of their lives become blended into a noble consistency in legends made living in the life of ages. Those men with whom we live we constantly modify in our minds, making them more real to us than they would be in a bare presentation. Men's ideal of womanhood and women's ideal of manliness are created by the imagination through a mental grouping of qualities and conducts according to our hopes and desires, and men and women consciously and unconsciously strive toward its attainment. In fact, they reach a degree of reality for each other according to their success in adapting these respective ideals to their own nature. To say that these ideals are imaginary and therefore not true is wrong in man's case. His true life is in his own creation, which represents the infinity of man. He is naturally indifferent to things that merely exist; they must have some ideal value for him, and then only his consciousness fully recognizes them as real. Men are never true in their isolated self, and their imagination is the faculty that brings before their mind the vision of their own greater being.

We can make truth ours by actively modulating its inter-relations. This is the work of art; for reality is not based in the substance of things but in the principle of relationship. Truth is the infinite pursued by metaphysics; fact is the infinite pursued by science, while reality is the definition of the infinite which relates truth to the person. Reality is human; it is what we are conscious of, by which we are affected, that which we express. When we are intensely aware of it, we are aware of ourselves and it gives us delight. We live in it, we always widen its limits. Our arts and literature represent this creative activity which is fundamental in man.

But the mysterious fact about it is that though the individuals are separately seeking their expression, their success is never individualistic in character. Men must find and feel and represent in all their creative works man the eternal, the creator. Their civilization is a continual discovery of the transcendental humanity. In whatever it fails it shows the failure of the artist, which is the failure in expression; and that civilization perishes in which the individual thwarts the revelation of the universal. For reality is the truth of man, who belongs to all times, and any individualistic madness of men against man cannot thrive for long.

Man is eager that his feeling for what is real to him must never die; it must find an imperishable form. The consciousness of this self of mine is so intensely evident to me that it assumes the character of immortality. I cannot imagine that it ever has been or can be non-existent. In a similar manner all things that are real to me are for myself eternal, and therefore worthy of a language that has a permanent meaning. We know individuals who have the habit of inscribing their names on the walls of some majestic monument of architecture. It is a pathetic way of associating their own names with some works of art which belong to all times and to all men. Our hunger for reputation comes from our desire to make objectively real that which is inwardly real to us. He who is inarticulate is insignificant, like a dark star that cannot prove itself. He ever waits for the artist to give him his fullest worth, not for anything specially excellent in him but for the wonderful fact that he is what he certainly is, that he carries in him the eternal mystery of being.

A Chinese friend of mine while traveling with me in the streets of Peking suddenly exclaimed with a vehement enthusiasm: "Look, here is a donkey!" Surely it was an utterly ordinary donkey, like an indisputable truism, needing no special introduction from him. I was amused; but it made me think. This animal is generally classified as having certain qualities that are not recommendable and then hurriedly dismissed. It was obscured to me by an envelopment of commonplace associations; I was lazily certain that I knew it and therefore I hardly saw it. But my friend, who possessed the artist mind of China, did not treat it with a cheap knowledge but could see it afresh and recognize it as real. When I say real, I mean that it did not remain at the outskirts of his consciousness tied to a narrow definition, but it easily blended in his imagination, produced a vision, a special harmony of lines, colors and life and movement, and became intimately his own. The admission of a donkey into a drawing-room is violently opposed; yet there is no prohibition against its finding a place in a picture which may be admiringly displayed on the drawing-room wall.

The only evidence of truth in art exists when it compels us to say, "I see." A donkey we may pass by in nature, but a donkey in art we must acknowledge even if it be a creature that disreputably ignores all its natural history responsibility, even if it resembles a mushroom in its head and a palm-leaf in its tail.

In the Upanishad it is said in a parable that there are two birds sitting on the same bough, one of which feeds and the other looks on. This is an image of the mutual relationship of the infinite being and the finite self. The delight of the bird which looks on is great, for it is a pure and free delight. There are both of these birds in man himself, the objective one with its business of life, the subjective one with its disinterested joy of vision.

A child comes to me and commands me to tell her a story. I tell her of a tiger which is disgusted with the black stripes on its body and comes to my frightened servant demanding a piece of soap. The story gives my little audience immense pleasure, the pleasure of a vision, and her mind cries out, "It is here, for I see!" She knows a tiger in the book of natural history, but she can see the tiger in the story of mine.

I am sure that even this child of five knows that it is an impossible

tiger that is out on its untigerly quest of an absurd soap. The delight-
fulness of the tiger for her is not in its beauty, its usefulness, or its
probability; but in the undoubted fact that she can see it in her mind
with a greater clearness of vision than she can the walls around her—
the walls that brutally shout their evidence of certainty which is
merely circumstantial. The tiger in the story is inevitable, it has the
character of a complete image, which offers its testimonial of truth
in itself. The listener's own mind is the eyewitness whose direct experience could not be contradicted. A tiger must be like every other
tiger in order that it may have its place in a book of science; there
it must be a commonplace tiger to be at all tolerated. But in the
story it is uncommon, it can never be reduplicated. We *know* a thing
because it belongs to a class; we *see* a thing because it belongs to itself.
The tiger of the story completely detached itself from all others of its
kind and easily assumed a distinct individuality in the heart of the
listener. The child could vividly see it, because by the help of her
imagination it became her own tiger, one with herself, and this union
of the subject and object gives us joy. Is it because there is no separation between them in truth, the separation being the *maya*, which is
creation?

There come in our history occasions when the consciousness of a
large multitude becomes suddenly illumined with the recognition of
a reality which rises far above the dull obviousness of daily happen-
ings. The world becomes vivid; we see, we feel it with all our soul.
Such an occasion there was when the voice of Buddha reached distant shores across physical and moral impediments. Then our life and
our world found their profound meaning of reality in their relation to
the central person who offered us emancipation of love. Men, in
order to make this great human experience ever memorable, determined to do the impossible; they made rocks to speak, stones to sing,
caves to remember; their cry of joy and hope took immortal forms
along the hills and deserts, across barren solitudes and populous
cities. A gigantic creative endeavor built up its triumph in stupendous carvings, defying obstacles that were overwhelming. Such heroic
activity over the greater part of the Eastern continents clearly answers
the question: "What is Art?" It is the response of man's creative soul
to the call of the real.

Once there came a time, centuries ago in Bengal, when the divine love drama that has made its eternal playground in human souls was vividly revealed by a personality radiating its intimate realization of God. The mind of a whole people was stirred by a vision of the world as an instrument, through which sounded an invitation to the meeting of bliss. The ineffable mystery of God's love-call, taking shape in an endless panorama of colors and forms, inspired activity in music that overflowed the restrictions of classical conventionalism. Our *kirtan* music of Bengal came to its being like a star flung up by a burning whirlpool of emotion in the heart of a whole people, and their consciousness was aflame with a sense of reality that must be adequately acknowledged.

The question may be asked as to what place music occupies in my theory that art is for evoking in our mind the deep sense of reality in its richest aspect. Music is the most abstract of all the arts, as mathematics is in the region of science. In fact these two have a deep relationship with each other. Mathematics is the logic of numbers and dimensions. It is therefore employed as the basis of our scientific knowledge. When taken out of its concrete associations and reduced to symbols, it reveals its grand structural majesty, the inevitableness of its own perfect concord. Yet there is not merely a logic but also a magic of mathematics which works at the world of appearance, producing harmony—the cadence of inter-relationship. This rhythm of harmony has been extracted from its usual concrete context, and exhibited through the medium of sound. And thus the pure essence of expressiveness in existence is offered in music. Expressiveness finds the least resistance in sound, having freedom unencumbered by the burden of facts and thoughts. This gives it a power to arouse in us an intimate feeling of reality. In the pictorial, plastic and literary arts, the object and our feelings with regard to it are closely associated, like the rose and its perfumes. In music, the feeling distilled in sound becomes itself an independent object. It assumes a tune-form which is definite, but a meaning which is undefinable, and yet which grips our mind with a sense of absolute truth.

It is the magic of mathematics, the rhythm which is in the heart of all creation, which moves in the atom and, in its different measures, fashions gold and lead, the rose and the thorn, the sun and the planets. These are the dance steps of numbers in the arena of time and space, which weave the *maya*, the patterns of appearance, the incessant flow of change, that ever is and is not. It is the rhythm that churns up images from the vague and makes tangible what is elusive. This is *maya*, this is the art in creation, and art in literature, which is the magic of rhythm.

And must we stop here? What we know as intellectual truth, is that also not a rhythm of the relationship of facts, that weaves the pattern of theory, and produces a sense of convincingness to a person who somehow feels sure that he knows the truth? We believe any fact to be true because of a harmony, a rhythm in reason, the process of which is analyzable by the logic of mathematics, but not its result in me, just as we can count the notes but cannot account for the music. The mystery is that I am convinced, and this also belongs to the *maya* of creation, whose one important, indispensable factor is this self-conscious personality that I represent.

And the Other? I believe it is also a self-conscious personality, which has its eternal harmony with mine.

FROM *Personality*

THE WORLD OF PERSONALITY

. . . There is a point where in the mystery of existence contradictions meet; where movement is not all movement and stillness is not all stillness; where the idea and the form, the within and the without, are united; where infinite becomes finite, yet not losing its infinity. If this meeting is dissolved, then things become unreal.

When I see a rose leaf through a microscope, I see it in a more extended space than it usually occupies for me. The more I extend the space the more it becomes vague. So that in the pure infinite it is neither rose-leaf nor anything at all. It only becomes a rose-leaf where the infinite reaches finitude at a particular point. When we disturb that point toward the small or the great, the rose-leaf begins to assume unreality.

It is the same with regard to time. If by some magic I could remain in my normal plane of time while enhancing its quickness with regard to the rose leaf, condensing, let us say, a month into a minute, then it would rush through its point of first appearance to that of its final disappearance with such a speed that I would hardly be able to see it. One can be sure that there are things in this world which are known by other creatures, but which, since their time is not synchronous with ours, are nothing to us. The phenomenon which a dog perceives as a smell does not keep its time with that of our nerves, therefore it falls outside our world.

Let me give an instance. We have heard of prodigies in mathematics who can do difficult sums in an incredibly short time. With regard to mathematical calculations their minds are acting in a different plane of time, not only from ours, but also from their own in other spheres of life. As if the mathematical part of their minds is living in a comet, while the other parts are the inhabitants of this earth. Therefore the process through which their minds rush into their results is not only invisible to us, it is not even seen by themselves.

It is a well-known fact that often our dreams flow in a measure of time different from that of our waking consciousness. The fifty minutes of our sundial of dreamland may be represented by five minutes of our clock. If from the vantage of our wakeful time we could watch these dreams, they would rush past us like an express train. Or if from the window of our swift-flying dreams we could watch the slower world of our waking consciousness, it would seem receding away from us at a great speed. In fact if the thoughts that move in other minds than our own were open to us, our perception of them would be different from theirs, owing to our difference of mental time. If we could adjust our focus of time according to our whims, we would see the waterfall standing still and the pine forest running fast like the waterfall of a green Niagara.

So that it is almost a truism to say that the world is what we perceive it to be. We imagine that our mind is a mirror, that it is more or less accurately reflecting what is happening outside us. On the contrary our mind itself is the principal element of creation. The world, while I am perceiving it, is being incessantly created for myself in time and space.

The variety of creation is owing to the mind seeing different phenomena in different foci of time and space. When it sees stars in a space which may be metaphorically termed as dense, then they are close to each other and motionless. When it sees planets, it sees them in much less density of sky and then they appear far apart and moving. If we could have the sight to see the molecules of a piece of iron in a greatly different space, they could be seen in movement. But because we see things in various adjustments of time and space therefore iron is iron, water is water, and clouds are clouds for us. . . .

Walt Whitman shows in his poems a great dexterity in changing his position of mind and thus changing his world with him from that of other people, rearranging the meaning of things in different proportions and forms. Such mobility of mind plays havoc with things whose foundations lie fixed in convention. Therefore he says in one of his poems:

> I hear it was charged against me that I sought
> to destroy institutions,
> But really I am neither for nor against institutions,
> (What indeed have I in common with them? or what
> with the destruction of them?)
> Only I will establish in the Mannahatta and in every
> city of these States inland and seaboard,
> And in the fields and woods, and above every keel little
> or large that dents the water,
> Without edifices or rules or trustees or any argument,
> The institution of the dear love of comrades.

Institutions which are so squarely built, so solid and thick, become like vapor in this poet's world. It is like a world of Röntgen rays, for which some of the solid things of the world have no existence whatever. On the other hand, love of comrades, which is a fluid thing in the ordinary world, which seems like clouds that pass and repass the sky without leaving a trace of a track, is to the poet's world more stable than all institutions. Here he sees things in a time in which the mountains pass away like shadows, but the rain clouds with their seeming transitoriness are eternal. He perceives in his world that this love of comrades, like clouds that require no solid foundation, is stable and true, is established without edifices, rules, trustees or arguments.

When the mind of a person like Walt Whitman moves in a time different from that of others, his world does not necessarily come to ruin through dislocation, because there in the center of his world dwells his own personality. All the facts and shapes of this world are related to this central creative power; therefore, they become interrelated spontaneously. His world may be like a comet among stars, different in its movements from others, but it has its own consistency because of the central personal force. It may be a bold world or even a mad world, with an immense orbit swept by its eccentric tail, yet it is a world.

But with science it is different. For she tries to do away altogether with that central personality, in relation to which the world is a world. Science sets up an impersonal and unalterable standard of space and time which is not the standard of creation. Therefore at its fatal touch the reality of the world is so hopelessly disturbed that it vanishes in an abstraction where things become nothing at all. For the world is not atoms and molecules or radio-activity or other forces, the diamond is not carbon, and light is not vibrations of ether. You can never come to the reality of creation by contemplating it from the point of view of destruction. Not only the world but God himself is divested of reality by science, which subjects him to analysis in the laboratory of reason outside our personal relationship and then describes the result as unknown and unknowable. It is a mere tautology to say that God is unknowable, when we leave altogether out of account the person who can and who does know him. It is the same thing as saying that food is uneatable when the eater is absent. Our dry moralists also play the same tricks with us in order to wean away our hearts from their desired objects. Instead of creating for us a world in which moral ideals find their natural places in beauty they begin to wreck the world that we have built ourselves, however imperfectly. They put moral maxims in the place of human personality and give us the view of things in their dissolution to prove that behind their appearances they are hideous deceptions. But when you deprive truth of its appearance, it loses the best part of its reality. For appearance is a personal relationship; it is for me. Of this appearance, which seems to be of the surface, but which carries the message of the inner spirit, Whitman has said:

Beginning my studies the first step pleas'd me so much,
The mere fact consciousness, these forms, the power
   of motion,
The least insect or animal, the senses, eye-sight,
   love,
The first step I say awed me and pleas'd me so much,
I have hardly gone and hardly wish'd to go any farther,
But stop and loiter all the time to sing it in ecstatic
   songs.

Our scientific world is our world of reasoning. It has its greatness and uses and attractions. We are ready to pay the homage due to it. But when it claims to have discovered the real world for us and laughs at the worlds of all simple-minded men, then we must say it is like a general grown intoxicated with his power, usurping the throne of his king. For the reality of the world belongs to the personality of man and not to reasoning, which is useful and great but which is not the man himself.

If we could fully know what a piece of music was in Beethoven's mind, we could ourselves become so many Beethovens. But because we cannot grasp its mystery, we may altogether distrust the element of Beethoven's personality in his sonata—though we are fully aware that its true value lies in its power of touching the depth of our own personality. But it is simpler to observe the facts when that sonata is played upon the piano. We can count the black and white keys of the keyboard, measure the relative lengths of the strings, the strength, velocity and order of sequence in the movements of fingers and triumphantly assert that this is Beethoven's sonata. Not only that, we can predict the accurate production of the same sonata wherever and whenever our experiment is repeated according to those observations. By constantly dealing with the sonata from this point of view we may forget that both in its origin and object dwell the personality of man, and however accurate and orderly may be the facts of the interactions of the fingers and strings they do not comprehend the ultimate reality of the music.

A game is a game where there is a player to play it. Of course, there is a law of the game which it is of use to us to analyze and to master. But if it be asserted that in this law is its reality, then we cannot accept it. For the game is what it is to the players. The game changes its aspects according to the personality of its players: for some its end is the lust of gain, in others that of applause; some find in it the means for satisfying their social instinct, and there are others who approach it in the spirit of disinterested curiosity for studying its secrets. Yet all through its manifold aspects its law remains the same. For the nature of reality is the variedness of its unity. And the world is like this game to us—it is the same and yet it is not the same to us all.

Science deals with this element of sameness, the law of perspective and color combination, and not with the pictures—the pictures which are the creations of a personality and which appeal to the personality of those who see them. Science does it by eliminating from its field of research the personality of creation and fixing its attention only upon the medium of creation.

What is this medium? It is the medium of finitude which the Infinite Being sets before him for the purpose of his self-expression. It is the medium which represents his self-imposed limitations—the law of space and time, of form and movement. This law is reason, which is universal—reason which guides the endless rhythm of the creative idea, perpetually manifesting itself in its ever changing forms.

Our individual minds are the strings which catch the rhythmic vibrations of this universal mind and respond in music of space and time. The quality and number and pitch of our mind strings differ and their tuning has not yet come to its perfection, but their law is the law of the universal mind which is the instrument of finitude upon which the Eternal Player plays his dance music of creation.

Because of the mind instruments which we possess we also have found our place as creators. We create not only art and social organizations, but our inner nature and outer surroundings, the truth of which depends upon their harmony with the law of the universal mind. Of course, our creations are mere variations upon God's great theme of the universe. When we produce discords, they either have to end in a harmony or in silence. Our freedom as a creator finds its highest joy in contributing its own voice in the concert of the world-music.

ON *Mahatma Gandhi*

. . . While India lay . . . cramped and divided, betrayed by its own idealism, it was called upon to meet the greatest trial in her history, the challenge of Western imperialism. For the Aryans and the Muslims may have deprived a few Dravidian and Hindu dynasties of their rule in India, but they settled down among the people and their achievements became India's heritage. But here was a new impersonal empire, where the rulers were over us but not among us, who owned our land but could never belong to it. So disintegrated and demoralized were our people that many wondered if India could ever rise again by the genius of her own people, until there came on the scene a truly great soul, a great leader of men, in line with the tradition of the greatest sages of old, whom we are today assembled to honor—Mahatma Gandhi.[1] Today no one need despair of the future of the country, for the unconquerable spirit that creates has already been released. Mahatma Gandhi has shown us a way which, if we follow, shall not only save ourselves but may also help other peoples to save themselves.

He who has come to us today is above all distinguished by his freedom from any bias of personal or national selfishness. For the selfishness of the Nation can be a grandly magnified form of that same vice; the viciousness is there all the same. The standard of conduct followed by the class called politicians is not one of high ideals. They think nothing of uttering falsehoods, they have no compunction in vitally hurting others for their own aggrandizement. . . . Such people plume themselves on being practical and do not hesitate to ally themselves with the forces of evil if they think that evil will accomplish their end. But tactics of this kind will not pass the audit of the Dispenser of our fortunes; so while we may admire their cleverness, we cannot revere them. Our reverence goes out to the Mahatma whose striving has ever been for truth; who, to the great good fortune of our country at this time of its entry into the new age, has never, for the sake of immediate results, advised or condoned any departure from the standard of universal morality.

He has shown the way how, without wholesale massacre, freedom may be won. There are doubtless but few amongst us who can rid our minds of a reliance on violence, who can really believe that victory may be ours without recourse to it. For even in the Mahabharata, not to speak of the "civilized" warfare of the modern age, we find *Dharma-yuddha* to be full of violence and cruelty. Now it has been declared that it is for us to yield up life, not to kill, and yet we shall win! A glorious message, indeed, not a counsel of strategy, not a means to a merely political end. In the course of unrighteous battle death means extinction; in the non-violent battle of righteousness something remains; after defeat victory, after death immortality. The Mahatma has realized this in his own life, and compels our belief in this truth.

As before, the genius of India has taken from her aggressors the most spiritually significant principle of their culture and fashioned of it a new message of hope for mankind. There is in Christianity the great doctrine that God became man in order to save humanity by taking the burden of its sin and suffering on Himself, here in this very world, not waiting for the next. That the starving must be fed, the ragged clad, has been emphasized by Christianity as no other religion has done. Charity, benevolence, and the like, no doubt have an important place in the religions of our country as well, but there they are in practice circumscribed within much narrower limits, and are only partially inspired by love of man. And to our great good fortune, Gandhiji was able to receive this teaching of Christ in a living way. It was fortunate that he had not to learn of Christianity through professional experts, but should have found in Tolstoi a teacher who realized the value of non-violence through the multifarious experience of his own life struggles. For it was this great gift from Europe that our country had all along been awaiting.

In the Middle Ages we also had received gifts from Muslim sources. Dadu, Kabir and other saints had proclaimed that purity and liberation are not for being hoarded up in any temple, but are wealth to which all humanity is entitled. We should have no hesitation in admitting freely that this message was inspired by contact with Islam. The best of men always accept the best of teaching, whenever and wherever it may be found, in religion, moral culture, or in the lives of individuals. But the Middle Ages are past, and we have stepped into a New Age. And now the best of men, Mahatma Gandhi, has come to us with this best of gifts from the West.

THE MODERN AGE

The terribly efficient method of repressing personality in the individuals and the races who have failed to resist it has, in the present scientific age, spread all over the world; and in consequence there have appeared signs of a universal disruption which seems not far off. Faced with the possibility of such a disaster, which is sure to affect the successful peoples of the world in their intemperate prosperity, the great powers of the West are seeking peace, not by curbing their greed, or by giving up the exclusive advantages which they have unjustly acquired, but by concentrating their forces for mutual security.

But can powers find their equilibrium in themselves? Power has to be made secure not only against power, but also against weakness; for there lies the peril of its losing balance. The weak are as great a danger for the strong as quicksand for an elephant. They do not assist progress because they do not resist, they only drag down. The people who grow accustomed to wield absolute power over others are apt to forget that by so doing they generate an unseen force which some day rends that power into pieces. The dumb fury of the downtrodden finds its awful support from the universal law of moral balance. The air which is so thin and unsubstantial gives birth to storms that nothing can resist. This has been proved in history over and over again, and stormy forces arising from the revolt of insulted humanity are openly gathering in the air at the present time.

Yet in the psychology of the strong the lesson is despised and no count taken of the terribleness of the weak. Have we never read of the castle of power, securely buttressed on all sides, in a moment dissolving in air at the explosion caused by the weak and outraged besiegers? Politicians calculate upon the number of mailed hands that are kept on the sword-like hilts; they do not possess the third eye to see the great invisible hand that clasps in silence the hand of the helpless and waits its time. The strong form their league by a combination of powers, driving the weak to form their own league alone with their God. I know I am crying in the wilderness when I raise the voice of warning; and while the West is busy with its organization of a machine-made peace, it will still continue to nourish by its iniquities the underground forces of earthquake in the Eastern Continent. The West seems unconscious that science, by providing it with more and more power, is tempting it to suicide and encouraging it to accept the challenge of the disarmed; it does not know that the challenge comes from a higher source.

Two prophecies about the world's salvation are cherished in the hearts of the two great religions of the world. They represent the highest expectation of man, thereby indicating his faith in a truth which he instinctively considers as ultimate—the truth of love. These prophecies do not have a vision of fettering the world and reducing it to tameness by means of a close-linked power forged in the factory of a political steel trust. One of the religions has for its meditation the image of the Buddha who is to come, Maitreya, the Buddha of love; and he is to bring peace. The other religion waits for the coming of Christ. For Christ preached peace when he preached love, when he preached the oneness of the Father with the brothers who are many. And this was the truth of peace. Christ never held that peace was the best policy. For policy is not truth. The calculation of self-interest can never successfully fight the irrational force of passion—the passion which is perversion of love, and which can only be set right by the truth of love. So long as the powers build a league on the foundation of their desire for safety, secure enjoyment of gains, consolidation of past injustice, and putting off the reparation of wrongs, while their fingers still wriggle for greed and reek of blood, rifts will appear in their union; and in future their conflicts will take greater force and magnitude. It is political and commercial egoism which is the evil harbinger of war. By different combinations it changes its shape and dimensions, but not its nature. This egoism is still held sacred, and made a religion; and such a religion, by a mere change of temple, and by new committees of priests, will never save mankind. We must know that, as through science and commerce, the realization of the unity of the material world gives us power, so the realization of the great spiritual unity of man alone can give us peace. . . .

. . . When we know this world as alien to us, then its mechanical aspect takes prominence in our mind, and then we set up our machines and our methods to deal with it and make as much profit as our knowledge of its mechanism allows us to do. This view of things does not play us false, for the machine has its place in this world. And not only this material universe, but human beings also may be used as machines and made to yield powerful results. This aspect of truth cannot be ignored; it has to be known and mastered. Europe has done so and has reaped a rich harvest. . . .

According to the true Indian view, our consciousness of the world, merely as the sum total of things that exist, and as governed by laws, is imperfect. But it is perfect when our consciousness realizes all things as spiritually one with it, and therefore capable of giving us joy. For us the highest purpose of this world is not merely living in it, knowing it and making use of it, but realizing our own selves in it through expansion of sympathy; not alienating ourselves from it and dominating it, but comprehending and uniting it with ourselves in perfect union. . . .

Strangely enough, in Shakespeare's dramas, like those of Kalidasa, we find a secret vein of complaint against the artificial life of the king's court—the life of ungrateful treachery and falsehood. And almost everywhere in his dramas, forest scenes have been introduced in connection with some working of the life of unscrupulous ambition. It is perfectly obvious in *Timon of Athens,* but there nature offers no message or balm to the injured soul of man. In *Cymbeline* the mountainous forest and the cave appear in their aspect of obstruction to life's opportunities. These only seem tolerable in comparison with the vicissitudes of fortune in the artificial court life. In *As You Like It,* the forest of Arden is didactic in its lessons. It does not bring peace, but preaches, when it says:

> Hath not old custom made this life more sweet
> Than that of painted pomp? Are not these woods
> More free from peril than the envious court?

In *The Tempest*, through Prospero's treatment of Ariel and Caliban we realize man's struggle with nature and his longing to sever connection with her. In *Macbeth*, as a prelude to a bloody crime of treachery and treason, we are introduced to a scene of a barren heath where the three witches appear as personifications of nature's malignant forces; and in *King Lear* it is the fury of a father's love turned into curses by the ingratitude born of the unnatural life of the court that finds its symbol in the storm on the heath. The tragic intensity of *Hamlet* and *Othello* is unrelieved by any touch of nature's eternity. Except in a passing glimpse of a moonlight night in the love scene in *The Merchant of Venice*, nature has not been allowed in other dramas of this series, including *Romeo and Juliet* and *Antony and Cleopatra*, to contribute her own music to the music of man's love. In *A Winter's Tale*, the cruelty of a king's suspicion stands bare in its relentlessness, and nature cowers before it, offering no consolation.

I hope it is needless for me to say that these observations are not intended to minimize Shakespeare's great power as a dramatic poet, but to show in his works the gulf between nature and human nature owning to the tradition of his race and time. It cannot be said that the beauty of nature is ignored in his writings; only that he fails to recognize in them the truth of the interpenetration of human life with the cosmic life of the world. We observe a completely different attitude of mind in the later English poets like Wordsworth and Shelley, which can be attributed in the main to the great mental change in Europe at that particular period, through the influence of the newly discovered philosophy of India which stirred the soul of Germany and aroused the attention of other Western countries.

In Milton's *Paradise Lost*, the very subject—man dwelling in the garden of Paradise—seems to afford a special opportunity for bringing out the true greatness of man's relationship with nature. But though the poet has described to us the beauties of the garden, though he has shown to us the animals living there in amity and peace among themselves, there is no reality of kinship between them and man. They were created for man's enjoyment; man was their lord and master. We find no trace of the love between the first man and woman gradually surpassing themselves and overflowing the rest of creation, such as we find in the love scenes in *Kumara-Sambhava* and

275

Shakuntala. In the seclusion of the bower, where the first man and woman rested in the garden of Paradise,

> Bird, beast, insect or worm
> Durst enter none, such was their awe of man.

Not that India denied the superiority of man, but the test of that superiority lay, according to her, in the comprehensiveness of sympathy, not in the aloofness of absolute distinction. . . .

FROM *Thoughts from Rabindranath Tagore*

Just as it does not do to have a writer entirely removed from the feeling to which he is giving expression, so also it does not conduce to the truest poetry to have him too close to it. Memory is the brush which can best lay on the true poetic color. Nearness has too much of the compelling about it, and the imagination is not sufficiently free unless it can get away from its influence. Not only in poetry, but in all art, the mind of the artist must attain a certain degree of aloofness—the creator within man must be allowed the sole control. If the subject matter gets the better of the creation, the result is a mere replica of the event, not a reflection of it through the artist's mind.

To be able to love material things, to clothe them with tender grace, and yet not be attached to them, this is a great service. Providence expects that we should make this world our own, and not live in it as though it were a rented tenement. We can only make it our own by some service, and that service is to lend it love and beauty from our soul. From your own experience you can see the difference between the beautiful, the tender, the hospitable; and the mechanically neat and monotonously useful.

There are truths which are of the nature of information, that can be added to our stock of knowledge from the outside. But there are other truths of the nature of inspiration, which cannot be used to swell the number of our accomplishments. These latter are not like food, but are rather the appetite itself, that can only be strengthened by inducing harmony in our bodily functions. Religion is such a truth. It establishes the right center for life's activities, giving them an eternal meaning. It maintains the true standard of value for the objects of our striving and inspires in us the spirit of renunciation which is the spirit of humanity.

Just as health is a condition of man's body, so is religion of his whole nature. Health cannot be given in the same way as money is put into one's palm. But it may be induced by bringing about suitable conditions. Religious teaching, likewise, cannot be left to a school committee to be put on their syllabus along with arithmetic and Euclid. No school inspector will be able to measure its progress. No examiner's blue pencil can assign it proper marks. An appropriate environment must be created in which religion may have its natural growth.

The question why there is evil in existence is the same as why there is imperfection, or, in other words, why there is creation at all. We must take it for granted that it could not be otherwise; that creation must be imperfect, must be gradual, and that it is futile to ask the question, "why are we?"

But this is the real question we ought to ask: is this imperfection the final truth, is evil absolute and ultimate? The river has its boundaries, its banks, but is a river all banks? Or are the banks the final facts about the river? Do not these obstructions themselves give its water an onward motion? The towing rope binds a boat, but is the bondage its meaning? Does it not at the same time draw the boat forward?

The current of the world has its boundaries, otherwise it could have no existence, but its purpose is not shown in the boundaries which restrain it, but in its movement, which is toward perfection. The wonder is not that there should be obstacles and sufferings in this world, but that there should be law and order, beauty and joy, goodness and love.

The idea of God that man has in his being is the wonder of all wonders. He has felt in the depths of his life that what appears as imperfect is the manifestation of the perfect, just as a man who has an ear for music realizes the perfection of a song, while in fact he is only listening to a succession of notes. Man has found out the great paradox, that what is limited is not imprisoned within its limits; it is ever moving, and therewith shedding its finitude every moment. In fact, imperfection is not a negation of perfectness, finitude is not contradictory to infinity; they are but completeness manifested in parts, infinity revealed within bounds.

The true universal finds its manifestation in the individuality which is true. Beauty is universal, and a rose reveals it because, as a rose, it is individually beautiful. By making a decoction of a rose, jasmine, and lotus, you do not get a realization of some larger beauty which is interfloral. The true universality is not breaking down the walls of one's own house, but the offering of hospitality to one's guests and neighbors.

As art creations are emotional representations of facts and ideas, they can never be like the product of a photographic camera which is passively receptive of lights and shadows in all their indiscriminate details. Our scientific mind is unbiased, it accepts facts with a cold-blooded curiosity that has no preference. The artistic mind is strongly biased, and that bias not only guides it in its fastidious selection of the subject, but also in that of its details. It throws the colored lights of emphasis on its theme in such a manner that it attains a character which clearly distinguishes it from its fellows. The skylarks of science offer corroboration of their truth through their similarity; the skylarks of artists and poets through their dissimilarity. If Shelley's poem on this bird had been just like that of Wordsworth, it would have been rejected for its lack of truth.

Children are living beings—more living than grown-up people who have built shells of habit around themselves. Therefore it is absolutely necessary for their mental health and development that they should not have mere schools for their lessons, but a world whose guiding spirit is personal love. It must be an ashram where men have gathered for the highest end of life, in the peace of nature; where life is not merely meditative, but fully awake in its activities; where boys' minds are not being perpetually drilled into believing that the ideal of the idolatry of the nation is the truest ideal for them to accept; where they are bidden to realize man's world as God's Kingdom to whose citizenship they have to aspire; where the sunrise and sunset and the silent glory of stars are not daily ignored; where nature's festivities of flowers and fruit have their joyous recognition from man; and where the young and the old, the teacher and the student, sit at the same table to take their daily food and the food of their eternal life.

Religion is not a fractional thing that can be doled out in fixed weekly or daily measures as one among various subjects in the school syllabus. It is the truth of our complete being, the consciousness of our personal relationship with the infinite; it is the true center of gravity of our life. This we can attain during our childhood by daily living in a place where the truth of the spiritual world is not obscured by a crowd of necessities assuming artificial importance; where life is simple, surrounded by fullness of leisure, by ample space and pure air and profound peace of nature; and where men live with a perfect faith in the eternal life before them.

That which I value most in my religion or my aspiration, I seek to find corroborated, in its fundamental unity, in other great religions, or in the hopes expressed in the history of other peoples. Each great movement of thought and endeavor in any part of the world may have something unique in its expression, but the truth underlying any of them never has the meretricious cheapness of utter novelty about it. The great Ganges must not hesitate to declare its essential similarity to the Nile of Egypt, or to the Yangtse-Kiang of China.

FROM *Our Universe*

However awe-inspiring we may find this immense magnitude in speed, distance and the measure of time regarding the world of stars, the inconceivable force, and the circumferences of their fiery revolving movements, we have yet to admit that what is still more miraculous is that man is aware of them, and surmounting all needs in life he is ever eager for knowledge of them. Smaller than small, perishable at any moment is his body. His presence occupies only a momentary corner in the history of the universe; a tiny spot in the vast universe that is ever turning where he dwells, and yet he keeps an account of the immense, the immeasurable and the formidable subtleties of a universe closing on infinity. There is no other splendor than this in the world, or perhaps, who knows, there may be, in the profusion of creation, some other world, which conquering the heart of another matter is expressing itself in some other form. But what man has proved is that the supreme is not in outward form, nor in weight, but in inward fulfillment.

FROM *Thought Relics*

We are like a stray line of a poem, which ever feels that it rhymes with another line and must find it, or miss its own fulfillment. This quest of the unattained is the great impulse in man which brings forth all his best creations. Man seems deeply to be aware of a separation at the root of his being; he cries to be led across it to a union, and somehow he knows that it is love which can lead him to a love which is final.

The horse harnessed to a carriage is only a part of it; the master is he who drives it unattached. We are enjoined to work with vigor and yet retain our detachment of mind. For our deeds must express our freedom above all, otherwise we become like wheels revolving because compelled. There is a harmony between doing and not doing, between gaining and renouncing which we must attain.

Our daily flow of prayer carries our self into the supreme Self, it makes us feel the reality of that fullness which we gain by utterly giving ourselves up, makes our consciousness expand in a large world of peace, where movements are beauty and all relations are truths because of their inner freedom, which is disinterestedness.

Love is not a mere impulse, it must contain truth, which is law. It accepts limitations from truth because of its own inner wealth. The child willingly exercises restraint to correct its bodily balance, because it has true pleasure in the freedom of its movements; and love also counts no cost as too great to realize its truth. Poetry is much more strict in its form of expression than prose, because poetry has the freedom of joy in its origin and end. Our love of God is accurately careful of its responsibilities. It is austere in its probity and it must have intellect for its ally. Since what it deals with is immense in value, it has to be cautious about the purity of its coins. Therefore, when our soul cries for the gift of immortality, its first prayer is, "Lead me from the unreal to truth."

We criticize nature from outside when we separate it in our mind from human nature, and blame it for being devoid of pity and justice. Let the wick burn with indignation at the want of light in the rest of the candle, but the truth is that the wick represents the whole candle in its illumination. Obstacles are necessary companions to expression, and we know that the positive element in language is not in its obstructiveness. Exclusively viewed from the side of the obstacle, nature appears inimical to the idea of morality. But if that were absolutely true, moral life could never come to exist. Life, moral or physical, is not a completed fact, but a continual process, depending for its movement upon two contrary forces, the force of resistance and that of expression. Dividing these forces into two mutually opposing principles does not help us, for the truth dwells not in the opposition but in its continual reconciliation.

Fear assumes unlimited dimensions in the dark, because it is the shadow of the self which has lost its foothold in the all, the self which is a doubter, an unbeliever, which puts its emphasis upon negation, exaggerating detached facts into fearful distortions. In the light we find the harmony of things and know that our world is great and therefore we are great; we know that with more and more extensive realization of truth, conflicts will vanish, for existence itself is harmony.

An acquaintance of mine has suddenly died and once again I come to know death, the tritest of all truisms in this world.

The moralist teaches us to know the world as unreal through the contemplation of death. But to make renunciation easy by calling the world names is neither true, nor brave. For that renunciation is no renunciation at all in which things have lost their value.

On the contrary, the world is so true, that death's wheel leaves no mark upon it. The untruth is in the belief that this self of ours for its own permanent use can rob this world of even a particle of its things. Death has its concern only with our self and not with this world. The world never loses an atom; it is our self which suffers.

There are men whose idea of life is static, who long for its continuation after death only because of their wish for permanence and not perfection; they love to imagine that the things to which they are accustomed will persist for ever. They completely identify themselves in their minds with their fixed surroundings and with whatever they have gathered, and to have to leave these is death for them. They forget that the true meaning of living is outliving, it is ever growing out of itself. The fruit clings to its stem, its skin clings to the pulp, and the pulp to the seed so long as the fruit is immature, so long as it is not ready for its course of further life. Its outer covering and its inner core are not yet differentiated and it only proves its life by its strength of tenacity. But when the seed is ripe its hold upon its surrounding is loosened, its pulp attains fragrance, sweetness and detachment, and is dedicated to all who need it. Birds peck at it and it is not hurt, the storm plucks it and flings it to the dust and it is not destroyed. It proves its immortality by its renunciation.

The life of the seed within the fruit is absolutely different from its life of growth as a tree. The life which is bound on all sides within the environment of our self, within the limited range of our senses must be so fundamentally different from the life of an emancipated soul that it is impossible to imagine the latter while we are immured in the sheath of self. And therefore, in our desire for eternal life we pray for an eternity of our habit and comfort, forgetting that immortality is in repeatedly transcending the definite forms of life in order to pursue the infinite truth of life. Those who think that life's true meaning is in the persistence of its particular forms which are familiar to us are like misers who have not the power to know that the meaning of money can only be found by spending it, by changing the symbol into truth.

The world of sleep is fundamental; it is the world of the mother's womb. It is the world where the grass and the trees live and find their beauty of reposefulness. Our consciousness has freed itself from its embrace, asserting its independence. It is the freedom of the fountain which must come over and over again to its origin to renew its play. The whole depth and spread of the still water finds its own play in the play of this little fountain. In like manner, it is in our own consciousness that the universe knows itself. Therefore this consciousness has to be great in order to be true. Our consciousness is the music of the world, its dance, its poem. It has its pauses in the bosom of the original sleep, to be fed with immortality at her breast.

But we cannot afford to fritter away our solitude where lies the throne of the infinite. We cannot truly live for one another if we never claim the freedom to live alone, if our social duties consist in helping one another to forget that we have souls. To exhaust ourselves completely in mere efforts to give company to each other is to cheat the world of our best, the best which is the product of the amplitude of our inner atmosphere of leisure. Society poisons the air it breathes, where it hems in the individual with a revolving crowd of distractions.

Some part of the earth's water becomes rarefied and ascends to the skies. With the movement and the music it acquires in those pure heights it then showers down, back to the water of the earth, making it wholesome and fresh. Similarly, part of the mind of humanity rises up out of the world and flies skyward; but this sky-soaring mind attains completeness only when it has returned to mingle with the earth-bound mind. This is the ventilation of religion, the circulation of man's ideals between heaven and earth.

Our greatest men have shown immense respect for mankind in their expectations. We come to believe in ourselves because of what is asked of us. Practical men base their arrangements upon their estimates of man's limitations. Therefore the great creations of history, the creations that have their foundations upon the faith in the infinite in man, have not their origin in the common sense of practical men. When Buddha said to men: "Spread thy thoughts of love beyond limits," when Christ said: "Love thine enemies," their words transcended the average standard of ideals belonging to the ordinary world. But they ever remind us that our true life is not the life of the ordinary world, and we have a fund of resources in us which is inexhaustible. It is not for us to despair, because the highest hope for mankind has been uttered by the great words of great men.

To fledgling birds, flight in the sky may appear incredible. They may with apparent reason measure the highest limit of their possibilities by the limited standard of their nests. But in the meanwhile they find that their food is not grown inside those nests; it is brought to them across the measureless blue. There is a silent voice that speaks to them, that they are more than what they are, and that they must not laugh at the message of soaring wings and glad songs of freedom.

The old is prudent but is not wise. Wisdom is that freshness of mind which enables one to realize that truth is not hoarded in caskets of maxims, it is free and living. Great sufferings lead us to wisdom because these are the birth-throes through which our mind is freed from its habit-environment, and comes naked into the arms of reality. Wisdom has the character of the child perfected through knowledge and feeling.

To alleviate pain, to try to remove its causes, is worthy of man. All the same, we must know that a great part of our sufferings should be ascribed to the beginning of our entrance into a new plane of existence to which our vital nature has not been completely adapted nor our mind thoroughly accustomed. From a narrow perfection of animality man has arrived in the imperfectness of spiritual life, where the civil war between the forces of our primitive past and those belonging to our future has robbed us of peace. Not having reached its normal stage, humanity is enveloped in the incandescent vapor of suffering.

We must know that to be provided with an exact apportionment of what we deserve and need is like traveling in a world whose flatness is ideally perfect, and therefore where the fluid forces of nature are held in suspense. We require ups and downs, however unpleasant they may be, in our life's geography, in order to make our thoughts and energies fluently active. Our life's journey is a journey in an unknown country, where hills and hollows come in our way unawares, keeping our minds ever active in dealing with them. They do not come according to our deserts, but our deserts are judged according to our treatment of them.

When we come to believe that we are in possession of our God because we belong to some particular sect it gives us such a complete sense of comfort, that God is needed no longer except for quarreling with others whose idea of God differs from ours in theoretical details.

Having been able to make provision for our God in some shadow-land of creed we feel free to reserve all the space for ourselves in the world of reality, ridding it of the wonder of the infinite, making it as trivial as our own household furniture. Such unlimited vulgarity only becomes possible when we have no doubt in our minds that we believe in God while our life ignores Him.

The pious sectarian is proud because he is confident of his right of possession in God. The man of devotion is meek because he is conscious of God's right of love over his life and soul. The object of our possession becomes smaller than ourselves, and without acknowledging it in so many words the bigoted sectarian has an implicit belief that God can be kept secured for certain individuals in a cage which is of their own make. In a similar manner the primitive races of men believe that their ceremonials have a magic influence upon their deities. Sectarianism is a perverse form of worldliness in the disguise of religion; it breeds a narrowness of heart in a greater measure than the cult of the world based upon material interest can ever do. For undisguised pursuit of self has its safety in its openness, like filth exposed to the sun and air. But the self-magnification with its consequent lessening of God that goes on unchecked under the cover of sectarianism loses its chance of salvation because it defiles the very source of purity.

Religion, like poetry, is not a mere idea, it is expression. The self-expression of God is in the endless variety of creation; and our attitude toward the Infinite Being must also in its expression have a variety of individuality ceaseless and unending. Those sects which jealously build their boundaries with too rigid creeds excluding all spontaneous movement of the living spirit may hoard their theology but they kill religion.

When religion is in the complete possession of the monotonous average, it becomes correct and comfortable, but loses the living spirit of art. For art is the expression of the universal through the individual, and religion in its outer aspect is the art of the human soul. It almost becomes a matter of pride and a sign of superior culture to be able to outrage all codes of decency imposed by an authorized religion bearing the stamp of approval of an organization which can persecute but has not the power to persuade.

As an analogous phenomenon, we have known literary men deliberately cultivating a dread of whatever has the reputation of goodness, and also men of art afraid of being suspected as lovers of the beautiful. They rebel against the fact that what is proper and what is true in beauty and in goodness have become mixed up in men's minds. The appraisement of what is proper does not require any degree of culture or natural sensitiveness of mind, and therefore it fetches a ready price in the market, outbids truth, becomes petty in its tyranny and leaves smudges of vulgarity upon things that are precious. To rescue truth from the dungeon of propriety has always been the mission of poets and artists, but in the time of revolution they are apt to go further by rejecting truth itself.

In our epic Ramayana, we find that when Prince Ramachandra won back his wife from the clutches of the giant who had abducted her, his people clamored for her rejection, suspecting defilement. Similarly, in art, fastidious men of culture are clamoring for the banishment of the beautiful because she has been allowed to remain so long in the possession of propriety.

In a lyrical poem, the meter and the idea are blended in one. Treated separately, they reveal themselves as two contrary forces;

and instances are common in which their natural antagonism has not been overcome, thus resulting in the production of bad poems.

We are the artists, before whom lie materials which are mutually obstructive. They continually clash, until they develop into a creation perfect in unity. Very often, in order to shirk trouble and secure peace, we sacrifice one of the contending parties. This makes the fight impossible, but also the creation. The restless spirit of nature divorced from the soul's repose drives us to the madness of work which piles up towers of things. On the other hand the spiritual being deprived of its world of reality lives only in the exile of abstraction, creating phantoms in which exaggerations, unchecked by the strict necessities of forms, run riot.

Our nature being complex, it is unsafe to generalize about things that are human, and it is an incomplete statement of truth to say that habits have the sole effect of deadening our mind. The habits that are helpful are like a channel, which helps the current to flow. It is open where the water runs onward, guarding it only where it has the danger of deviation. The bee's life in its channel of habit has no opening, it revolves within a narrow circle of perfection. Man's life has its institutions which are its organized habits. When these act as enclosures, then the result may be perfect, like a beehive of wonderful precision of form, but unsuitable for the mind which has unlimited possibilities of growth.

For the current of our spiritual life creeds, rituals are channels that may thwart or help, according to their fixity or openness. When a symbol or spiritual idea becomes rigidly elaborate in its construction, it supplants the idea which it should support. In art and literature metaphors which are the symbol of our emotional perceptions excite our imagination but do not arrest it. For they never claim a monopoly of our attention; they leave open the way for the endless possibility of other metaphors. They lose their artistic value if they degenerate into fixed habits of expression. Shelley, in his poem on the skylark, pours out images which we value because they are only a few sugges-tions of the immeasurableness of our enjoyment. But if, because of their fitness and beauty, a law were passed that while thinking about a skylark these images should be treated as final and no others admitted, then Shelley's poem would at once become false; for its truth is in its fluidity, in its modesty, which tacitly admits that it has not the last word.

The question is asked, if life's journey be endless where is its goal? The answer is, it is everywhere. We are in a palace which has no end, but which we have reached. By exploring it and extending our relationship with it we are ever making it more and more our own. The infant is born in the same universe where lives the adult of ripe mind. But its position is not like a schoolboy who has yet to learn his alphabet, finding himself in a college class. The infant has its own joy of life because the world is not a mere road, but a home, of which it will have more and more as it grows up in wisdom. With our road the gain is at every step, for it is the road and the home in one; it leads us on yet gives us shelter.

A block of stone is unplastic, insensitive, inert; it offers resistance to the creative idea of the artist. But for a sculptor its very obstacles are an advantage and he carves his image out of it. Our physical existence is an obstacle to our spirit, it has every aspect of a bondage, and to all appearance it is a perpetual humiliation to our soul. And therefore it is the best material for our soul to manifest herself through it, to proclaim her freedom by fashioning ornaments out of her fetters. The limitations of our outer circumstances are only to give opportunities to our soul, and by being able to defy them she realizes her truth.

When I was a child, God also became a child with me to be my playmate. Otherwise my imperfections would have weighed me down, and every moment it would have been a misery to be and yet not fully to be. The things that kept me occupied were trifling and the things I played with were made of dust and sticks. But nevertheless my occupations were made precious to me and the importance that was given to my toys made them of equal value with the playthings of the adult. The majesty of childhood won for me the world's homage, because there was revealed the infinite in its aspect of the small.

And the reason is the same, which gives the youth the right to claim his full due and not to be despised. The divinity which is ever young, has crowned him with his own wreath, whispering to his ears that he is the rightful inheritor of all the world's wealth.

The infinite is with us in the beauty of our childhood, in the strength of our youth, in the wisdom of our age, in play, in earning, and in spending.

The world of senses in which animals live is limited. Our reason has opened the gate for our mind into the heart of the infinite. Yet this freedom of reason is but a freedom in the outer courtyard of existence. Objects of knowledge maintain an infinite distance from us who are the knowers. For knowledge is not union. Therefore the further world of freedom awaits us there where we reach truth, not through feeling it by senses or knowing it by reason, but through union of perfect sympathy. This is an emancipation difficult fully to imagine; we have but glimpses of its character. We perceive the fact of a picture by seeing it, we know about it by measuring its lines, analyzing its colors and studying the laws of harmony in its composition. But even then it is no realization of the picture, for which we want an intimate union with it immediate to ourselves.

The picture of a flower in a botanical book is information; its mission ends with our knowledge. But in pure art it is a personal communication. And therefore until it finds its harmony in the depth of our personality it misses its mark. We can treat existence solely as a textbook furnishing us lessons, and we shall not be disappointed, but we know that there its mission does not end. For in our joy in it, which is an end in itself, we feel that it is a communication, the final response to which is not the response of our knowing but the response of our being.

POETRY

Several unusual factors are involved when a poet becomes his own translator, and a lyricist, more than others, knows that the inspired word, phrase, or rhyme in the language of his subconscious cannot be repeated or replaced. A creative writer is intimately responsible to his own original, symbolic expression, and it was exceptional historical and personal inducements, one feels, that made Tagore conquer the natural resistance of an artist. One factor was perhaps the peculiar nature of the Indian culture itself during the Indo-Anglian phase when artists as well as ordinary Indians lived and absorbed, in a manner almost unprecedented in the annals of cultural duality, not only the new learning and incentives of the modern West, channeled in the new India through the English language, but also the feeling tone, accent of thought, and adventurous thrust of Western thought. This, in Tagore's case, was an auxiliary stream which met and mingled with the great currents of Sanskrit and Bengali traditions which were the main source of his continuing poetic expression. We find in Tagore's life a process of absorption, an atmospheric quickening of his imagination through the deep reading of English poetry, especially in the area of English lyricism. His eager delight in Shakespeare, in early nineteenth century English poetry, later in Browning and then in Whitman enriched the creative force of his own Bengali writing where he went from one level of excellence to another in outgrowing a technique which had already revolutionized Bengali poetry.

Secondly, Tagore's conscious faith in the need for East-West reciprocity, as part of the essential progress of civilization, seems to have played an important role in making him his own translator into English. He felt that modern civilization demanded to some extent an outbreak beyond the immediate horizon of local and indigenous art forms fashioned in the normal vernacular context. The English language which he knew and loved, even though he learned it later than the average educated Indian of his day, was for him the language of an expanding era, and the speech currency for the greater part of global mankind. From this came his partly deliberate sponsorship, when he was nearly fifty, of the language of Wordsworth, Keats, and Shelley, and his experiments with translations from modern English poetry in the later period of his life.

Added to this is the part played by personal demands made upon him by his English visitors and friends, mainly Ramsay Macdonald and William Rothenstein, and his colleagues at Santiniketan like C. F. Andrews, who knew no Bengali and did not claim citizenship in the realm of creative English writing, but were persons dedicated to the cause of international and Indo-European cooperation at spiritually relevant levels. The genesis of the *Gitanjali* translation by Tagore is given in another section of this volume. (See letter to Indira Devi, May 6, 1913, page 20.)

Tagore was not only an artist, but a craftsman who used and perfected the tools of Bengali poetry in a systematic and chiseled manner for nearly seventy years. Therefore, he knew even at an earlier stage of his artistry how completely untranslatable poetry is. The Bengali language, rich in syllabic sound and natural melody, offered the same problems as Indian music itself which uses subtle quarter notes that defy the notational system of Europe. Tagore knew this, and even when fame descended upon his translation of *Gitanjali* in 1912, when he was fifty-two years old, he could not at heart, or more precisely, in his literary mind, reconcile himself to this strange and unexpected acceptance by the West in terms of the creative element in his own translations. It is true that he felt the novelty and excitement of trying out his ideas in English, but he felt baffled and even a sense of self-betrayal in confronting what he knew to be the untranslatable core of Bengali lyricism, over which he had no more right as a translator than any other translator of poetry.

While Tagore, with a singular intention, and with a competence born not only of genius but of repeated intellectual exercise, reached unique success in putting his Bengali poetry into English, he perhaps paid the price of getting used to the process, in spite of inward rebellion. The translations sensitively enhanced a relationship of understanding between the East and West, and also between different parts of the East, and even between different parts of India which did not yet have a measurably successful national language. But Tagore heavily lost his position in the artistic society of the West, even though he was one of the great world poets. The meter and rhyme, the associational words, the irreplaceable symbols in his Bengali poetry, were discarded in favor of rhythmic "prose-poems" in English, and soon strained the responsive capacity of his readers. It must be pointed out, however, contrary to repeated assertions by many Western and Indian literary critics of today, that some of his own later translations from his Bengali poems were as fine, and sometimes superior to anything done by him in *Gitanjali* or *Gardener* ("Our Lane Is Torturous," in *The Fugitive*, The Macmillan Company, New York, 1921, and much later, "Once More the Night Has Waned," *Poems*, Visva-Bharati, 1942). But this whole literary problem will continue to intrigue, inspire, and frustrate genuine lovers of poetry.

Time will cast aside the temporal, while the enduring contributions of Tagore's own English translations will remain. We have here attempted to select the best. Care has been taken to eliminate any duplication of form and style, and where possible, to present poems in English which carry even a faint and transferred suggestion of the light and bloom of Bengali verse. All the published volumes in English, including Tagore's own English translations, have been represented; some of his own translations, posthumously published in book form, or published in Indian journals and almost unknown to the greater part of the Western world have also been used.

"The Child," published by Allen & Unwin, was the only poem directly written by Tagore in English free verse; he did this while in Berlin and Munich at the request of a German film company, UFA, who wanted a script from him for a pageant of Indian life. The scheme did not materialize, but the poem remains and is included in this section.

Translations made by this editor, mostly of Tagore's Bengali poems composed or dictated shortly before his death, as well as translations made by other Bengali contemporaries, are included. This latest phase of Tagore's poetry is represented for reasons of chronological and literary inclusiveness. The editor is delighted to acknowledge the help and advice, sensitively and artistically rendered, of Donald Junkins in regard to the revisions of first translations made by the editor from some of Tagore's Bengali poems. Fidelity to the Bengali original and a recognition of the needs of modern literary English had to be combined, though the same, almost insurmountable, barriers remain in regard to translation from one language to another.

Poems, published by Visva-Bharati, has been used, as well as the resources of volumes of the *Visva-Bharati Quarterly*, in order to illustrate the later phase of Tagore's Bengali poetry. Other sources, magazines and books, are mentioned in the footnotes. It is important to add that Tagore's later Bengali poems became increasingly terse, luminous and precise in the use of imagery. A modern and experimental artistry marks another phase in the plenitude of his poetic genius.

I am thankful to Henry Braun for his research assistance in tracing Tagore's influence on the poetry of Hart Crane.

FROM *Gitanjali*

Thou hast made me endless, such is thy pleasure. This frail vessel thou emptiest again and again, and fillest it ever with fresh life.

This little flute of a reed thou hast carried over hills and dales, and hast breathed through it melodies eternally new.

At the immortal touch of thy hands my little heart loses its limits in joy and gives birth to utterance ineffable.

Thy infinite gifts come to me only on these very small hands of mine. Ages pass, and still thou pourest, and still there is room to fill.

When thou commandest me to sing, it seems that my heart would break with pride; and I look to thy face, and tears come to my eyes.

All that is harsh and dissonant in my life melts into one sweet harmony—and my adoration spreads wings like a glad bird on its flight across the sea.

I know thou takest pleasure in my singing. I know that only as a singer I come before thy presence.

I touch by the edge of the far-spreading wing of my song thy feet which I could never aspire to reach.

Drunk with the joy of singing I forget myself and call thee friend who art my lord.

Life of my life, I shall ever try to keep my body pure, knowing that thy living touch is upon all my limbs.

I shall ever try to keep all untruths out from my thoughts, knowing that thou art that truth which has kindled the light of reason in my mind.

I shall ever try to drive all evils away from my heart and keep my love in flower, knowing that thou hast thy seat in the inmost shrine of my heart.

And it shall be my endeavor to reveal thee in my actions, knowing it is thy power gives me strength to act.

※

I ASK for a moment's indulgence to sit by thy side. The works that I have in hand I will finish afterwards.

Away from the sight of thy face my heart knows no rest nor respite, and my work becomes an endless toil in a shoreless sea of toil.

Today the summer has come at my window with its sighs and murmurs; and the bees are plying their minstrelsy at the court of the flowering grove.

Now it is time to sit quiet, face to face with thee, and to sing dedication of life in this silent and overflowing leisure.

※

HERE is thy footstool and there rest thy feet where live the poorest, and lowliest, and lost.

When I try to bow to thee, my obeisance cannot reach down to the depth where thy feet rest among the poorest, and lowliest, and lost.

Pride can never approach to where thou walkest in the clothes of the humble among the poorest, and lowliest, and lost.

My heart can never find its way to where thou keepest company with the companionless among the poorest, the lowliest, and the lost.

※

LEAVE this chanting and singing and telling of beads! Whom dost thou worship in this lonely dark corner of a temple with doors all shut? Open thine eyes and see thy God is not before thee!

He is there where the tiller is tilling the hard ground and where the pathmaker is breaking stones. He is with them in sun and in shower, and his garment is covered with dust. Put off thy holy mantle and even like him come down on the dusty soil!

Deliverance? Where is this deliverance to be found? Our master himself has joyfully taken upon him the bonds of creation; he is bound with us all for ever.

Come out of thy meditations and leave aside thy flowers and incense! What harm is there if thy clothes become tattered and stained? Meet him and stand by him in toil and in sweat of thy brow.

THE song that I came to sing remains unsung to this day.

I have spent my days in stringing and in unstringing my instrument.

The time has not come true, the words have not been rightly set; only there is the agony of wishing in my heart.

The blossom has not opened; only the wind is sighing by.

I have not seen his face, nor have I listened to his voice; only I have heard his gentle footsteps from the road before my house.

The livelong day has passed in spreading his seat on the floor; but the lamp has not been lit and I cannot ask him into my house.

I live in the hope of meeting with him; but this meeting is not yet.

MY desires are many and my cry is pitiful, but ever didst thou save me by hard refusals; and this strong mercy has been wrought into my life through and through.

Day by day thou art making me worthy of the simple, great gifts that thou gavest to me unasked—this sky and the light, this body and the life and the mind—saving me from perils of overmuch desire.

There are times when I languidly linger and times when I awaken and hurry in search of my goal; but cruelly thou hidest thyself from before me.

Day by day thou art making me worthy of thy full acceptance by refusing me ever and anon, saving me from perils of weak, uncertain desire.

CLOUDS heap upon clouds and it darkens. Ah, love, why dost thou let me wait outside at the door all alone?

In the busy moments of the noontide work I am with the crowd, but on this dark lonely day it is only for thee that I hope.

If thou showest me not thy face, if thou leavest me wholly aside, I know not how I am to pass these long, rainy hours.

I keep gazing on the far-away gloom of the sky, and my heart wanders wailing with the restless wind.

ON the day when the lotus bloomed, alas, my mind was straying, and I knew it not. My basket was empty and the flower remained unheeded.

Only now and again a sadness fell upon me, and I started up from my dream and felt a sweet trace of a strange fragrance in the south wind.

That vague sweetness made my heart ache with longing and it seemed to me that it was the eager breath of the summer seeking for its completion.

I knew not then that it was so near, that it was mine, and that this perfect sweetness had blossomed in the depth of my own heart.

IN the deep shadows of the rainy July, with secret steps, thou walkest, silent as night, eluding all watchers.

Today the morning has closed its eyes, heedless of the insistent calls of the loud east wind, and a thick veil has been drawn over the ever-wakeful blue sky.

The woodlands have hushed their songs, and doors are all shut at every house. Thou art the solitary wayfarer in this deserted street. Oh, my only friend, my best beloved, the gates are open in my house —do not pass by like a dream.

ART thou abroad on this stormy night on thy journey of love, my friend? The sky groans like one in despair.

I have no sleep tonight. Ever and again I open my door and look out on the darkness, my friend!

I can see nothing before me. I wonder where lies thy path!

By what dim shore of the ink-black river, by what far edge of the frowning forest, through what mazy depth of gloom art thou threading thy course to come to me, my friend?

IN the night of weariness let me give myself up to sleep without struggle, resting my trust upon thee.

Let me not force my flagging spirit into a poor preparation for thy worship.

It is thou who drawest the veil of night upon the tired eyes of the day to renew its sight in a fresher gladness of awakening.

OBSTINATE are the trammels, but my heart aches when I try to break them.

Freedom is all I want, but to hope for it I feel ashamed.

I am certain that priceless wealth is in thee, and that thou art my best friend, but I have not the heart to sweep away the tinsel that fills my room.

The shroud that covers me is a shroud of dust and death; I hate it, yet hug it in love.

My debts are large, my failures great, my shame secret and heavy; yet when I come to ask for my good, I quake in fear lest my prayer be granted.

"Prisoner, tell me, who was it that bound you?"

"It was my master," said the prisoner. "I thought I could outdo everybody in the world in wealth and power, and I amassed in my own treasure-house the money due to my king. When sleep overcame me I lay upon the bed that was for my lord, and on waking up I found I was a prisoner in my own treasure-house."

"Prisoner, tell me, who was it that wrought this unbreakable chain?"

"It was I," said the prisoner, "who forged this chain very carefully. I thought my invincible power would hold the world captive leaving me in a freedom undisturbed. Thus night and day I worked at the chain with huge fires and cruel hard strokes. When at last the work was done and the links were complete and unbreakable, I found that it held me in its grip."

By all means they try to hold me secure who love me in this world. But it is otherwise with thy love which is greater than theirs, and thou keepest me free.

Lest I forget them they never venture to leave me alone. But day passes by after day and thou art not seen.

If I call not thee in my prayers, if I keep not thee in my heart, thy love for me still waits for my love.

When it was day they came into my house and said, "We shall only take the smallest room here."

They said, "We shall help you in the worship of your God and humbly accept only our own share of his grace"; and then they took their seat in a corner and they sat quiet and meek.

But in the darkness of night I find they break into my sacred shrine, strong and turbulent, and snatch with unholy greed the offerings from God's altar.

LET only that little be left of me whereby I may name thee my all.

Let only that little be left of my will whereby I may feel thee on every side, and come to thee in everything, and offer to thee my love every moment.

Let only that little be left of me whereby I may never hide thee.

Let only that little of my fetters be left whereby I am bound with thy will, and thy purpose is carried out in my life—and that is the fetter of thy love.

WHERE the mind is without fear and the head is held high;

Where knowledge is free;

Where the world has not been broken up into fragments by narrow domestic walls;

Where words come out from the depth of truth;

Where tireless striving stretches its arms toward perfection;

Where the clear stream of reason has not lost its way into the dreary desert sand of dead habit;

Where the mind is led forward by thee into ever-widening thought and action—

Into that heaven of freedom, my Father, let my country awake.

THIS is my prayer to thee, my lord—strike, strike at the root of penury in my heart.

Give me the strength lightly to bear my joys and sorrows.

Give me the strength to make my love fruitful in service.

Give me the strength never to disown the poor or bend my knees before insolent might.

Give me the strength to raise my mind high above daily trifles.

And give me the strength to surrender my strength to thy will with love.

THAT I want thee, only thee—let my heart repeat without end. All desires that distract me, day and night, are false and empty to the core.

As the night keeps hidden in its gloom the petition for light, even thus in the depth of my unconsciousness rings the cry—"I want thee, only thee."

As the storm still seeks its end in peace when it strikes against peace with all its might, even thus my rebellion strikes against thy love and still its cry is—"I want thee, only thee."

WHEN the heart is hard and parched up, come upon me with a shower of mercy.

When grace is lost from life, come with a burst of song.

When tumultuous work raises its din on all sides shutting me out from beyond, come to me, my lord of silence, with thy peace and rest.

When my beggarly heart sits crouched, shut up in a corner, break open the door, my king, and come with the ceremony of a king.

When desire blinds the mind with delusion and dust, O thou holy one, thou wakeful, come with thy light and thy thunder.

THE rain has held back for days and days, my God, in my arid heart. The horizon is fiercely naked—not the thinnest cover of a soft cloud, not the vaguest hint of a distant cool shower.

Send thy angry storm, dark with death, if it is thy wish, and with lashes of lightning startle the sky from end to end.

But call back, my lord, call back this pervading silent heat, still and keen and cruel, burning the heart with dire despair.

Let the cloud of grace bend low from above like the tearful look of the mother on the day of the father's wrath.

THE day was when I did not keep myself in readiness for thee; and entering my heart unbidden even as one of the common crowd, unknown to me, my king, thou didst press the signet of eternity upon many a fleeting moment of my life.

And today when by chance I light upon them and see thy signature, I find they have lain scattered in the dust mixed with the memory of joys and sorrows of my trivial days forgotten.

Thou didst not turn in contempt from my childish play among dust, and the steps that I heard in my playroom are the same that are echoing from star to star.

Have you not heard his silent steps? He comes, comes, ever comes.

Every moment and every age, every day and every night he comes, comes, ever comes.

Many a song have I sung in many a mood of mind, but all their notes have always proclaimed, "He comes, comes, ever comes."

In the fragrant days of sunny April and through the forest path he comes, comes, ever comes.

In the rainy gloom of July nights on the thundering chariot of clouds he comes, comes, ever comes.

In sorrow after sorrow it is his steps that press upon my heart, and it is the golden touch of his feet that makes my joy to shine.

I had gone a-begging from door to door in the village path, when thy golden chariot appeared in the distance like a gorgeous dream and I wondered who was this King of all kings!

My hopes rose high and methought my evil days were at an end, and I stood waiting for alms to be given unasked and for wealth scattered on all sides in the dust.

The chariot stopped where I stood. Thy glance fell on me and thou camest down with a smile. I felt that the luck of my life had come at last. Then of a sudden thou didst hold out thy right hand and say, "What hast thou to give to me?"

Ah, what a kingly jest was it to open thy palm to a beggar to beg!

I was confused and stood undecided, and then from my wallet I slowly took out the least little grain of corn and gave it to thee.

But how great my surprise when at the day's end I emptied my bag on the floor to find a least little grain of gold among the poor heap! I bitterly wept and wished that I had the heart to give thee my all.

THUS it is that thy joy in me is so full. Thus it is that thou hast come down to me. O thou lord of all heavens, where would be thy love if I were not?

Thou hast taken me as thy partner of all this wealth. In my heart is the endless play of thy delight. In my life thy will is ever taking shape.

And for this, thou who art the King of kings hast decked thyself in beauty to captivate my heart. And for this thy love loses itself in the love of thy lover, and there art thou seen in the perfect union of two.

LIGHT, my light, the world-filling light, the eye-kissing light, heart-sweetening light!

Ah, the light dances, my darling, at the center of my life; the light strikes, my darling, the chords of my love; the sky opens, the wind runs wild, laughter passes over the earth.

The butterflies spread their sails on the sea of light. Lilies and jasmines surge up on the crest of the waves of light.

The light is shattered into gold on every cloud, my darling, and it scatters gems in profusion.

Mirth spreads from leaf to leaf, my darling, and gladness without measure. The heaven's river has drowned its banks and the flood of joy is abroad.

LET all the strains of joy mingle in my last song—the joy that makes the earth flow over in the riotous excess of the grass, the joy that sets the twin brothers, life and death, dancing over the wide world, the joy that sweeps in with the tempest, shaking and waking all life with laughter, the joy that sits still with its tears on the open red lotus of pain, and the joy that throws everything it has upon the dust, and knows not a word.

THOU hast made me known to friends whom I knew not. Thou hast given me seats in homes not my own. Thou hast brought the distant near and made a brother of the stranger.

I am uneasy at heart when I have to leave my accustomed shelter; I forget that there abides the old in the new, and that there also thou abidest.

Through birth and death, in this world or in others, wherever thou leadest me it is thou, the same, the one companion of my endless life who ever linkest my heart with bonds of joy to the unfamiliar.

When one knows thee, then alien there is none, then no door is shut. Oh, grant me my prayer that I may never lose the bliss of the touch of the one in the play of the many.

THOU art the sky and thou art the nest as well.

O thou beautiful, there in the nest it is thy love that encloses the soul with colors and sounds and odors.

There comes the morning with the golden basket in her right hand bearing the wreath of beauty, silently to crown the earth.

And there comes the evening over the lonely meadows deserted by herds, through trackless paths, carrying cool draughts of peace in her golden pitcher from the western ocean of rest.

But there, where spreads the infinite sky for the soul to take her flight in, reigns the stainless white radiance. There is no day nor night, nor form nor color, and never, never a word.

THE same stream of life that runs through my veins night and day runs through the world and dances in rhythmic measures.

It is the same life that shoots in joy through the dust of the earth in numberless blades of grass and breaks into tumultuous waves of leaves and flowers.

It is the same life that is rocked in the ocean-cradle of birth and of death, in ebb and in flow.

I feel my limbs are made glorious by the touch of this world of life. And my pride is from the life-throb of ages dancing in my blood this moment.

DELIVERANCE is not for me in renunciation. I feel the embrace of freedom in a thousand bonds of delight.

Thou ever pourest for me the fresh draught of thy wine of various colors and fragrance, filling this earthen vessel to the brim.

My world will light its hundred different lamps with thy flame and place them before the altar of thy temple.

No, I will never shut the doors of my senses. The delights of sight and hearing and touch will bear thy delight.

Yes, all my illusions will burn into illumination of joy, and all my desires ripen into fruits of love.

THE day is no more, the shadow is upon the earth. It is time that I go to the stream to fill my pitcher.

The evening air is eager with the sad music of the water. Ah, it calls me out into the dusk. In the lonely lane there is no passer-by, the wind is up, the ripples are rampant in the river.

I know not if I shall come back home. I know not whom I shall chance to meet. There at the fording in the little boat the unknown man plays upon his lute.

TIME is endless in thy hands, my lord. There is none to count thy minutes.

Days and nights pass and ages bloom and fade like flowers. Thou knowest how to wait.

Thy centuries follow each other perfecting a small wild flower.

We have no time to lose, and having no time we must scramble for our chances. We are too poor to be late.

And thus it is that time goes by while I give it to every querulous man who claims it, and thine altar is empty of all offerings to the last.

At the end of the day I hasten in fear lest thy gate be shut; but I find that yet there is time.

IN desperate hope I go and search for her in all the corners of my room; I find her not.

My house is small and what once has gone from it can never be regained.

But infinite is thy mansion, my lord, and seeking her I have come to thy door.

I stand under the golden canopy of thine evening sky and I lift my eager eyes to thy face.

I have come to the brink of eternity from which nothing can vanish—no hope, no happiness, no vision of a face seen through tears.

Oh, dip my emptied life into that ocean, plunge it into the deepest fullness. Let me for once feel that lost sweet touch in the allness of the universe.

I KNOW that the day will come when my sight of this earth shall be lost, and life will take its leave in silence, drawing the last curtain over my eyes.

Yet stars will watch at night, and morning rise as before, and hours heave like sea waves casting up pleasures and pains.

When I think of this end of my moments, the barrier of the moments breaks and I see by the light of death thy world with its careless treasures. Rare is its lowliest seat, rare is its meanest of lives.

Things that I longed for in vain and things that I got—let them pass. Let me but truly possess the things that I ever spurned and overlooked.

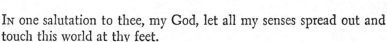

I was not aware of the moment when I first crossed the threshold of this life.

What was the power that made me open out into this vast mystery like a bud in the forest at midnight?

When in the morning I looked upon the light I felt in a moment that I was no stranger in this world, that the inscrutable without name and form had taken me in its arms in the form of my own mother.

Even so, in death the same unknown will appear as ever known to me. And because I love this life, I know I shall love death as well.

The child cries out when from the right breast the mother takes it away, in the very next moment to find in the left one its consolation.

When I go from hence let this be my parting word, that what I have seen is unsurpassable.

I have tasted of the hidden honey of this lotus that expands on the ocean of light, and thus am I blessed—let this be my parting word.

In this playhouse of infinite forms I have had my play and here have I caught sight of him that is formless.

My whole body and my limbs have thrilled with his touch who is beyond touch; and if the end comes here, let it come—let this be my parting word.

In one salutation to thee, my God, let all my senses spread out and touch this world at thy feet.

Like a rain-cloud of July hung low with its burden of unshed showers let all my mind bend down at thy door in one salutation to thee.

Let all my songs gather together their diverse strains into a single current and flow to a sea of silence in one salutation to thee.

Like a flock of homesick cranes flying night and day back to their mountain nests let all my life take its voyage to its eternal home in one salutation to thee.

FROM *The Crescent Moon*

ON THE SEASHORE

On the seashore of endless worlds children meet.

The infinite sky is motionless overhead and the restless water is boisterous. On the seashore of endless worlds the children meet with shouts and dances.

They build their houses with sand, and they play with empty shells. With withered leaves they weave their boats and smilingly float them on the vast deep. Children have their play on the seashore of worlds.

They know not how to swim, they know not how to cast nets. Pearl-fishers dive for pearls, merchants sail in their ships, while children gather pebbles and scatter them again. They seek not for hidden treasures, they know not how to cast nets.

The sea surges up with laughter, and pale gleams the smile of the sea-beach. Death-dealing waves sing meaningless ballads to the children, even like a mother while rocking her baby's cradle. The sea plays with children, and pale gleams the smile of the sea-beach.

On the seashore of endless worlds children meet. Tempest roams in the pathless sky, ships are wrecked in the trackless water, death is abroad and children play. On the seashore of endless worlds is the great meeting of children.

THE SOURCE

The sleep that flits on baby's eyes—does anybody know from where it comes? Yes, there is a rumor that it has its dwelling where, in the fairy village among shadows of the forest dimly lit with glow-worms, there hang two shy buds of enchantment. From there it comes to kiss baby's eyes.

The smile that flickers on baby's lips when he sleeps—does anybody know where it was born? Yes, there is a rumor that a young pale beam of a crescent moon touched the edge of a vanishing autumn cloud, and there the smile was first born in the dream of a dew-washed morning—the smile that flickers on baby's lips when he sleeps.

The sweet, soft freshness that blooms on baby's limbs—does anybody know where it was hidden so long? Yes, when the mother was a young girl it lay pervading her heart in tender and silent mystery of love—the sweet, soft freshness that has bloomed on baby's limbs.

SLEEP-STEALER

Who stole sleep from baby's eyes? I must know.

Clasping her pitcher to her waist mother went to fetch water from the village near by.

It was noon. The children's playtime was over; the ducks in the pond were silent.

The shepherd boy lay asleep under the shadow of the banyan tree.

The crane stood grave and still in the swamp near the mango grove.

In the meanwhile the Sleep-stealer came and, snatching sleep from baby's eyes, flew away.

When mother came back she found baby traveling the room over on all fours.

Who stole sleep from our baby's eyes? I must know. I must find her and chain her up.

I must look into that dark cave, where, through boulders and scowling stones, trickles a tiny stream.

I must search in the drowsy shade of the *bakula* grove, where pigeons coo in their corner, and fairies' anklets tinkle in the stillness of starry nights.

In the evening I will peep into the whispering silence of the bamboo forest, where fireflies squander their light, and will ask every creature I meet, "Can anybody tell me where the Sleep-stealer lives?"

Who stole sleep from baby's eyes? I must know.
Shouldn't I give her a good lesson if I could only catch her!
I would raid her nest and see where she hoards all her stolen sleep.
I would plunder it all, and carry it home.

I would bind her two wings securely, set her on the bank of the river, and then let her play at fishing with a reed among the rushes and the water lilies.

When the marketing is over in the evening, and the village children sit in their mothers' laps, then the night birds will mockingly din her ears with:

"Whose sleep will you steal now?"

WHEN AND WHY

WHEN I bring you colored toys, my child, I understand why there is such a play of colors on clouds, on water, and why flowers are painted in tints—when I give colored toys to you, my child.

When I sing to make you dance, I truly know why there is music in leaves, and why waves send their chorus of voices to the heart of the listening earth—when I sing to make you dance.

When I bring sweet things to your greedy hands, I know why there is honey in the cup of the flower, and why fruits are secretly filled with sweet juice—when I bring sweet things to your greedy hands.

When I kiss your face to make you smile, my darling, I surely understand what pleasure streams from the sky in morning light, and what delight the summer breeze brings to my body—when I kiss you to make you smile.

VOCATION

WHEN the gong sounds ten in the morning and I walk to school by our lane,

Every day I meet the hawker crying, "Bangles, crystal bangles!"

There is nothing to hurry him on, there is no road he must take, no place he must go to, no time when he must come home.

I wish I were a hawker, spending my day in the road, crying, "Bangles, crystal bangles!"

When at four in the afternoon I come back from the school,

I can see through the gate of that house the gardener digging the ground.

He does what he likes with his spade, he soils his clothes with dust, nobody takes him to task if he gets baked in the sun or gets wet.

I wish I were a gardener digging away at the garden with nobody to stop me from digging.

Just as it gets dark in the evening and my mother sends me to bed,

I can see through my open window the watchman walking up and down.

The lane is dark and lonely, and the street-lamps stand like a giant with one red eye in its head.

The watchman swings his lantern and walks with his shadow at his side, and never once goes to bed in his life.

I wish I were a watchman walking the streets all night, chasing the shadows with my lantern.

BENEDICTION

BLESS this little heart, this white soul that has won the kiss of heaven for our earth.

He loves the light of the sun, he loves the sight of his mother's face.

He has not learned to despise the dust, and to hanker after gold.

Clasp him to your heart and bless him.

He has come into this land of an hundred crossroads.

I know not how he chose you from the crowd, came to your door, and grasped your hand to ask his way.

He will follow you, laughing and talking, and not a doubt in his heart.

Keep his trust, lead him straight and bless him.

Lay your hand on his head, and pray that though the waves underneath grow threatening, yet the breath from above may come and fill his sails and waft him to the heaven of peace.

Forget him not in your hurry, let him come to your heart and bless him.

THE CHILD-ANGEL

They clamor and fight, they doubt and despair, they know no end to their wranglings.

Let your life come amongst them like a flame of light, my child, unflickering and pure, and delight them into silence.

They are cruel in their greed and their envy, their words are like hidden knives thirsting for blood.

Go and stand amidst their scowling hearts, my child, and let your gentle eyes fall upon them like the forgiving peace of the evening over the strife of the day.

Let them see your face, my child, and thus know the meaning of all things; let them love you and thus love each other.

Come and take your seat in the bosom of the limitless, my child. At sunrise open and raise your heart like a blossoming flower, and at sunset bend your head and in silence complete the worship of the day.

FROM *The Gardener*

I AM restless. I am athirst for far-away things.
    My soul goes out in a longing to touch the skirt of the dim distance.
    O Great Beyond, O the keen call of thy flute!
    I forget, I ever forget, that I have no wings to fly, that I am bound in this spot evermore.

    I am eager and wakeful, I am a stranger in a strange land.
    Thy breath comes to me whispering an impossible hope.
    Thy tongue is known to my heart as its very own.
    O Far-to-seek, O the keen call of thy flute!
    I forget, I ever forget, that I know not the way, that I have not the winged horse.

    I am listless, I am a wanderer in my heart.
    In the sunny haze of the languid hours, what vast vision of thine takes shape in the blue of the sky!
    O Farthest End, O the keen call of thy flute!
    I forget, I ever forget, that the gates are shut everywhere in the house where I dwell alone!

THE tame bird was in a cage, the free bird was in the forest.
    They met when the time came, it was a decree of fate.
    The free bird cries, "O my love, let us fly to the wood."
    The cage bird whispers, "Come hither, let us both live in the cage."
    Says the free bird, "Among bars, where is there room to spread one's wings?"
    "Alas," cries the cage bird, "I should not know where to sit perched in the sky."

    The free bird cries, "My darling, sing the songs of the woodlands."
    The cage bird says, "Sit by my side, I'll teach you the speech of the learned."

The forest bird cries, "No, ah no! songs can never be taught."
The cage bird says, "Alas for me, I know not the songs of the woodlands."

Their love is intense with longing, but they never can fly wing to wing.
Through the bars of the cage they look, and vain is their wish to know each other.
They flutter their wings in yearning, and sing, "Come closer, my love!"
The free bird cries, "It cannot be, I fear the closed doors of the cage."
The cage bird whispers, "Alas, my wings are powerless and dead."

"Trust love even if it brings sorrow. Do not close up your heart."
"Ah, no, my friend, your words are dark, I cannot understand them."

"The heart is only for giving away with a tear and a song, my love."
"Ah, no, my friend, your words are dark, I cannot understand them."

"Pleasure is frail like a dewdrop, while it laughs it dies. But sorrow is strong and abiding. Let sorrowful love wake in your eyes."
"Ah, no, my friend, your words are dark, I cannot understand them."

"The lotus blooms in the sight of the sun, and loses all that it has. It would not remain in bud in the eternal winter mist."
"Ah, no, my friend, your words are dark, I cannot understand them."

Peace, my heart, let the time for the parting be sweet,
    Let it not be a death but completeness.

Let love melt into a memory and pain into songs.

Let the flight through the sky end in the folding of the wings over the nest.

Let the last touch of your hands be gentle like the flower of the night.

Stand still, O Beautiful End, for a moment, and say your last words in silence.

I bow to you and hold up my lamp to light you on your way.

At midnight the would-be ascetic announced:

"This is the time to give up my home and seek for God. Ah, who has held me so long in delusion here?"

God whispered, "I," but the ears of the man were stopped.

With a baby asleep at her breast lay his wife, peacefully sleeping on one side of the bed.

The man said, "Who are ye that have fooled me so long?"

The voice said again, "They are God," but he heard it not.

The baby cried out in its dream, nestling close to its mother.

God commanded, "Stop, fool, leave not thy home," but still he heard not.

God sighed and complained, "Why does my servant wander to seek me, forsaking me?"

She dwelt on the hillside by the edge of a maize-field, near the spring that flows in laughing rills through the solemn shadows of ancient trees. The women came there to fill their jars, and travelers would sit there to rest and talk. She worked and dreamed daily to the tune of the bubbling stream.

One evening the stranger came down from the cloud-hidden peak; his locks were tangled like drowsy snakes. We asked in wonder, "Who are you?" He answered not but sat by the garrulous stream and silently gazed at the hut where she dwelt. Our hearts quaked in fear and we came back home when it was night.

Next morning when the women came to fetch water at the spring by the deodar trees, they found the doors open in her hut, but her voice was gone and where was her smiling face? The empty jar lay on the floor and her lamp had burnt itself out in the corner. No one knew where she had fled to before it was morning—and the stranger had gone.

In the month of May the sun grew strong and the snow melted, and we sat by the spring and wept. We wondered in our mind, "Is there a spring in the land where she has gone and where she can fill her vessel in these hot thirsty days?" And we asked each other in dismay, "Is there a land beyond these hills where we live?"

It was a summer night; the breeze blew from the south; and I sat in her deserted room where the lamp stood still unlit. When suddenly from before my eyes the hills vanished like curtains drawn aside. "Ah, it is she who comes. How are you, my child? Are you happy? But where can you shelter under this open sky? And, alas! our spring is not here to allay your thirst."

"Here is the same sky," she said, "only free from the fencing hills, —this is the same stream grown into a river,—the same earth widened into a plain." "Everything is here," I sighed, "only we are not." She smiled sadly and said, "You are in my heart." I woke up and heard the babbling of the stream and the rustling of the deodars at night.

FROM *Fruit-Gathering*

WHERE roads are made I lose my way,
   In the wide water, in the blue sky there is no line of a track.
   The pathway is hidden by the birds' wings, by the star-fires, by the flowers of the wayfaring seasons.
   And I ask my heart if its blood carries the wisdom of the unseen way.

No: it is not yours to open buds into blossoms.

Shake the bud, strike it; it is beyond your power to make it blossom.

Your touch soils it, you tear its petals to pieces and strew them in the dust.

But no colors appear, and no perfume.

Ah! it is not for you to open the bud into a blossom.

He who can open the bud does it so simply.

He gives it a glance, and the life-sap stirs through its veins.

At his breath the flower spreads its wings and flutters in the wind.

Colors flush out like heart-longings, the perfume betrays a sweet secret.

He who can open the bud does it so simply.

SUDĀS, the gardener, plucked from his tank the last lotus left by the ravage of winter and went to sell it to the King at the palace gate.

There he met a traveler who said to him, "Ask your price for the last lotus,—I shall offer it to Lord Buddha."

Sudās said, "If you pay one golden *māshā* it will be yours."

The traveler paid it.

At that moment the King came out and he wished to buy the flower, for he was on his way to see Lord Buddha, and he thought, "It would be a fine thing to lay at his feet the lotus that bloomed in winter."

When the gardener said he had been offered a golden *māshā* the King offered him ten, but the traveler doubled the price.

The gardener, being greedy, imagined a greater gain from him for whose sake they were bidding. He bowed and said, "I cannot sell this lotus."

In the hushed shade of the mango grove beyond the city wall Sudās stood before Lord Buddha, on whose lips sat the silence of love and whose eyes beamed peace like the morning star of the dew-washed autumn.

317

Sudās looked in his face and put the lotus at his feet and bowed his head to the dust.

Buddha smiled and asked, "What is your wish, my son?"

Sudās cried, "The least touch of your feet."

※

Sanātan was telling his beads by the Ganges when a Brahmin in rags came to him and said, "Help me, I am poor!"

"My alms-bowl is all that is my own," said Sanātan. "I have given away everything I had."

"But my lord Shiva came to me in my dreams," said the Brahmin, "and counseled me to come to you."

Sanātan suddenly remembered he had picked up a stone without price among the pebbles on the riverbank, and thinking that some one might need it hid it in the sands.

He pointed out the spot to the Brahmin, who wondering dug up the stone.

The Brahmin sat on the earth and mused alone till the sun went down behind the trees, and cowherds went home with their cattle.

Then he rose and came slowly to Sanātan and said,

"Master, give me the least fraction of the wealth that disdains all the wealth of the world."

And he threw the precious stone into the water.

※

"Who among you will take up the duty of feeding the hungry?" Lord Buddha asked his followers when famine raged at Shravasti.

Ratnākar, the banker, hung his head and said, "Much more is needed than all my wealth to feed the hungry."

Jaysen, the chief of the King's army, said, "I would gladly give my life's blood, but there is not enough food in my house."

Dharmapāl, who owned broad acres of land, said with a sigh, "The drought demon has sucked my fields dry. I know not how to pay King's dues."

Then rose Supriyā, the mendicant's daughter.
She bowed to all and meekly said, "I will feed the hungry."
"How!" they cried in surprise. "How can you hope to fulfill that vow."

"I am the poorest of you all," said Supriyā, "that is my strength. I have my coffer and my store at each of your houses."

"Sire," announced the servant to the King, "the saint Narottam has never deigned to enter your royal temple.

"He is singing God's praise under the trees by the open road. The temple is empty of worshipers.

"They flock round him like bees round the white lotus, leaving the golden jar of honey unheeded."

The King, vexed at heart, went to the spot where Narottam sat on the grass.
He asked him, "Father, why leave my temple of the golden dome and sit on the dust outside to preach God's love?"
"Because God is not there in your temple," said Narottam.
The King frowned and said, "Do you know, twenty millions of gold went to the making of that marvel of art, and it was consecrated to God with costly rites?"

"Yes, I know it," answered Narottam. "It was in that year when thousands of your people whose houses had been burned stood vainly asking for help at your door.

"And God said, 'The poor creature who can give no shelter to his· brothers would build my house!'

"And he took his place with the shelterless under the trees by the road.

319

"And that golden bubble is empty of all but hot vapor of pride."
The King cried in anger, "Leave my land."
Calmly said the saint, "Yes, banish me where you have banished my God."

WHEN, mad in their mirth, they raised dust to soil thy robe, O Beautiful, it made my heart sick.

I cried to thee and said, "Take thy rod of punishment and judge them."

The morning light struck upon those eyes, red with the revel of night; the peace of the white lily greeted their burning breath; the stars through the depth of the sacred dark stared at their carousing —at those that raised dust to soil thy robe, O Beautiful!

Thy judgment seat was in the flower-garden, in the birds' notes in springtime: in the shady river-banks, where the trees muttered in answer to the muttering of the waves.

O my Lover, they were pitiless in their passion.

They prowled in the dark to snatch thy ornaments to deck their own desires.

When they had struck thee and thou wert pained, it pierced me to the quick, and I cried to thee and said, "Take thy sword, O my Lover, and judge them!"

Ah, but thy justice was vigilant.

A mother's tears were shed on their insolence; the imperishable faith of a lover hid their spears of rebellion in its own wounds.

Thy judgment was in the mute pain of sleepless love; in the blush of the chaste; in the tears of the night of the desolate; in the pale morning light of forgiveness.

O Terrible, they in their reckless greed climbed thy gate at night, breaking into thy storehouse to rob thee.

But the weight of their plunder grew immense, too heavy to carry or to remove.

Thereupon I cried to thee and said, "Forgive them, O Terrible!"

Thy forgiveness burst in storms, throwing them down, scattering their thefts in the dust.

Thy forgiveness was in the thunderstone; in the shower of blood; in the angry red of the sunset.

❦

BRING beauty and order into my forlorn life, woman, as you brought them into my house when you lived.

Sweep away the dusty fragments of the hours, fill the empty jars, and mend all that has been neglected.

Then open the inner door of the shrine, light the candle, and let us meet there in silence before our God.

THANKSGIVING

THOSE who walk on the path of pride crushing the lowly life under their tread, covering the tender green of the earth with their footprints in blood;

Let them rejoice, and thank thee, Lord, for the day is theirs.

But I am thankful that my lot lies with the humble who suffer and bear the burden of power, and hide their faces and stifle their sobs in the dark.

For every throb of their pain has pulsed in the secret depth of thy night, and every insult has been gathered into thy great silence.

And the morrow is theirs.

O Sun, rise upon the bleeding hearts blossoming in flowers of the morning, and the torchlight revelry of pride shrunken to ashes.

FROM *Lover's Gift*

COME to my garden walk, my love. Pass by the fervid flowers that press themselves on your sight. Pass them by, stopping at some chance joy, which like a sudden wonder of sunset illumines, yet eludes.

For love's gift is shy, it never tells its name, it flits across the shade, spreading a shiver of joy along the dust. Overtake it or miss it for ever. But a gift that can be grasped is merely a frail flower, or a lamp with a flame that will flicker.

※

SHE dwelt here by the pool with its landing-stairs in ruins. Many an evening she had watched the moon made dizzy by the shaking of bamboo leaves, and on many a rainy day the smell of the wet earth had come to her over the young shoots of rice.

Her pet name is known here among those date-palm groves and in the courtyards where girls sit and talk while stitching their winter quilts. The water in this pool keeps in its depth the memory of her swimming limbs, and her wet feet had left their marks, day after day, on the footpath leading to the village.

The women who come today with their vessels to the water have all seen her smile over simple jests, and the old peasant, taking his bullocks to their bath, used to stop at her door every day to greet her.

Many a sailing-boat passes by this village; many a traveler takes rest beneath that banyan tree; the ferryboat crosses to yonder ford carrying cows to the market; but they never notice this spot by the village road, near the pool with its ruined landing-stairs,—where dwelt she whom I love.

※

THERE is a looker-on who sits behind my eyes. It seems he has seen things in ages and worlds beyond memory's shore, and those forgotten sights glisten on the grass and shiver on the leaves. He has seen under new veils the face of the one beloved, in twilight hours of many a

nameless star. Therefore his sky seems to ache with the pain of countless meetings and partings, and a longing pervades this spring breeze,
—the longing that is full of the whisper of ages without beginning.

I TRAVELED the old road every day, I took my fruits to the market,
my cattle to the meadows, I ferried my boat across the stream and all
the ways were well known to me.

One morning my basket was heavy with wares. Men were busy
in the fields, the pastures crowded with cattle; the breast of earth
heaved with the mirth of ripening rice.

Suddenly there was a tremor in the air, and the sky seemed to kiss
me on my forehead. My mind started up like the morning out of mist.

I forgot to follow the track. I stepped a few paces from the path,
and my familiar world appeared strange to me, like a flower I had
only known in bud.

My everyday wisdom was ashamed. I went astray in the fairyland
of things. It was the best luck of my life that I lost my path that
morning, and found my eternal childhood.

THE evening was lonely for me, and I was reading a book till my heart
became dry, and it seemed to me that beauty was a thing fashioned
by the traders in words. Tired I shut the book and snuffed the candle.
In a moment the room was flooded with moonlight.

Spirit of Beauty, how could you, whose radiance overbrims the sky,
stand hidden behind a candle's tiny flame? How could a few vain
words from a book rise like a mist, and veil her whose voice has
hushed the heart of earth into ineffable calm?

FROM *Crossing*

ACCEPT me, my lord, accept me for this while.

Let those orphaned days that passed without thee be forgotten.

Only spread this little moment wide across thy lap, holding it under thy light.

I have wandered in pursuit of voices that drew me yet led me nowhere.

Now let me sit in peace and listen to thy words in the soul of my silence.

Do not turn away thy face from my heart's dark secrets, but burn them till they are alight with thy fire.

WHEN thou savest me the steps are lighter in the march of thy worlds.

When stains are washed away from my heart it brightens the light of thy sun.

That the bud has not blossomed in beauty in my life spreads sadness in the heart of creation.

When the shroud of darkness will be lifted from my soul it will bring music to thy smile.

I KNOW that this life, missing its ripeness in love, is not altogether lost.

I know that the flowers that fade in the dawn, the streams that strayed in the desert, are not altogether lost.

I know that whatever lags behind in this life laden with slowness is not altogether lost.

I know that my dreams that are still unfulfilled, and my melodies still unstruck, are clinging to some lute-strings of thine, and they are not altogether lost.

When I awake in thy love my night of ease will be ended.

Thy sunrise will touch my heart with its touchstone of fire, and my voyage will begin in its orbit of triumphant suffering.

I shall dare to take up death's challenge and carry thy voice in the heart of mockery and menace.

I shall bare my breast against the wrongs hurled at thy children, and take the risk of standing by thy side where none but thee remains.

No guest had come to my house for long, my doors were locked, my windows barred; I thought my night would be lonely.

When I opened my eyes I found the darkness had vanished.

I rose up and ran and saw the bolts of my gates all broken, and through the open door your wind and light waved their banner.

When I was a prisoner in my own house, and the doors were shut, my heart ever planned to escape and to wander.

Now at my broken gate I sit still and wait for your coming.

You keep me bound by my freedom.

I lived on the shady side of the road and watched my neighbors' gardens across the way reveling in the sunshine.

I felt I was poor, and from door to door went with my hunger.

The more they gave me from their careless abundance the more I became aware of my beggar's bowl.

Till one morning I awoke from my sleep at the sudden opening of my door, and you came and asked for alms.

In despair I broke the lid of my chest open and was startled into finding my own wealth.

You hide yourself in your own glory, my King.

The sand-grain and the dew-drop are more proudly apparent than yourself.

The world unabashed calls all things its own that are yours—yet it is never brought to shame.

You make room for us while standing aside in silence; therefore love lights her own lamp to seek you and comes to your worship unbidden.

I REMEMBER my childhood when the sunrise, like my playfellow, would burst in to my bedside with its daily surprise of morning; when the faith in the marvelous bloomed like fresh flowers in my heart every day, looking into the face of the world in simple gladness; when insects, birds and beasts, the common weeds, grass and the clouds had their fullest value of wonder; when the patter of rain at night brought dreams from the fairyland, and mother's voice in the evening gave meaning to the stars.

And then I think of death, and the rise of the curtain and the new morning and my life awakened in its fresh surprise of love.

COMRADE of the road,
Here are my traveler's greetings to thee.
O Lord of my broken heart, of leave-taking and loss, of the gray silence of the dayfall,
My greetings of the ruined house to thee!
O Light of the new-born morning,
Sun of the everlasting day,
My greetings of the undying hope to thee!
My guide,
I am a wayfarer of an endless road,
My greetings of a wanderer to thee!

FROM *Stray Birds*

THE mighty desert is burning for the love of a blade of grass who shakes her head and laughs and flies away.

SORROW is hushed into peace in my heart like the evening among the silent trees.

I SIT at my window this morning where the world like a passer-by stops for a moment, nods to me and goes.

THAT I exist is a perpetual surprise which is life.

O BEAUTY, find thyself in love, not in the flattery of thy mirror.

THE trees come up to my window like the yearning voice of the dumb earth.

HIS own mornings are new surprises to God.

WOMAN, when you move about in your household service your limbs sing like a hill stream among its pebbles.

THE fish in the water is silent, the animal on the earth is noisy, the bird in the air is singing.
   But Man has in him the silence of the sea, the noise of the earth and the music of the air.

YOUR idol is shattered in the dust to prove that God's dust is greater than your idol.

WE come nearest to the great when we are great in humility.

NEVER be afraid of the moments—thus sings the voice of the everlasting.

CHASTITY is a wealth that comes from abundance of love.

EVERY child comes with the message that God is not yet discouraged of man.

BE still, my heart, these great trees are prayers.

IF you shut your door to all errors truth will be shut out.

THIS rainy evening the wind is restless.
 I look at the swaying branches and ponder over the greatness of all things.

WHEN I traveled to here and to there, I was tired of thee, O Road, but now when thou leadest me to everywhere I am wedded to thee in love.

BY plucking her petals you do not gather the beauty of the flower.

THEY hated and killed and men praised them.
 But God in shame hastens to hide its memory under the green grass.

MEN are cruel, but Man is kind.

THE false can never grow into truth by growing in power.

WHEN I stand before thee at the day's end thou shalt see my scars and know that I had my wounds and also my healing.

SOME day I shall sing to thee in the sunrise of some other world, "I have seen thee before in the light of the earth, in the love of man."

THOU wilt find, Eternal Traveler, marks of thy footsteps across my songs.

WHEN all the strings of my life will be tuned, my Master, then at every touch of thine will come out the music of love.

MAN's history is waiting in patience for the triumph of the insulted man.

LET this be my last word, that I trust in thy love.

FROM *The Fugitive, and Other Poems*

"WHY these preparations without end?"—I said to Mind—"Is some one to come?"

Mind replied, "I am enormously busy gathering things and building towers. I have no time to answer such questions."

Meekly I went back to my work.

When things were grown to a pile, when seven wings of his palace were complete, I said to Mind, "Is it not enough?"

Mind began to say, "Not enough to contain—" and then stopped.

"Contain what?" I asked.

Mind affected not to hear.

I suspected that Mind did not know, and with ceaseless work smothered the question.

His one refrain was, "I must have more."

"Why must you?"

"Because it is great."

"What is great?"

Mind remained silent. I pressed for an answer.

In contempt and anger, Mind said, "Why ask about things that are not? Take notice of those that are hugely before you—the struggle and the fight, the army and armaments, the bricks and mortar, and laborers without number."

I thought, "Possibly Mind is wise."

I REMEMBER the day.

The heavy shower of rain is slackening into fitful pauses, renewed gusts of wind startle it from a first lull.

I take up my instrument. Idly I touch the strings, till, without my knowing, the music borrows the mad cadence of that storm.

I see her figure as she steals from her work, stops at my door, and retreats with hesitating steps. She comes again, stands outside leaning against the wall, then slowly enters the room and sits down. With head bent, she plies her needle in silence; but soon stops her work, and looks out of the window through the rain at the blurred line of trees.

Only this—one hour of a rainy noon filled with shadows and song and silence.

WHILE stepping into the carriage she turned her head and threw me a swift glance of farewell.

This was her last gift to me. But where can I keep it safe from the trampling hours?

Must evening sweep this gleam of anguish away, as it will the last flicker of fire from the sunset?

Ought it to be washed off by the rain, as treasured pollen is from heartbroken flowers?

Leave kingly glory and the wealth of the rich to death. But may not tears keep ever fresh the memory of a glance flung through a passionate moment?

"Give it to me to keep," said my song; "I never touch kings' glory or the wealth of the rich, but these small things are mine for ever."

WHEN we two first met my heart rang out in music, "She who is eternally afar is beside you for ever."

That music is silent, because I have grown to believe that my love is only near, and have forgotten that she is also far, far away.

Music fills the infinite between two souls. This has been muffled by the mist of our daily habits.

On shy summer nights, when the breeze brings a vast murmur out of the silence, I sit up in my bed and mourn the great loss of her who is beside me. I ask myself, "When shall I have another chance to whisper to her words with the rhythm of eternity in them?"

Wake up, my song, from thy languor, rend this screen of the familiar, and fly to my beloved there, in the endless surprise of our first meeting!

SHE went away when the night was about to wane.

My mind tried to console me by saying, "All is vanity."

I felt angry and said, "That unopened letter with her name on it, and this palm-leaf fan bordered with red silk by her own hands, are they not real?"

The day passed, and my friend came and said to me, "Whatever is good is true, and can never perish."

"How do you know?" I asked impatiently; "was not this body good which is now lost to the world?"

As a fretful child hurting its own mother, I tried to wreck all the shelters that ever I had, in and about me, and cried, "This world is treacherous."

Suddenly I felt a voice saying—"Ungrateful!"

I looked out of the window, and a reproach seemed to come from the star-sprinkled night,—"You pour out into the void of my absence your faith in the truth that I came!"

THE name she called me by, like a flourishing jasmine, covered the whole seventeen years of our love. With its sound mingled the quiver of the light through the leaves, the scent of the grass in the rainy night, and the sad silence of the last hour of many an idle day.

Not the work of God alone was he who answered to that name; she created him again for herself during those seventeen swift years.

Other years were to follow, but their vagrant days, no longer gathered within the fold of that name uttered in her voice, stray and are scattered.

They ask me, "Who should fold us?"

I find no answer and sit silent, and they cry to me while dispersing, "We seek a shepherdess!"

Whom should they seek?

That they do not know. And like derelict evening clouds they drift in the trackless dark, and are lost and forgotten.

I WAS walking along a path overgrown with grass, when suddenly I heard from some one behind, "See if you know me?"

I turned round and looked at her and said, "I cannot remember your name."

She said, "I am that first great Sorrow whom you met when you were young."

Her eyes looked like a morning whose dew is still in the air.

I stood silent for some time till I said, "Have you lost all the great burden of your tears?"

She smiled and said nothing. I felt that her tears had had time to learn the language of smiles.

"Once you said," she whispered, "that you would cherish your grief for ever."

I blushed and said, "Yes, but years have passed and I forget."

Then I took her hand in mine and said, "But you have changed."

"What was sorrow once has now become peace," she said.

THE General came before the silent and angry King and saluting him said: "The village is punished, the men are stricken to dust, and the women cower in their unlit homes afraid to weep aloud."

The High Priest stood up and blessed the King and cried: "God's mercy is ever upon you."

332

The Clown, when he heard this, burst out laughing and startled the Court. The King's frown darkened.

"The honor of the throne," said the Minister, "is upheld by the King's prowess and the blessing of Almighty God."

Louder laughed the Clown, and the King growled—"Unseemly mirth!"

"God has showered many blessings upon your head," said the Clown; "the one he bestowed upon me was the gift of laughter."

"This gift will cost you your life," said the King, gripping his sword with his right hand.

Yet the Clown stood up and laughed till he laughed no more.

A shadow of dread fell upon the Court, for they heard that laughter echoing in the depth of God's silence.

I HAVE looked on this picture in many a month of March when the mustard is in bloom—this lazy line of water and the gray of the sand beyond, the rough path along the river-bank carrying the comradeship of the field into the heart of the village.

I have tried to capture in rhyme the idle whistle of the wind, the beat of the oar-strokes from a passing boat.

I have wondered in my mind how simply it stands before me, this great world: with what fond and familiar ease it fills my heart, this encounter with the Eternal Stranger.

How often, great Earth, have I felt my being yearn to flow over you, sharing in the happiness of each green blade that raises its signal banner in answer to the beckoning blue of the sky!

I feel as if I had belonged to you ages before I was born. That is why, in the days when the autumn light shimmers on the mellowing ears of rice, I seem to remember a past when my mind was everywhere, and even to hear voices as of playfellows echoing from the remote and deeply veiled past.

When, in the evening, the cattle return to their folds, raising dust from the meadow paths, as the moon rises higher than the smoke ascending from the village huts, I feel sad as for some great separation that happened in the first morning of existence.

THE kingfisher sits still on the prow of an empty boat, while in the shallow margin of the stream a buffalo lies tranquilly blissful, its eyes half closed to savor the luxury of cool mud.

Undismayed by the barking of the village cur, the cow browses on the bank, followed by a hopping group of *saliks* hunting moths.

I sit in the tamarind grove, where the cries of dumb life congregate —the cattle's lowing, the sparrows' chatter, the shrill scream of a kite overhead, the crickets' chirp, and the splash of a fish in the water.

I peep into the primeval nursery of life, where the mother Earth thrills at the first living clutch near her breast.

IN the evening my little daughter heard a call from her companions below the window.

She timidly went down the dark stairs holding a lamp in her hand, shielding it behind her veil.

I was sitting on my terrace in the starlit night of March, when at a sudden cry I ran to see.

Her lamp had gone out in the dark spiral staircase. I asked, "Child, why did you cry?"

From below she answered in distress, "Father, I have lost myself!"

When I came back to the terrace under the starlit night of March, I looked at the sky, and it seemed that a child was walking there treasuring many lamps behind her veils.

If their light went out, she would suddenly stop and a cry would sound from sky to sky, "Father, I have lost myself!"

THE day came for the image from the temple to be drawn round the holy town in its chariot.

The Queen said to the King, "Let us go and attend the festival."

Only one man out of the whole household did not join in the pilgrimage. His work was to collect stalks of spear-grass to make brooms for the King's house.

The chief of the servants said in pity to him, "You may come with us."

He bowed his head, saying, "It cannot be."

The man dwelt by the road along which the King's followers had to pass. And when the Minister's elephant reached this spot, he called to him and said, "Come with us and see the God ride in his chariot!"

"I dare not seek God after the King's fashion," said the man.

"How should you ever have such luck again as to see the God in his chariot?" asked the Minister.

"When God himself comes to my door," answered the man.

The Minister laughed loud and said, "Fool! 'When God comes to your door!' yet a King must travel to see him!"

"Who except God visits the poor?" said the man.

OUR Lane is tortuous, as if, ages ago, she started in quest of her goal, vacillated right and left, and remained bewildered for ever.

Above in the air, between her buildings, hangs like a ribbon a strip torn out of space: she calls it her sister of the blue town.

She sees the sun only for a few moments at midday, and asks herself in wise doubt, "Is it real?"

In June rain sometimes shades her band of daylight as with pencil hatchings. The path grows slippery with mud, and umbrellas collide. Sudden jets of water from spouts overhead splash on her startled pavement. In her dismay, she takes it for the jest of an unmannerly scheme of creation.

The spring breeze, gone astray in her coil of contortions, stumbles like a drunken vagabond against angle and corner, filling the dusty air with scraps of paper and rag. "What fury of foolishness! Are the Gods gone mad?" she exclaims in indignation.

But the daily refuse from the houses on both sides—scales of fish mixed with ashes, vegetable peelings, rotten fruit, and dead rats— never rouses her to question, "Why should these things be?"

She accepts every stone of her paving. But from between their chinks sometimes a blade of grass peeps up. That baffles her. How can solid facts permit such intrusion?

On a morning when at the touch of autumn light her houses wake up into beauty from their foul dreams, she whispers to herself, "There is a limitless wonder somewhere beyond these buildings."

But the hours pass on; the households are astir; the maid strolls back from the market, swinging her right arm and with the left clasping the basket of provisions to her side; the air grows thick with the smell and smoke of kitchens. It again becomes clear to our Lane that the real and normal consist solely of herself, her houses, and their muck-heaps.

THE man had no useful work, only vagaries of various kinds.

Therefore it surprised him to find himself in Paradise after a life spent perfecting trifles.

Now the guide had taken him by mistake to the wrong Paradise— one meant only for good, busy souls.

In this Paradise, our man saunters along the road only to obstruct the rush of business.

He stands aside from the path and is warned that he tramples on sown seed. Pushed, he starts up: hustled, he moves on.

A very busy girl comes to fetch water from the well. Her feet run on the pavement like rapid fingers over harp-strings. Hastily she ties a negligent knot with her hair, and loose locks on her forehead pry into the dark of her eyes.

The man says to her, "Would you lend me your pitcher?"

"My pitcher?" she asks, "to draw water?"

"No, to paint patterns on."

"I have no time to waste," the girl retorts in contempt.

Now a busy soul has no chance against one who is supremely idle.

Every day she meets him at the well, and every day he repeats the same request, till at last she yields.

Our man paints the pitcher with curious colors in a mysterious maze of lines.

The girl takes it up, turns it round and asks, "What does it mean?"

"It has no meaning," he answers.

The girl carries the pitcher home. She holds it up in different lights and tries to con its mystery.

At night she leaves her bed, lights a lamp, and gazes at it from all points of view.

This is the first time she has met with something without meaning.

On the next day the man is again near the well.

The girl asks, "What do you want?"

"To do more work for you!"

"What work?" she enquires.

"Allow me to weave colored strands into a ribbon to bind your hair."

"Is there any need?" she asks.

"None whatever," he allows.

The ribbon is made, and thenceforward she spends a great deal of time over her hair.

The even stretch of well-employed time in that Paradise begins to show irregular rents.

The elders are troubled; they meet in council.

The guide confesses his blunder, saying that he has brought the wrong man to the wrong place.

The wrong man is called. His turban, flaming with color, shows plainly how great that blunder has been.

The chief of the elders says, "You must go back to the earth."

The man heaves a sigh of relief: "I am ready."

The girl with the ribbon round her hair chimes in: "I also!"

For the first time the chief of the elders is faced with a situation which has no sense in it.

GIVE me the supreme courage of love, this is my prayer—the courage to speak, to do, to suffer at thy will, to leave all things or be left alone. Strengthen me on errands of danger, honor me with pain, and help me climb to that difficult mood which sacrifices daily to thee.

Give me the supreme confidence of love, this is my prayer—the confidence that belongs to life in death, to victory in defeat, to the power hidden in frailest beauty, to that dignity in pain which accepts hurt but disdains to return it.

FROM His eternal seat Christ comes down to this earth, where, ages ago, in the bitter cup of death He poured his deathless life for those who came to the call and those who remained away.

He looks about Him, and sees the weapons of evil that wounded His own age.

The arrogant spikes and spears, the slim, sly knives, the scimitar in diplomatic sheath, crooked and cruel, are hissing and raining sparks as they are sharpened on monster wheels.

But the most fearful of them all, at the hands of the slaughterers, are those on which has been engraved His own name, that are fashioned from the texts of His own words fused in the fire of hatred and hammered by hypocritical greed.

He presses His hand upon His heart; He feels that the age-long moment of His death has not yet ended, that new nails, turned out in countless numbers by those who are learned in cunning craftsmanship, pierce Him in every joint.

They had hurt Him once, standing at the shadow of their temple; they are born anew in crowds.

From before their sacred altar they shout to the soldiers, "Strike!"

And the Son of Man in agony cries, "My God, My God, why hast Thou forsaken me?"

RAIDAS, the sweeper, sat still, lost in the solitude of his soul, and some songs born of his silent vision found their way to the Rani's heart,—the Rani Jhali of Chitore.

Tears flowed from her eyes, her thoughts wandered away from her daily duties, till she met Raidas who guided her to God's presence.

The old Brahmin priest of the King's house rebuked her for her desecration of sacred law by offering homage as a disciple to an outcaste.

"Brahmin," the Rani answered, "while you were busy tying your purse-strings of custom ever tighter, love's gold slipped unnoticed to the earth, and my Master in his divine humility has picked it up from the dust.

"Revel in your pride of the unmeaning knots without number, harden your miserly heart, but I, a beggar woman, am glad to receive love's wealth, the gift of the lowly dust, from my Master, the sweeper."

 Fireflies

I touch God in my song
    as the hill touches the far-away sea
      with its waterfall.

The butterfly counts not months but moments,
    and has time enough.

Let my love, like sunlight, surround you
    and yet give you illumined freedom.

Love remains a secret even when spoken,
    for only a lover truly knows that he is loved.

Emancipation from the bondage of the soil
    is no freedom for the tree.

In love I pay my endless debt to thee
    for what thou art.

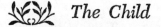 *The Child*

"What of the night?" they ask.
No answer comes.
For the blind Time gropes in a maze and knows not its path or
    purpose.
The darkness in the valley stares like the dead eye-sockets of a giant,
    the clouds like a nightmare oppress the sky,
        and the massive shadows lie scattered like the torn limbs of the
            night.
A lurid glow waxes and wanes on the horizon—
is it an ultimate threat from an alien star,
    or an elemental hunger licking the sky?
Things are deliriously wild,
they are a noise whose grammar is a groan,
    and words smothered out of shape and sense.
They are the refuse, the rejections, the fruitless failures of life,
abrupt ruins of prodigal pride—
fragments of a bridge over the oblivion of a vanished stream,
godless shrines that shelter reptiles,
    marble steps that lead to blankness.
Sudden tumults rise in the sky and wrestle
    and a startled shudder runs along the sleepless hours.

Are they from desperate floods
   hammering against their cave walls,
or from some fanatic storms
   whirling and howling incantations?
Are they the cry of an ancient forest
   flinging up its hoarded fire in a last extravagant suicide,
or screams of a paralytic crowd scourged by lunatics
   blind and deaf?
Underneath the noisy terror a stealthy hum creeps up
   like bubbling volcanic mud,
     a mixture of sinister whispers, rumors and slanders, and hisses of
       derision.
The men gathered there are vague like torn pages of an epic.
Groping in groups or single, the torchlight tattoos
   their faces in chequered lines, in patterns of frightfulness.
The maniacs suddenly strike their neighbors on suspicion
and a hubbub of an indiscriminate fight bursts forth,
   echoing from hill to hill.
The women weep and wail,
   they cry that their children are lost in a wilderness
     of contrary paths with confusion at the end.
Others defiantly ribald shake with raucous laughter
   their lascivious limbs unshrinkingly loud,
   for they think that nothing matters.

There on the crest of the hill
   stands the Man of faith amid the snow-white silence,
   He scans the sky for some signal of light,
   and when the clouds thicken and the nightbirds scream as they fly,
   he cries, "Brothers, despair not, for Man is great."
But they never heed him,
   for they believe that the elemental brute is eternal
   and goodness in its depth is darkly cunning in deception.
When beaten and wounded they cry, "Brother, where art thou?"
   The answer comes, "I am by your side."—
But they cannot see in the dark
   and they argue that the voice is of their own desperate desire,

that men are ever condemned to fight for phantoms
  in an interminable desert of mutual menace.

The clouds part, the morning star appears in the East,
  a breath of relief springs up from the heart of the earth,
  the murmur of leaves ripples along the forest path, and the early
      bird sings.
"The time has come," proclaims the Man of faith.
"The time for what?"
"For the pilgrimage."
They sit and think, they know not the meaning,
  and yet they seem to understand according to their desires.
The touch of the dawn goes deep into the soil
  and life shivers along through the roots of all things.
"To the pilgrimage of fulfillment," a small voice whispers, nobody
      knows whence.
Taken up by the crowd
  it swells into a mighty meaning.
Men raise their heads and look up,
  women lift their arms in reverence,
  children clap their hands and laugh.
The early glow of the sun shines like a golden garland on the forehead
      of the Man of faith,
and they all cry: "Brother, we salute thee!"

Men begin to gather from all quarters,
  from across the seas, the mountains and pathless wastes,
They come from the valley of the Nile and the banks
  of the Ganges,
  from the snow-sunk uplands of Tibet,
  from high-walled cities of glittering towers,
  from the dense dark tangle of savage wilderness.
Some walk, some ride on camels, horses and elephants,
  on chariots with banners vying with the clouds of dawn,
The priests of all creeds burn incense, chanting verses as they go.
The monarchs march at the head of their armies,
  lances flashing in the sun and drums beating loud.

Ragged beggars and courtiers pompously decorated,
   agile young scholars and teachers burdened with learned age jostle
      each other in the crowd.
Women come chatting and laughing,
mothers, maidens and brides,
   with offerings of flowers and fruit,
   sandal paste and scented water.
Mingled with them is the harlot,
   shrill of voice and loud in tint and tinsel.
The gossip is there who secretly poisons the well
   of human sympathy and clucks.
The maimed and the cripple join the throng with the blind and the
      sick,
   the dissolute, the thief and the man who makes a trade of his God
      for profit and mimics the saint.
"The fulfillment!"
   They dare not talk aloud,
but in their minds they magnify their own greed,
   and dream of boundless power,
   of unlimited impunity for pilfering and plunder,
   and eternity of feast for their gluttonous flesh.

The Man of faith moves on along pitiless paths strewn with flints over
      scorching sands and steep mountainous tracks.
They follow him, the strong and the weak, the aged and young,
   the rulers of realms, the tillers of the soil.
Some grow weary and footsore, some angry and suspicious.
They ask at every dragging step,
   "How much further is the end?"
The Man of faith sings in answer;
they scowl and shake their fists and yet they cannot resist him;
   the pressure of the moving mass and indefinite hope push them
      forward.
They shorten their sleep and curtail their rest,
   they out-vie each other in their speed,
they are ever afraid lest they may be too late for their chance
   while others be more fortunate.

343

The days pass,
the ever-receding horizon tempts them with renewed lure of the unseen till they are sick.
Their faces harden, their curses grow louder and louder.

It is night.
The travelers spread their mats on the ground under the banyan
tree.
A gust of wind blows out the lamp
and the darkness deepens like a sleep into a swoon.
Someone from the crowd suddenly stands up
and pointing to the leader with merciless finger breaks out:
"False prophet, thou has deceived us!"
Others take up the cry one by one,
women hiss their hatred and men growl.
At last one bolder than others suddenly deals him a blow.
They cannot see his face, but fall upon him in a fury of destruction
and hit him till he lies prone upon the ground, his life extinct.
The night is still, the sound of the distant waterfall comes muffled,
and a faint breath of jasmine floats in the air.

The pilgrims are afraid.
The women begin to cry, the men in an agony of wretchedness
shout at them to stop.
Dogs break out barking and are cruelly whipped into silence broken
by moans.
The night seems endless and men and women begin to wrangle as to
who among them was to blame.
They shriek and shout and as they are ready to unsheathe their knives
the darkness pales, the morning light overflows the mountain tops.
Suddenly they become still and gasp for breath as they gaze at the
figure lying dead.
The women sob out loud and men hide their faces in their hands.
A few try to slink away unnoticed,
but their crime keeps them chained to their victim.
They ask each other in bewilderment,
"Who will show us the path?"
The old man from the East bends his head and says:
"The Victim."

They sit still and silent.
  Again speaks the old man,
  "We refused him in doubt, we killed him in anger,
    now we shall accept him in love,
  for in his death he lives in the life of us all,
    the great Victim."
And they all stand up and mingle their voices and sing,
    "Victory to the Victim."

"To the pilgrimage" calls the young,
  "to love, to power, to knowledge, to wealth overflowing,"
"We shall conquer the world and the world beyond this,"
  they all cry exultant in a thundering cataract of voices,
The meaning is not the same to them all, but only the impulse,
  the moving confluence of wills that recks not death and disaster.
No longer they ask for their way,
  no more doubts are there to burden their minds
    or weariness to clog their feet.
The spirit of the leader is within them and ever
    beyond them—
the Leader who has crossed death and all limits.
They travel over the fields where the seeds are sown,
  by the granary where the harvest is gathered,
and across the barren soil where famine dwells
  and skeletons cry for the return of their flesh.
They pass through populous cities humming with life,
  through dumb desolation hugging its ruined past,
  and hovels for the unclad and unclean,
  a mockery of home for the homeless.
They travel through long hours of the summer day,
  and as the light wanes in the evening they ask the man who reads
    the sky:
"Brother, is yonder the tower of our final hope and peace?"
The wise man shakes his head and says:
  "It is the last vanishing cloud of the sunset."
"Friends," exhort the young, "do not stop.
  Through the night's blindness we must struggle into the Kingdom
    of living light."
They go on in the dark.

345

The road seems to know its own meaning
and dust underfoot dumbly speaks of direction.
The stars—celestial wayfarers—sing in silent chorus:
"Move on, comrades!"
In the air floats the voice of the Leader:
"The goal is nigh."

The first flush of dawn glistens on the dew-dripping leaves of the
forest.
The man who reads the sky cries:
"Friends, we have come!"
They stop and look around.
On both sides of the road the corn is ripe to the horizon,
—the glad golden answer of the earth to the morning light.
The current of daily life moves slowly
between the village near the hill and the one by the river bank.
The potter's wheel goes round, the woodcutter brings fuel to the
market,
the cowherd takes his cattle to the pasture,
and the woman with the pitcher on her head walks to the well.
But where is the King's castle, the mine of gold, the secret book of
magic,
the sage who knows love's utter wisdom?
"The stars cannot be wrong," assures the reader of the sky.
"Their signal points to that spot."
And reverently he walks to a wayside spring
from which wells up a stream of water, a liquid light,
like the morning melting into a chorus of tears and laughter.
Near it in a palm grove surrounded by a strange hush stands a leaf '
thatched hut,
at whose portal sits the poet of the unknown shore, and sings:
"Mother, open the gate!"

A ray of morning sun strikes aslant at the door.
The assembled crowd feel in their blood the primeval chant of
creation:
"Mother, open the gate!"
The gate opens.

The mother is seated on a straw bed with the babe on her lap,
  Like the dawn with the morning star.
The sun's ray that was waiting at the door outside falls on the head
    of the child.
The poet strikes his lute and sings out:
  "Victory to Man, the new-born, the ever-living."
They kneel down—the king and the beggar, the saint and the sinner,
  the wise and the fool—and cry:
  "Victory to Man, the new-born, the ever-living."
The old man from the East murmurs to himself:
      "I have seen!"

 Poems Old and New

      Be not ashamed, my brothers, to stand
          before the proud and the powerful
          with your white robes of simpleness.
      Let your crown be of humility, your
          freedom the freedom of the soul.
      Build God's throne daily upon the ample
          bareness of your poverty, and know
          that what is huge is not great and
          pride is not everlasting.[1]

Far as I gaze at the depth of Thy immensity
I find no trace there of sorrow or death or separation.
Death assumes its aspect of terror
and sorrow its pain
only when, away from Thee,
I turn my face toward my own dark self.
Thou All Perfect,

everything abides at Thy feet
for all time.
The fear of loss only clings to me
with its ceaseless grief,
but the shame of my penury
and my life's burden
vanish in a moment
when I feel Thy presence
in the center of my being.[2]

Let the earth and the water, the air and
the fruits of my country be sweet,
my God.
Let the homes and marts, the forests
and fields of my country be full,
my God.
Let the promises and hopes, the deeds
and words of my country be true,
my God.
Let the lives and hearts of the sons and
daughters of my country be one,
my God.[3]

Thou art the ruler of the minds of all people,
Thou Dispenser of India's destiny.
Thy name rouses the hearts
of the Punjab, Sind, Gujrat and Maratha,
of Dravid, Orissa and Bengal.
It echoes in the hills of the Vindhyas and
Himalayas,
mingles in the music of Jumna and Ganges,
and is chanted by the waves of the Indian Sea.
They pray for thy blessing and sing thy praise,

Thou Dispenser of India's destiny,
Victory, Victory, Victory to thee.

Day and night, thy voice goes out from land to land,
calling Hindus, Buddhists, Sikhs and Jains
        round thy throne
and Parsees, Mussalmans and Christians.
Offerings are brought to thy shrine by
        the East and the West
to be woven in a garland of love.
Thou bringest the hearts of all peoples
        into the harmony of one life,
Thou Dispenser of India's destiny,
Victory, Victory, Victory to thee.

Eternal Charioteer, thou drivest man's history
along the road rugged with rises and falls
        of Nations.
Amidst all tribulations and terror
thy trumpet sounds to hearten those that
        despair and droop,
and guide all people in their paths of
        peril and pilgrimage.
Thou Dispenser of India's destiny,
Victory, Victory, Victory to thee.

When the long dreary night was dense with gloom
and the country lay still in a stupor,
thy Mother's arms held her,
thy wakeful eyes bent upon her face,
till she was rescued from the dark evil
        dreams
that oppressed her spirit,
Thou Dispenser of India's destiny,
Victory, Victory, Victory to thee.[4]

Thou hast given us to live.
Let us uphold this honor with all our
　　strength and will;
For thy glory rests upon the glory that we are.
Therefore in thy name we oppose the power that
　　would plant its banner upon our soul.
Let us know that thy light grows dim in the
　　heart that bears its insult of bondage,
That the life, when it becomes feeble,
　　timidly yields thy throne to untruth,
For weakness is the traitor who betrays our soul.
Let this be our prayer to thee—

Give us power to resist pleasure where it
　　enslaves us,
To lift our sorrow up to thee as the summer
　　holds its midday sun.
Make us strong that our worship may
　　flower in love, and bear fruit in work.
Make us strong that we may not insult the weak
　　and the fallen,
That we may hold our love high where all things
　　around us are wooing the dust.

They fight and kill for self-love, giving
　　it thy name,
They fight for hunger that thrives on
　　brother's flesh,
They fight against thine anger and die.
But let us stand firm and suffer with strength
for the true, for the good, for the
　　eternal in man,
for thy kingdom which is in the union
　　of hearts,
for the freedom which is of the soul.[5]

A beast's bony frame lies bleaching on the grass.
Its dry white bones—time's hard laughter—cry to me:
Thy end, proud man, is one with the end of the cattle that graze no
        more,
for when thy life's wine is spilt to its last drop
the cup is flung away in final unconcern.
I cry in answer:
Mine is not merely the life that pays its bed and board
with its bankrupt bones, and is made destitute.
Never can my mortal days contain to the full
all that I have thought and felt, gained and given,
listened to and uttered.
Often has my mind crossed time's border,—
Is it to stop at last for ever at the
boundary of crumbling bones?
Flesh and blood can never be the measure of the truth that is myself;
the days and moments cannot wear it out with their passing kicks;
the wayside bandit, dust, dares not rob it of all its possessions.

Death, I refuse to accept from thee
that I am nothing but a gigantic jest of God,
a blank annihilation built with all the wealth of the Infinite.[6]

You were born to the joy of all:
the blue sky,
birds,
your mother's eyes;
Sravan's rains, *sarat*'s moist air,
these were the first welcome of life.
Your birth was given in an instant
an endless gift,
the call of home to the home-dweller.

Death be yours in distant loneliness at night,
greet you where sea-waves rhythm the dance of the homeless,
where a chant rises from the unknown forest,

where the foreign waterfall claps its hands in a farewell song,
where unfamiliar stars offer light to the infinite,
where nothing calls back to return.
The door is open: oceans and hills all point to the road.
The night near your head will stand silent
For death is a call to the wayfarer.[7]

The worshiper offers leaves and flowers to the river
    and ends his worship.
So I fill my basket and offer songs to Ganges, water of life;
    and I too worship.

This is love's current from high Vaikuntha,
    from the tangled locks of Siva,
      the water purified by his fiery sacrifice.
Ages of sin have dissolved in these waters,
    and its waves resound the future.
Each bank and bend beckons at the endless current.

By touch
    it has rescued me from dust,
      swung its waves into my limbs, murmured in my voice,
      rippled light and color in my eyes.
Removing the mantle of the infinite,
    what form and joy, dear stream, you have revealed.

My song is my flower-offering to the waters.
What if no flower floats for long,
    with whom, then, do I quarrel?
Under the firmament, in this grass-thrilled earth,
    in the cycle of spring and rain,
    in the procession of summer and winter,
I have worshiped each day with song.
And at the end, may my song be complete, be blessed
    and carried away.[8]

When I was a boy,
At two in the afternoon
    My head against the door
    Of my room on the roof
My mat spread out,
I spent the sunny hours.
Far in the sky the eagle called,
The *shishu* leaves glittered in the breeze,
Its beak parted in thirst, the crow
Lighted on the stone wall.
Sparrows fluttered
To the rafters of my room.
Across the lane came the hawker's cry:
On a distant roof somebody was flying a kite.
The unknown,
The far-away beyond the eyes
Played a tune that won my heart
From home.
Love and pain mingled without reason,
Wove dreams with no beginning
And no end.
It seemed I saw—
    The friend of one without a friend.

I have stepped to seventy,
Toward the shore's end.
    I open the window of my heart
    As in the childhood
Gazing. My hours pass.
In this burning heat
The *shirish* branches quiver
Near the well by the tamarind tree.
The neighborhood dog is asleep;
Freed from the cart, the bullock
Lies on the ground.

The *gandharajas* wilt on the gravel.
My eyes touch all,
My thoughts are in each thing.
Free as a naked child, my mind
Is with the forest shade
And with the sky.
The conch-shell of the unknown
      Sounds in all that I know.[9]

The world today is wild with the delirium
      of hatred,
the conflicts are cruel and unceasing in
      anguish,
crooked are its paths, tangled its bonds
      of greed.
All creatures are crying for a new birth
      of thine,
Oh Thou of boundless life,
save them, rouse thine eternal voice of hope,
let Love's lotus with its inexhaustible
      treasure of honey
open its petals in thy light.
O Serene, O Free,
in thine immeasurable mercy and goodness
wipe away all dark stains from the heart
      of this earth.

Thou giver of immortal gifts
give us the power of renunciation
and claim from us our pride.
In the splendor of a new sunrise of wisdom
let the blind gain their sight
and let life come to the souls that are dead.
O Serene, O Free,
in thine immeasurable mercy and goodness

354

wipe away all dark stains from the heart
      of this earth.

Man's heart is anguished with the fever
      of unrest,
with the poison of self-seeking,
with a thirst that knows no end.
Countries far and wide flaunt on their
      foreheads
the blood-red mark of hatred.
Touch them with thy right hand,
make them one in spirit,
bring harmony into their life,
bring rhythm of beauty.
O Serene, O Free,
in thine immeasurable mercy and goodness
wipe away all dark stains from the heart
      of this earth.[10]

Those who struck Him once
in the name of their rulers,
are born again in this present age.

They gather in their prayer-halls
      in a pious garb,
they call their soldiers,
"Kill, Kill," they shout;
in their roaring mingles the music of
      their hymns,
while the Son of Man in His agony
      prays, "O God,
fling, fling far away this cup filled with
      the bitterest of poisons." [11]

From afar I thought you
Invincible, merciless;
The world trembled in fear.
Awesome,
Your greedy flames
Consumed broken hearts.
The trident in your hand
Rose to the storm-clouds
To draw down the thunder.

My heart trembled;
I stood before you.
At the sight of your scowling brow
Danger rose like a wave.
Down came the blow.
Pressing my hand against my heart
I asked,
"Is there more,
The last of your thunderbolts?"
Down came the blow.
Just this?
My fear disappeared.
When you held your thunderbolt aloft
You seemed mightier than I.
Your blow brought you down
To my world.
You became small
And my fear was gone.
However great,
You were not mightier than death.

That I am mightier,
Will be my last word
When I leave.[12]

Door, always open
Only the blind eye is shut.
He fears to enter
Who does not know the inner way.

Door, your call resounds in light and dark,
Your welcome music solemn.
You unbar in the risen sun
And in the darkness of stars.

Door, from seed to sprout
You lead from flower to fruit.
Through ages you unravel,
From death to life.

Oh door, world's life
Journeys from death to death.
You beckon to freedom's pilgrim;
"Never fear" comes from the despairing night.[13]

Scattered in this room
Dumb, deaf things intermingle;
Some strike my eyes, others I barely see:
The corner flower jar,
There the teapot darkly hides its face;
The cabinet articles, miscellaneous,
Crowd into nothingness;
Two window-panes lie broken there behind the screen,
Suddenly, I even see that red screen itself;
I see but do not see.
And the morning light traces intricate rug designs.
There—the green desk cloth; I had fancied it before,
Its color flaming in my eyes.
Today the green lies buried, as if ashes smoked,
And it is there, but it is gone.

The drawers are here, layers crammed with papers
I forgot to throw away.
The calendar slanting on the table
Reminds me it is the eighth day of the month.
A lavender bottle catches light;
The clock ticks; I hardly look.
Near the wall
An almirah, full of books—
Most of them remain unknown.
Those pictures which I hung
Appear like ghosts, forgotten.
The carpet lines once spoke clear language,
Now are almost silent.
Those days gone before and this day now
Lie unconnected.
In this small room
Some things are intimate, so many are alien,
And in passing the table
From shut-eyed habit
I miss most of what there is to see.
Inattentively, I cross and re-cross
Between the known and unknown.
Some one has placed a childhood photograph
Under the mirror-frame; the faded print
Is little more than shadows.
In my mind I am Rabindranath,
Like this room.
In dim, torn language,
Some things throng clear, some
Hide away in corners.
Most of it I merely forgot to remove.
Like these lost meanings,
The past days diminish,
Rubbing off their right to be:
Shadows lost amidst the new.
And the alphabet which holds their meanings,
Nobody can read.[14]

The journey nears the road-end
　　where the shadows deepen with death.
The setting sun unties the last strings of its gifts,
　　Squanders gold with both hands.
Death is lighted with festive colors;
　　Life is before me.

With this word my breath will stop:
　　I loved.
Love's overbrimming mystery
　　joins death and life. It
Has filled my cup of pain
　　with joy.

The *Vaisakh* storm lashed sorrow's road
　　Where I walked, a lonely pilgrim,
Many nights bereft of light.
　　Yet beckonings reached my heart.
Slander's thorn pricked me
　　As a garland of triumph.

Gazing at the face of earth
　　I never exhausted wonder.
Lakshmi, grace in the lotus of beauty,
　　Touched me.
I caught in my flute
　　The breath that rocks with laughs and cries.

I claimed for my soul
　　Those human voices of the divine.
Many defeats, much fear and shame,
　　Yet I saw greatness.
In the midst of agony and striving
　　The door suddenly opened.

I gained the right of birth;
  That glory was mine.
I shared the stream that flows from ages,
  in wisdom, work and thought.
If a vision were mine
  It belonged to all.

Sitting in the dust, I saw the supreme
  in light beyond the light,
Smaller than the smallest, great beyond the greatest,
  Transcending the senses.
I often beheld the unquenchable flame
  Rending the body.

Wherever a saint atoned,
  I gained.
Whoever triumphed over delusion,
  I knew myself in him;
Wherever a hero died with ease,
  My place is in his history.

Perfect beyond perfection, even if I forgot His name
    I offered Him worship.
The quiet sky reached me,
  At dawn I received the radiance.
My death will be fulfilled
  In this earth with the splendor of life.

Today in the farewell of the year,
  Death, remove your veil.
Much has fallen aside, love's tenderness often left me,
  Lightless memory faded on the road
But at this deathless moment of life, O Death
  Your hands are filled with treasure.[15]

In the center of the universe
Age to age, there gathers
Unforgiveness.
Unaware, a single error
Multiplies in time and
Suddenly destroys itself.
The seeming solid base
Heaves an earthquake dance.
Creatures come in hordes,
Power-packed, illusory:
The burden grows, and grows
To self-destruction.
Piercing through errors beyond our ken
It rends relationships;
Mistakes of a gesture or of a gleaming spark
Impede the backward path, forever:
Destruction at the bidding of the Perfect.
What new creation will it yield at last?
Disobedient clay is crushed, resistance all removed,
Now green sprouts will bear new life.
Unforgiveness,
Strength in creation,
Your feet trample the thorns
On the path of peace.[16]

The war-drums are sounded.
Men force their features into frightfulness
    and gnash their teeth;
and before they rush out to gather raw
    human flesh for death's larder,
they march to the temple of Buddha,
    the compassionate,
to claim his blessings,
while loud beats the drum rat-a-tat
and earth trembles.

They pray for success;
for they must raise weeping and wailing
in their wake, sever ties of love,
plant flags on the ashes of desolated
        homes,
devastate the centers of culture
and shrines of beauty,
mark red with blood their trail
across green meadows and populous
        markets,
and so they march to the temple of Buddha,
        the compassionate,
to claim his blessings,
while loud beats the drum rat-a-tat
and earth trembles.

They will punctuate each thousand of
        the maimed and killed
with the trumpeting of their triumph,
arouse demon's mirth at the sight
of the limbs torn bleeding from women
        and children;
and they pray that they may befog minds
        with untruths
and poison God's sweet air of breath,
and therefore they march to the temple
        of Buddha, the compassionate,
to claim his blessings,
while loud beats the drum rat-a-tat
and earth trembles.[17]

I have won blessings in this life
of the beautiful.
In the vessel of man's affection I taste His own divine nectar.
Sorrow, difficult to bear,

has shown me the unconquered, unhurt soul.
On the day when I saw death's impending shadow,
I was not defeated by fear.
Great human beings
have not deprived me of their touch;
I have stored undying words in my heart.
I received grace from the god of life:
let me leave this memory
in grateful words.[18]

On the bank of Rup-Narain
I awake:
This world
Is not a dream.
In words of blood I saw
My being.
I knew myself
Through hurts
And pain.
Truth is hard
And never deceives.
I loved that hardness.
Death-long *tapasya* of suffering
To win truth's terrible value
And to pay all debts
In death.[19]

Here in the universe
Revolves a gigantic wheel of pain;
Stars and planets burst;
Sparks of far-flung, fiery dust
Scatter at a gaping speed
Enveloping first creation's anguish.

In the armory of pain
Glowing on the stretches of consciousness
Torture instruments clang;
Bleeding wounds gape.
Man's body is so small,
His strength of suffering so immense.
Where chaos and creation meet
Why does man hold up his fiery cup
In the weird festival of the gods,
Titan-drunk—O why
Fill his clay body, deliriously
With the red tide of tears?
Each moment offers value.
Man's sacrifice,
His burning body—
Can anything compare
In all the suns and stars?
Such prowess, endurance
Indifference to death—
This triumphal march where hundreds
Trample embers
To reach the limit of sorrow—
Where else is such a guest,
Where such a pilgrimage,
Such service, breaking like water through
Igneous rocks,
Where else such endless stores of love? [20]

Once again I wake up when the night has waned,
when the world opens all its petals once more,
and this is an endless wonder.
Vast islands have sunk in the abyss unnamed,
stars have been beggared of the last flicker
    of their light,

countless epochs have lost all their ladings.
World-conquerors have vanished into the
      shadow of a name
behind dim legends,
great nations raised their towers of triumph
as a mere offering to the unappeasable
      hunger of the dust.
Among this dissolving crowd of the discarded
my forehead receives the consecration of light,
and this is an endless wonder.
I stand for another day with the Himalayas,
with constellations of stars.
I am here where in the surging sea-waves
the infuriate dance of the Terrible
is rhythmed with his boisterous laughter.
The centuries on which have flashed up
      and foundered
kingly crowns like bubbles
have left their signature on the bark of
      this aged tree,
where I am allowed to sit under its ancient
      shade for one more day,
and this is an endless wonder.[21]

How little I know of this world:
deeds of men, cities, rivers,
mountains, arid wastes, unknown
creatures, unacquainted trees.
The great Earth teems
and I know merely a niche.
Deprived, I travel with my eyes
gathering word-glimpses, pictures
that fill my areas of inexperience
with wealth.

I am a poet of the earth:
my flute re-plays its tunes.
I fill its callings with my dreams
and hear the harmony in the
silent hours of my heart.
Inaccessible snowy ranges
call me ever again
with music unheard.
The Polar star, far, alone,
has touched my sleepless eyes.
The waterfall
dances in my heart as I have heard
the primal song of nature.
I have heard the symphony of being.

Man stands farthest in this mystery,
hidden in time and space.
To know him is to commune and love.
Seldom have I won access,
my ways of life have intervened.
The tiller,
the weaver,
the fisherman
all sustain the world with labor.
I have known them from my corner of renown,
unable to enter the intimate precincts.
I know the song basket is empty
if filled with trinkets when links are gone
between life and life.
And I know my failure
whenever my song has been incomplete,
wherever it has missed the all.

So I am here waiting for the message
from the poet of the world,
of the peasant, the comrade
whose words and deeds have concurred.
May his words reveal, not hoodwink,

nor tempt the eye alone.
May he give what I have not.
May he save himself from a
mimic sympathy for laborers.

Come, poet of the multitudes,
sing songs of obscure man,
reveal his unspoken soul,
soothe his humiliated heart,
restore life and song
to this dry land.
Resuscitate the failing hearts
of hidden men.
May your voice reflect
those standing bowed.
Let the one-stringed minstrel, also,
add his tune
to the great court anthem of the muse.
Come, poet of the new age,
lead me to those hearts
so far away, those hearts so near.
May they know themselves through you
whom I salute.[22]

Sheltered by the distant throne
The kingdom flaunts
The difference between rulers and the ruled,
Keeps disaster hidden under awnings.
Hapless the reign which
Reduces the symbol of power to shame.
Even if the suffering of multitudes
Does not touch the rulers—
Finally it draws the providential curse.

Under the shadow of great wealth
Starvation moves across the land,

Where drinking water is impure and drying up—
Where the body has no winter clothes.
And the door of death is open—
Where, worse than death, the lives worn to the skin,
Day and night, are subjected to unchecked disease.
There,
The dying cannot help the kingdom,
They are only burdens.
The bird whose wing is shriveled up,
Cannot remain steady in the storm,
It falls to the dust, broken.
The reckoning comes.
When possessions topple down,
From the ruins
The penury which was destitute
Re-builds its state.[23]

On that birthday morning,
With deference
I lifted my eyes to the sunrise.
I saw the dawn
Consecrate
The white forehead of the mountain ranges.
I beheld
The great distance
In creation's heart
On the throne of the lord of mountains.
From ages, majestic,
He has preserved the unknown
In the trackless forest;
The sky-cleaving, far-away,
Encircled
In sunrise and sunset.

On this birthday,
The great distance grows in my heart.

The starry path is nebular,
Mysterious;
And my own remoteness
Impenetrable.
The pilgrim moves, his path unseen,
The consequence unknown.
Today
I hear that traveler's footsteps
From my lonely seashore.[24]

Shunned at the temple-gates
by the pious;
the outcastes,
uninitiates,
seek their God
beyond the artificial,
inwardly,
in midnight skies,
in forest flowers,
in love
and separation.
Their image of God
is not manhandled,
or imprisoned by temple walls.
Along the edge of the Padma,
whose waves sweep away
old temples,
I have seen one of them
alone with his *ektara*
seeking his soul's companion
through songs.
I am an
—outcaste,
whose offerings cannot reach
the imprisoned God.

369

The priest asks,
"Did you see your God?"
"No"—I say.
Surprised, he asks,
"Do you know the path?"
"No"—I say.
He questions sadly,
"Are you not of caste then?"
"No"—I say.

As a boy
I felt in my blood the radiance
of the primal light.
I spread my spirit
upon the bosom of the Eternal
and marveled,
that for millions of years
a spark lay hidden
until it burst into the flame
that was I.
This wonder
has been
ritual for me every day,
my worship
outside the temple-gates;
I am the outcaste, the uninitiate.
Born in the household
of exile,
I was rejected by the respectable.
Out of grace with playmates,
a nameless stranger
to the neighborhood,
I could but peep across
the bristling hedge
to their house
sanctimonious in pride.
And from a distance I watched
the crowds pouring

along the traveled paths.
Away from the crowd,
I pursued my fancies
at the crossing of the roads.
For their worship they plucked
flowers prescribed by scripture
and left for me and my God
the garden of blossoms
blessed by the sun.
By the contempt of the pious
I was thrust
into the arms of man.
And I found solitary friends
whose light and voice
made history.
The heroes and sages
who made death divine
are my associates:
They are seekers after truth
and inheritors of life.
I have prayed:
Deliver us,
O man of men,
from the creed
which flaunts
exclusion;
rescue me from the boredom
of observances
that insult humanity.
I am blessed
who have known you
in the fellowship
of sons of the immortal,
—even I, the outcaste, the uninitiate.
Whose offerings are
to Him in the heavens,
and to the inner man in me,
whose love is joy forever.[25]

Floating on time's stream
My mind gazes at the
Beyond.
Along that track of emptiness
Shadow pictures form,
Conquerors processing through the past
With power's arrogant speed.
Empire-hungry Pathans have come,
And the Mughals:
Victory's chariot-wheels
Churning dust;
Triumphant banners have fluttered.
Today in the empty path
I see no traces.
The blue space, age to age,
Is colored by sunrise and sunset.

Again, in that emptiness,
Iron-bound,
Fire-breathing,
The powerful English
Scattering energy.
Time's current will
Sweep away Empire's nets.
Their merchandise troops
Will leave no sign
On the path of the stars.
On this earth
I see the moving
Multitudes,
Age to age,
Urged by mankind's needs in life,
and death.

They pull the oars,
Hold the helm;

In the fields they
Sow and cut the corn.
They work.
The kingly scepter breaks, the war-drums cease,
Victory columns gape, stupidly
Oblivious:
Blood-stained weapons and blood-shot eyes
Hide in children's storybooks.
They work,
In Anga, in Banga, in Kalinga's seas and river-ghats,
In Punjab, Bombay, and Gujrat.
Voices hum
Night and day
The world's livelihood.
Sorrows and joys
Chant life.
On hundreds of empire ruins
They work.[26]

You have covered the path of your creation
in a mesh of varied wiles,
Guileful One.
Deftly you have set a snare of false beliefs
in artless lives.
With your deception
you have set the great man on trial
taking from him the secrecy of night.
Your star lights for him
the translucent path of his heart,
illumined by a simple faith.
Though tortuous outside
it is straight within,
and there is his pride.
Though men call him futile,
in the depth of his heart he finds truth
washed clean by the inner light.

373

Nothing can deprive him;
he carries to his treasure-house
his last reward.
He who could easily bear your wile,
receives from you the right
to everlasting peace.[27]

There lies the ocean of peace,
Helmsman, launch the boat.
You will always be his comrade.
Take, O take him to your heart.
In the path of the Infinite
will shine the *Dhruva-tara*.
Giver of freedom, your forgiveness, your mercy
will be wealth inexhaustible
in the eternal journey.
May the mortal bonds perish,
May the vast universe take him in its arms,
And may he know in his fearless heart
The great unknown.[28]

The first day's sun
asked
at the new manifestation of being—
Who are you?
No answer came.
Year after year went by,
the last sun of the day
the last question utters
on the western sea-shore,
in the silent evening—
Who are you?
He gets no anwser.[29]

Soon, I feel
the time comes near to leave.
With sunset shadings
screen the parting day.
Let the hour be silent; let it be peaceful.
Let not any pompous memories or meetings
create a sorrow's trance.
May the trees at the gate
raise the earth's chant of peace
in a cluster of green leaves.
May the night's blessings be
in the light of the seven stars.[30]

NOTES

TRAVEL

Occasional changes in the verb tenses of the English translations are intentional. The original Bengali verbs possess qualities which give the sense of both the past and the present, and in order to convey this dual sense of what one could call the reminiscent past and the discursive present, it has seemed best to use both the past and present tenses of the English verbs.

1. Charlie. C. F. Andrews.
2. Yokoyama Taikan. Renowned nineteenth century landscape painter.
3. "Rural England." The reading at Rothenstein's referred to in the preface is discussed in Rathindranath Tagore's *On the Edges of Time* (Orient Longmans, Bombay, 1958), p. 116, where he says, "The historic evening at Rothenstein's, when Yeats read out the *Gitanjali* poems in his musical, ecstatic voice to a choice group of people like Ernest Rhys, Alice Meynell, Henry Nevinson, Ezra Pound, May Sinclair, Charles Trevelyan, C. F. Andrews and others gathered in the drawing-room. . . ."

LETTERS

Salutations have been omitted from letters translated from the Bengali, due to the impossibility of rendering precise connotations into English.

1. Tagore's wife, Mrinalini Devi, was born in 1872 and died in 1902.
2. Rathi. Rathindranath, Tagore's son.

3. "Meghdut." A well known Sanskrit poem by Kalidas.

4. Bela. His first daughter.

5. Fultala. His wife's birthplace.

6. The Sturge Moore letters are from the private collection of Elinor Wolf, used with her permission. Thomas Sturge Moore (1870–1944) was an English poet, man of letters, and wood engraver.

7. Tagore does not mean to suggest that Valentine Chirol is one of the leading Mohammedan gentlemen; rather, he was a British administrator.

8. *Crescent Moon*. A collection of poems translated into English by Tagore himself (1913); all but half a dozen were taken from *Sisu*, poems written for his children during 1903–1904 after the death of his twenty-nine-year-old wife.

9. Havell. 1861–1934. E. B. Havell, art critic, Principal of Calcutta School of Art, Administrator of the Government Art Gallery, 1896–1906.

10. *Chitra*. Anglicized title of *Chitrangada*, published in 1892. The original Bengali was a poetic drama which was later set to music and dance, similar to the Elizabethan masque.

11. C. F. Andrews. Most of *Letters to a Friend* was written to Tagore's close friend, C. F. Andrews, during the years 1913–1922. Andrews (1871–1940) was born and educated in England, but after a period of service as a missionary on the staff of St. Stephen's College, Delhi, joined Tagore at Santiniketan in 1912. Andrews devoted the rest of his life to the cause of India, both in England and abroad; he championed Indian laborers in South Africa, Fiji, British Guiana, and Kenya, and played a large role in the abolition of the indenture system, in the Gandhi-Smuts agreement, and in the 1927 agreement between India and the South African Union. His friendship with Gandhi and Tagore made him the best interpreter of Indian aspirations to both the East and the West. He died April 5, 1940, and was buried in Calcutta.

12. W. W. Pearson. William Winstanley Pearson was a friend and close associate of Tagore during 1912–1923. He began his work in India in the London Missionary Society at Bhowanipur in Calcutta. After joining Tagore at Santiniketan, he later traveled in different parts of the world with Tagore and C. F. Andrews. The *Manchester Guardian* called him "the best loved Englishman in India." During World War I, the British Home Government ordered his departure from Peking as "undesirable," from where he was sent to England under guard and placed on parole in Manchester. He died as a result of a railway accident in Italy, in 1923.

13. *Post Office*. English translation by Tagore (1914) of the drama *Dakghar* (1912).

14. Gagan. Tagore's cousin, Gaganendranath Tagore, a distinguished painter.

15. Aban. Tagore's cousin, the well known artist Abanindranath Tagore.

16. Haricharan Babu. The late Haricharan Bandopadhyaya, a scholar and staff member of Santiniketan.

17. Texas, 1921. During this and other visits to the United States, Tagore met and talked with such American writers as Sinclair Lewis, Theodore Dreiser, Hart Crane, Carl Sandburg, and Robert Frost. It might be interesting to include here a poem by Theodore Dreiser which he sent to Tagore shortly after they met in 1930 and which appeared in *The Golden Book of Tagore*, ed. Ramananda Chatterji (Golden Book Committee, Calcutta, 1931).

THE PROCESS

That which was crooked straightened
That which was defeated
Joined with that which was beautiful
Blended
With that which was ill planned
To be separated
And made crooked
Or straight again.

18. Leonard Elmhirst. Met Tagore in New York in 1920, and after receiving a B.Sc. degree in agriculture from Cornell, joined Tagore at Santiniketan in 1921. On February 6, 1922, he began the work of Sriniketan Center of Rural Reconstruction under Tagore's guidance. In 1924–1925, Elmhirst traveled with Tagore to China and Japan, Argentina and Italy.

19. "Genesis of Gitanjali." The following is a quote from Harriet Monroe's article "Poetry: A Magazine of Verse": ". . . *Poetry: A Magazine of Verse* had the honor of being the first occidental publication to print Tagore's poems in English. His six *Gitanjali* poems, appearing in *Poetry* for December, 1912, preceded by a few weeks the London India Society's private edition, which, though dated 1912, was not distributed until 1913.

"*Poetry*, published in Chicago, was far away from India and even from London where the Bengali poet was sojourning, and its founder and editor had never heard of Tagore. But Ezra Pound, our foreign correspondent, had met him in London and had induced him to permit the sending of some of the *Gitanjali* poems to the new little poets' magazine."

This article was also published in *The Golden Book of Tagore*.

20. Rothenstein. Sir William Rothenstein (1872–1945), English artist, author, principal of the Royal College of Art, 1920–1935. Noted for *Men and Memories*, 2 vols. (New York, 1931–32).

SHORT STORIES

1. "Cabuliwallah." It is said that Tagore's eldest daughter, Bela, was a little chatterbox, somewhat like Mini. As to the story, Tagore once said, "Of course there used to be a Cabuliwallah who came to our house and became very familiar with us. I imagined that he too must have a daughter left behind in his motherland. . . ."

2. "The Hungry Stones." Before leaving for England when he was seventeen, Tagore spent some time with his elder brother Satyendranath in an old Muslim palace in Shahibag, and in his imagination relived the court life of the Mughal kings. He said that here "My mind received the first suggestion for the story of 'Hungry Stones.'" Edward Thompson, writing on Tagore's famous poem, "Taj Mahal," refers to "The Hungry Stones": "The Mughal Empire always touches his imagination, and we find an atmosphere as eerie and glamorous as that of 'Hungry Stones.'" Edward Thompson, *Rabindranath Tagore* (Oxford University Press, London, 1926), p. 237.

AUTOBIOGRAPHICAL

For further information about Tagore's life see *Rabindranath Tagore* by Marjorie Sykes (Longmans, Green and Company, Ltd., London, 1943) and *Rabindranath Tagore, His Personality and Work* by V. Lesny, trans. Guy McKeever Phillips (George Allen Unwin, Ltd., London, 1939).

The following extract throws some outside light on the material included in this section: "Tagore's life history is mainly the biography of ideas and artistic creations. . . . In other words, Tagore's crises are all subjective, begotten by this spirit, even if nursed by the objective situation. That jealous guard over his soul completely defeats Western biographers and baffles any Indian writer of this century who has accepted their model. In another language, the life of Tagore cannot be composed on the symphonic pattern of Goethe's, whose variety of creative work most resembled his. Tagore's life-pattern was essentially melodic, with numerous improvisations, indeed, but it was built around the regnant notes. This does not at all mean that he did not share in the tragedies of his country and the world. That he did, but his actions remained essentially personal, spiritual." Dhurjati Prasad Mukerji, *Tagore—A Study* (Padma Publications, Ltd., Bombay, 1943), p. 15.

1. Raja Rammohan Roy. Considered by Tagore to be the maker of the Modern Age in India. He was an Indian religious reformer (1774–1833); founder of the Brahma Samaj or Theistic Church for the worship of God. He was the enemy of idol worship, supported the abolition of suttee, and worked hard to promote education among his countrymen. He visited England and France in 1832; died on September 27, 1833, at Bristol.

2. Bankim Chandra Chatterji. Bengali novelist (1838–1894), the first in Bengal to take the B.A. degree (1858), entered the government service, from which he retired in 1894. He was the greatest Indian novelist of the nineteenth century, and some of his work was modeled on Scott's historical novels. His influence even at present is considerable; among the literary young men he gathered round him was Rabindranath Tagore. He is the author of the first Indian national anthem, "Vande Mataram."

3. Vaishnava poems. Vaishnavism is the name given to the Hindu sect the members of which in a special way worship Vishnu of the Hindu trinity. The erotic tendency of some Vaishnava poetry, especially in connection with degenerate forms of the cult of Radha and Krishna, had aroused opposition among the more sober-minded Hindus.

4. King's Palace. Corresponds to Wonderland.

CONVERSATIONS

Unfortunately, meetings with other great thinkers and artists were not recorded, but evidences of such meetings are available in letters, telegrams, and messages, of which the following are examples:

Telegram from G. B. Shaw

"10 January, 1933
"R.M.S. The Empress of Britain
"My dear Rabindranath Tagore,
"Unfortunately I am not really visiting India; but the ship in which I am going round the world to get a little rest and do a little work has to put in at Bombay and Colombo to replenish her tanks; and on such occasions I step ashore for a few hours and wander about the streets and such temples as are open to European untouchables.

"The organizers of the tour urge me to see India by spending five days and nights in a crowded railway carriage and being let out for a few minutes occasionally to lunch at a hotel and see the Tajmahal; but I am too old a traveler to be taken by such baits, and too old a man (76½) to endure such hardships without expiring.

"My only regret is that I shall be unable to visit you. My consolation is that the present situation in India will not bear being talked about. I understand it only too well.

"Faithfully,
"G. Bernard Shaw"

Letter from Albert Einstein, 1931

This was a personal address to Tagore at the end of an article contributed by Einstein to *The Golden Book of Tagore*.

"You saw the fierce strife of creatures, a strife that wells forth from need and dark desire. You saw the withdrawal in calm meditation and in creation of beauty. Cherishing these, you serve mankind all through a long and fruitful life, spreading everywhere a gentle and free thought in a manner such as the seers of your people have proclaimed as the ideal."

Letter from Albert Schweitzer, 1936

Following is an excerpt from a letter which Schweitzer wrote to Tagore when he sent him a copy of his book, *Indian Thought and Its Development*. Dated Gunsbach, près Munster, Alsace, France, August 15, 1936, the letter is quoted in A. Aronson, *Rabindranath Through Western Eyes* (Kitabistan, Allahabad, 1943), p. 131.

"I do not think that you agree with everything as regards my analysis; neither will you agree with everything I say about you. But I still believe that you will feel in this book my deep understanding of the greatness of Indian thought and the sympathy I have for it. Let me tell you on this occasion the great love I have for you and your thought. When I call you in this book the Goethe of India that is because, in my opinion, you are as important for India as Goethe was for Europe."

Message from Robert Frost

In a letter of September 19, 1959, to this editor, Robert Frost reminisced about his meeting with Tagore in Williamstown, Massachusetts, during the fall of 1930. The friendship that developed as a result of this meeting was communicated by Frost in a message to the Embassy of India in Washington, D.C., on May 7, 1959.

"Fortunately Tagore's poetry overflowed national bounds to reach us in his own English. He belongs little less to us than to his own country. He was my friend and I am proud to take part in celebrating his greatness."

DRAMA

Concerning Tagore's development as a dramatist, Edward Thompson wrote (*Rabindranath Tagore, Poet and Dramatist*, Geoffrey Cumberlege: Oxford University Press, 2nd ed., 1948), pp. 292–293:

"Tagore's dramas fall into three main groups: (1) the earliest, non-symbolic, of which *Sacrifice* is the best as drama, and *Chitrāngadā* and *Mālini* the loveliest as poetry. All of these, except *Mālini*, are in blank verse; they are of the Shakespearian type, with five acts. (2) The group of short dramas based on Sanskrit (or, in the case of *Sati*, later) heroic story. These are in rhymed couplets and are symbolical. Whatever fire of human interest was present in the earlier plays is fading out; ideas gain the mastery, almost the monopoly, of the poet's stage."

Thompson reports Tagore's conversation with him about the genesis of *Sacrifice* on p. 54:

"I wanted a serial for *Bālak*, and was thinking about one. I was going to visit Ramnarayan Basu. The train was crowded, and an Englishman wouldn't allow the lamp to be hidden, so it burnt brightly all night and I couldn't sleep. But I dozed, and dreamed of a father and a girl before a temple. Blood was running out over the steps, and the girl was deeply pained. 'Why is this blood? Why is this blood?' she kept asking, and tried to wipe it away. Her father was very troubled, and couldn't answer her, so tried to silence her, really to silence his own mind. I woke up, and determined to put this in my story. And I used also the story of the Raja of Tripura, who introduced Vaishnavism into his state, and was banished by his brother."

Commenting on the religious and social criticism in *Sacrifice*, Thompson wrote (pp. 91–92):

"The theme of *Sacrifice* had been implicit in many an obscure page of Indian religious thought. But Rabindranath's play first gave its protest a reasoned and deliberate place in art. He attacks bigotry with the weapon most dangerous to it, the sarcasm of parody."

Concerning the writing of the *Post Office* (and also *Gitanjali*, which was written during the same period), Edward Thompson (pp. 215, 216) reports the following excerpt from a conversation with Tagore:

"I was very restless, just as I am now. That gave me the idea of a child pining for freedom, and the world anxious to keep it in its bounds, for it has its duties there. . . . I was anxious to know the world. At that time, I thought that it was in the West that the spirit of humanity was experimenting and working. My restlessness became intolerable. I wrote *Dakghar* in three or four days. About the same time I wrote *Gitanjali*. Most of the pieces were written at Santiniketan. I used to write almost every day and sometimes at night. I did not intend to publish them. I knew people would be disappointed, and would say that after *Sonar Tari* [*The Golden Boat*] they were very poor. But I knew that they were very intimately my own."

In connection with the staging of the *Post Office* in England, Ernest Rhys, in *Rabindranath Tagore, A Biographical Study* (Macmillan, New York, 1916), pp. 79, 80, says:

"Of the two plays acted over here, the *Post Office* (*Dakghar* in the original) and *The King of the Dark Chamber*, I saw the first when it was produced at the Court Theatre, with Synge's mordant comedy, *The Well of the Saints*. . . . As it was acted, even with the drawback of having a partly Irish, instead of an Indian, characterization of its village humors, it proved moving and particularly effective in the stroke of tragedy redeemed at the close. . . ."

Concerning the staging in India, Rathindranath, Tagore's son, describes the Calcutta opening in his book, *On the Edges of Time* (Orient Longmans, Calcutta, 1958), p. 105.

"The stage was set up at one end of the Vichitra Hall, leaving enough room for only about one hundred and fifty persons to make the audience. The arrangement could not have been better. Many of the delicate nuances of the play would have been lost in a less intimate atmosphere. The conception of the stage was entirely Gaganendranath's. It was novel and daring. A cottage with a real thatched roof and bamboo walls was erected by him on the stage platform. The decorations were simple but artistic as only the eye of a connoisseur could select and apply with sure effect.

"The performance was meant to be a private show for the benefit of the members of the Vichitra Club, but it was such a unique treat and people were so eager to see it that it had to be repeated several times. After every show when I wanted to pull down the stage, a demand was made for another repeat performance and thus Amal's three-walled cottage remained a fixture in the Vichitra Hall for many weeks. I believe the seventh and last performance was given for the entertainment of the delegates of the Indian National Congress then being held in Calcutta."

1. Buddhist legend. The original title of the Buddhist legend is *Sārdūlakarnavadānā*. Sukumar Sen, *History of Bengali Literature* (Sahitya Akademi, New Delhi, 1960), p. 310.

2. *Chandalika.* Dance sequences which obviously cannot be translated, but which constitute an integral part of the charm and color in the staging of the play, have not been indicated.

3. Uma. In the Puranic legend ·Uma imposed on herself a terrible penance in order to win the love of Siva.

4. "He who has called me." This speech is followed by a song in the original, which has been omitted. In this translation, all the songs except two have been omitted. These omissions occur after the following speeches:

"Was there no water to be had anywhere else in this whole village?"
"You won't understand, Mother, you won't."
"I do not fear what does not fear me."
"Do not be so afraid, Mother."
"How can I bring him back?"
"To undo this spell may cost me my life."
"Until that moment let the spell work."
"I knew something greater than fear."
"Keep trying. Don't give up."
"I am afraid to, Mother."

5. Pali (Buddha's language). The word for monk is actually Bhikku, which means one who has been initiated into the Buddhist order. In many instances in the original the word wayfarer is substituted, because these monks were often wanderers.

6. See note 4 above.

7. "Blessed am I says the flower who belongs to the earth." This song is based on a translation by Tagore.

8. See note 4 above.

9. See note 4 above.

10. See note 4 above.

11. A chant of four lines beginning "To the most pure Buddha, ocean of mercy."

12. See note 4 above.

13. See note 4 above.

14. See note 4 above.

15. See note 4 above.

16. See note 4 above.

17. See note 4 above.

Encouragement for Tagore's ideas on the necessity for a supernational consciousness has been expressed in all corners of the world. The following quotations from *The Golden Book of Tagore* are printed here as examples:

"Nationalism, especially when it urges us to fight for freedom, is noble and life-giving. But often it becomes a narrow creed, and limits and encompasses its votaries and makes them forget the many-sidedness of life. But Rabindranath Tagore has given to our nationalism the outlook of internationalism and has enriched it with art and music and the magic of his words, so that it has become the full-blooded emblem of India's awakened spirit."

Jawaharlal Nehru
Allahabad, 1931

"Perhaps the most valuable contribution which can be made to our perplexing age is a revelation of the essential unity and validity of all human experiences, that our intellectual and emotional understanding may approach our commercial and political arrangements. In spite of the magnificent methods of communication modern science has placed at our disposal, such a revelation can be made only in the age-old way—through the spirit of genius. This message to be natural and inevitable must be varied as well as profound, romantic as well as classical, delightful as well as poignant; above all it must be clothed in Beauty sufficient to carry it over the gulfs lying between different peoples, especially those who live in the East and those who live in the West.

"Rabindranath Tagore has met all the requirements of genius combined in a man who is at once a poet, a philosopher, a humanitarian, an educator. . . . He has once more made clear to us the saying we so often used in the early days of the University Settlement—the things that make us alike are finer and deeper than the things that make us different."

Jane Addams
Hull House
Chicago, 1931

EDUCATION

In order not to give the impression that Tagore neglected the purely practical element in education, the following statement by Prabodh Chandra Bagchi, the late Vice-Chancellor of Visva-Bharati, Santiniketan is included (from *Visva-Bharati News*, Silver Jubilee Number, 1957, pp. 32–34):

"Our education under foreign rule was planned to produce clerks only, as Macaulay admitted. The replacement of our *Pathsala* by an urban system of education helped the growth of the number of clerks in the country, but almost the entire nation remained sunk in the stupor of ignorance, because in India, villages largely outnumber the towns and our agriculturists are so many. To this vast mass of humanity the fruits of our new system of education did not reach. The existing schools in the villages also began to close down. The fruits of this new system of education did not reach them. Gurudeva [Tagore] recognized the malady and started this institution, not with a view to prepare clerks but to give effect to the concept of total education. He wished that, along with the cultivation of knowledge, the students would do manual labor as well, and that they should not be ashamed of it. Thus he wanted to spread education in every walk of life. To it were added art, music, handicrafts, etc., so that the students might come out with more accomplishment and ability.

"Having had this objective in view, Gurudeva established Sriniketan side by side with Santiniketan, because he thought that there would be no real emancipation of our country if the so-called education of the townsmen remained as their monopoly and failed to reach the vast multitude in the countryside. So he took up the upliftment of our villages. Sriniketan became the center. It explains how Santiniketan by not being divorced from the interests of Sriniketan was not converted into a mere replica of urban education.

"Along with rural education, Sriniketan has developed Cooperative Health Societies. Hundreds of families within the jursidiction of Bolpur Police Station are members of these societies and have been deriving enormous benefits. Cooperative storehouses have also been organized for storing paddy at times of good harvests and for distribution of paddy at times of bad ones.

"Sriniketan has been carrying on other important activities with no mean results. One of these is in connection with the organization of *Bratibalaka*. Very often there is a tendency to confuse these *bratibalakas* with scouts. In fact it is not so. The main purpose of the *bratibalaka* organization is to do away with the caste prejudices. These *bratibalakas* are composed of boys of different castes and religion. It is hoped that they live together in a cooperative manner. Also that they will foster social welfare through voluntary service to the community. Sriniketan has been also helping the villagers by initiating better farming methods and techniques and by effecting a system of improved communication. In short, it has been trying to create the constituents of joy by providing manifold opportunities to live and let others live.

"In this connection another important feature of Sriniketan's activities deserves mention. It is cottage industry training, development and extension. To provide better means of work and to ensure marketability of their products Sriniketan has been training up the village craftsmen in better techniques of production and creating markets for sale of their products." [Editor's note. Leonard and Dorothy Elmhirst and the late Kalimohan Ghosh played a great role in the development of the rural welfare units of Visva-Bharati at Sriniketan, the sister institution two miles from Santiniketan.]

Tagore discussed his educational theories and projects with such internationally known educators as Madame Montessori, the pioneer in children's education in the West, and with John Dewey. In this light, the following excerpt from a letter to Tagore by Helen Keller (published in *The Golden Book of Tagore,* 1931) is included:

". . . With observing eye and listening ear you journeyed, and saw the curse of division, the darkness of prejudice, the deafness of hate in which men live as strangers and enemies. But, looking long and patiently, you found the dynamic force of love hidden in humanity. . . .

"Your school at Visva-Bharati is a bright pledge of a nobler civilization; for it is a meeting-ground of the East and the West. There you teach in object-lessons of sympathy and goodwill that the true happiness of individuals and nations is identified with the highest good of mankind. When this supreme truth is grasped, the dream of all the greatest teachers spoken through the ages shall be fulfilled; wars will be dead; hatred will be dead; dogmas will be dead; man will live, he will possess something greater than all these, . . . the whole of earth for his country and the whole of Heaven for his hope."

Tagore's idea of bringing education to the homes and farms of Indian villagers was greatly extended and applied on a nationwide basis in the Basic Education Program of Mahatma Gandhi.

ART AND LITERARY CRITICISM

Tagore's Western tour in 1930, during which he gave the Hibbert Lectures at Oxford, acquainted the West with another aspect of his artistic expression. Exhibitions of his paintings and drawings appeared in Paris, Birmingham, London, Berlin, Dresden, Munich, Copenhagen, Moscow, New York, and Boston.

About this new form of expression, Tagore once wrote:

"The only training which I had from my young days was the training in rhythm, the rhythm in thought, the rhythm in sound! I had come to know that rhythm gives reality to that which is desultory, which is insignificant in itself. And therefore, when the scratches in my manuscript cried, like sinners, for salvation, and assailed my eyes with the ugliness of their irrelevance, I often took more time in rescuing them into a merciful finality of rhythm than in carrying on what was my obvious task."

Rabindra Sadana, the Tagore Memorial Museum at Santiniketan, has a collection of nearly eighteen hundred paintings and drawings of Tagore. A number also are in various public and private collections in India and abroad. The total number amounts to well over two thousand paintings and drawings, and are generally datable between 1925–1939.

1. These lines are from Wordsworth's sonnet "Why Art Thou Silent?" *Complete Poetical Works of William Wordsworth*, Student's Cambridge Edition (Houghton Mifflin, Boston, 1904), p. 740.

2. William Blake's poem, "Never Seek to Tell Thy Love," *The Poems of William Blake*, ed. John Sampson (Florence Press, London, 1921), p. 141.

3. Duhshashan. One of the Kaurava brothers (Mahabharata) who tried to insult Draupadi (queen of the Pandavas) by disrobing her in public.

4. Amy Lowell's "A Lady," from *A Shard of Silence* (Twayne, New York, 1957), p. 29.

5. "Red Slippers." Published in *Poetry* VI, 1915, pp. 10–11.

6. "A Study in Aesthetics," *Selected Poems* (Faber and Faber, London, 1934), p. 78.

7. T. S. Eliot, "Preludes," *Collected Poems 1909–1935*, copyright, 1936, by Harcourt, Brace and Company, Inc. Reprinted by permission of Harcourt, Brace and Company, New York, and Faber and Faber, Ltd.; London.

8. "In the Mountains," *The Works of Li Po the Chinese Poet*, trans. Shigeyoshi Obata, 1928.

9. "Nocturne."

10. "A Summer Day."

11. "Two Letters from Chang-Kan."

12. "Richard Cory," Edwin Arlington Robinson, *Collected Poems* (Macmillan, New York, 1937), p. 82.

PHILOSOPHICAL MEDITATIONS

1. Mahatma Gandhi. To the world outside India, Tagore and Gandhi were the two great personalities who represented the spiritual genius of India. Apart from their specific contributions in the area of literature and national service, both of them met on the common ground of a profound concern for humanity, and exemplified the great traditions of Indian thought. Gandhi's recognition of Tagore, not only as a poetic personality, but as a man of pure thought, is applicable here. In *The Golden Book of Tagore* (1931) he wrote:

"In common with thousands of his countrymen I owe much to one who by his poetic genius and singular purity of life has raised India in the estimation of the world. Did he not harbor in Santiniketan the inmates of my Ashram who had preceded me from South Africa? The other ties and memories are too sacred to bear mention in a public tribute."

As a general note to Tagore's philosophic and religious thought, it is significant to quote here Sarvepalli Radhakrishnan's summary in his *Great Indians* (Hind Katabs, Ltd., Bombay, 1949), p. 92:

"In all Rabindranath's work three features are striking: (1) The ultimateness of spiritual values to be obtained by inward honesty and cultivation of inner life; (2) the futility of mere negation or renunciation and the need for a holy or a whole development of life; and (3) the positive attitude of sympathy for all, even the lowly and the lost. It is a matter for satisfaction to find an Indian leader insisting on these real values of life at a time when so many old things are crumbling away and a thousand new ones are springing up."

POETRY

Tagore was critical about his own English translations. In a letter to William Rothenstein quoted in Rothenstein's *Men and Memories* (Coward-McCann, Inc., New York, 1932), p. 301, he wrote:

"My translations are frankly prose—my aim is to make them simple with just a suggestion of rhythm to give them a touch of the lyric, avoiding all archaism and poetical conventions."

André Gide, who translated *Gitanjali* and *Post Office*, from Paris sent the following statement to be included in *The Golden Book of Tagore* (1931).

"Rabindranath Tagore ne comptait encore, en Angleterre même, que de très rares lecteurs, lorsque en 1912, je traduisis son *Gitanjali*. L'incomparable pureté poétique de ce petit livre rayonnait à mes yeux d'un tel éclat que je tiens à honneur d'en apporter un reflet à la France. A travers la guerre, au dessus de toutes nos dissensions politiques ou confessionnelles cette étoile fixe a continué de luire et de verser sur la monde une tranquille lumière d'amour, de confiance et de paix. Je suis heureux d'apporter aujourd'hui mon tribut d'hommage et de reconnaissance à la grande figure que vous vous proposez d'honorer."

The same volume included the following letter from Yeats in Dublin:

"Since we met I have married, I have now two children, a boy and a girl, and feel more knitted into life; and life, when I think of it as separated from all that is not itself, from all that is complicated and mechanical, takes to my imagination an Asiatic form. That form I found first in your books and afterwards in certain Chinese poetry and Japanese prose writers. What an excitement the first reading of your poems, which seemed to come out of the fields and the rivers and have their changelessness!"

Brown Weber, in *Hart Crane, A Biographical and Critical Study*, The Bodley Press, New York, 1948, includes the following statements about Tagore's relationship with Hart Crane:

"From Mrs. Moody, too, Hart heard news of the poets and novelists in and about Chicago, many of whom shared her hospitality while in that city. One of these writers was Rabindranath Tagore of India, whose first visit to Chicago had occurred in 1913, shortly after several of his poems from his *Gitanjali* appeared in an issue of the newly-founded *Poetry*. When Tagore came again to the United States in 1916, he stopped off in Cleveland. One of the few interviews he granted at that time was to Hart, who returned home impressed of the Indian writer and philosopher. Hart was now at a stage where he easily appreciated Tagore's insistence upon the fusion of religion with everyday life, as well as his distaste for the supremacy of American business and scientific ideals over the values of art.

"Undoubtedly he read the cadenced English translations of Tagore's Bengali poems and responded to the poet's . . . conception of God's immanence, his imagery of infinite sky and bottomless ocean depths, and his faith in the motive-power of love. In later years, one of Tagore's poems was to make a strange reappearance in a poem written by Crane" [pp. 9–10].

"During September, [1921] Crane completed 'The Bottom of the Sea Is Cruel' which, after rejection by *The Dial* and *The Little Review,* was printed in *Secession* in 1923, and finally took its place in *White Buildings* as 'Voyages I.' The poem treats the sea as the same cruel agency of 'The Bridge of Estador.' It is difficult to tell when Crane began to write the poem, for it is strikingly reminiscent of Tagore's 'On the Seashore' (*The Crescent Moon,* 1913), which Crane probably read many years before. Tagore describes children playing on the beach with 'empty shells' and 'withered leaves' who are aware only that 'the sea surges up with laughter'; they fail to observe that 'the death-dealing waves sing meaningless ballads . . . like a mother while rocking her baby's cradle.' In Crane's poem, too, the sea is an ambivalent force, alternately attracting and repelling with surges of maternal love and clutching death. The poet watches colorfully-dressed children playing on the shore . . ." [pp. 105–106]. [Note: This passage was brought to the attention of the editor by Henry Braun, Boston University.]

1. "Be not ashamed"—Bengali original in *Naivedya,* 1901; poet's own translation, in *Poems* (Visva-Bharati, Calcutta, 1942).

2. "Far as I gaze"—Bengali original in *Naivedya,* 1901; poet's own translation, in *Poems* (Visva-Bharati, Calcutta, 1942).

3. "Let the earth and the water"—Bengali original in 1905, published in *Gàn,* 1908; poet's own translation, in *Poems* (Visva-Bharati, Calcutta, 1942).

4. "Thou art the ruler"—Bengali original (song), 1912; poet's own translation, in *Poems* (Visva-Bharati, Calcutta, 1942); India's new national anthem.

5. "Thou hast given us to live"—Several Bengali poems used by the poet in his English version made for the Indian National Congress, 1917; published in present form in *Poems* (Visva-Bharati, Calcutta, 1942).

6. "A beast's bony frame"—Bengali original, 1924, published in *Puravi,* 1925; poet's own translation, in *Poems* (Visva-Bharati, Calcutta, 1942).

7. "You were born"—Bengali original, November 3, 1929, published in *Puravi;* translated by the editor for this volume.

8. "The worshiper offers leaves and flowers"—Bengali original, January 16, 1925, published in *Puravi*; translated by the editor for this volume.

9. "When I was a boy"—Bengali original, May 4, 1931, published in *Parishesh*, 1932; translated by the editor for this volume.

10. "The world today"—Bengali original, 1927; poet's own translation in *Poems* (Visva-Bharati, Calcutta, 1942).

11. "Those who struck Him once"—Bengali original, Christmas Day 1939; poet's own translation in *Poems* (Visva-Bharati, Calcutta, 1942).

12. "From afar I thought"—Bengali original, July 1, 1932; published in *Parishesh*; translation by Kshitis Roy in *Visva-Bharati Quarterly*, August-October, 1943; revised for this volume.

13. "Door, always open"—Bengali original, 1924, published in *Parishesh*; translated by the editor for this volume.

14. "Scattered in this room — Bengal original in *Akashpradit*, 1938; translated by the editor for this volume.

15. "The journey nears the road-end"—Bengali original, April 13, 1924, published in *Parishesh*; translated by the editor for this volume.

16. "In the center of the universe"—Bengali original, November 13, 1940, *Rogashajyay*; translated by the editor for this volume.

17. "The war-drums are sounded"—Bengali original, January 7, 1938, *Navajatak*; poet's own translation in *Poems* (Visva-Bharati, Calcutta, 1942).

18. "I have won blessings"—original Bengali, January 28, 1941; published in posthumous volume *Shesh Lekha*; translated by the editor in *Poems* (Visva-Bharati, Calcutta, 1942), revised.

19. "On the bank of Rup-Narain"—Bengali original, May 13, 1941; translated by the editor in *Poems* (Visva-Bharati, Calcutta, 1942); revised.

20. "Here in the universe"—Bengali original, November 4, 1940; translated by the editor in *Poems* (Visva-Bharati, Calcutta, 1942); revised.

21. "Once again I wake up"—Bengali original, 1932, *Parishesh*; poet's own translation in *Poems* (Visva-Bharati, Calcutta, 1942).

22. "How little I know of this world"—Bengali original, January 21, 1941; translated by Kshitis Roy and the editor, published in the *Modern Review*, Calcutta, March 1921; revised.

23. "Sheltered by the distant throne"—Bengali original, January 24, 1941, *Janmadine*; translated by the editor in *Asian Horizon*, Calcutta, 1947; revised.

24. "On that birthday morning"—Bengali original, February 21, 1941, *Janmadine*; translated by the editor for this volume.

25. "Shunned at the temple-gates"—Bengali original, May 1, 1936,

Patraput; translated by Kshitis Roy in *Visva-Bharati Quarterly*, November, 1938; revised.

26. "Floating on time's stream"—Bengali original, February 23, 1941, *Arogya*; translated by the editor in *Poems* (Visva-Bharati, Calcutta, 1942); revised.

27. "You have covered the path of your creation"—This was the last poem dictated by the poet, July 30, 1941, and could not be corrected by him; published in posthumous volume *Shesh-lekha*; translated by the editor in *Poems* (Visva-Bharati, Calcutta, 1942); revised.

28. "There lies the ocean of peace"—Bengali original, December 3, 1939, published posthumously in *Shesh-lekha* (1941); translated by the editor in *Poems* (Visva-Bharati, Calcutta, 1942); revised.

29. "The first day's sun"—Bengali original, July 27, 1941, *Rogashaj-yay*; translated by the editor in *Poems* (Visva-Bharati, Calcutta, 1942); revised.

30. "Soon, I feel"—Bengali original, February 1941; *Arogya*, translated by the editor in *Poems* (Visva-Bharati, Calcutta, 1942); revised.

GLOSSARY

AMALAKI   The emblic myrobalan, green berrylike fruit.

AMAN   Autumnal crop of paddy rice.

ANDAMANS   A group of islands in the Bay of Bengal, formerly used by the British Government in India as a prison for criminals and also for political revolutionaries.

ANNA BRAHMA   The Lord in the form of food; food conceived as the Lord.

ANUBHUTI   Feeling, perception.

APIPASA   Without desire, absence of thirst or desire.

ARJUN, ARJUNA   A legendary warrior and one of the principal heroes of the epic, Mahabharata, for whose benefit Lord Krishna is said to have uttered the discourses of the Bhagavat Gita.

ARYAN   Fair-skinned Caucasian invaders of India; their descendants.

ASHRAM, ASHRAMA   One of the four stages or orders of life of a Hindu; a hermitage; a monastery; a refuge.

ASWATH   Sanskrit: aswattha; the holy fig tree, the peepul; *ficus religiosa.*

AVATAR   Manifestation; incarnation of a deity.

BADSHAH   A king (generally used in India for Muslim kings).

BAITARANI   In Hindu mythology, a river of hell; also name of a river in Orissa.

BALHIC   Balkh, in Afghanistan.

BARA LOK   Belonging to the upper or rich class.

BHAGAVAT-GITA   The standard classic of Hindu philosophy of life (in Sanskrit verse), popularly attributed to Lord Krishna.

Bhagavat Purana   One of the eighteen puranas, or sacred legends; consists of 18,000 verses.

Bhagavatas   Beings devoted to the Supreme deity; godly.

Bharat-varsha   The ancient name of India, still in use in Indian languages.

Bhrigu   A Vedic sage, founder of the race of the Bhrigus or Bhargavas.

Brahma   The all-pervading Divine Essence; the universal spirit; the Supreme Being; God.

Brahmin   Belonging to the supposed highest caste among the Hindus.

Bulbul   The Indian nightingale.

Chaitra   The last month of the Bengali year (March-April).

Chāmar   A kind of deer; the yak; a long brush made of the tail-hair of the yak and used as a fan.

Chāmār   Belonging to a "low caste" among the Hindus; a cobbler.

Champa   Name of a flower; *Michelia Champaka*.

Chandal, Chandala   The "lowest caste" among the Hindus, regarded by the orthodox as outcaste.

Chandalika, Chandalini   A chandal girl.

Chatus-pathis   A college where the four Vedas are taught; a school of Sanskrit learning.

Chetana   Consciousness; an awakening.

Choto Lok   People of "low caste"; poor people; humble folk.

Chitragiri   Legendary hill.

Cowrie   Small shell used as a token of money; used also as ornament.

Dada   Elder brother; also used to address a person older than oneself.

Dada Moshay   Grandfather.

Dada of Phalguni   A character in Tagore's play *Phalguni* (Eng. *the Cycle of Spring*).

Dak Bungalow   Halting place; a rest house provided by the government for its officers and other visitors.

Dal   Split peas or pulses; soup of split peas or pulses. In Bengali it also means a branch of a tree when the word is pronounced with *d* hard.

Darwan   Gatekeeper.

Dharma   Righteousness; religion; law; duty.

Dharma-yuddha   "A war for a holy cause"; a crusade.

Dhoti   A common form of male dress in India consisting of a long piece of cloth worn round the waist.

Dhruva-tārā   The Pole Star, signifying steadfastness, brightness.

DRAVIDIANS   The original inhabitants of India before the advent of the Aryans.

DWIJA   "Twice born"; spiritually reborn.

EKTARA   One-string instrument greatly in favor with India's wandering minstrels.

ELA   Character in Tagore's novel *Char Adhyay*.

FAKIR   Muslim mendicant.

GAMELAN   Muscial instrument used in Indonesia.

GANDHAR, GANDHARA   Ancient name for Afghanistan; name of the art in that area and in North India, influenced by Greece.

GHAZALS   A popular form of poetry in Urdu, which can also be sung.

GHEE   Clarified butter used in Indian cooking.

GUHAKA   King of the hunter tribe who befriended Rama in his exile.

GURU   A religious teacher; a spiritual preceptor or guide.

HENNA   White flowered evergreen; dye made from it (Arabic).

HILSA   Sablefish, a favorite dish in Bengal.

HUNAS   A race belonging to the Middle Asia who invaded India frequently during the Gupta and Harsha periods.

ISOPANISHAT   One of the principal Upanishads.

JALATARANGA   Literally "water waves"; a musical instrument consisting of porcelain bowls of various sizes which are filled with the requisite quantity of water to produce musical notes when struck with wooden ladles.

JANAKA   King of Mithila, and father of Sita, the heroine of Ramayana.

JANAMEJAYA   A great king, son of Parikshit and great-grandson of Arjuna, the famous character of Mahabharata.

JATRAS   Bengali folk plays played on open-air stage; a pilgrimage; procession.

KABAB   Roasted meat.

KAILAS   Fabled abode of Siva in the high Himalayas; the name of a mountain pilgrimage in the Himalayas.

KAJRI   A type of folk song and dance in the eastern part of Uttar Pradesh, India.

KAMBOJ   Ancient geographical name of an area in the Punjab.

KAMYAK   Name of a forest in the ancient Indian legends.

KARMA   Literally "action." Generally used in connection with the common Indian belief that the fruit of one's action persists through many lives.

KARTAVIRYA   Son of Krita-Virya, King of Haiheyas. This is his patronymic, by which he is best known; his real name was Arjuna (not to be confused with the hero of Mahabharata).

KARTIK   Bengali month corresponding to October-November; name of a deity.

KASHI   Benares, pilgrim city.

KIRATAS   Foresters and mountaineers living in the east of Hindustan.

KIRTANS   A particular type of devotional songs in Bengal.

KRISHNA   The legendary hero of Bhagavat, worshiped by some Hindus as a divine incarnation.

KSHATRIYA   Belonging to the "second highest caste" among Hindus, traditionally warriors.

KUMARA SAMBHAVA   A Sanskrit epic written by the great poet Kalidasa, dealing with the birth and exploits of Kartikeya, son of the god Siva and Parvati.

KUNDA   A character in one of the novels of Bankim Chandra Chatterji.

LABANGALATÌKA   A creeper with delicate white flowers; name of a Bengali sweetmeat.

MAHABHARATA   The great epic poem of the Hindus, dealing with the conflict between the Pandavas and the Kauravas, said to be composed by the sage, Vedavyasa.

MAHAJANI   Of the rich, of the banker; usury, money-lending business.

MAHAVIRA   Literally, "the great warrior." Epithet commonly used for the "monkey-god" Hanuman who served Rama. Also the name of the founder of the Jain religion.

MALATI   A kind of jasmine creeper.

MANTRAS   Sacred couplets and hymns in Sanskrit scriptures.

MANU   Name of the first lawgiver of the Hindus. Also the mythological progenitor and ruler of mankind.

MARICH   A demon in the Ramayana who metamorphosed himself as a golden deer and was killed by Rama; name for chili.

MASTER-MASHAI   A respectful term for the teacher.

MAYA   Literally "illusion," or partial reality. Popularly used as a concept in Indian philosophy applied to appearance as against reality.

Mayavin Person having power of illusion or spell; a charmer.

Mehedi Name of a plant the leaves of which are crushed and applied on the palms and the feet as aids to beauty.

Mela A fair; a crowd.

Mochlai Of the moghals; generally applied to richly cooked meat dishes favored by Muslim aristocracy.

Nag Serpent; mountain, elephant.

Naga Name of a tribe in East India.

Nahabat Originally, kettledrum. Generally used for ceremonial playing of music in a king's palace.

Namaz Prayer offered by the followers of Islam.

Narghileh Pipe with flexible tube and attached vase of water through which smoke is drawn (Persian).

Nirvana Final deliverance of self in Buddhist and Jaina philosophy; transcendence.

Padma Name of a great river which flows through East Pakistan.

Palanquin A carriage consisting of a covered wooden box with a pole on either side, carried on the shoulders by bearers.

Palmyra A species of palm tree.

Pan A preparation of betel leaf, betel nut, and some other ingredients, popular with Indians.

Parasu-rama A character in Hindu mythology, warrior and sworn enemy of the Kshatriyas.

Peepul A common Indian tree. Also held sacred because the Buddha is supposed to have meditated and attained enlightenment under it; known as the Bodhi tree.

Phalgun Bengali month corresponding to January-February; the spring season.

Pillau A popular dish of rice with meat.

Pujah Literally, "worship." The term is used in Bengal for the important festival *Durga puja* and holiday season (October-November).

Purani Of the past, ancient.

Ragas Melodic patterns in Indian music.

Raghu The mythological king of Ikshwaku dynasty, forefather of Rama.

Raginis Subdivisions of musical patterns belonging to one raga or the other.

Rajasthan Literally, "home of the Rajputs"; one of the states in western India.

RAMACHANDRA   The hero of Ramayana.

RAMAYANA   The great Sanskrit epic composed by the sage Valmiki dealing with the story of Rama.

RIG   Earliest of the four Vedas, the most ancient hymns of the Aryans.

SAHEB   A European, or Europeanized Indian.

SAKAS   Name of a tribe in Middle Asia who invaded India; the era founded by King Salivahana seventy-eight years before the Christian era.

SAKUNTALA   Variant of Shakuntala.

SAL   Name of a tree.

SALAM   The Muslim way of greeting; literally, "peace be on you."

SANAI   A musical instrument (like a bagpipe) used on festive occasions and celebrations.

SANTINIKETAN   Literally "abode of peace"; name of the famous place about a hundred miles from Calcutta, where Tagore founded his school, and later his international University, Visva-Bharati.

SANYASI, SANNYASINS   An order of Hindu sprital aspirants who have renounced the world; ascetic.

SARENG   Captain of a ferry steamer.

SATARA   Town in the state of Maharashtra.

SAYANACHARYA   Celebrated commentator on Rig-Veda.

SEPOY   Indian soldier; infantryman.

SETAR   A stringed musical instrument.

SHAKUNTALA, SAKUNTALA   The heroine of the famous Sanskrit play of that name by Kalidasa.

SHANKARA   Great Indian philosopher of *Advaita* (monist) school.

SHELIDAH   Former headquarters of the Tagore estate (now in East Pakistan).

SIRIS, SIRISH   Name of a tree with bright red flowers.

SIVA   One of the Hindu trinity, representing God in his destructive aspect.

SOLA   Indian pith helmet.

SRIJUT   Indian equivalent of Mister.

SUDRA   "Low caste" Hindus.

SURYA   The sun god.

SUSTA   Name of a river.

SUZERAIN   Sovereign; feudal lord.

TAPASYA   Spiritual discipline; penance.

TAXILA   Seat of learning and sculpture of great antiquity, situated in West Pakistan.

UPANISHADS The later part of Vedas dealing with the exposition of Hindu ontology and philosophical meditations.

UTTARAYANA Name of a house in Santiniketan where Tagore lived; at present used for the Tagore Museum.

VAIKUNTHA Heaven.

VAISHNAVA Name of a religious sect among the Hindus who emphasize personal devotion to God.

VARNA Literally, "color"; social division according to profession in the Aryan society, later perpetuated into castes or classes by birth.

VARUNA Water god of the Hindu pantheon, comparable to the Greek Neptune.

VEDAS Literally, "to know"; holy books which are the foundation of Hindu religion written in an old form of Sanskrit.

VEDIC-RUDRA The forerunner of Siva; the god of destruction mentioned in the Vedas.

VISHNU One of the Hindu trinity; the god of sustenance.

VISWAMITRA The Vedic sage; father of Sakuntala and preceptor of many Vedic hymns.

YAJNAVALKYA The Vedic sage; composer of a prominent Smriti; code of behavior.

YAK-TAIL Tail of the yak, oxlike animal of Tibet.

YAMADAGNI A Vedic sage, father of Parasurama.

ZAMINDARS Landlords.

ZENANA Quarters segregated for ladies.